Resilient and Sustainable Destinations After Disaster

Tourism Security-Safety and Post Conflict Destinations

Series editors: Maximiliano E. Korstanje and Hugues Seraphin

Since the turn of the century, the international rules surrounding security and safety have significantly changed, specifically within the tourism industry. In the age of globalization, terrorism and conflict have moved beyond individual high-profile targets; instead, tourists, travellers, and journalists are at risk. In response to this shift, the series invites authors and scholars to contribute to the conversation surrounding tourism security and postconflict destinations.

The series features monographs and edited collections to create a critical platform which not only explores the dichotomies of tourism from the theory of mobilities but also provides an insightful guide for policymakers, specialists, and social scientists interested in the future of tourism in a society where uncertainness, anxiety, and fear prevail.

Tourism Security-Safety and Post Conflict Destinations explores research approaches and perspectives from a wide range of ideological backgrounds to discuss topics such as:

- Studies related to comparative cross-cultural perceptions of risk and threat
- Natural and human-caused disasters
- Post-disaster recovery strategies in tourism and hospitality
- Terror movies and tourism
- Aviation safety and security
- Crime and security issues in tourism and hospitality
- Political instability, terrorism, and tourism
- Thanatourism
- War on terror and Muslim tourism
- The effects of global warming on tourism destinations
- Innovative quantitative/qualitative methods for the study of risk and security issues in tourism and hospitality
- Virus outbreaks and tourism mobility
- Disasters, trauma, and tourism
- Apocalyptic theories and tourism as a form of entertainment

Advisory Board

Stanislav Ivanov
Varna University of Management, Bulgaria

Metin Kozak
Dokuz Eylul University, Turkey

Sharad K. Kulshreshtha
North Eastern Hill University Shillong Meghalaya, India

Dominic Lapointe
University of Quebec at Montreal, Canada

Duncan Light
Bournemouth University, UK

Claudio Milano
The Autonomous University of Barcelona, Spain

Andreas Papatheodorou
University of Aegean, Greece

Cesar Augusto Oliveros
University of Guadalajara, Mexico

Daniel Olsen
Brigham Young University, USA

Alexandros Paraskevas
Oxford Brookes University, UK

Lorri Pennington Gray
University of Florida, USA

Arie Reichel
Ben-Gurion University of the Negev, Israel

Claudia Seabra
University of Coimbra, Portugal

Anukrati Sharma
University of Kota, India

Richard A. Sharpley
University of Central Lancashire, UK

Jonathan Skinner
University of Roehampton, UK

Geoffrey Skoll
Buffalo State College, USA

Marta Soligo
University of Nevada, USA

Dallen Timothy
Arizona State University, USA

Abraham Pizam
University of Central Florida, USA

Peter Tarlow
Texas A&M University, USA

Marcelo Tomé de Barros
State University of Fluminense, Brazil

Diego R. Toubes
University of Vigo, Spain

Rodanthi Tzanelli
University of Leeds, UK

Ghialy Yap
Edith Cowan University, Australia

Resilient and Sustainable Destinations After Disaster: Challenges and Strategies

EDITED BY

JEETESH KUMAR
Taylor's University, Malaysia

GÜL ERKOL BAYRAM
University of Sinop, Turkey

And

ANUKRATI SHARMA
University of Kota, India

United Kingdom – North America – Japan – India – Malaysia – China

Emerald Publishing Limited
Howard House, Wagon Lane, Bingley BD16 1WA, UK

First edition 2023

Reprints and permissions service
Contact: permissions@emeraldinsight.com

British Library Cataloging in Publication Data
A catalog record for this book is available from the British Library

ISBN: 978-1-80382-022-4 (Print)
ISBN: 978-1-80382-021-7 (Online)
ISBN: 978-1-80382-023-1 (Epub)

Printed and bound by CPI Group (UK) Ltd, Croydon, CR0 4YY

INVESTOR IN PEOPLE

Table of Contents

About the Contributors   *xi*

Introduction   *1*
Jeetesh Kumar, Gül Erkol Bayram and Anukrati Sharma

**A Road Map for Two Decades of Sustainable Tourism Development
Framework**   *9*
*Asik Rahaman Jamader, Shahnawaz Chowdhary and Srijib Shankar
Jha*

**The Benefits of Being a Smart Destination in the Post-COVID-19
Period**   *19*
Emre Ozan Aksoz and Ipek Itir Can

**Tourism Sustainable Planning in Low Density Territories and the
Post (Disaster) Pandemic Context**   *41*
*Pedro Liberato, Bruno Barbosa Sousa, Márcia Costa and Dália
Liberato*

**Building Positive Zimbabwean Tourism Festival and Event
Destination Brand Image and Equity**   *63*
*Farai Chigora, Brighton Nyagadza, Chipo Katsande and Promise
Zvavahera*

**Destination Marketing as an Orienting Tool in Zimbabwe's Tourism
Image and Publicity Crisis**   *75*
*Farai Chigora, Brighton Nyagadza, Chipo Katsande and Promise
Zvavahera*

Pandemic and Tourism: From Health Emergency to Standard Operating Procedures (SOPs) Adherence—Insights of Novel Adaptations in the New Normal   *87*
Farhad Nazir, Norberto Santos and Luis Avila Silveira

Post-disaster Tourism: Building Resilient and Sustainable Communities   *97*
Gina B. Alcoriza and John Ericson A. Policarpio

Rebuilding Tourism in Asia for Future (Post-COVID-19)   *109*
Syed Haider Ali Shah, Kamran Jamshed, Sharjeel Saleem, Basheer M. Al-Ghazali and Ozair Ijaz Kiani

Synthesizing Theories for Resilient Medical Tourism   *121*
Kasturi Shukla and Avadhut Patwardhan

Tourists' Harassment During Pilgrimage: A Case Study of TripAdvisor's Review for the Hindu Pilgrim Centers in India   *139*
Debasish Batabyal, Nilanjan Ray, Sudin Bag and Kaustav Nag

Communication Effectiveness in Rebuilding and Raising Awareness for Safe and Innovative Future Tourism in Oman   *157*
Sangeeta Tripathi and Muna Al Shahri

Responsible Sustainable Tourism Product Planning and Design for Recovery   *179*
Sweety Jamgade and Puja Mondal

Vulnerability and Resilience of Tourism: Recovery Plans and Strategies of Countries   *195*
Derya Toksoz and Ali Dalgic

Rebuilding Senior Tourism Destinations in the Post-COVID Era   *213*
Sultan Nazmiye Kılıç

Spirituality and Yoga for Well-being in a Post-disaster Scenario: Linking the Qualitative Facets of Traditional Indian Ways of Life   *227*
Manpreet Arora and Roshan Lal Sharma

Smart Technologies and Tour Guides Beyond COVID-19 *241*
Gül Erkol Bayram, Jeetesh Kumar and Anukrati Sharma

Regenerative Tourism and Resilience in COVID-19 Pandemic: From Strategic Principles to Sustainability *251*
Parag S. Shukla and Sofia Devi Shamurailatpam

Revamping Hotel Industry in South East Asian Region: Outlook of Existing Situation After COVID-19 *267*
Syed Haider Ali Shah, Nosheen Rafique, Sharjeel Saleem, Rafia Amjad and Bilal Arshad

Harnessing the Potential of Ecotourism for Sustainability *277*
Deeksha Dave

Rebuilding Tourism Industry Through Sustainability Practices and Opportunities in the Postpandemic Era *287*
Shivani Trivedi and Santosh K. Patra

Index *299*

About the Contributors

Emre Ozan Aksoz, PhD, completed his primary, secondary, and high school education at T.E.D Ankara College, Ankara, Turkey. He completed his associate degree in Hacettepe University, Tourism and Hotel Management program in 1996. Later, in 1999, he received his undergraduate degree from Anadolu University School of Tourism and Hotel Management. After graduating, he worked in hotels in the United States for a year. He enrolled in Hacettepe University, Department of Business Administration/Tourism Management Master's Program, in 2000 and received his master's degree in 2003. At the end of 2001, he started to work as a Research Assistant at Anadolu University School of Tourism and Hotel Management. In 2010, he completed his PhD at Anadolu University, Institute of Social Sciences, Department of Business Administration, in the department of Marketing. He was appointed as an assistant professor at Anadolu University in 2012. He received the title of associate professor in 2017. He still works as a lecturer, associate professor, and vice dean at Anadolu University, Faculty of Tourism.

Dr Gina B. Alcoriza is the Campus Coordinator for International Affairs and for Office of Student Affairs Services of Partido State University, San Jose Campus, Camarines Sur, Philippines. She served as Tourism Management Program Chairperson at the University of Santo Tomas – Legazpi. She was the Vice President of the Union of the Filipino Tourism Educators (UFTE) and a Membership Ambassador of the Philippine Association of Researchers in Tourism and Hospitality (PARTH). She served as Tourism Consultant of some Local Government Units and a Tourist Police Trainer, an Honorary Member of SKEDUx International Educators Network, and an Executive Council Member, Fater Academy India (FAI) Council. She is also a speaker/lecturer and researcher on Tourism, Hospitality, and Business topics, a research reviewer and editorial board member of some international journals, and one of the editors of the book, *Marketing Tourist Destinations in Emerging Economies.*

Dr Basheer M. Al-Ghazali joined King Fahd University of Petroleum & Minerals (KFUPM), Saudi Arabia, in 2018 as Assistant Professor and is currently working as a coordinator of the Department of Business Administration-DCC. He earned a PhD in Management from Universiti Teknologi Malaysia (UTM) in 2016. He holds a bachelor's degree in Computer Engineering from KFUPM (2000) and an MBA from KFUPM as well (2006). Before joining KFUPM, Dr Basheer held a position as Assistant Professor in Business Administration at Applied Science

University (ASU) in Bahrain. He has more than 10 years of experience in the IT industry in various roles. His research interests cover CSR, Entrepreneurship, Technology Adoption, Leadership, and HRM. His research has been published in several well-reputed peer-reviewed journals including *Technology in Society*, *Leadership & Organization Development*, *Corporate Social Responsibility and Environmental Management*, *European Journal of Innovation Management*, *Sustainability*, and *Frontiers in Psychology*.

Ms Muna Al Shahri is an Assistant Lecturer at the University of Technology and Applied Sciences, Salalah, Oman, since 2013. She has a masters degree in international communication and development from Swansea University, UK. She is involved in research work in media impact-related areas such as communication, tourism, new media, women empowerment, and new media. In addition, she has conducted workshops for local institutions in aspects such as IP skills and stress management. Recently, her research project titled "Advance Communication Role in Creating Consensus and Acceptability for Innovative Tourism to Support Diversified Economy Drive in The Sultanate" was approved by The Research Council (TRC), Ministry of Higher Education, Research and Innovation, Oman.

Rafia Amjad completed her MPhil in the Department of Management Sciences, Bahria University Islamabad, Pakistan.

Dr (Ms) Manpreet Arora is Senior Assistant Professor of Management in the School of Commerce and Management Studies, Central University of Himachal Pradesh Dharamshala, India. A gold medalist at undergraduate and distinction holder at postgraduate level, she is a merit holder. Her areas of research interest include Accounting and Finance, Strategic Management, Entrepreneurship, Qualitative Research, Case Study Development, Communication Skills, Sustainability, and Microfinance. Having published more than 25 papers in various journals of national and international repute (including SCOPUS, WOS, and category journals), she has also worked as content developer of MHRD "e-PG Pathshala" Project and OER's for IGNOU. She has written 30 book chapters in national as well as international books/handbooks/volumes published with Routledge, CABI, Apple Academic Press, IGI, Taylor and Francis and the latest with Springer Nature etc. With four edited books to her credit, she is a persistent researcher in the field of Management.

Bilal Arshad completed his MS from the Department of Management Sciences, Bahria University Islamabad, Pakistan.

Dr Sudin Bag is an Assistant Professor, Department of Business Administration, Vidyasagar University, Midnapore, West Bengal, India. Dr Bag has more than 10 years of working experience which is inclusive of corporate exposure as well as teaching in management academic in colleges and university. His areas of interest include Marketing Management, Services Marketing, Research Methodology, Consumer Behavior, and International Marketing. Dr Bag has published 18 research papers in reputed national and international journals, contributed a good number of research papers in the edited volume including Springer Nature, and also authored two books (including one edited volume) with high repute. Dr Bag is associated with various academic institutions as well as professional bodies. Dr Bag has received an IARA Best Faculty Award – 2019 in the field of Management and was awarded ICSSR research project under special call for studies focusing on Social Science Dimension of COVID-19.

Dr Debasish Batabyal has been teaching Travel and Tourism Management at the Department of Travel and Tourism, Amity University, Kolkata, West Bengal. A postgraduate in Business Management with specialization in tourism, Dr Batabyal received a doctorate degree from the Department of Business Administration, University of Burdwan, in the year 2013. His areas of research interest include religious tourism, cultural tourism, sustainable development, and social solidarity economy. He has written two books and edited two more with reputed international publishing houses.

Gül Erkol Bayram, PhD, is currently working as an Associate Professor in the School of Tourism and Hotel Management, Department of Tour Guiding, University of Sinop, Sinop, Turkey. Dr Erkol Bayram has worked as an internal trainer in the tour guiding arena. Her doctorate is in Tourism Management from the Sakarya University, Turkey, and she completed her dissertation research on Tour Guiding in Turkey. Her core subjects are Tourism, tour guiding, tourism policy and planning, and women studies. She has many book chapters in the international arena and published her books as an editor in the national arena. She has edited a book on *Women and Tourism and Tour Guiding – Past, Present, Future* under Detay Publishing, Turkey. Currently, she is working as editor on her books, *Resilient and Sustainable Destinations after Disaster: Challenges and Strategies* under the Emerald Publishing, *Practical Book for Tour Guides* in Nobel Publishing, and *Dynamics of Tourism Industry Post-Pandemic and Disasters* in Apple Academic Press, USA. She also has more than 30 book chapters under Cambridge, Emerald, CABI, IGI Global, Springer, etc. She has been invited for many talks/lectures/panel discussions by different universities like the University of Mumbai, India, International Multidisciplinary Conference, College for Women, Parade Ground, Jammu India, International Faculty Development Program, etc. The Government of India has invited her to deliver a talk on Tour Guiding and the University of Kota about a career in tourism, Taylor's University on Tour Guiding. Also, she has a member of many organizations, Universities Board of Studies as an examiner and evaluator. She was invited as special guest and guest of honor to many conferences and organizations. She was awarded by several organizations. Erkol Bayram has also worked as a professional tour guide in Turkey.

Ipek Itir Can is a PhD student and a research assistant in the Department of Tourism Management at the Faculty of Tourism, Anadolu University, Turkey. She obtained her BA and MA in Tourism Management at Istanbul University, Turkey. She previously worked as a research assistant at Nisantasi and Mardin Artuklu University. She has authored or coauthored several articles, book chapters, and conference papers in the field of tourism. In addition to her academic career, she works as a board member/accountant at the Tourism and Destination Development Association (TDGD), and as a member at International Federation for Information Technologies in Travel and Tourism (IFITT) and Tourism Academics Association (TUADER). Her research interests center around the intersection of destination management and marketing, recreation, and tourism technologies.

Farai Chigora has a doctorate in Business Administration from the University of KwaZulu-Natal (South Africa) and is a Senior Lecturer in Business Science in the College of Business, Peace Leadership and Governance, Africa University in Zimbabwe. He is a branding specialist with interest in destination branding, strategic marketing, business research, and related business areas which he has authored in various refereed international journals.

Dr Shahnawaz Chowdhary (UGC National Fellowship Awardee) is an Assistant Professor at Baba Ghulam Shah Badshah University Rajouri (J&K), India. He is a seasoned professional with AHLEA, USA certification in "The Resort Management," and an Academic Counselor to Government P. G College Rajouri, IGNOU Center no. 1207 (since November 2016). His experience includes having been a visiting faculty in different Government Degree colleges and universities. His research interest includes Sustainable Tourism Development, Community-based Tourism, Ecotourism, and Hospitality Management. He has authored two books and recently completed a six-week Post Crisis Hospitality Management Certificate Program at Muma College of the Business University of Florida, as well as the Research Methodology course on Partial least squares (SEM), at Taylor's University in Malaysia. A number of his research papers have been published in reputed peer-reviewed journals and books.

Márcia Costa holds a Master's degree in Tourism Management and is a Researcher at the Polytechnic Institute of Porto, School of Hospitality and Tourism, Portugal.

Ali Dalgic was born in Antalya, Turkey, in 1987. He worked as research assistant in the Department of Tourism Management at Mersin University. He completed his MSc in Management at Adnan Menderes University, Aydin/Turkey in December 2013. He obtained a PhD in Tourism Management at Mersin University. He is working at Isparta University of Applied Sciences Faculty of Tourism as an assistant professor. His research interests include event management, alternative tourism, and strategic management.

Dr Deeksha Dave is Assistant Professor, Environmental Studies, School of Interdisciplinary Studies and Transdisciplinary Studies, Indira Gandhi National Open University, New Delhi, India. She has an MSc (Gold Medalist) and PhD in Environmental Sciences from M. L. Sukhadia University, Udaipur. She has a rich experience of more than 15 years of teaching and research in Environmental Studies. She has authored several textbooks on Environmental Studies published by reputed publishers. To her credit are several book chapters, research papers, and articles in various journals and magazines. She has also participated and presented her research work in several national and international seminars and conferences.

Mr Asik Rahaman Jamader is associated in the Department of Tourism & Hotel Management at Bharathiar University, Coimbatore, Tamil Nadu, India. His research interest is Sustainable Tourism and Innovative Technique implemented in the Hospitality Industry. He has 23 granted patents (National/International) and 12 registered and published patents (National/International), as well as 12 international authored book publications, including a few journal and conference publications in reputed journals like CRC, Springer, and IEEE.

Dr Sweety Jamgade is the Head of Management Studies, Hospitality Department, and Associate Professor in FHMCT, Ramaiah University of Applied Sciences. She has completed her doctorate in the faculty of Science and Technology in the domain of Ecotourism. She treasures the topper award in her postgraduation in her Master's in Hospitality Management. She is specialized in hospitality, tourism, and management studies. She is a member of the Responsible Tourism Society of India, TIES, etc. Her research focus area includes Sustainable Tourism Business and Hospitality Management. She has published several research papers and is the editor, journal reviewer, travel writer, blogger, and vlogger on various platforms.

Kamran Jamshed is currently a PhD aspirant and holds a Master's degree in Management Studies from the Business School of Bahria University Islamabad, Pakistan. His published work is on Green Leadership, Green Training, Green Process Innovation, Ethical Leadership, Work Performance, Perceived Organizational Politics, and Political Skills. His current research interests include small businesses, family-oriented businesses, family businesses hotels, travel, and tourism industry focusing on GHRM and sustainable development, Human Resource Development, Human trafficking and sustainability in the hospitality industry, strategic management, and organizational behavior and their implications in the industry. He worked in the telecom industry of Saudi Arabia under Mobily (Etisalat) for more than 7 years on different roles and overall, he has industrial experience of more than 10 years.

Dr Srijib Shankar Jha is an accomplished academician, researcher, and author with more than two decades of expertise in industry, education, training, and project management. He has a PhD in Performance Management, and is a Google-certified Data Analyst, with UGCNET and an IATA (Canada) certifications. He is a member of several international organizations and a reviewer of reputed international journals. He has published numerous research papers in international journals and conferences and organized various seminars, workshops, FDPs, and MDPs. His patent work also is in progress simultaneously, and it will be filed to the German Patent Office for a possible grant of the same invention.

Chipo Katsande is a Lecturer in Information Systems and Computer Science at Manicaland State University of Applied Sciences, Department of Information

Systems and Computer Science, Zimbabwe. She is a holder of Master of Computer Science and Master of Business Administration from the University of Zimbabwe. She has vast experience as a Software Engineer, Systems Analyst and Development. Her interest and publications are in systems development, administration and security, software engineering, database development and administration, information security, data analytics, artificial intelligence, algorithms, programming, and web applications.

Ozair Ijaz Kiani was an MS student having completed the degree from the Department of Management Sciences, Bahria University Islamabad, Pakistan.

Sultan Nazmiye Kılıç is Research Assistant Doctor at Balıkesir University, Faculty of Tourism, Türkiye. She started to work here in 2014, after three years' experience in the tourism sector. She has a PhD as well as a master's degree in Tourism Management, Balıkesir University, and an undergraduate degree in Tourism Management, Boğaziçi University. Her research interests are mainly related to the aspects associated with the tourism field.

Jeetesh Kumar is Senior Lecturer at the School of Hospitality, Tourism, and Events and Associate Director for Information Management & Documentation at the Center for Research and Innovation in Tourism (CRiT), Taylor's University, Malaysia. His doctorate is from Taylor's University in Hospitality and Tourism, with research on Economic Impacts of Business Events in Malaysia. He has two postgraduate degree specialities: a Professional Master's in Hospitality Management and International Tourism from University of Toulouse, France, and the other in Business Administration (MBA – Marketing) from Hamdard University, Pakistan. His research areas include Economic Impacts, Economic Modeling, MICE, Medical Tourism, and Behavioral Studies. He has worked on consultancy and research projects at the national/international level and authored 45 publications including research articles and book chapters. 15 postgraduate students have graduated under his supervision, and currently he is supervising seven PhD scholars. Along with being an active member of several national and international associations, conferences, and journals, he is also serving as an associate editor for *Asia-Pacific Journal of Innovation in Hospitality and Tourism* (APJIHT).

Pedro Liberato holds a PhD in Tourism and is Tourism Professor at the Polytechnic Institute of Porto, School of Hospitality and Tourism, Portugal. He is also coordinator of the Master's Program in Tourism Management, and Head of Tourism and Leisure Department. He is a researcher in CiTUR, IELT | Nova FCSH and CEI – ISCAP (Portugal).

Dália Liberato holds a PhD in Tourism and is Tourism Professor at the Polytechnic Institute of Porto, School of Hospitality and Tourism, Portugal. She is coordinator of Tourism Activities Management Degree and researcher in CiTUR, IELT | Nova FCSH and CEI – ISCAP (Portugal).

Puja Mondal is a student of MBA in Hospitality Management, FHMCT, Ramaiah University of Applied Sciences, Bangalore, India. She is interested in travel and tourism studies. Her interest in travel and tourism began during her internship period in 2021 when she got an opportunity to learn deeply about the tourism industry. She spends most of her time traveling and cooking. She aspires to become a successful entrepreneur in the travel and tourism industry.

Mr Kaustav Nag a post graduate in Tourism Administration from Amity Institute of Travel and Tourism, Kaustav Nag has been working with Victoria Travels in Kolkata, India. His area of research interest is online travel agency business and travel portal analysis.

Farhad Nazir is Lecturer at the Institute of Cultural Heritage, Tourism, and Hospitality Management ICHTHM, University of Swat, Pakistan. Before joining the University of Swat, he has served as coordinator at Marriott Hotel International. Presently, he is pursuing a Doctorate in Tourism, Heritage, and Territory at the Department of Geography & Tourism, University of Coimbra, Portugal. He has an MPhil in Development Studies from the Pakistan Institute of Development Economics PIDE. He obtained his MA in Tourism & Hospitality from Hazara University, Pakistan, and was awarded a Gold Medal on distinguished performance. His research lines corroborate Cultural Tourism Sites and Cultural Identity, Islamic Legislation and Tourism Laws, and Hospitality Laws in the Islamic preview. During his career at Marriott Hotel Islamabad, he demonstrated various training sessions as Master Trainer.

Brighton Nyagadza is a full-time Lecturer and A/Chairperson in the Department of Marketing (digital marketing) at Marondera University of Agricultural Sciences and Technology (MUAST), Zimbabwe, a full member of the Marketers Association of Zimbabwe (MAZ), an Associate of The Chartered Institute of Marketing (ACIM), United Kingdom, and Power Member of the Digital Marketing Institute (DMI), Dublin, Ireland. He has published several book chapters in Routledge books of Taylor & Francis Publishers, New York (USA), Emerald Insight, United Kingdom (UK), Lexington books of the Rowan & Littlefield Publishers, Maryland (USA), and in reputable international journals such as the *Journal of Digital Media & Policy* (JDMP) (Intellect Publishers, Bristol, UK), *Sustainable Technology & Entrepreneurship* (STE) (Elsevier), *Journal of Fashion Marketing & Management* (JFMM) (Emerald Insight, UK), *Journal of Environmental Media* (JEM) (Intellect, Bristol, UK), *European Journal of Innovation Management* (EJIM) (Emerald Insight, UK), *Africa Review* (Brill, Leiden, The Netherlands), *Tourism Critiques: Practice & Theory* (TCPR) (Emerald Insight, UK), *Journal of Asian & African Studies* (JAAS) (SAGE, London, UK), *PSU Research Review* (PRR) (Emerald Insight, UK), *Youth & Society* (SAGE, London, UK), *Cogent Business & Management, Cogent Economics & Finance, Cogent Psychology, Cogent Social Sciences* (Taylor & Francis, England & Wales, UK), *The Marketing Review* (TMR) (Westburn Publishers, Scotland), and others.

Dr Santosh K. Patra has 17 years of work experience in teaching, research, and academic administration. He has held various positions at MICA, Ahmedabad,

IMT-Ghaziabad, and has been associated with different IIMs like the Indian Institute of Management, Indore (IIMI), and other business schools in the capacity of visiting faculties and also serving as a member of different academic councils. He has completed his master's in Sociology, MPhil in Political Economy and Development Sociology, and PhD in Digital Sociology from Jawaharlal Nehru University (JNU), New Delhi. His teaching and research interest cuts across different subfields in media and entertainment management, social studies, which includes media sociology, digital sociology, self and cyberspace, and theories of political economy.

Dr Avadhut Patwardhan holds a Fellow NITIE degree from the National Institute of Industrial Engineering, Mumbai, India. He is presently working as an Assistant Professor with Somaiya Vidyavihar University (SVU) at K.J. Somaiya Institute of Management (KJSIM), Vidyavihar East, Mumbai. His research areas emphasize on Technology Adoption and Services Management. He has published his research work in refereed journals including *Journal of Medical Marketing* and *International Journal of Healthcare Marketing*. He has coauthored research works published in the *International Journal of Product Development* and *International Journal of Electronic Banking*.

John Ericson A. Policarpio is an Assistant Professor and Program Chairperson of the Tourism & Hospitality Management Department of PATTS College of Aeronautics, Philippines. He is a Tourism Professional and currently a candidate for Doctor of Business Administration degree. He is an immediate past Board Member of the Union of Filipino Tourism Educators (UFTE), South Manila Membership Ambassador of the Philippine Association of Researchers for Tourism & Hospitality (PARTH), and a Senior Fellow at the Asia Pacific Institute for Events Management (APIEM). His research interests are in Special Interest or Niche Tourism, Tourism Marketing, Destination Management, and Events Management.

Nosheen Rafique has an MPhil scholarship from the Department of Management Sciences, Bahria University Islamabad. She is working on numerous research papers and book chapters under the supervision of Dr Syed Haider Ali Shah. Her research interest are proenvironmental behavior, employee turnover, motivation enhancing practices, green HR practices, and emotional intelligence.'

Dr Nilanjan Ray is from Kolkata, India, and presently associated as an Associate Professor and Head of the Department at Department of Management Studies, Institute of Leadership Entrepreneurship and Development and Director IQAC. Prior to joining iLEAD, Dr Ray was at Adamas University as an Associate Professor of Marketing Management and Centre Coordinator for Research in Business Analytics at Adamas University in Department of Management, School of Business and Economics, West Bengal, India. Dr Ray has obtained certified *Accredited Management Teacher Award from All India Management Association*, New Delhi, India. He has obtained his PhD(Mktg); M.Com (Mktg); MBA (Mktg), STC FMRM (IIT-Kgp). He has more than 13 years teaching and 6 years Research experience, awarded two Doctoral Scholars, and guided around 56 Post

Graduate students' project also. Dr Ray has contributed over 90 research papers in reputed National and International Referred, Peer Reviewed Journals, Proceedings, and 13 Edited Research Hand Books from Springer, IGI-Global USA, and Apple Academic Publisher CRC Press (A Taylor & Francis Group), USA. He has obtained one Patent from Germany and one Copyright from India. He has also associated himself as a reviewer of Tourism Management Elsevier, Journal of Service Marketing Emerald Group Publishing Limited, Journal of Business and Economics, Research Journal of Business and Management Accounting and as an Editorial Board Member of several referred Journals. Dr Ray has organized several FDPs, National and International Conference, Management Doctoral Colloquium. Dr Ray is a life-member of the International Business Studies Academia, Fellow Member of Institute of Research Engineers and Doctors Universal Association of Arts and Management Professionals (UAAMP) New York, USA Calcutta Management Association (CMA).

Sharjeel Saleem (Assoc Prof, Dr) obtained his PhD in Management from the University of Vienna, Austria. His research interests include international human resource management, specifically expatriate adjustment, organizational behavior, and leadership. He has published his work in highly reputed international journals including *Personnel Review, The Service Industries Journal, Journal of Hospitality and Tourism Management, Journal of Management Development*, etc. He has presented in renowned international conferences, including the Academy of Management Conference, International Congress of Psychology, Academy of Human Resource Development Conference, and Australian & New Zealand Academy of Management Conference. He is currently reviewing for well-reputed journals, including the *International Journal of Human Resource Management, Personnel Review*, and *International Journal of Contemporary Hospitality Management*, among others. He has vast experience in industry and academia. Currently, he is working as an Associate Professor at Lyallpur Business School, Government College University Faisalabad, Pakistan.

Norberto Santos is Full Professor at the University of Coimbra. He has published more than 55 articles in specialized magazines and dozens of works in proceedings of events. He has around 50 book chapters and 14 published and/or edited books. It has 155 technical production items. He participated in 24 events abroad and 121 in Portugal. He supervised 14 doctoral theses and co-supervised 1, supervised more than 50 master's dissertations in the areas of Tourism and Leisure, Economic, and Social Geography and Cultural Geography. He participated in nine research projects and coordinated one of these. He works in the areas of Social Sciences with an emphasis on Tourism, Tourism Destination Management, Economic and Social Geography, in Cultural and Heritage Tourism, in Tourism Management and in Local Development. In his professional activities, he interacted with more than 55 collaborators in coauthorship of scientific works. The most frequent terms in the context of its scientific and technological production are: Tourism, Development, Heritage, Local Development, Coimbra, Gastronomy, Leisure, City, Geography, World Heritage, and Intangible Cultural Heritage.

Dr Syed Haider Ali Shah is the Senior Assistant Professor/Research Cell Coordinator at Business Studies Department, BUIC. He holds a PhD from the University of Malaya, Malaysia. His area of specialization is HR Practices, Leadership, and Management with a special research interest in HR Practices, Green HR Practices, Talent Management, Green HR Practices, Leadership Styles, CSR Practices, and Pro-environmental behavior. Dr. Haider has more than 10 years of experience in Industry and Academia. He has multiple research publications in multiple impact factor journals, ABDC, ABS, Scopus Data Base, and HEC-recognized journals and various book chapters. Moreover, he has presented papers at both national and international conferences. In addition to that, he chaired various sessions at different international and national conferences. Further, he is a reviewer of various reputed journals and works on various projects nationally and internationally. Dr. Haider Shah is engaged in many academic activities and professional training both nationally and internationally. He has been conducting training through different platforms like Leadership Development Center (LDC), Bahria University, and CALWASS. His training activities/Seminars/Webinars on CLAWASS "Center for Academic Learning Writing and Support Services (CALWASS)" can be accessed at https://www.calwass.com, YouTube Channel (CALWASS).

Dr Sofia Devi Shamurailatpam has a PhD in Economics with specialization in the areas of Banking and Financial Economics. Currently she is serving as an Assistant Professor in the Department of Banking and Insurance, Faculty of Commerce, The Maharaja Sayajirao University of Baroda. She has published several research papers to her credit and authored a book entitled *Banking Reforms in India: Consolidation, Restructuring and Performance*, published by Palgrave Macmillan, UK (2017). Her major research area of interests includes Economics of Banking, Financial Economics, Economics of Gender, Agricultural Economics, and Development Economics particularly Contemporary Issues on Sustainability.

Roshan Lal Sharma is Professor of English in the Department of English and European Languages, Central University of Himachal Pradesh, Dharamshala. He has been a Senior Fulbright Fellow at the University of Wisconsin-Madison (USA) during 2007–2008. He has authored *Raja Rao's Shorter Fiction: The Enlightenment Theme* (2009), *Walt Whitman* (2000), coauthored *Som P. Ranchan: Dialogue Epic in Indian English Poetry* (2012), coedited *Communication in Contemporary Scenario: Its Multiple Dimensions* (2017) and *Mapping Diaspora Identities* (2017). He has more than 60 published papers and book chapters to his credit. His areas of interest include contemporary literary and cultural theory, communication studies, and new media ecology.

Dr Anukrati Sharma is the Head and Associate Professor of the Department of Commerce and Management at the University of Kota (a state government university) in Kota, Rajasthan, India. She is the Director of the Skill Development Center of the same University. She is also Dean (Honorary) of two faculties, Tourism and Hospitality and Aviation and Aerospace at Rajasthan Skill University (a government state university) in Jaipur. In 2015, she received a Research

Award from the University Grants Commission (UGC), New Delhi, for her project "Analysis of the Status of Tourism in Hadoti and Shekhawati Region/ Circuit (Rajasthan): Opportunities, Challenges, and Future Prospects." Her doctorate from the University of Rajasthan is in Tourism Marketing, and she completed her dissertation research on Tourism in Rajasthan – Progress and Prospects. She has two postgraduate degree specialties – one in International Business (Master of International Business) and the other in Business Administration (Master of Commerce). Her special interest areas are Tourism, Tourism Marketing, Strategic Management, and International Business Management. Dr Sharma is a featured author of Routledge publishers. Dr Sharma is the Book Series Editor of "Building the Future of Tourism" under Emerald Publishing, UK. She is also the book series editor of *Insights in Tourism* book series, Routledge. She has edited books on *Tourism – Opportunities and Ventures, on Maximizing Business Performance and Efficiency through Intelligent Systems*, under IGI Global (Scopus Indexed), *Tourism Sustainable Tourism Development Futuristic Approaches* under Apple Academic Press (CRC Press, a Taylor & Francis Group), USA, under the series *Advances in Hospitality and Tourism* and book titled *Tourism Events in Asia Marketing and Development*, Routledge, USA, under *Advances in Events Research* series, *Sustainable Destination Branding and Marketing: Strategies for Tourism Development* under CABI, UK, *Future of Tourism: An Asian Perspective*, under Springer, Singapore, *Over-tourism as Destination Risk: Impacts and Solutions*, Emerald Publishing UK under the *Tourism Security – Safety Series*, *Over-tourism, Technology Solutions and Decimated Destinations*, Springer, Singapore, *Event Tourism in Asian Countries: Challenges and Prospects* under Apple Academic Press (Taylor & Francis Group), USA, and *The Emerald Handbook of ICT in Tourism and Hospitality* under Emerald Publishing UK. She also authored a book entitled *Event Management and Marketing Theory, Practical Approaches and Planning*. Another book she wrote is entitled *International Best Practice in Event Management* and it was published by the United Kingdom Event Industry Academy Ltd and Prasetiya Mulya Publishing, Indonesia. Her current projects include editing a book on *COVID-19 and Tourism Sustainability: Ethics, Responsibilities, Challenges and New Directions* for Routledge, USA, *Festivals and Event Tourism: Building Resilience and Promoting Sustainability* for CABI, UK, *The Emerald Handbook of Destination Recovery in Tourism and Hospitality*, Emerald Publishing, UK, *COVID-19 and the Tourism Industry: Sustainability, Resilience & New Directions*, Routledge, UK, *Event Tourism & Sustainable Community Development: Advances, Effects and Implications*, Apple Academic Press, USA, *Crisis, Resilience and Recovery in Tourism and Hospitality*, Springer Nature, Singapore, *Strategic Tourism Planning for Communities: Restructuring and Rebranding*, Nova Science Publishers, USA, *Dynamics of Tourism Industry Post-Pandemic and Disasters*, Apple Academic Press, USA, and *Resilient and Sustainable Destinations after Disaster: Challenges and Strategies*, Emerald Publishing, UK. She is also working on a major research project under Mahatma Gandhi National Council of Rural Education, Ministry of Human Resource Development Government of India. A member of 10 professional bodies, she has attended a number of national and international conferences and presented 45 papers. She has been invited as keynote speaker and panel member by different countries such as Sri Lanka, Uzbekistan, Nepal, and Turkey. She has been invited as Visiting Professor to Kazakhstan and Uzbekistan.

Dr Kasturi Shukla is a trained Hospital Administrator and has completed her PhD (Doctorate) in Health-Related Quality of Life in the adolescent population. She is presently working as Associate Professor, She is Presently working as Associate Professor, Symbiosis Institute of Health Sciences, Symbiosis International (Deemed University), Pune, India, and has more than 18 years' experience in industry, research, and academics. She has published more than 30 original research articles in journals of national and international repute and has published books on applied areas of Hospital Management and Conceptual Frameworks of Quality of Life. She is on the review board of some of the reputed health journals. She has taught Medical Tourism for several years to Health Management students and has delivered invited lectures for students of the Indian Institute of Tourism and Travel Management, India. Besides hospital management and healthcare quality, her core research interest includes Health-Related Quality of Life, Resilience, Medical Value Travel, Sustainability, and Green practices in Business.

Dr Parag S. Shukla has been working as an Assistant Professor in the Faculty of Commerce at the Maharaja Sayajirao University of Baroda (MSUB), Vadodara, Gujarat. Moreover, he has been serving as Honorary Assistant Coordinator at the Management Development Center (MDC) at the Trivenidevi Kashinath Agrawal Management Development Center, and he is also appointed as an Assistant Coordinator of the Main Building at the Faculty of Commerce. Parag Shukla holds a PhD (Commerce), an MCom, BCom, and PG diploma in Marketing Management from the Maharaja Sayajirao University of Baroda. Dr Shukla holds teaching and research experience of more than 10 years. He has been actively associated with various academic organizations like All India Management Association [AIMA], Indian Society of Training and Development [ISTD], and MTC Global, to name a few. Dr Shukla is the recipient of the Best Business Academic of the Year Award [BBAY]. He has also received accolades for his research papers from various academias. Dr Shukla has presented more that 70 research papers in national and international conferences and seminars. He has to his credit more than 30 research papers published in national and international journals.

Luis Avila Silveira has completed his PhD in Tourism, Leisure, and Culture in 2016 from University of Coimbra, Master in Human Geography – Territory and Development and Bachelor in Geography from the University of Coimbra. He is Integrated Researcher at the Center for Studies on Geography and Spatial Planning, Assistant Professor at the University of Coimbra (Department of Geography and Tourism), Sub-director of the journal *Cadernos de Geografia* in the University of Coimbra, and published 12 articles in journals. He has seven section(s) of books. He has supervised one PhD thesis and cosupervised 1. He has also supervised eight MSc dissertation(s) and received 5 awards and/or honors. He participates and/or participated as Research Fellow in one project(s) and was Researcher in seven project(s). In his curriculum Ciência Vitae the most frequent terms in the context of scientific, technological, and artistic-cultural output are: Development; Azores; territories; nautical; Leisure; Marina; impacts; Islands; Figueira da Foz; Vegetable garden; Tourism; Nautical tourism; Recreational Boating; Finland; Tourism; and Portugal.

Bruno Barbosa Sousa, PhD in Marketing and Strategy, is a Professor in the Polytechnic Institute of Cávado and Ave (IPCA, Portugal), Head of Master Program – Tourism Management. He is a researcher at CiTUR and Applied Management Research Unit (UNIAG), Portugal.

Derya Toksoz graduated from Ege University, Department of Hospitality Management in 2012. She completed her MSc and PhD in the field of Tourism Management at Mersin University. Toksoz is continuing her academic career at Isparta University of Applied Sciences Tourism Faculty. Her research interests are mainly focused on tourism planning, cultural heritage management, visitor management, and tour guiding.

Dr Sangeeta Tripathi is currently an Assistant Professor of Mass Communication at the University of Technology and Applied Sciences, Oman, and was previously associated with the Institute of Management Studies, Noida, India. Dr Sangeeta has completed her education at Banaras Hindu University and M.G.K.V., State University, India. She started her career as a TV journalist. Later she embarked on an academic career. She has been active in Communication and Mass Media Research. Her area of research is communication, tourism, public relations, advertising, media education, and online media. She attended Oxford Media Summer Policy School 2019. She has presented her research papers to different international conferences in Dubai, Thailand, Turkey, Hungary, London, the SAUnited States, and India. Recently her research project titled "Advance Communication Role in Creating Consensus and Acceptability for Innovative Tourism to Support Diversified Economy Drive in The Sultanate" was approved by The Research Council (TRC), Ministry of Higher Education, Research and Innovation, Oman.

Shivani Trivedi is a doctoral scholar at MICA, Ahmedabad, India. Her interest area is in Tourism Marketing. Previously she worked at IIM, Indore, as an Academic Associate in Marketing for three years. She has participated in several national and international management and marketing conferences.

Promise Zvavahera holds a PhD in Human Capital Management from the National University of Science and Technology, Zimbabwe. He is the Deputy Registrar-Human Resources & Administration at Africa University. He is a Visiting Lecturer at the Great Zimbabwe University and a part-time Lecturer at Africa University, Zimbabwe. His areas of research are talent acquisition and retention, gender, higher education, marketing, change management, corporate governance, works ethics, and artificial intelligence.

Introduction

Jeetesh Kumar, Gül Erkol Bayram and Anukrati Sharma

Abstract

This book is essential for anyone in destination management in the tourism industry or government. The book includes both theoretical and practical writings for stakeholders. In all chapters, we provide titles including pandemic and disaster descriptions, crises during and after disasters and the motivation and safety of tourists, the regeneration of the tourism industry only after the global epidemic, the revamp of the tourism industry as well as the existence of a reshaping, crisis planning and control upon crises as well as pandemic after the restoration of the tourism sector of the tourism industry, and tourism issues are discussed in the management plans of the centralization. This book provides cases and empirical studies that deal in depth with the current situation, challenges, solutions and future strategies after the outbreaks and natural disasters from a sustainable perspective, for readers with an equitable interest or involvement with the organizations in inquiry.

Keywords: Resilient and sustainable destinations; sustainable tourism; pandemics; crises; destination management; tourism industry

Introduction

Crises refer to a negative situation or a periodic process that leads to consequences. Although it is not desirable to live, it occurs suddenly at certain times and takes a long time to compensate, leaving deep scars. Crises, which can occur in almost any area of daily life, can sometimes refer to a physical illness, an unexpected economic loss, a national famine, a shortage of products, a diplomatic mess, or a severe flood, storm, or earthquake. Regardless of the way it occurs, duration, impact force, social perception, or the negative meaning with which it is associated, crises have significant adverse effects on the tourism sector.

The tourism industry has been the source of livelihood for millions of people worldwide from the past to the present. In addition, tourism offers billions of people the opportunity to introduce their own cultures and get to

Resilient and Sustainable Destinations After Disaster, 1–7
Copyright © 2023 Jeetesh Kumar, Gül Erkol Bayram and Anukrati Sharma
Published under exclusive licence by Emerald Publishing Limited
doi:10.1108/978-1-80382-021-720231001

know different cultures. Tourism is vital for some countries, providing a large part of their income directly and indirectly from the tourism sector. However, the tourism sector has a dynamic structure that is very quickly affected by emerging crises and can give sudden reactions. Tourism, a sector sensitive to the socioeconomic development level of countries, their political stability, and negative developments in the world economic conjuncture, is negatively affected by structural and cyclical problems in the country to various extents and negatively.

The tourism sector has a dynamic structure that can react positively or negatively to different situations in demand. Followed with interest on a global scale, providing a stream of visitors in the regions that they were in severe numbers in creative activities or income in the host country and the impact that tourism destinations and attractions that makes them unique, while making a positive impact on revenues from the sector; several unexpected and undesirable situations, such as terrorist attacks, political events, and epidemics, also have negative consequences for the tourism sector, such as changing travel plans globally, canceling reservations and closing borders to citizens of countries where the epidemic is observed. Epidemics, among the unpredictable situations, also decimate the confidence in the destination where they occur. But unlike epidemics, terrorist attacks, or political events, it requires several measures to be taken globally since they have a spreading effect outside the origin destinations.

This book is about destination resilience and sustainability in pandemics and disasters that cause significant damage to the current functioning of tourism and threaten its future. The book offers theoretical and practical content for academics, researchers, students, tourism employees, business managers, tourist guides, and representatives of local and national institutions. In this context, the book covers topics such as definitions of pandemic & disaster, tourist motivation & safety, disaster recovery of the tourism sector after the pandemic, redesigning tourism activities, creating restructuring, crisis management, recovery of the tourism sector and tourism policy & planning beyond pandemics. Government policies and strategies significantly impact sustainable and regenerative tourism after pandemics. Therefore, climate change, disasters, and pandemics are critical issues of tourism management & marketing. This book includes cases and empirical studies that deal with the current situation, challenges, solutions, and future strategies after epidemics and natural disasters from a sustainable perspective. Almost the entire world is in a difficult situation in this process, but we must overcome it as soon as possible, start tourism movements, and take precautions. At this point, destinations are considered a great mission and the trigger of the world economy and development.

In the **first chapter**, Jamader, Chowdhary, and Jha address the history of pandemics and disasters, tourist motivation and safety during and after pandemics and disasters, recovery of the tourism industry after pandemics and disasters, redesign, reconstruction, and creation of tourism activities, crisis management and planning after pandemic and disasters, post-pandemic tourism industry recovery the routes and tourism plans, the role of governments in the management of the tourism industry, government policies, laws and strategies after the pandemic and disasters, the role of sustainable tourism for durable tourism after the pandemic, the current situation of the hotel industry in the new world, the competitive marketing strategies of tourism management after the pandemic, alternative tourism after the pandemic, reflections of climate change on tourism, and future trends after the pandemic with theoretical and practical content.

In the **second chapter**, Aksoz and Itır Can argue the recovery strategies in the post-crisis period and "smart destinations", one of the most popular topics of recent years. In this chapter, the author presents information within the context of some data from United Nations World Tourism Organization (UNWTO). The chapter discusses resilient and sustainable destinations after the disaster on behalf of challenges and strategies.

In the **third chapter**, Liberato, Sousa, Costa, and Liberato focus on creating a tourism monitoring system for Arouca (Portugal), a territory classified as a low-density territory with specific characteristics. The further chapter also includes planning and management of a database at the disposal of all stake-holders, ensuring that the tourism flows in the analysis do not get overwhelmed, allowing the discussion of opportunities and threats for the territory, based on the partnership between the population, public and private sector, adjusted to the social, cultural, economic, and environmental perception.

In the **fourth chapter**, Chigora, Nyagadza, Katsande, and Zvavahera argue about Zimbabwean tourism and the effect of festivals and events on brand image and equity. Since Zimbabwe, as a tourism destination, has also experienced various changes due to globalization induced by its socioeconomic and political state of affairs, this chapter deals with some issues for surviving the changing market demands. As a tourism destination, Zimbabwe has also adopted branding as a marketing strategy to hold a highly valued global market position through extensive brand identity.

In the **fifth chapter**, Chigora, Nyagadza, Katsande, and Zvavahera seek answers to the marketing strategies used in Zimbabwe tourism destination; the leading tourism sectors involved in tourism destination marketing; factors that affect the image of a tourism destination; the competitive environment in tourism destination; the stages in Zimbabwe tourism destination area life cycle; the marketing efforts that have been practiced in Zimbabwe tourism destination; and the marketing mixes for Zimbabwe tourism destination success. This chapter shall explore the destination marketing position for the Zimbabwe tourism industry.

In the **sixth chapter**, Nazir, Santos, and Silveira identify new offerings in a different normal, more worried about health issues, ethical behaviors, and trips with a social purpose to contribute to local development. Also, an archival analysis of studies anchored on this issue. While critically contemplating the existing studies, this study implicates the new offerings duly implemented during the new normal. Recommendations were acquired from these literature-based implications on specific and generic grounds.

Alcoriza and Policarpio in the **seventh chapter**, deal with building resilient and sustainable societies post-disaster tourism. According to the chapter, tourism communities must be resilient to maintain economic benefits. These issues need a strategic approach to local tourism development with solid public–private partnerships (PPPs) and collaboration. Resilient and sustainable local tourism communities must be guided by carefully defined goals and objectives depending on the dynamics and resources and critical areas to focus on as economy, environment, emergency management and response, disaster risk management, community-based participation, post-disaster tourism recovery management, psychological behavior of people, nature-based tourism, dark tourism, responsive consumer behavior, and transportation.

In the **eighth chapter**, Shah, Jamshed, Saleem, Al-Ghazali, and Kiani focus on pre-pandemic tourism history in Asia and the effects on the tourism industry during the existing phases of COVID-19, including the facts and available stats of Asia, which will help in the understanding of how these countries are rebuilding the tourism industry in the post-pandemic situation by literature review. The chapter provides an overview of the measures taken by top tourism countries of Asia regarding the post-pandemic situations and their plans, whichever they are planning. According to the chapter, some countries work on domestic tourism while others offer travel bubbles for neighboring countries. Some countries in the Middle East, like Saudi Arabia (Riyadh Season, 2021) and UAE (EXPO-2020), are bringing entertainment events to attract international tourists.

In the **ninth chapter**, Shukla and Patwardhan discuss systematically reviewing the literature for identifying recovery strategies to create a resilient healthcare sector. This study deployed the systematic literature review/synthesis approach. The various databases like Google Scholar, ProQuest, and EBSCO were searched for predefined keywords. This study considered articles published between 2000 and 2021 due to the narrow focus on a specific sector like healthcare. As a result of an online literature search, 116 studies were identified. The relevance to the sector was considered as an inclusion criterion. Considering the inclusion and exclusion criteria, 30 were retained for the systematic review. The results show that collective resilience consists of individual resilience and organizational resilience.

In the **tenth chapter**, Batabyal, Ray, Bag, and Nag seek to answer their question of what factors are responsible for pilgrim tourist harassment in major Hindu pilgrim centers in India. The study is confined to ill treatment and related sociocultural issues, only avoiding the lack of facilities and scarcity of services in the pilgrim centers. To appreciate the extent of harassment encountered by tourists, an in-depth study was conducted on the reviews provided by tourists on TripAdvisor's (Indian) website. This study characterizes harassment through an ethnographic research approach of published reviews. According to TripAdvisor, a total of 260 reviews of 28 top Hindu temples are considered for all the states and union territories where the top Hindu pilgrim centers are located (excluding Nagaland). This study has also shown how tourists respond when they face such situations. The study is impactful as it can question many policy issues and temple management procedures. Also, it raises and highlights many illegitimate and unsustainable practices that need to be investigated further for policies and procedures to be reviewed and updated accordingly.

Tripathi and Al Shahri, in the **eleventh chapter**, reveal to promote safe and innovative tourism for the sustainable growth of Oman and to explore different communication strategies to enhance public and private partnerships, to offer tremendous socioeconomic benefits by stimulating the development of local and long-term establishment that benefits many generations, to encourage investment climate in the country. This chapter discussed communication effectiveness and significance for attracting tourists to the country and called for the community to participate in facilitating visitors. The quantitative method would be applied to reach out to the findings. The samples have been obtained from the Dhofar region through the survey. Tabulation and coding have been done.

Jamgade and Mondal, in the **twelfth chapter**, determine to provide the conceptual knowledge of sustainable and responsible tourism product planning for the recovery of the tourism industry that is severely bruised by the COVID-19 pandemic using secondary data. The chapter will also highlight the cases of responsible tourism products in India and Belize. According to the chapter, the tourism sector was severely hit by the pandemic. Thus, it created an introspection phase for the tourism stakeholders to check and control their activities for a better recovery. Responsible tourism product development in this VUCA (volatile, uncertain, complex, and ambiguous) world needs controlled planning and a duty-bound PPP product model.

In the **thirteenth chapter**, Toksoz and Dalgıc examine the measures and recovery plans taken by the countries to increase the resilience of the tourism industry against crises/disasters. This book chapter seeks answers to what can be done to prepare and fortify destinations in times of risk and disasters. This chapter is provided with vulnerability and resilience terms. In addition, the strengthening practices against the tourism crises will be examined and presented. The chapter will be concluded with recommendations.

Kılıç, in the **fourteenth chapter**, focuses on the policy regulations of destinations for senior tourism by secondary source scanning and the development and changes in the process by examining academic studies on the subject. This chapter highlights the destinations' restrictive and encouraging policies and strategies. The qualitative method and document analysis technique was used to analyze the emerging codes in MAXQDA qualitative analysis program.

In the **fifteenth chapter** Arora and Lal Sharma focus on spirituality, yoga, and meditation as strategies for well-being. The qualitative analysis of the literature will serve as secondary data on various government portals that will serve as indicators. For content analysis in the public domain, Nvivo software will be used. The traditional Indian scriptures and their excerpts will be used to support the arguments. This chapter presents well-being, spirituality, and yoga as strategies post-disaster, traditional ways for better wellness tourism, and the role of tourism as a bridge for achieving well-being in a post-disaster scenario.

In the **sixteenth chapter**, Erkol Bayram, Kumar, and Sharma argue the levels of utilization of smart tourism applications by tourist guides, their activities in the

COVID-19 period, and the transformation that tour guiding will undergo in the future. In this chapter, smart tourism applications used in tours with opportunities and challenges and current practices were explained according to previous papers. In addition, the reflection of the guided cultural tours in the future has been evaluated. According to this chapter, tourist guides, one of the essential service providers of tourism, have effected greatly by smart tourism technology during the COVID-19 period.

Shukla and Shamurailatpam, in the **seventeenth chapter**, examined the concept of regenerative tourism to build resilience, particularly during the post-COVID-19 pandemic. The result shows various strategies for implementing regenerative tourism, framework approach not recovery of tourism and renewing tourism. Additionally, implications of regenerative tourism and a roadmap provided for the tourism stakeholders could be foreseen.

In the **eighteenth chapter**, Shah, Rafique, Saleem, Amjad, and Arshad identify the revamping of the hospitality and hotel industry in the Southeast Asian region after the COVID-19 pandemic. The chapter also focuses on how a crisis management plan revamps this industry after the most significant destruction. According to this chapter, reconstruction of this tourism depends upon the advanced techniques and practices to boost up this sector after the crisis. Therefore, implementing such practices highly depends on highly educated and aware managers.

In the **nineteenth chapter**, Dave explores the ecotourism potential of the Vagad region of the State of Rajasthan in India. The subsequent sections in the chapter describe the unexplored ecotourist spots in the region having environmental and social importance. Tourism here means an encounter with experiencing nature in the lap of rich cultural heritage. It underlies exploring the mixed deciduous forests, heritage forts, picturesque landscapes, and tribal communities and discovering unmapped natural and sociocultural heritage, highlighting sustainability's importance.

In the **twentieth chapter**, Trivedi and Patra discussed the implementation of post-pandemic sustainable practices and revealed how these practices could benefit India's travel and tourism sector. The epidemic has forced everyone to confront the environmental issues that people have exacerbated. Vacationers would hold a crucial role in ecological concerns following the outbreak. The chapter will focus on the challenges and opportunities facing the travel industry following the COVID-19 situation.

The editors believe that this book will fill a significant gap in identifying, managing, and controlling pandemics and disasters that will always impact destinations. Pandemics and disasters have affected people since the beginning of the historical era. Today, it affects and will continue to affect humanity and many lines of business. The book is made up of collective experiences. The book evaluates the issues related to pandemics and disasters from a broad perspective within the scope of destination resilience and sustainability. The book will provide a good and original understanding and approach to academics, students, and researchers. It will provide information about the problems, challenges, and future implications of pandemics and disasters that control the success and resilience of destinations.

This book is a laborious and ambitious effort by professionals and academics in various countries. We are grateful to the authors from India, Turkey, Spain, Pakistan, Zimbabwe, Oman, Malaysia, Portugal, and the Philippines, who believe in us and support us.

A Road Map for Two Decades of Sustainable Tourism Development Framework

Asik Rahaman Jamader, Shahnawaz Chowdhary and Srijib Shankar Jha

Abstract

Sustainability, innovation, and corporate identity were the guiding ideas in a research. Professional discussion was used to get information. The research yielded four possibilities for a sustainable tourist business in 2040, each defined by the fundamental variables that will shape that future. This theoretical chapter is dedicated to the conceptualization of fairness concepts in relation to local knowledge sharing and addresses practical implications for how varied claims of justice by local actors might be handled in the development of sustainable tourism. The Sustainable Improvement Goals (SIGs) and the management ecology of tourism are investigated using a "heterogeneous respondents completed" methodology.

Keywords: Sustainable tourism; Sustainable Improvement Goals (SIGs); sustainable tourist business; methodology; development framework; tourism

Introduction

The fact that tourism policymakers, including industry and destination marketing organizations, and tourism scholars, place a lot of emphasis on sustainable development has evolved to be accepted as a given. For instance, the World Tourism Organization (UNWTO), the leading UN body, lists sustainable growth as one of the webpage primary categories for what it does in the case of the former. Regarding the above, several manuals and journal articles – possibly making up even more a 5% of publication output – as well as a specific journal focusing on sustainable tourism are available. Because of the importance of sustainable tourism to public policy, 2022 was designated as the UN's official

Resilient and Sustainable Destinations After Disaster, 9–18
doi:10.1108/978-1-80382-021-720231002

International Year of Sustainable Tourism for Advancement (Ip, Leung, & Law, 2011). However, actual data suggest that, globally, tourist industry is really less sustainable than ever despite this interest and overt attention. Obtainable to pursue a crowd of elite assortment unbearable explanation to ecotourism development in places like Spain, India, as well as Northern Italy, which are part of a larger sector as well as the government representative reactions to the alleged "achievement" of tourism, concerns about tourism's contribution to sustainable development have also emerged at the local-level report on Controlling Crowdedness in Tourism Destinations: Coping with Achievement (Law, Buhalis, Cobanoglu, 2014).

As part of a new sustainable development agenda, the UN 2040 Agenda for Sustainable Development lays out a number of Sustainable Development Goals (SDGs) for the year 2040, including "to eradicate inequality, safeguard the environment, and provide affluence for everyone." Considering the UNWTO's focus on sustainability tourism and the sector's economic importance, the Sustainable Improvement Goals (SIGs) and their related Millennium Improvement Goals (MIGs) have emerged as key areas of research for tourism's role in sustainable development and the integrity of hospitality as a whole. Notwithstanding the this, tourism is only mentioned multiple times in the UN 2040 Agenda for Sustainable Development resolution: once in relation to the sustainable use of marine resources to boost the economic benefits to small-island developing states and least developed countries and once in relation to the creation of jobs and the promotion of local culture and items (Yoo, Lee, & Bai, 2011). However, although some criticisms of the methods used to achieve the objectives, the prevailing narrative frequently adopts the strategies as well as motifs of the narrative of tourism's "adventure" to the SIGs. The connection for sustainability is founded on the premise that the way communities are currently organized around the world is unsustainable, or, to put it another way, does not take into account Earth's natural limits and is not capable of providing a sense of well-being for the people within these limits, both now and in the long term (Williams, 2006).

This chapter offers a known antiviewpoint on how the tourism industry has approached the SIGs and how conceptualized solution fits. This is principally made in response to the accepted understanding of the dominant social paradigm in tourism, which describes the fundamental assumptions and behaviors of buyers and sellers in the tourist trade as they are expressed in the current price structures as well as the behaviors of actors who reinforce the paradigm within related formal institutions (Wang, & Qualls, 2007). Giant business players, nationwide trade bodies, as well as tourism boards, along with internationally renowned organizations like the UNWTO and the World Travel and Tourism Council (WTTC), are crucial players in promoting the economy's significance, expansion, competitive pressure, as well as the "strategic planning" of issues.

Numerous universities and the professors who work there also firmly support this viewpoint. This is given the high inconsistencies here between viewpoints as sustainable development, which are demonstrated by the loss of biodiversity, the concentration of wealth in the hands of a few number of people, as well as the mounting reality of climate change. Instead, there are many different methods to know and many different claims to reflect reality, making knowledge essentially plural. This structuralism viewpoint contrasts with realist beliefs that a fact-based analysis will disclose the reality to which coping strategies may logically react. As a result, in accordance with the prevailing exchange patterns, a "heterogeneous constructionist" method is used to build the SIGs and tourism. While studying leisure as well as the SIGs, in especially as they were created mostly by UNWTO, the nature of this approach is examined first. Sustainable development comprises an economic-social aspect in addition to an environmental aspect (Pirnar, Icoz, & Icoz, 2010). Although since 1970s, it has been understood that although the phenomenon might be resolved, sustainability also requires addressing social challenges like poverty reduction and the development of skills. Although while most sectors have seen improvement, as the UN's yearly report on the Millennium Development Goals (MDGs) demonstrates, there are still urgent societal challenges that must be tackled, particularly but not primarily in poor nations. As a result, it might be said that our digital age is untenable from an environmental and social standpoint. The generally accepted traditional idea of green tourist industry suggested by the Ministry Of Environment and UNWTO aims to ensure that tourism lessens its negative impacts and increases its positive impacts on the environment and public health of the project: Hospitality which "gets complete explanation of its present as well as prospective financial, sociological, and implications, meeting the requirements of tourists, the sector, the ecosystem, including local community" is referred to as tourism development. In order to be considered acting upon sustainability, a tourism industry must add value on all three of the triple bottom lines of revenue, persons, as well as the ecosystem (DiPietro & Wang, 2010).

Corporate Identification as Well as the Genetic Structure

In recent years, there has been an increase in interest in how to incorporate sustainability into a company's guiding principles and business strategy. The aim of corporate plan is to create a sustainable strong position in the market. Companies that want to succeed must make their offerings as relevant to their clients as possible and stand out from those of their competitors. In other respects, businesses have to both generate distinguishing key marketing features that set themselves excluding the competition and to achieve the fundamental requirements required to succeed in a market, known as the key achievement determinants. A company's positioning, or unique combination of relevance and distinctiveness, defines its position in the marketplace. The first step in enhancing business performance is location. The approach, which may include a sustainable effective policy, is said to follow when the standing is obvious (Tuomi, Tussyadiah, & Stienmetz, 2021). As was said before, the sustainability movement puts an emphasis on the long-term prospects, as well as for companies to participate in it, they must cause a stronger, coming generations strategy. It's challenging to see the future, especially the long-term future. There are several causes for this. First, only a portion of the future can be changed by human actions because of past and current actions and decisions that have an impact on the future, as well as the paradigms that are used to make those decisions. Furthermore, given its intricacy, business is challenging to understand as well as, consequently, to affect (Inanc–Demir & Kozak, 2019).

Throughout the increasingly globalized as well as a densely civilization, tourist industry is closely linked to other population, financial, cultural, innovative, environmental, diplomatic, and institutional developments. Tourist industry is made up of a number of domains that are highly interconnected and interdependent (such as sports, hospitality, recreation, culture and the arts, events, and travel), each with their own dynamics and perspectives the services and facilities in the tourism opportunity Third, there is a lot of uncertainty about the future because of the shifting customer demand and the enormous rise in consumer understanding. With the help of professional counsel, foresight has been used in this study to promote sustainable tourist expansion (Damnjanović, Lončarić, & Dlačić, 2020). Although since 1960s, both in commercial practice and in the scientific community, foresight has evolved as an alternative to prediction. The intricacies, dynamism, inherent partially of the modern world are accepted by clairvoyance, in contrast to traditional forecasts. This method projects the future into the present rather than the past and the present into the tomorrow.

Scenarios are created based on the results after the main drivers of change and significant uncertainties have been investigated. Such possibilities depict a vision as intended as mentioned in the preceding section since they are dynamic descriptions of conceivable possibilities rather than quantitative forecasts. All of the scenarios might come true because they are based on the hides. Combined, the alternatives paint a picture of how the globe might eventually seem. For corporates, the main task is to be ready for each of these possibilities. This kind of forward thinking will make companies more resilient ahead. It suggests a shift in behavior from being reactive to being proactive and believes that this is crucial for the ability of tourist groups as well as enterprises to compete (Leonidou, Leonidou, Fotiadis, & Zeriti, 2013).

Two key inconsistencies that, in the opinion of the specialists, will drive the sustainable development of the tourism industry through the year 2040, as well as the opposing guidance in which these uncertainties may develop, were identified through an analysis of the findings of both consultation rounds. The term "essential uncertainty" describes the factors that are both highly significant and very uncertain about the result of transformation. The sociopolitical environment in Europe and India's resource base are the two key uncertainties that have been highlighted. The contrasting paths where one or both may conceivably evolve by 2040 were used to illustrate the unpredictability of these elements (Kuo, Chen, & Tseng, 2017). The sociopolitical environment also might result in India having a reasonably strong economic position or a worse economic one. The economic base might result in total reliance on (old) nonsustainable resources or analysis includes on conventional resources. Four different scenarios are framed by a cross with two axes that is based on the two major assumptions described earlier and their opposing growth paths (Nayak, Mishra, Das, Jamader, & Acharya, 2022). These have been described as being from the 1970s, being in terror, putting one's arms on the steering, and also being globally unique. The situations intersect in

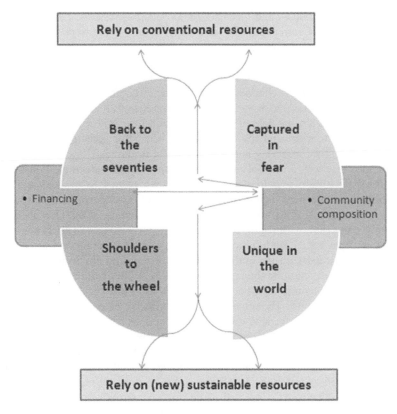

Fig. 1.   Road Map for a Healthy Tourist Sector by 2040 With Four
Scenarios.

Fig. 1. The outputs of the detailed analysis as well as the data flow model diagram
were used to provide coherent explanations for the situations (Pappas, 2015).

Differentiated Methodological Individualism

The heterogeneity standardized conditions try to stay away from dualism classifications that view environment as a purely human institution with no independent reality or as an external domain that serves as a resource for, limit to,
determiner of, or background to modern civilization. Contrarily, the heterogeneous materialist viewpoint holds that ecology and the environment are actually,
consequently learning about them is a continually and existentially shifting
endeavour (Sigala, 2003). For instance, the growth of companies based on the
natural world, such as the ecotourism industry, demonstrates how biophysical
processes shape some sectors, especially those that are biologically based, by

offering both possibilities and obstacles for production systems. Lacking experience of the world, Castree argues, "we can never fully come to comprehend the nature to which these learning's pertain. ..." To structure our interactions with phenomena we categorize as "normal," we employ both implicit and explicit knowledge. In a nutshell, there is no unhindered accessibility to the beauty of nature free from existing theories. However, the structure it offers is frequently overlooked without taking into account the "suppositions that orchestrate as well as, notably, constrain the field of analysis," which have had a significant impact on research on tourism and the environment. The SIGs seek to enable growth while concurrently conserving nature and natural resources.

The idea of effect, a symbol rooted from the physical realism metaphysics of traditional positivism and frequently utilized with regard to tourism and sustainability, notably with regard to the SIGs as well as conceptions of "tourism impacts," is the best illustration of this (Buhalis & Sinarta, 2019). For instance, the study states that, with regard to "Enhancing metrics to ensure effect as well as sharing information," "Both nations and enterprises need frameworks to collect, aggregate, and report on the entire economic, social, and environmental implications of tourism," despite the fact that the study defines sustainable tourism as "travel that fully accounts for its current and prospective financial, sociological, or ecological implications" The attention on the "effects" of population growth on economic growth, society, and environment as one of the "three pillars" of sustainability has favored explanations that rely on correlation in time and space and methodologies that are entirely focused on hooking up as well as specific pictures, to the disadvantage of the quest for techniques of link and proximate cause instead of simple correlation. The focus on the impression moment(s) is predicated on a baseline that is assumed to be stable in terms of nature, society, or economy, as well as an experimental design where just one factor is altered. Additionally, such a method is ineffective for comprehending complicated as well as changing political and social processes (Cline, 1999).

As a Management Ecology, Tourism and the SIGs

Environmental and resource management, as described by managerial ecology, entails the use of science and utilitarian economic theories for the purpose of asset utilization as well as productivity expansion. Administrative environmentalism, which is distinguished by an "unquestionable confidence in administration as the answer to underground ecological and societal issues," aims to maximize energy output, economic returns, and environmental quality through ecosystem modeling, manipulation, and result prediction. Zwier and Blok interpret the anthropogenic notion as a result of management ecology thinking, contrary to Merchant's contention that managerial ecology's historical roots are in reductionist utilitarian approaches to the human–nature connection. However, despite the fact that complexity science emphasizes uncertainty and the limits of predictability and control, this has not led to "a wholesale rejection of the idea of management, rather it has resulted in redefinition, redeployment and relocation of management, supervisors, as well as the handled," as stated in the article.

Since this aims to end whether at as well as highlights the importance of engineering and innovation in dealing with crises, management is crucial in its perceived ability to handle challenging problems, like those addressed either by SIGs. In comparison, relatively new progress in political and social thinking has brought to light not just the multiscale dynamic complexity of sustainability concerns but also the manner in which values as well as the sociopolitical environment of judgments are used to influence the government. In a managerial ecology paradigm, the effects of complexity vary depending on the viewpoint. If intricacy is viewed from an epistemological standpoint as a fundamental naturally occurring phenomenon, it is obvious that there must be constraints on control and that alternative surviving or adapting mechanisms are necessary (Jamader, Das, & Acharya, 2019). The analysis presented indicates how significantly the leadership ecology of the large tourism organisations to the SIGs, which has a neoliberal concentration, is impacting how the ecosystem is handled, how people relate to the world around them, as well as it could be argued, how investigation should be undertaken. Capitalism is predicated on the idea that the market mediates how citizens interact with the state and other people. Neoliberalism scientific management, also known as new public management, entails incarcerating technological innovations that are infused with commercial ideals in order to rule. In the case of the UNWTO, there has been a gradual but significant trend away from sustainability and toward market principles.

This, obviously, partly improved the performance in governmentality elsewhere, but significantly, it hasn't made tourism any more sustainable; in fact, as was mentioned at the start of this chapter, tourism has actually gotten less sustainable overall by the majority of scientific measurements (Sagayam et al., 2022). If the expansion in tourism activity, their reflecting higher, as well as the performance improved from initiatives greatly exceed high product efficiency per tourist, then the emphasis on greater efficiency in tourism – for example, in terms of per tourist consumption – makes little difference to the industry's overall absolute sustainability and the achievement of the SDGs' development sustainability.

The world has a language to it. Even if it is important, this goes beyond simply defining what defines sustainable tourism since it also establishes how we should view vacation as well as its connection to the SIGs. While capitalism is the dominant political, financial, as well as cultural fictitious concept of today's culture, comprehended as "a mindset communicated in a society by regular folk, the prevalent conceptions which complement existing practises potential, offering people sense and legitimacy," it is frequently presented as apolitical. This is especially true of neoliberal approaches, such as those portrayed in the UNWTO's approach to the SIGs. Despite the fact that neoliberal economics comes in many forms, there's still enough evidence of its similarities to show that the report and related UNWTO activities related to the SDGs are helping to reembed sustainable tourism in various political, legal, and cultural frameworks that prioritize business and corporate interests as well as the financialization and mercerization of sustainability (Das, Jamader, Acharya, & Das, 2019). The WTTC's attempts to further this perspective are probably unsurprising given that it is an organization serving corporate interests. Contrarily, the UNWTO is intended to have a broader authority but nonetheless support the idea that the private sector and competitive markets should bear greater responsibility in the provision of tourism infrastructure and services and, as a result, act to further support the commoditization of the environment by tourism. As the following quote from the UNWTO suggests: "Turning sustainability into eco-business... is altering the nature of environmentalism, increasing its power to accelerate some forms of change, but it also increases its power to promote biotic." The concept of sustainability can be radical since it calls for modifications to not just the game's rules but also to the event altogether.

Additionally, adopting the vocabulary of adaptability, specifically in regard to SIG "decarbonisation," to support particular characteristics of sustainability acts as a form of "capitalist conservationism" that views the exhaustion of ecologies as a problem of global security for which the only solution is the securitization as well as securitization of the biodiversity (Jamader, Das, Acharya, & Hu, 2021). In fact, the UNWTO as well as the WTTC seem to be promoting "much of the same" neoliberal methods despite of the fact that they are failing because to the general feeling of major challenge either by SIGs, responsible tourism, especially, extra recently, tourism impacts.

Conclusion

The SIGs' universal call to sustainable development and its conceptualization speak to a feeling of intercultural competence. The SIGs are apparently meant to address economic, environmental, and social problems; however, such appeals "steer attention away from the difficult politics that result from differentiated social groups having different interests in causing and alleviating" these issues, even though they are not necessarily unjustified, especially in areas like individual rights. The method, which is common to much of the research on sustainable tourism, aims to "tune out" viewpoints that are at odds with neoliberalist managerial ecosystems, including some that raise doubts regarding specific problem-solving presumptions as well as the relative contributions of the industry, businesses, as well as the government. Highlighting the interpersonal linkages its production includes and demystifying the managerial ecology, tourist knowledge, and policymaking are not needed to indicate skepticism about perhaps that understanding or the realities it reflects. Shall consist continued, that there could clearly be no discussion of doing without science given its crucial role in aiding in the understanding of the natural concerns like environmental issues. The difficulty is in learning to comprehend as well as deal with it effectively.

It is necessary to disrupt the status quo of ongoing tourist expansion as well as consumption in order to achieve the holy grail of manageability championed by the UNWTO and others: the notion that all issues can be resolved by expending more effort and demanding more efficiency. In fact, if the SIGs and its tourist supporters are serious about making tourism a "sector of hope," they must clearly commit to living within the ecological boundaries of the ecosystems of which we are a part, rather than continuing to promote expansion.

References

Buhalis, D., & Sinarta, Y. (2019). Real-time co-creation and nowness service: Lessons from tourism and hospitality. *Journal of Travel & Tourism Marketing, 36*(5), 563–582.

Cline, R. S. (1999). Hospitality 2000—The technology: Building customer relationships. *Journal of Vacation Marketing, 5*(4), 376–386.

Damnjanović, V., Lončarić, D., & Dlačić, J. (2020). Teaching case study: Digital marketing strategy of Accor Hotels: Shaping the future of hospitality. *Tourism and Hospitality Management, 26*(1), 233–244.

Das, P., Jamader, A. R., Acharya, B. R., & Das, H. (2019, May). HMF based QoS aware recommended resource allocation system in mobile edge computing for IoT. *2019 International Conference on Intelligent Computing and Control Systems (ICCS)* (pp. 444–449). IEEE.

DiPietro, R. B., & Wang, Y. R. (2010). Key issues for ICT applications: Impacts and implications for hospitality operations. *Worldwide Hospitality and Tourism Themes.* doi:10.1108/17554211011012595

Inanc–Demir, M., & Kozak, M. (2019). Big data and its supporting elements: Implications for tourism and hospitality marketing. In *Big data and innovation in tourism, travel, and hospitality* (pp. 213–223). Singapore: Springer.

Ip, C., Leung, R., & Law, R. (2011). Progress and development of information and communication technologies in hospitality. *International Journal of Contemporary Hospitality Management.* doi:10.1108/09596111111130029

Jamader, A. R., Das, P., & Acharya, B. R. (2019, May). BcIoT: Blockchain based DDoS prevention architecture for IoT. In *2019 International Conference on Intelligent Computing and Control Systems (ICCS)* (pp. 377–382). IEEE.

Jamader, A. R., Das, P., Acharya, B., & Hu, Y. C. (2021). Overview of security and protection techniques for microgrids. In *Microgrids* (pp. 231–253). Boca Raton, FL: CRC Press.

Kuo, C. M., Chen, L. C., & Tseng, C. Y. (2017). Investigating an innovative service with hospitality robots. *International Journal of Contemporary Hospitality Management.* doi:10.1108/IJCHM-08-2015-0414

Law, R., Buhalis, D., & Cobanoglu, C. (2014). Progress on information and communication technologies in hospitality and tourism. *International Journal of Contemporary Hospitality Management.* doi:10.1108/IJCHM-08-2013-0367

Leonidou, L. C., Leonidou, C. N., Fotiadis, T. A., & Zeriti, A. (2013). Resources and capabilities as drivers of hotel environmental marketing strategy: Implications for competitive advantage and performance. *Tourism Management, 35*, 94–110.

Nayak, D. K., Mishra, P., Das, P., Jamader, A. R., & Acharya, B. (2022). Application of deep learning in biomedical informatics and healthcare. In *Smart healthcare analytics: State of the art* (pp. 113–132). Singapore: Springer.

Pappas, N. (2015). Marketing hospitality industry in an era of crisis. *Tourism Planning & Development, 12*(3), 333–349.

Pirnar, I., Icoz, O., & Icoz, O. (2010). *The new tourist: Impacts on the hospitality marketing strategies* (pp. 25–28). Amsterdam: EuroCHRIE.

Sagayam, K. M., Das, P., Jamader, A. R., Acharya, B. R., Bonyah, E., & Elngar, A. A. (2022). DeepCOVIDNet: COVID-19: Detection of chest image using deep learning model. *Research Square.* doi:10.21203/rs.3.rs-1725511/v1

Sigala, M. (2003). Developing and benchmarking internet marketing strategies in the hotel sector in Greece. *Journal of Hospitality & Tourism Research*, *27*(4), 375–401.

Tuomi, A., Tussyadiah, I. P., & Stienmetz, J. (2021). Applications and implications of service robots in hospitality. *Cornell Hospitality Quarterly*, *62*(2), 232–247.

Wang, Y., & Qualls, W. (2007). Towards a theoretical model of technology adoption in hospitality organizations. *International Journal of Hospitality Management*, *26*(3), 560–573.

Williams, A. (2006). Tourism and hospitality marketing: Fantasy, feeling and fun. *International Journal of Contemporary Hospitality Management*. doi:10.1108/09596110610681520

Yoo, M., Lee, S., & Bai, B. (2011). Hospitality marketing research from 2000 to 2009: Topics, methods, and trends. *International Journal of Contemporary Hospitality Management*. doi:10.1108/09596111111130010

The Benefits of Being a Smart Destination in the Post-COVID-19 Period

Emre Ozan Aksoz and Ipek Itir Can

Abstract

The aim of the study is to determine the benefits of transforming a destination into smart destination (SD) to restart tourism after the COVID-19 outbreak, to match the dimensions of SD with restarting strategies, and to make conceptual inferences to serve this. For this purpose, two reports published by the World Tourism Organization (WTO) in 2020 were examined: Priorities for Tourism Recovery and Global Guidelines to Restart Tourism. Then, the contents of these reports and the dimensions of SDs were matched and a guiding model for tourism decision-makers was developed.

Keywords: COVID-19 pandemic; restart strategies; restart tourism; smart destination; smart city; tourism recovery

Introduction

The outbreak of COVID-19, which first appeared in Wuhan, China, in December 2019 (Medical News Today, 2022) was declared as a "global health emergency" by the World Health Organization (WHO) on January 30, 2020 (Foo, Chin, Tan, & Phuah, 2021). The COVID-19 pandemic, which affected the whole world from 2020 to 2022 and became a major concern, infected a total of 537,591,764 people and led to the death of 6,319,395 people according to the data of the WHO dated June 20, 2022 (WHO, 2022). This global pandemic caused by a new type of coronavirus (SAR-CoV-2) has had a significant negative impact on economic development around the world (Bakar & Rosbi, 2020). So much so that Kristalina Georgieva, the Director-General of the International Monetary Fund (IMF), described COVID-19 as "*a crisis like no other,*" emphasizing the devastating impact of this crisis on the global economy (World Economic Forum, 2020). The social distancing measures, lockdown practices, and travel restrictions intended to

Resilient and Sustainable Destinations After Disaster, 19–39
Copyright © 2023 Emre Ozan Aksoz and Ipek Itir Can
Published under exclusive licence by Emerald Publishing Limited
doi:10.1108/978-1-80382-021-720231003

reduce the spread of the pandemic have globally transformed people's lifestyles, habits, and, thus, the functioning of sectors.

One of the changed habits of people has undoubtedly been about their travel and tourism preferences. This transformation has significantly affected and still significantly affects the tourism sector. Therefore, the changes that the COVID-19 outbreak will bring about in the functioning of the tourism sector emerge as a prominent research area. The COVID-19 pandemic has also once again underlined the importance of sustainability (Jones & Comfort, 2020) and given opportunities to destinations that follow the sustainable development goal. In the last 3 years (in 2017, 2018, and 2019) until 2020, when the pandemic struck globally, overtourism was a hot topic, but the concept of nontourism appears to be trending starting from the first quarter of 2020 (Gössling, Scott, & Hall, 2020). This provides decision-makers with the opportunity to develop tourism in a more conscious and sustainable way after the elimination of nontourism and the transition to the recovery phase. Various strategies have been developed to restart tourism activities in destinations after the COVID-19 outbreak and to ensure the sustainability of tourism. These strategies are presented in the reports entitled the "Priorities for Tourism Recovery" and "Global Guidelines for Restart Tourism" published by the Global Tourism Crisis Committee affiliated with the WTO on May 28, 2020. The principles and priorities set in these reports for restarting tourism seem to coincide with the dimensions of smart destinations (SDs). That said, the aim of the study is to determine the benefits of transforming a destination into SD to restart tourism after the COVID-19 outbreak, to match the dimensions of SD with restarting strategies, and to make conceptual inferences to serve this.

Literature Review

The Effects of the COVID-19 Pandemic on Tourism

According to the 2019 data of the WTO, the international tourism sector is the third largest export sector in the world after the crude oil and pharmaceuticals sectors. International tourism, which alone accounts for 7% of the world's total exports and 28% of the world's service exports, generated a total of $1.7 trillion in international exports in 2019, including transportation costs. In 2019, the number of international tourists increased by 4% compared to the previous year to 1.460 million; international tourism revenue increased by 3% to $1.481 billion. From 2009 to 2019, the real growth in international tourism revenues (54%) exceeds the real growth in the world's gross domestic product (44%) (UNWTO, 2020a). The tourism sector, which has been constantly growing during this period, has come to a standstill due to the COVID-19 pandemic in 2020. In fact, the COVID-19 pandemic has had heavier imprints on the tourism sector than both the SARS epidemic in 2003 and the global economic crisis in 2009. The SARS epidemic and the global economic crisis reduced the number of international tourists by 0.4% and 4%, respectively. That said, the COVID-19 pandemic, which led to a drop of 74%, can be described as the greatest crisis experienced by the tourism sector since 1990.

According to the report of the WTO, as of April 20, 2020, all destinations around the world imposed travel restrictions due to the pandemic; in 45% of the destinations, borders were completely closed to tourists, while international flights were completely or partially suspended in 35%. As a result of travel restrictions, lockdowns, social distancing measures, stay-at-home orders, and fear of coming into contact with foreigners, the tourism sector faced a sharp decline in 2020 (Duro, Perez-Laborda, Turrion-Prats, & Fernández-Fernández, 2021; Gursoy & Chi, 2020). In 2020, the number of tourists worldwide fell by 74% compared to 2019 to $381 million; export income generated by international tourism fell by 76% to $4 billion (UNWTO, 2021a). In other words, 2020 witnessed the loss of 1 million international tourists and $1.3 trillion in international tourism exports. Tourism plunged to its level in the 1990s. This also jeopardized the employment of 100–120 million people.

Although the number of international tourists in 2021 increased by 4% compared to 2020, it was still 72% less than 2019. Further, it is remarkable that the export revenue generated by tourism increased to $7 billion, which is over $4 billion recorded in 2020, but is still well below the $1.7 trillion revenue in 2019 (UNWTO, 2022a). Though the tourism sector experienced major challenges in 2020 and 2021, when the strict restrictions of the COVID-19 pandemic were imposed, the sector started to recover in 2022. In the first quarter of 2021, the number of international tourists was 41 million, and this reached 117 million in the first quarter of 2022. To put it another way, the number of international tourists increased by almost three times in the first quarter of 2022 compared to the same period in 2021. A substantial part of this increase occurred in March, and this is considered a sign that tourism movements will gain even greater momentum (UNWTO, 2022b).

The tourism sector has started to revive as the effects of the COVID-19 outbreak, which appears to be one of the biggest crises experienced by the tourism sector, mitigate and restrictions are lifted. It is important to note here that, as the WTO has emphasized, the experiences from 2020 and 2021 are critical for creating a more inclusive, innovative and sustainable tourism sector in line with the reset vision (UNWTO, 2021b, 2022c). In other words, the tourism sector, which plunged to its level in the 1990s in 2020 and 2021 and needs time to recover, will most probably continue to strengthen and grow if it manages the future process properly. To that end, the Global Tourism Crisis Committee of the WTO published two reports on May 28, 2020. The first is titled the "Priorities for Tourism Recovery" and the second is the "Global Guidelines to Restart Tourism." Thus, this study further examines the content of these reports, matches the content with the dimensions of SD, and discusses the benefits of transforming a destination into a SD to restart tourism in the post-COVID-19 period.

Restarting Strategies in Destinations After the COVID-19 Pandemic

Priorities for Tourism Recovery[1]

The report titled "Priorities for Tourism Recovery" was prepared by the leadership of the WTO with the help of the representatives of the member countries, the International Civil Aviation Organization (ICAO), and the International Maritime Organization (IMO), the International Labor Organization (ILO), the World Bank (WB), the Airports Council International (ACI), the Cruise Lines International Association (CLIA), the International Air Transport Association (IATA), and WTTC as well as the Government of Spain. The priorities for the improvement of the tourism sector are presented in the report under seven headings as follows (UNWTO, 2020b):

(1) Provide liquidity and protect jobs.
(2) Recover confidence through safety and security.
(3) Public–private collaboration for an efficient reopening.
(4) Open borders with responsibility.
(5) Harmonize and coordinate protocols and procedures.
(6) Added value jobs through new technologies.
(7) Innovation and sustainability as the new normal.

Provide liquidity and protect jobs: This priority concerns employers and employees in the tourism sector. It highlights the priorities of creating tourism support programs for small and medium-scaled businesses, entrepreneurs, and self-employed business owners, designing financial instruments to increase liquidity, providing grants and benefits for self-employed and workers, expanding social benefits, ensuring dialogue between companies and workers' unions, reviewing cancellation policies taking into account consumers' rights and the urgency of liquidity for companies, and supporting job seekers' transition into new jobs.

Recover confidence through safety and security: This priority is associated with minimizing risks throughout the value chain and in all steps of the traveler's journey. It emphasizes the priorities of determining safety and hygiene protocols, providing information to travelers about current measures in destinations and tourism companies, informing visitors about their rights in case they are infected with COVID-19 during their travels, focusing on human-centered and two-way communication, and creating communication campaigns for confidence-building that focus on safety and empathy.

Public–private collaboration for an efficient reopening: This priority overall emphasizes the importance of the collaboration of the public and private sectors. It highlights the priorities of establishing mechanisms in which the public and private sectors cooperate in the definition and implementation of health-related protocols, ensuring coordination with health authorities to create scientific-based and applicable protocols, establishing mechanisms for the adaptation of destinations and tourism companies and for the training of their staff, sharing knowledge and good practices with the public and private sectors as well as investing in data systems for a more effective sharing of knowledge and good practices.

Open borders with responsibility: This priority includes opening borders to tourism movements and facilitating tourism activities without risking public health considering the spread of the epidemic. It underlines the priorities of enhancing the use of technology for secure, seamless and touchless travel, identifying the roles and responsibilities of stakeholders in this process and embracing e-visa/no visa policies to support demand.

Harmonize and coordinate protocols and procedures: This priority is associated with the harmonization of health protocols and procedures related to tourism at the global level. It emphasizes the priorities of ensuring international coordination to reopen the borders, establishing an internationally coordinated system to monitor the health of visitors and ensuring coordination between tourism, health, internal affairs, foreign affairs, and transportation authorities.

Added value jobs through new technologies: This priority is linked to the acceleration of the digitalization process of destinations and tourism companies, and the adoption of new technologies by employers and employees. It underlines the priorities of supporting companies to accelerate digital transformation; strengthening emphasis on cybersecurity, big data analytics, data science in tourism; equipping job seekers with new skills, better training staff on service delivery, new technologies and language skills; and promoting online free training on tourism.

Innovation and sustainability as the new normal: This priority pertains to the consolidation of the national and global innovation ecosystem and the promotion of sustainability. It underlines the priorities of fostering opportunities for major companies to work with start-ups in ensuring easier, quicker and more efficient processes, encouraging start-ups and entrepreneurs to develop innovative solutions, valuing innovation, accelerating the transition to a circular economy, and investing in digital transformation for a more effective destination planning and management. With regard to sustainability, it emphasizes using resources more efficiently toward a greener tourism, defining and managing carrying capacity for destinations, using a high value-added, data evidence-based tourism measurement system, and building a more sustainable and responsible tourism sector.

Global Guidelines to Restart Tourism[2]

The same institutions and organizations that prepared the previous report prepared this report titled "Global Guidelines to Restart Tourism." This report sets global principles under eight different headings listed below (UNWTO, 2020c).

(1) Safe and seamless border management (air, sea, and ground travel)
(2) Private sector – cross-cutting measures
(3) Safe air travel

(4) Hospitality
(5) Tour operators and travel agencies
(6) Meetings and events
(7) Attractions and thematic parks
(8) Destination planning and management

As the focus of this study is "destination planning and management," other headings are discussed briefly.

Safe and seamless border management (air, sea, and ground travel): The principles of introducing and adapting border processes, defining roles and responsibilities for tourism stakeholders, ensuring both regional and international coordination and intersectoral coordination in reopening borders, improving the use of technology for safe, seamless, and touchless travel, and increasing practices to encourage and facilitate travel.

Private sector – Cross-cutting measures: This principle includes implementing global health, hygiene, and safety protocols, ensuring safe and hygienic service delivery, informing visitors about protocols and responsibilities through digital channels and social media channels, promoting social dialogue, and strengthening the dialogue between the public and private sectors.

Safe air travel: This principle addresses implementing health control procedures, increasing the frequency of cleaning the aircraft and cabin, complying with mask, distance, and hygiene rules, limiting cabin baggage, ensuring the coordination of tourism stakeholders with the processes of the ICAO.

Hospitality: This principle consists of three subheadings. These are hygiene and operation, product and marketing, and partnerships. The subheading of hygiene and operation is related to ensuring hygiene rules and health safety in common areas and rooms, increasing contactless transactions and complying with distance rules. The subheading of product and marketing pertains to adding new services considering COVID-19, promoting domestic tourism and carrying out promotional activities to communicate corporate values to domestic tourism and employees. Partnerships, on the other hand, include working in cooperation with the health sector and being in contact with local actors (such as destination management and marketing organizations).

Tour operators and travel agencies: This principle, similar to the principle of hospitality, consists of three subheadings, which are "hygiene and operation, product and marketing, and partnerships." Hygiene and operation includes implementing health and safety protocols related to hygiene as well as promoting digital communication. Product and marketing is linked to developing sustainable products for small groups, focusing on ecotourism and cultural tourism, featuring storytelling in the promotion of tourism experiences, and incentivizing domestic tourism. Lastly, partnership includes cooperation with the banking and insurance sectors, increasing cooperation with airline companies, and developing loyalty reward systems.

Meetings and events: This principle addresses creating special guides for meeting and event planners to restart tourism, offering digital events first and then organizing medium-sized events for domain-specific sectors in the domestic market.

Attractions and thematic parks: This principle presents prioritizing hygiene and health safety issues, monitoring the area capacity, managing density of people in areas, communicating the density to traveler guests in real time, and implementing augmented reality or virtual reality technologies.

Destination planning and management: The information on this principle is presented as follows in the report (UNWTO, 2020c, pp. 25–26).

- Introduce and adapt actionable and harmonized processes and procedures in line with public health evidence-based risk assessment and in full coordination with relevant public- and private-sector partners.
- Support companies in the implementation and training of their staff on the new protocols (financing and training).
- Enhance the use of technology for safe, seamless and touchless travel in your destination.
- Provide reliable, consistent and easy-to-access information on protocols to the private sector and to travelers (send SMS to tourists to inform them of national and local heath protocols and relevant health contacts).
- Create programs and campaigns to incentivize the domestic market in cooperation with the private sector (incentive schemes, possible revision of holiday dates, transport facilities, vouchers, etc.) and integrate destinations.
- Promote new products and experiences targeted at individual and small-group travelers, such as special interest, nature, rural tourism, gastronomy, wine, sports, etc.
- Consider the data privacy policies when there is a proposal of developing tracing apps.
- Enhance and communicate medical capacity and protocols at the destination (e.g., safety seals).
- Ensure coordination among tourism, health, and transport policies.
- Define roles and responsibilities for governments, private sectors, and travelers.

In the simplest terms, tourist destinations that are the central elements of the tourism system (Kozak & Rimmington, 1999) are defined as the country, city, region, or areas where tourism is one of its mainstays (Jenkins, 1999). For this reason, it is reasonable to say that tourist destinations can be expressed as a whole of tourism products. Destinations that consider the COVID-19 pandemic crisis as an opportunity to shape and redesign the tourism of tomorrow will probably gain an important competitive advantage in the post-pandemic period (Destination Think, 2021). Thus, decision-makers in the tourism sector need to take into account the long-term consequences of the crisis and the structural transformation required to build a stronger, sustainable, innovative, and reliable tourism. It is believed that as efforts are made to add the "smartness" attribute to a destination, that is, as what is necessary to transform a destination a "smart destination" is achieved, it will be easier to implement the principles and measures described in the above reports and ensure a restart in tourism.

Smart Destination

Tourism takes place in the areas of destinations that attract tourists for various activities and have natural, cultural, and human features (Jovicic, 2019). The concept of SD is derived from the concept of "smart city" (Xiang, Tussyadiah, & Buhalis, 2015), which envisages that in the urban development strategy to transform city infrastructure and services, the fields of economy, environment, mobility, life, people, and governance (Chourabi et al., 2012) are based on the use of information and communication technology. The reason why the concept of smart city emerged before the concept of SD can be explained by the high awareness of the problems caused by the excessive increase in the urban population and potentially greater investment in cities compared to small settlements. Destinations can be described as "the area in which the economic, physical and social effects of tourism occur; the countries, regions and cities in which tourism is one of the economic mainstays" (Gretzel & Scarpino-Johns, 2018) and SDs apply smart city principles to all tourist areas, taking into account the experience and mobility of tourists and local people, resource availability and allocation, efforts to support quality of life, and sustainability (Cimbaljević, Stankov, & Pavluković, 2019; Gretzel, Reino, Kopera, & Koo, 2015). From this standpoint, it can be argued that a city that carries out tourism activities and has "smart" features can also be considered as a SD (Yavuz, 2019).

There are many different definitions of SD in the literature. According to Dirks and Keeling (2008), SDs are destinations that can best utilize interconnected information through information communication technologies to optimize the use of scarce resources and control their activities; Dameri and Rosenthal-Sabroux (2014) state that they are environments where technology is embedded in destinations in synergy with social components to create public value. Del Chiappa and Baggio (2015) define SD as areas that support cooperation, knowledge-sharing, and innovation, seek to create a digital environment, have a technological infrastructure, and develop a networked ecosystem of stakeholders in the provision of services to tourists. Thus, it is predicted that the current state of information and communication technologies (ICTs) and their predictable development in the future are creating/will create a new scenario for destination management, which depends on the development of SD (Ivars-Baidal, Celdrán-Alic, Mazón, & Perles-Ivars, 2019). Building upon the existing definitions, SDs emerge as destinations that use ICTs to support the production and development of tourism processes (Wang, Li, & Li, 2013).

However, it is reported that SDs are not technological developments that cause their residents to be inactive and prevent deliberation; rather, they should be a mechanism of thought and sharing that invites the residents to work more actively and to be decision-making actors in solving various problems of the region they live in (Buhalis & Amaranggana, 2014). Similarly, SEGITTUR (Sociedad

Mercantil Estatal para la Gestión de la Innovación y las Tecnologías Turísticas), the Spanish State Mercantile Society for Management of Innovation and Tourist Technologies, defines SD as "an innovative tourism destination, based on an infrastructure of state-of-the-art technology, which guarantees the sustainable development of universally accessible tourist areas, enabling visitors to integrate and interact with their surroundings, raising the quality of their experience at the destination, and improving residents' quality of life" (SEGITTUR, 2022). Thus, in order for a destination to qualify as "smart," it must use technology, but more importantly, make the transportation, energy, environment, and society elements of the destination more sustainable and efficient through technology and to unite the tourism actors on a common ground (Chourabi et al., 2012).

Guo, Liu, and Chai (2014) and Zhu, Zhang, and Li (2014) report that SDs can be defined as destinations that benefit from existing technology to create value, pleasure, and experience for tourism actors. From this standpoint, it is critical to ask the following question: "What are the elements/dimensions that add value and pleasure to a destination and enhance the quality of a destination's experience?" The Sustainable Smart Cities Initiative groups these elements under four main headings, which as "transportation, energy, environment, and society" (DSEIN, 2022) and emphasizes that technology is a facilitator that ensures sustainability of these four elements and makes the destination more "livable." Giffinger et al. (2007) discuss the dimensions of SD under six headings and offer the following definition: "SD is the intelligent combination of activities of economy, management, transportation, human, environment and quality of life in well performing, forward–looking destinations." Giffinger et al. (2007) list the dimensions of SD as follows: smart economy, smart mobility, smart governance, smart environment, smart people, and smart life. These dimensions, also acknowledged by the European Union (Lazaroiu & Roscia, 2012), are outlined as follows (Giffinger et al., 2007, p. 12):

- Smart Economy: includes elements of innovation, entrepreneurship, transformation, economic image and trademarks, efficiency and productivity, flexibility of the labor market, and integration in the international market, and pertains to economic competitiveness.
- Smart Governance: includes common participation in decision-making processes, functioning of public and social services, transparent governance, and political strategies and perspectives, and is related to the sustainability of the political aspect of a destination.
- Smart Mobility: includes the elements of local, national, and international accessibility, infrastructure of ICTs, availability of sustainable, innovative, and modern transportation systems, and is linked to the mobility/movement of people in a destination.
- Smart People: includes the element of the level of competence and education of local people, their tendency to lifelong learning, flexibility, creativity, open-mindedness, attitude toward social and ethnic pluralism, and participation in public life. It is linked to social and human capital.

- Smart Environment: The attractiveness of natural resources (climate, green area, flora, fauna, etc.) includes elements of pollution, environmental protection, and sustainable resource management. It is associated with all efforts to protect natural resources and the environment.
- Smart Living: includes elements of cultural facilities, educational facilities, health facilities, individual security, quality of housing, touristic attraction, and social solidarity, and is linked to the quality of life in a destination.

Considering the features listed above, for a destination to qualify as smart, it should have innovative, efficient, and competitive economy; a transportation infrastructure powered with ICTs; management with an emphasis on transparency and public participation; a sensitive and effective system in the fields of environment, waste management, and sustainability; an area where independent, educated, open-minded, and conscious citizens reside, and where basic needs such as accommodation, food and beverage, education, security, health, and various needs including art, culture, and socialization are all provided in a quality manner.

Another concept developed on the dimensions of SD is the "Smart City Wheel" model put forward by Cohen (2012). The model proposed by Cohen is a kind of modeled version of the elements listed by Giffinger et al. (2007). This model assumes that a SD consists of six basic dimensions (smart economy, smart governance, smart mobility, smart people, smart environment, and smart living) that three main components are required for each dimension and the performance of destinations are monitored through over 100 indicators linked to these components (Lekamge & Marasinghe, 2013). The dimensions of SD are listed as follows (Cohen, 2012):

- Smart economy components: Entrepreneurship and innovation, efficiency, national and international integration.
- Smart governance components: Activating supply- and demand-side policies, transparency and open data, ICTs, and e-management.
- Smart mobility components: Mixed-method access, clean and nonmotorized options, and ICTs.
- Smart people components: An inclusive and creative society educated for the twenty-first century.
- Smart environment components: Green buildings, green energy, and green urban planning.
- Smart living components: Health, safety, cultural vitality, and happiness.

Underlining the importance to take into account each destination's population density, social structure, topography, culture, values, technological infrastructure, and transportation systems, Cohen stated that destinations need to determine their vision and mission before applying this model and this process should be carried out based on common sense. It is further significant that destinations may stand out in one of the dimensions in the model when moving toward being "smart," but it is a prerequisite to meet the requirements of each dimension and its related components (Lekamge & Marasinghe, 2013).

ICTs for smart tourism destinations should be implemented considering the dimensions of smart tourism proposed by Giffinger et al. (2007) and Cohen (2012) (Smart economy, smart mobility, smart governance, smart environment, smart people, and smart living). That is, prior to the design and implementation of a technology, its potential contributions to the smartness of the destination should be evaluated. The benefits of ICTs are gaining significance every day in the tourism industry as well as in all areas. Destinations that have established a strong ICT infrastructure grow rapidly in a short period of time, and tourism companies that benefit from such ICT generate more revenue by enhancing their consumer satisfaction. The key point here is that the dimensions of SD (smart economy, smart mobility, smart governance, smart environment, smart people, and smart living) should not be ignored while making technological investments.

Conclusion and Discussion

First offering a conceptual basis for the restarting strategies in the post-COVID-19 period and for the concept of SD, this study then discusses the benefits of SD considering the restarting strategies and matches the dimensions of SD with the principles and priorities of the restarting strategies.

Benefits of SDs in the Context of Restart Strategies

Table 1 below presents the matching of dimensions of SD, which seek to make the economy, management, transportation, human, environment, and quality of life dimensions of destinations more sustainable and efficient through ICT and to unite tourism actors on a common ground, with the priorities in the report titled Priorities for Tourism Recovery and the principles of destination planning and management in the report titled Global Guidelines to Restart Tourism.

Smart economy, the first dimension of SDs (Cohen, 2012; Giffinger et al., 2007), is directly linked to the economic competitiveness of a destination. It is characterized by innovative spirit, entrepreneurship, city image, productivity, labor market, and international embeddedness (Ates & Onder, 2019). This dimension is congruent with the priorities to provide liquidity and protect jobs and innovation and sustainability as the new normal in the Priorities for Tourism Recovery report. The priority of providing liquidity and protecting jobs is related to employers and employees in the tourism sector. It involves designing programs to support small and medium-sized (SMEs) and entrepreneurs in the sector, providing grants and benefits, reducing job losses and layoffs, and creating financial instruments. Innovation and sustainability as the new normal are about strengthening the national and global innovation ecosystem and supporting sustainability. The dimension of smart economy matches the principle of creating programs and campaigns to enhance the domestic market in cooperation with the private sector and integrating destinations under the heading of the destination

Table 1. Matching SD Dimensions With Restart Strategies.

Dimensions of SD	Priorities for Tourism Recovery	Global Guidelines to Restart Tourism – Destination Planning and Management
Smart Economy	• Provide liquidity and protect jobs. • Innovation and sustainability as the new normal.	• Create programs and campaigns to incentivize the domestic market in cooperation with the private sector and integrate destinations.
Smart Governance	• Public–private collaboration for an efficient reopening. • Harmonize and coordinate protocols and procedures.	• Introduce and adapt actionable and harmonized processes and procedures in line with public-health evidence-based risk assessment and full coordination with relevant public- and private-sector partners. • Consider the data privacy policies when there is a proposal of developing tracing apps. • Define roles and responsibilities for governments, private sectors, and travelers. • Ensure coordination among tourism, health, and transport policies.
Smart Mobility	• Open borders with responsibility.	• Enhance the use of technology for safe, seamless, and touchless travel in your destination. • Ensure coordination among tourism, health, and transport policies.
Smart People	• Innovation and sustainability as the new normal. • Added value jobs through new technologies.	• Support companies in the implementation and training of their staff on the new protocols (financing and training).
Smart Environment	• Innovation and sustainability as the new normal.	• Promote new products and experiences targeted at individual and small-groups travelers, such as special interest, nature, rural tourism, gastronomy, wine, sports, etc.

Table 1. *(Continued)*

Dimensions of SD	Priorities for Tourism Recovery	Global Guidelines to Restart Tourism – Destination Planning and Management
Smart Living	• Recover confidence through safety and security.	• Provide reliable, consistent, and easy-to-access information on protocols to the private sector and to travelers • Enhance and communicate medical capacity and protocols at the destination. • Ensure coordination among tourism, health, and transport policies.

Source: Created by the authors based on two reports, Priorities for Tourism Recovery and Global Guidelines to Restart Tourism.

planning and management in the report titled the Global Guidelines to Restart Tourism. The motivation behind this principle is that domestic tourism is considered to be the market that will grow the fastest in the post-COVID-19 period. Destinations that develop programs and campaigns to boost domestic tourism and create an economic campaign will achieve to recover faster during this period.

Smart governance is directly linked to the engagement of a destination. Political awareness pertains to cooperation between public and private services, and efficient and transparent management (Celik & Topsakal, 2017). This dimension is related to the priorities of public–private collaboration for an efficient reopening, and harmonizing and coordinating protocols and procedures in the report titled the Priorities for Tourism Recovery. These priorities include creating mechanisms that run through the cooperation of the public and private sectors, ensuring coordination between stakeholders, sharing information between the public and private sectors, and designing a coordinated system. The dimension of smart governance matches the four principles under the heading of the destination planning and management in the report titled the Global Guidelines to Restart Tourism. These principles are as follows: (1) Introduce and adapt actionable public health and harmonized processes and procedures in line with evidence-based risk assessment and full coordination with relevant public- and private-sector partners, (2) consider the data privacy policies of developing a business proposal when there are tracing apps, (3) define the roles and interests of governments, the private sector, and travelers, (4) ensure coordination among tourism, health, and transport policies in the form of ranking. These principles define the processes that need to be coordinated in a destination. The large number of principles in the dimension of smart governance demonstrates the importance of participation in the processes for restarting after crises.

Smart mobility is about the accessibility of a destination. Further, a transportation system supported by ICTs and infrastructure is deemed critical for smart mobility (Benevolo, Dameri, & D'Auria, 2016). This dimension is linked to the priority of opening borders with responsibility in the report titled the Priorities for Tourism Recovery. This priority involves increasing the use of technology for touchless travel and applying e-visa/visa-free travel procedures to encourage travel. The dimension of smart mobility also pertains to the principles of enhancing the use of technology for safe, seamless, and touchless travel in your destination and ensuring coordination among tourism, health, and transport policies under the heading of destination planning and management in the report titled the Global Guidelines to Restart Tourism. It is evident that it is of great significance to include ICTs in accessibility processes and also to ensure coordination between tourism, health, and transportation processes.

Smart people refer to the social and human dimension of a destination. This dimension highlights people's education, level of lifelong learning, creativity, social and ethnic diversity, and tolerance and open-mindedness as some of the critical indicators of benefiting from the human potential of a destination (Gupta, Mustafa, & Kumar, 2017). This dimension is related to the priorities of innovation and sustainability as the new normal and added value jobs through new technologies in the report titled the Priorities for Tourism Recovery. While the first priority involves making people aware of innovation and sustainability, the second one pertains to improving people's knowledge (tourism-sector stakeholders) on digitalization, new technologies, foreign languages, and tourism awareness. The dimension of smart people matches the principle of supporting companies in the implementation and training of their staff on the new protocols under the heading of the destination planning and management in the report titled the Global Guidelines to Restart Tourism. This principle includes training staff considering the restarting strategies.

Smart environment is about the environmental sustainability of a destination. Sustainable resource management is related to ecological awareness, air, water, and environmental quality (Kar, Mustafa, Gupta, Ilavarasan, & Dwivedi, 2017). This dimension relates to the principle of innovation and sustainability as the new normal in the Priorities for Tourism Recovery report. This priority focuses on using resources more efficiently toward a greener tourism, defining and managing carrying capacity for destinations, using a high value-added, data evidence–based tourism measurement system, and building a more sustainable and responsible tourism sector. It is further linked to the principle of promoting new products and experiences targeted at individual and small-group travelers (such as special interest, nature, rural tourism, gastronomy, wine, sports, etc.) presented under the heading of the destination planning and management in the report titled the Global Guidelines to Restart Tourism. Considering that despite the environmental destructiveness of mass tourism, alternative types of tourism respect nature, support sustainability, and are balanced in terms of carrying capacity, it will not be surprising that SDs should turn to alternative types of tourism for the dimension of environment.

Smart living is about the quality of life in a destination. It is associated with cultural opportunities of the destination, educational opportunities and equipment, health facilities, personal security and quality of housing, quality of communication systems, and availability of touristic activities (Celik & Topsakal, 2017). Smart living pertains to the priority of recovering confidence through safety and security in the report titled the Priorities for Tourism Recovery. This priority highlights determining safety and hygiene protocols, maximizing health facilities, focusing on human-centered and two-way communication, and conducting communication campaigns that will provide trust to people by prioritizing safety and empathy. The dimension of smart living is linked to the three principles presented under the heading of destination planning and management in the report titled the Global Guidelines to Restart Tourism: (1) Providing reliable, consistent, and easy-to-access information on protocols to the private sector and to travelers, (2) enhancing and communicating medical capacity and protocols at the destination, (3) ensuring coordination among tourism, health, and transport policies. Based on these principles, it is plausible to argue that health facilities and communication systems in particular will be the foci in the restarting principles in the post-COVID-19 period.

This present study offers a guiding model that takes into account the restarting strategies in the post-COVID-19 period and the dimensions of SDs for tourism decision-makers. This model is shown in Fig. 1.

The tourism sector is a sector open to the negative effects of crises. Therefore, crisis management is of pivotal importance in the tourism sector (Ritchie, 2009). The management and planning of destinations, which is the most inclusive dimension of tourism, needs to be addressed comprehensively due to their complex nature. The resilience of destinations to crises, in other words, their ability to be sustainable, can be achieved by proper management, planning, and marketing efforts. The "smart" attribute of destinations, undoubtedly, allows destinations to be more resistant to crises and thus more sustainable. The advantages of being a SD against crises can be outlined as follows:

- SDs have the advantage of economic competitiveness. Entrepreneurship, innovation, and productivity are encouraged in SDs. SDs that can internationally adapt in the economy provide a competitive advantage. In SDs in the tourism sector, SMEs and entrepreneurs in the tourism sector are supported; grants and assistance are offered during crises; and plans are developed to minimize job losses and layoffs. Also, financial instruments are designed to maintain liquidity.
- There is a coordinated structure among the stakeholders of SDs and the management is transparent. In particular, harmony prevails between the public sector and private sector. Multirationality delays the production of fast and effective solutions in the tourism sector. In contrast, it is much easier to take

Fig. 1.   Guiding Model for Tourism Decision-Makers. *Source:*
Created by the authors based on two reports, Priorities for Tourism Recovery
and Global Guidelines to Restart Tourism.

quick measures against crises and to carry out efforts toward this end in
tourism planning performed with a common mind and full coordination.
- Accessibility is prioritized in SDs; transport systems are supported by ICT; and
  travel is encouraged. This facilitates managing the carrying capacity of a

destination, providing visitors with information about the density of the destination, offering information about the places to visit, and offering the opportunity to travel much more comfortably. Destinations that are smart in terms of mobility provide visitors and local people with a much higher quality of travel experience, and therefore are more preferred.

- Local people in SDs are much more educated, knowledgeable, tolerant, respectful, and conscious. These characteristics among local people also enhance the quality of experience of visitors in destinations. Communication and interaction with local residents make visitors content as well. Furthermore, these characteristics among local people help raise awareness on sustainability. Thus, it is possible to preserve the natural, cultural, historical, and human attractions of the destination.

- SDs stand out in that they ensure environmental sustainability and protect natural resources. Considering that consumers will be much more sensitive to the environment in the post-COVID-19 period (Abbas, Mubeen, Iorember, Raza, & Mamirkulovab, 2021; Hall, Scott, & Gössling, 2020; Stankov, Filimonau, & Vujičić, 2020) and that alternative types of tourism will attract greater attention (Hall et al., 2020; Romagosa, 2020), it is reasonable to state that destinations that protect the environment do not disrupt natural resources and feature natural elements which will be much more attractive.

- The supporting services of SDs (cultural facilities, educational facilities, health facilities, security, housing quality, quality of communication systems, etc.) are also of better quality. Destinations that offer strong supporting services achieve significant attractiveness and are more successful in attracting tourists (Buhalis, 2000).

- Every subdimension of SDs is integrated with ICT infrastructure. Given that digitalization in the tourism sector will become more important than ever in the future (Alaeddinoglu & Rol, 2020; Özaltın Türker, 2020; Strielkowski, 2020), it is reasonable to argue that destinations using ICTs will overcome crises more easily. Even when it is not possible to physically visit a destination, SDs achieve to generate tourism revenue by using technologies such as virtual reality and augmented reality. Further, it is known that coordination is high in SDs, big data are constantly analyzed, tourist markets are assessed effectively, and visitors are provided with experiences in a much easier and more effective way. These allow for much more efficient planning and marketing activities in destinations both in crisis periods and noncrisis periods.

Notes

1. This section offers an overview of the report titled the "Priorities for Tourism Recovery" published by UNWTO on May 28, 2020.
2. This section is based on an overview of the report titled the "Global Guidelines to Restart Tourism" published by UNWTO on May 28, 2020.

References

Abbas, J., Mubeen, R., Iorember, P. T., Raza, S., & Mamirkulovab, G. (2021). Exploring the impact of COVID-19 on tourism: Transformational potential and implications for a sustainable recovery of the travel and leisure industry. *Current Research in Behavioral Sciences, 2*(100033), 1–11. doi:10.1016/j.crbeha.2021. 100033

Alaeddinoglu, F., & Rol, S. (2020). Covid-19 Pandemic and its effects on tourism. *Van Yüzüncü Yıl University the Journal of Social Sciences Institute, Outbreak Diseases Special Issue* (pp. 233–258).

Ates, M., & Onder, D. E. (2019). Akıllı şehir kavramı ve dönüşen anlamı bağlamında eleştiriler [The concept of smart city and criticism within the context of its transforming meaning]. *Megaron Yıldız Teknik Üniversitesi Mimarlık Fakültesi Dergisi, 14*(1), 41–50.

Bakar, N. A., & Rosbi, S. (2020). Effect of Coronavirus disease (COVID-19) to tourism industry. *International Journal of Advanced Engineering Research and Science, 7*(4), 189–193. doi:10.22161/ijaers.74.23

Benevolo, C., Dameri, R. P., & D'Auria, B. (2016). Smart mobility in smart city. In T. Torre, A. Braccini, & R. Spinelli (Eds.), *Empowering organizations. Lecture notes in information systems and organisation* (pp. 13–28). Cham: Springer. doi:10.1007/ 978-3-319-23784-8_2

Buhalis, D. (2000). Marketing the competitive destination of the future. *Tourism Management, 21*(1), 97–116.

Buhalis, D., & Amaranggana, A. (2014). Smart tourism destinations. In Z. Xiang & I. Tussyadiah (Eds.), *Information and communication technologies in tourism* (pp. 553–564). Cham: Springer.

Celik, P., & Topsakal, Y. (2017). Akıllı turizm destinasyonları: Antalya destinasyonunun akıllı turizm uygulamalarının incelenmesi [Smart tourism destinations: Review of smart tourism applications of Antalya, Antalya destination]. *Journal of Travel and Hospitality Management, 14*(3), 149–166.

Chourabi, H., Nam, T., Walker, S., Gil-Gracia, R., Mellouli, S., Nahon, K., & Prado, T. (2012, June 04–07). Understanding smart cities: An integrative framework. In *45th Hawaii International Conference on System Sciences*, Maui, USA (pp. 2289–2997).

Cimbaljević, M., Stankov, U., & Pavluković, V. (2019). Going beyond the traditional destination competitiveness: Reflections on a smart destination in the current research. *Current Issues in Tourism, 22*(20), 2472–2477. doi:10.1080/13683500. 2018.1529149

Cohen, B. (2012). What exactly is a smart city? Fast company. Retrieved from https:// www.fastcompany.com/1680538/what-exactly-is-a-smart-city

Dameri, R. P., & Rosenthal-Sabroux, C. (2014). Smart city and value creation. In R. P. Dameri & C. Rosenthal-Sabroux (Eds.), *Smart city how to create public and economic value with high technology in urban space* (pp. 1–12). Cham: Springer. doi: 10.1007/978-3-319-06160-3_1

Del Chiappa, G., & Baggio, R. (2015). Knowledge transfer in smart tourism destinations: Analyzing the effects of a network structure. *Journal of Destination Marketing & Management, 4*(3), 145–150. doi:10.1016/j.jdmm.2015.02.001

Destination Think. (2021). *Mitigate COVID-19's impact on your destination: Phase 1 of 3* Destination Think! Professional Services Inc. Retrieved from https://destinationthink.com/blog/mitigate-covid-19-impact-destination/

Dirks, S., & Keeling, M. (2008). *A vision of smarter cities, how cities can lead the way into a prosperous and sustainable future.* Indianapolis, IN: IBM Global Services Publication.

DSEIN. (2022). Sürdürülebilir Akıllı Şehirler İnisiyatifi [Sustainable smart cities initiative]. Retrieved from https://www.surdurulebilir-sehirler.com/hakkimizda/

Duro, J. A., Perez-Laborda, A., Turrion-Prats, J., & Fernández-Fernández, M. (2021). COVID-19 and tourism vulnerability. *Tourism Management Perspectives, 38*, 100819. doi:10.1016/j.tmp.2021.100819

Foo, L. P., Chin, M. Y., Tan, K. L., & Phuah, K. T. (2021). The impact of COVID-19 on tourism industry in Malaysia. *Current Issues in Tourism, 24*(19), 2735–2739. doi:10.1080/13683500.2020.1777951

Giffinger, R., Fertner, C., Kramar, H., Kalasek, R., Milanović, N., & Meijers, E. (2007). Final report: Smart cities ranking of European medium-sized cities. Vienna Centre of Regional Science and Vienna University of Technology, Vienna.

Gössling, S., Scott, D., & Hall, M. (2020). Pandemics, tourism and global change: A rapid assessment of COVID-19. *Journal of Sustainable Tourism, 29*(1), 1–20. doi:10.1080/09669582.2020.1758708

Gretzel, U., Reino, S., Kopera, S., & Koo, C. (2015). Smart tourism challenges. *Journal of Tourism, 16*(1), 41–47.

Gretzel, U., & Scarpino-Johns, M. (2018). Destination resilience and smart tourism destinations. *Tourism Review International, 22*(3–4), 263–276. doi:10.3727/154427218X15369305779065

Guo, Y., Liu, H., & Chai, Y. (2014). The embedding convergence of smart cities and tourism internet of things in China: An advance perspective. *Advances in Hospitality and Tourism Research, 2*(1), 54–69.

Gupta, S., Mustafa, S. Z., & Kumar, H. (2017). Smart people for smart cities: A behavioral framework for personality and roles. In A. K. Kar, M. P. Gupta, P. V. Ilavarasan, & Y. K. Dwivedi (Eds.), *Advances in smart cities.* New York, NY: Chapman and Hall/CRC. doi:10.1201/9781315156040

Gursoy, D., & Chi, C. G. (2020). Effects of COVID-19 pandemic on hospitality industry: Review of the current situations and a research agenda. *Journal of Hospitality Marketing & Management, 29*(5), 527–529. doi:10.1080/19368623.2020.1788231

Hall, C. M., Scott, D., & Gössling, S. (2020). Pandemics, transformations and tourism: Be careful what you wish for. *Tourism Geographies, 22*(3), 577–598. doi:10.1080/14616688.2020.1759131

Ivars-Baidal, J. A., Celdrán-Alic, M. A., Mazón, J. N., & Perles-Ivars, Á. F. (2019). Smart destinations and the evolution of ICTs: A new scenario for destination management? *Current Issues in Tourism, 13*(22), 1581–1600. doi:10.1080/13683500.2017.1388771

Jenkins, O. H. (1999). Understanding and measuring tourist destination images. *International Journal of Tourism Research, 1*(1), 1–15. doi:10.1002/(SICI)1522-1970(199901/02)1:1<1::AID-JTR143>3.0.CO;2-L

Jones, P., & Comfort, D. (2020). The COVID-19 crisis, tourism and sustainable development. *Athens Journal of Tourism, 7*(2), 75–86.

Jovicic, D. Z. (2019). From the traditional understanding of tourism destination to the smart tourism destination. *Current Issues in Tourism, 22*(3), 276–282. doi:10.1080/13683500.2017.1313203

Kar, A. K., Mustafa, S. Z., Gupta, M. P., Ilavarasan, P. V., & Dwivedi, Y. K. (2017). Understanding smart cities: Inputs for research and practice. In A. K. Kar, M. P. Gupta, P. V. Ilavarasan, & Y. K. Dwivedi (Eds.), *Advances in smart cities* (pp. 1–7). New York, NY: Chapman and Hall/CRC. doi:10.1201/9781315156040

Kivilcim, B. (2020). COVID-19 (yeni koronavirüs) salgınının turizm sektörüne muhtemel etkileri [Probable effects of COVID-19 (new coronavirus) pandemic on tourism sector]. *USOBED Uluslararası Batı Karadeniz Sosyal ve Beşeri Bilimler Dergisi, 4*(1), 17–27.

Kozak, M., & Rimmington, M. (1999). Measuring tourist destination competitiveness: Conceptual considerations and empirical findings. *International Journal of Hospitality Management, 18*(3), 273–283. doi:10.1016/S0278-4319(99)00034-1

Lazaroiu, G., & Roscia, M. (2012). Definition methodology for the smart cities model. *Energy, 47*(1), 326–332.

Lekamge, S., & Marasinghe, A. (2013). Developing a smart city model that ensures the optimum utilization of existing resources in cities of all sizes. In *International Conference on Biometrics and Kansei Engineering* (pp. 202–207). Institute of Electrical and Electronics Engineers, Tokyo, Japan.

Medical News Today. (2022). COVID-19 live updates: WHO monitoring Delta-Omicron recombinant virus. *Medical News Today*. Retrieved from https://www.medicalnewstoday.com/articles/live-updates-coronavirus-covid-19#1

Ozaltın Turker, G. (2020). COVID-19 salgını turizm sektörünü nasıl etkiler? Turizm akademisyenleri perspektifinden bir değerlendirme [How COVID-19 pandemic affects tourism sector? An evaluation from tourism academics perspective]. *International Journal of Social Sciences and Education Research, 6*(2), 207–224. doi:10.24289/ijsser.760790

Ritchie, B. W. (2009). *Aspects of tourism: Crisis and disaster management for tourism*. Bristol: Channel View Publications. doi:10.21832/9781845411077-002

Romagosa, F. (2020). The COVID-19 crisis: Opportunities for sustainable and proximity tourism. *Tourism Geographies, 22*(3), 690–694. doi:10.1080/14616688.2020.1763447

SEGITTUR. (2022). *Smart destinations*. SEGITTUR. Retrieved from https://www.segittur.es/en/smart-tourism-destinations/dti-projects/smart-destinations/

Stankov, U., Filimonau, V., & Vujičić, M. D. (2020). A mindful shift: An opportunity for mindfulness-driven tourism in a post-pandemic world. *Tourism Geographies, 22*(3), 703–712. doi:10.1080/14616688.2020.1768432

Strielkowski, W. (2020). International tourism and COVID-19: Recovery strategies for tourism organisations. *Preprints*, 1–6. doi:10.20944/preprints202003.0445.v1

UNWTO. (2020a). *International tourism highlights* (2020 Edition). Madrid: UNWTO.

UNWTO. (2020b). *Priorities for tourism recovery*. Madrid: World Tourism Organization.

UNWTO. (2020c). *Global guidelines to restart tourism*. Madrid: World Tourism Organization.

UNWTO. (2020d). *Global guidelines to restart tourism*. Madrid: World Tourism Organization.

UNWTO. (2021a). *2020: A year in review.* World Tourism Organization. Retrieved from https://www.unwto.org/covid-19-and-tourism-2020

UNWTO. (2021b). *World tourism day 2021 | tourism for inclusive growth.* World Tourism Organization. Retrieved from https://www.unwto.org/wtd2021

UNWTO. (2022a). *Tourism grows 4% in 2021 but remains far below pre-pandemic levels.* World Tourism Organization. Retrieved from https://www.unwto.org/news/tourism-grows-4-in-2021-but-remains-far-below-pre-pandemic-levels

UNWTO. (2022b). *Tourism recovery gains momentum as restrictions ease and confidence returns.* World Tourism Organization. Retrieved from https://www.unwto.org/news/tourism-recovery-gains-momentum-as-restrictions-ease-and-confidence-returns#:~:text=According%20to%20the%20latest%20UNWTO,41%20million%20in%20Q1%202021

UNWTO. (2022c). *2021: Tourism united, resilient and determined.* World Tourism Organization. Retrieved from https://www.unwto.org/2021-a-year-in-review adresinden alındı

Wang, D., Li, X. R., & Li, Y. (2013). China's "smart tourism destination" initiative: A taste of the service-dominant logic. *Journal of Destination Marketing & Management, 2*(2), 59–61.

WHO. (2022). *WHO Coronavirus (COVID-19) dashboard.* World Health Organization. Retrieved from https://covid19.who.int/adresinden alındı

World Economic Forum. (2020). *COVID-19 sparked an economic crisis "like no other" but these measures can help now.* WHO and IMF. Retrieved from https://www.weforum.org/agenda/2020/04/who-briefing-0403-economic-response-vulnerable/

Xiang, Z., Tussyadiah, I., & Buhalis, D. (2015). Smart destinations: Foundations, analytics, and applications. *Journal of Destination Marketing & Management, 4*(3), 143–144.

Yavuz, M. C. (2019). Akıllı destinasyon: Turizm, inovasyon, girişimcilik ve çözüm bekleyen konular [Smart destination: Tourism, innovation, entrepreneurship, challenges]. *Journal of Tourism Theory and Research, 5*(2), 203–211. doi:10.24288/jttr.524534

Zhu, W., Zhang, L., & Li, N. (2014). Challenges, function changing of government and enterprises in Chinese smart tourism. In Z. Xiang & L. Tussyadiah (Eds.), *Information and communication technologies in tourism* (pp. 553–564). Dublin: Springer.

Tourism Sustainable Planning in Low Density Territories and the Post (Disaster) Pandemic Context

Pedro Liberato, Bruno Barbosa Sousa, Márcia Costa and Dália Liberato

Abstract

The evolution of tourism must be framed into policies that aim a development model perspective for the destinations, based on the analysis of economic, political, and social indicators. Therefore, emerging destinations, located in territories with low population density, should be a target of a careful strategy policy, considering the characteristics of the region. In particular, the disaster caused by the pandemic context (i.e., COVID-19) implied profound changes in tourism thinking, planning, and development of regions in Portugal and throughout the world. The present chapter proposes the creation of a tourism monitoring system for Arouca (Portugal), a territory classified as Low-Density Territory, with specific characteristics. The monitoring will involve the planning and management of database, at the disposal of all *stakeholders*, ensuring that the tourism flows in analysis do not get overwhelmed, allowing the discussion of opportunities and threats for the territory, based on the partnership between the population, public and private sector, adjusted to the social, cultural, economic, and environment perception. Will also be considered the perspective of the local community from Arouca's region, the main actors from the territory such as Geopark Association of Arouca and the City Council, according to the surveys used as data basis of this study, along with statistics analysis.

Keywords: Disaster; geopark; low-density territories; sustainable planning; tourism; destination management; sustainability cluster

Resilient and Sustainable Destinations After Disaster, 41–62
Copyright © 2023 Pedro Liberato, Bruno Barbosa Sousa, Márcia Costa and Dália Liberato
Published under exclusive licence by Emerald Publishing Limited
doi:10.1108/978-1-80382-021-720231004

Introduction

The regions where the low-density territories are inserted may assume a potential for growth and development, when combined with the three regional policy objectives such as convergence, regional competitiveness and employability, and territorial cooperation (Mascarenhas, Coelho, & Subtil, 2010). The National Program for Territorial Cohesion (PNCT) highlights the importance of empowering these territories, structuring policies capable of achieving this end, with specific measures to promote and enhance endogenous resources, identify and stimulate structuring projects, invest in smart economic development and strengthen networking activities, thus ensuring the sustainable prosperity of inland regions (Government of the Portuguese Republic: Lisbon, 2018) often referred to as low population density territories. The low density and rurality of a destination are increasingly perceived as a positive externality, as places of rest, tranquility, and own identity, difficult to duplicate (Government of the Portuguese Republic: Lisbon, 2018). Hence, the promotion of tourism in rural areas grants vitality to the territory, counteracts demographic challenges by reducing migration, promotes the endogenous resources of the territory as well as its traditions while educating tourists about the essence of rural life (UNWTO, 2020).

It is crucial to identify and understand the agents involved in the economic promotion of a tourism product and verify their environment. From Porter's perspective (1998), these are geographical concentrations in which companies and institutions are united in a particular field. The territorial cooperation necessary for the economic promotion of these territories are called clusters, sectors that work and collaborate with each other, which have an important role in the development of the industry, stimulating positive economic and social externalities and competitiveness among regions (Ketels & Memedovic, 2008). When the concept of cluster is applied to tourism, in addition to the factors described above, it is important to emphasize the quality of the visitor experience, which depends not only on the main attractions but also on the quality and efficiency of complementary services and products such as hotels, restaurants, stores, and transportation services (Porter, 1998), also based on government action as well as other institutions—such as universities (The Metropolitan Policy Program at Brookings: Washington, D.C., 2018). Several authors identify a tourism cluster as an essential strategy in emerging economies of less developed areas, especially in communities that want to activate tourism in their region as a strategic component of their economy (The Metropolitan Policy Program at Brookings: Washington, D.C., 2018).

To enhance these territories, it will be necessary to make them attractive and capable of combining "anchor investments" related to the following pairs of elements: environment and economic activity, tourism and leisure, culture, and science. Investments made in these areas will have to be proposed and implemented according to the attributes of the territory and according to a medium- and long-term strategy (Covas, 2007). As these territories are small-scale economies—micro clusters, the co-location of complementary and competing businesses that produce synergies that enhance market, employability, and product growth is crucial for specialization and competitiveness for small tourism destinations (Michael, 2003). Identifying clusters at the regional level can make a significant contribution to economic growth. This requires capturing the advantages of all stakeholders to work as one, clustering, acquiring and sharing new information to specialize (The Metropolitan Policy Program at Brookings: Washington, D.C., 2018). Cooperation in the long run will reduce the costs of specialization and in turn increase the quality of products reflecting in an increased value of the product leading to its value in the market (Nowaczyk, 2019).

It is also important to remember that the growth and promotion of tourism activities often starts through small family businesses, with limited skills and capital, and it is in this way that the governmental role becomes crucial to guide and design integrated tourism planning strategies, fundamental to the success of a tourist destination. It will then be crucial for local stakeholders to specialize in their tourism product, instead of looking for external help, from multinational companies with capital and knowledge because otherwise, what has become a source of economic growth for the population can turn into the loss of autonomy and capital (Scholz, Breuste, Bourlon, Rojas, & Torres Salinas, 2012, p. 356).

To delineate the micro cluster for the region under study (Arouca), the model of Tapachai (2019) was used which proposed a tourism micro cluster defined as "the concentration and connection of businesses and income generated in tourism-related activities in a rural village" which aims to take advantage of local resources and aptitude applied in the philosophy of economic autonomy, where all businesses or profitable activities in the cluster will be driven toward a balanced business method based on three principles—moderation, weighting, and independence along with acquired knowledge and morality. In short, a micro cluster is defined by the context in which it is inserted and by the identification of its product, determined according to the values of rural communities. Considering that the members of the micro cluster are based on trust and daily cooperation, it will contribute positively to the specialization of the tourism product, creating a value-added business network, through the combination of services that provide a unique experience, sought by the visitor and tourist (Michael, 2003; Sigurðardóttir & Steinthorsson, 2018).

However, there must be effective connection between the communities/ stakeholders to be able to claim that it is a successful micro cluster. Otherwise, it will just be a cluster of institutions in a short place (Tapachai, 2019). According to Michael (2003), the demand for tourism in micro clusters should focus on aspects of economic growth/strategy and planning; geographic location analysis (synergies); marketing (cooperation programs); and microeconomic management (niche markets that generate tourism demand) that promotes local development. This type of cluster generates opportunities for economies of scale (increasing in scale), giving the possibility for companies to specialize around the tourism product and gain market power against potential competitors (Nowaczyk, 2019; The Metropolitan Policy Program at Brookings: Washington, D.C., 2018).

Sustainable Development Applied to the Territories

Before understanding tourism sustainability, the concept of sustainable development should be exposed. The World Commission and Environment and Development defined sustainable development in 1987 as "development that addresses the needs of present generations without compromising future generations." In this same period, concerns about the tourism economy began to emerge, along with the goals of tourism sustainability (WCDE, 1987). In this perspective, the UNWTO defined sustainable tourism as "tourism activity that takes into consideration the present and future economic, social and environmental impacts, taking into account the needs of visitors, industry, environment and local communities" (UNWTO, 2013). Tourism sustainability of a destination can be achieved by exalting the positive impacts of tourism over the negative ones when preserving the environment, fostering economic development, and conserving social equity (Vehbi, 2012).

According to the World Economic Forum (2019), the preservation of natural and cultural resources is a challenge that the tourism industry presents. The list of intangible cultural heritage continues to grow, thus indicating the key to tourist attraction in destinations. From this perspective, it is crucial to optimally manage the environment and its resources, maintaining the essential ecological processes of the activity, and helping to conserve natural heritage and biodiversity. Respect for the cultural heritage of local communities, a key element for sustainable development, through the contribution of intercultural understanding and tolerance and conservation of cultural heritage, its traditions and urban regeneration of places (Turismo de Portugal, 2017).

Long-term economic viability is also paramount, to ensure the narrowing of economic and social gaps, through a holistic approach that allows individuals, businesses, and organizations to integrate sustainable practices into their daily operations, enabling the equitable management of socioeconomic benefits by all, thereby ensuring stable employment, profitable economic opportunities, and social services for local communities (Henriques, Castro, Félix, & Carvalho, 2020; Heslinga, Groote, & Vanclay, 2019; Ramos & Fernandes, 2016; UNWTO, 2013). Tourism, being a significant component of global development, the United Nations (UN) decreed 2017 as the International Year of Sustainable Tourism in order to raise awareness of sustainability around tourism, as it is an inclusive sector that enables economic sustainability, social inclusion and poverty reduction through job creation, and the reduction of environmental resources; enhances cultural values, diversity and authenticity; incites mutual understanding, peace, and security (UN, 2017).

At present, and due to the outbreak of the global pandemic COVID-19, the United Nations Organization was faced with an unprecedented economic and social imbalance. In this context, it was necessary to rethink the goals around sustainable development to "turn recovery into an opportunity to do the right thing for the future." The Sustainable Development Goals, coupled with tourism, are vital for a sustainable, economically inclusive, strengthened and more resilient recovery for societies, and 17 goals are enacted in the 2030 Agenda for Sustainability and Development and the Paris Climate Change Summit: end poverty of all forms, in all regions; ensure educational equity and inclusion, promoting opportunities for all; achieve gender equality and empowerment of all women and girls; promote sustainable and inclusive economic growth, through appropriate employment for all (the promotion of equal employment opportunities around geotourism is one of the pillars of the UNESCO Geoparks network. Local communities enjoy opportunities associated with tourism, allowing the promotion of local culture and its products), make cities and communities inclusive, safe, resilient, and sustainable (by protecting and safeguarding the cultural heritage of the territories where the UNESCO Geoparks are inserted, grants a perception of security and pride in the region from the perspective of residents, fortifying the local identity); act in the face of climate change and its impacts (the UNESCO Geoparks ensure, in its principles, the change of behaviors and adaptation of communities to the effects introduced by climate change); strengthen and revitalize partnerships for sustainable development (based on one of the premises of the UNESCO Geoparks network, the partnership and cooperation between local stakeholders and between international and local organizations, whose knowledge, ideals, and best practices of sustainability are shared in network toward a common goal: reaching the full potential of geoparks).

It is the responsibility of sustainable development in tourism, to achieve its fullness in order to avoid the degradation of the territory, allowing the enjoyment of future generations, based on its main dimensions (Agyeiwaah, McKercher, & Suntikul, 2017; Marujo & Carvalho, 2010): Social—considered the process that leads to continuous growth development, with a decrease in social differences (quality of life); Cultural—, by seeking solutions of local scope, conserving cultural identity and the local way of life, as well as the participation of the population in decision-making processes and in the formulation of tourism development plans; Ecological—supported by the theory that tourism development should limit the consumption of natural resources and cause little damage to life support systems (nonrenewable resources management); Economic Sustainability—enabling economic growth for current generations, as well as responsible handling of natural resources that should have the role of meeting the needs of future generations (economic viability); Spatial Sustainability—based on the most balanced geographical distribution of tourist settlements to avoid exceeding carrying capacity; Political Sustainability—grounded in negotiating the diversity of interests involved in key issues ranging from local to global (Agyeiwaah et al., 2017; Marujo & Carvalho, 2010).

All elements of the destination are essential to ensure its tourism sustainability. From the tourism agents responsible for promoting and boosting the destination to the development of measures implemented by political agents, which ensure the sustainable viability of the destination to agents that are not directly linked to tourism (infrastructure, transport, and restaurants).

Tourism Sustainability Indicators

In each dimension of sustainability, it is possible to synthesize some of the main indicators that are important for the viability of a destination (Agyeiwaah et al., 2017; Vehbi, 2012) (Table 1).

Table 1. Tourism Sustainability Indicators.

Economic	Growth of tourism jobs; Unemployment rate; Seasonality of tourism and production; Growth of prices of goods and services; Percentage of tourist accessibility in the destination.
Environmental	Loss of renewable resources (air quality, water, and soil pollution levels); Loss of nonrenewable resources (vegetation, species, natural spaces); Territory infrastructures (degradation of historical centers, infrastructure development).
Social	Community reception and the perception around tourism development; Community Health and Safety; Social Cohesion; Accessibility.
Cultural	Maintenance of local and cultural tradition; Authenticity; Maintenance of cultural spaces.

Source: Own elaboration according to Vehbi (2012) and Agyeiwaah et al. (2017).

Sustainable tourism indicators can outline guidelines capable of making decisions in terms of the development of priority strategies, which are essential information for the definition of long- and medium-term planning measures, along with other activities (Ocampo, Ebisa, Ombe, & Geen Escoto, 2018). Implementing sustainable development practices in territories with low population density attributes, coupled with a strategic plan for progressive growth with government action and the Tourism Strategic Plan 2027, is essential for smart growth. In this perspective, applying tourism sustainability goals to territories characterized by increasing depopulation, stagnation, backwardness, and by the evident social and economic gap that is difficult to combat, due to lower levels of development (Brito, 2012) will counter their trends, valuing and preserving the authenticity and experience of local communities (Turismo de Portugal, 2017). One of the priorities of the Strategic Plan (Turismo de Portugal, 2017) is to position Portugal as one of the most competitive and sustainable tourism destinations in the world through the enhancement of the territory, connectivity, and knowledge-sharing, as the main lines of action to boost the national economy projecting Portugal as a tourism destination of excellence, based on the principles of sustainability and its indicators, demonstrating the constant commitment to territorial and social cohesion, innovation, entrepreneurship, technology, and above all, people as the main link of differentiation and strategy.

However, the complexity of how the tourism industry operates includes variables that may pose risks to the intended sustainability. The stakeholder perspective will facilitate awareness among all stakeholders in the territory (Heslinga et al., 2019). Regarding the receiving community, the support of residents is essential since hospitality is one of the factors that tourists value most in a destination, influencing their degree of satisfaction (Sánchez del Río-Vázquez, Rodríguez-Rad, & Revilla-Camacho, 2019) regarding the destination and tourist experience. Involving the local community in local sustainability processes induces a greater contribution to the conservation of the territory because they are active agents in the territory and the greatest stakeholders in the benefits generated by tourism activities in the region (Ginting, Marpaung, Sinaga, Narisa, & Siregar, 2020). People must remain at the center of the tourism strategy, being essential to verify all the attributes of the community where the tourism product is inserted and create synergies between all elements (territory managers, stakeholders, and residents) since the hotel component, transport, catering, and cultural activities (Brito, 2012; Turismo de Portugal, 2017), based on a systematic process and intercommunication between all, aiming effective and pragmatic results (Marujo & Carvalho, 2010).

The need for planning and monitoring of a destination is imperative. Based on this perspective, the European Union presented some indicators, developed by Ambiente Italia Research Institute (2003) which aim to involve local authorities as the main authors of the process. These indicators intend to represent in an integrated way the common policies in the European space, contributing to the intermunicipal sustainable concern. Planning is determinant for tourism development (Marujo & Carvalho, 2010) so it is necessary to select indicators and indexes that convey to the various stakeholders of a destination, in real time, vital information to react in a proactive perspective in favor of sustainable tourism development of the destination of which they are part. The choice of sustainability indicators should be based on the opinion of the *stakeholders of* a region by their degree of real knowledge of the place where they are located, adjusted to local needs (Farsani, Coelho, & Costa, 2011; Feil & Schreiber, 2017; Remoaldo et al., 2017). Since *stakeholders* are the main actors in local development, if there is dialogue, cooperation, and collaboration among all, there will be a minimization of possible risks and threats and development of practices to preserve cultural and natural resources of communities (Brito, 2012; Farsani et al., 2011; Remoaldo et al., 2017).

Given the large number of sustainability indicators present in the literature, Mascarenhas et al. (2010) used the PCA (Principal Component Analysis) method, coupled with the sustainability indicators based on the *stakeholders'* opinion. This method allows to analyze the relationship between variables and how they differ, taking as a starting point a wide set of indicators being possible to determine the most accurate indicators. Already Tanguay, Rajaonson, and Therrien (2013), consider 507 sustainability indicators and in seven steps, starting by determining the most important categories for the study, the frequency of use of the indicators, the main problems in tourism sustainability and the measurement of the indicators in time (in order to obtain comparison and analysis throughout the period under study), the availability of information, compatibility with policies applied at the destination, and the validation of the indicators selected by the *stakeholders*. In a more simplified perspective, Kunasekaran et al. (2017) considered the literature around the Indigenous ethnic context and gathered 61 indicators around this topic, determining the degree of importance of the indicators through a questionnaire. Qiu Zhang, Fan, Tse, and King (2017), on the other hand, chose to collect the indicators based on the literature review and then assess these indicators in interviews with key Hong Kong *stakeholders* and residents to get a holistic perspective of the sustainability of the destination.

Despite the existence of various methods for selecting indicators, Vehbi (2012) points out that each destination should define its indicators according to its geographical, social, environmental, and economic structure, with their relevance varying according to the ultimate purpose of its monitoring.

The municipality of Arouca belongs to the NUT III classification, the Metropolitan Area of Porto (Northern Portugal), with about 22,500 inhabitants and an area of 329 km², constituting the lowest population density of the area with 63.2 hab/km² (total population density of the Metropolitan Area of Porto 845.2 hab/km²) (PORDATA, 2019). It is noted the concern of national entities regarding the low population density of the municipality of Arouca, compared to the previous study (population density in the year 2001 was 73.6 hab/km²), was being identified in the PNCT (Government of the Portuguese Republic, 2018). Prepared by intermunicipal communities, higher education institutions, local action groups and business associations and supervised by the Mission Unit for the Enhancement of the Interior (UMVI), the PNCT's main objective is to promote measures for the development of the interior territory of nature.

This program is based on eight objectives defined for the inland territories around challenges and issues preponderant for its development: Aging with Quality; Rural–Urban Relationship; Innovation of the Economic Base; Digital Accessibility; Territorial Capital; Territorial Attractiveness; Cross-border Cooperation; Approaches, Networks; and Participation. In the context of these eight objectives, the main challenges that are directly or indirectly related to tourism development were highlighted, in which the municipality of Arouca committed itself in the current mandate as key elements of action: Promotion of biosphere reserves and geoparks—Nature Tourism: Geopark of Arouca as the main tourism product of the municipality; Heritage Reserve Platform—website specialized in the geopark product; Stimulation of employment—creation of new opportunities for the professional achievement of young people; Promotion of areas with interest to nature conservation—development of actions of external promotion of the network protected areas (Geotourism); and encourage the aggregation of municipal sanitation systems.

As a tourism anchor of the municipality, the Arouca Geopark allows the geological understanding of the space and its esthetic appreciation, involving the populations. It is understood as a new concept of rural territory where the geological heritage is the basis of a strategy that promotes the well-being of populations, while maintaining maximum respect for the environment (National Commission of UNESCO—Portugal, 2014). This new way of categorization of protected area allows to understand Nature conservation and to reconcile it with a sustainable tourism, enabling an improvement of the living conditions of its inhabitants. The Arouca Geopark is part of the European Geoparks Network (EGN), created in 2000, to encourage the exchange of experiences and to benefit from EU rural development programs, having already demonstrated a strong growth of response that meets the interests of municipalities, businesses, and scientific and academic associations. The development strategy of the Arouca

Geopark goes through a participatory methodology between public and private entities, based on local initiative, valuing the assets that make up the territory, in order to promote innovation and foster growth and competitiveness of the region, through the development of the geological heritage and the remaining natural and cultural heritage, stimulating activities and products for the territory; promotion of the quality of life of residents and planning policies in the area of environment, agriculture, and forestry; promotion of education for sustainability; promotion of geotourism, focusing on the qualification, organization, strategic promotion, and marketing of its tourism products; promotion of a territorial dynamics around the sociocultural animation, strengthening the sense of belonging (local authenticity) and strengthening and boosting cooperation, partnerships, and networking among stakeholders (Arouca Geopark Association, 2021).

In addition to the dynamics previously mentioned, key strategies for cultural sustainability were also adopted (Torabi Farsani, Coelho, & Costa, 2012): Encouraging students from local schools to dress as trilobites, rafting down the Paiva River, hiking and other activities associated with the geopark; creating a geobrew recipe book; and organizing a "Geo-art" contest for local artists.

In economic terms, it is possible to verify through a study conducted in 2014, by the National UNESCO Commission, that UNESCO classifications boost benefits for the surrounding region, which can be analyzed through indicators such as the number of visitors, average spending/visitor, average length of stay, and local job creation. Between 2014 and 2020, the number of hotel establishments (4–14), the number of overnight stays per 100 inhabitants (40.2–88.6), and the total income of the lodgings increased; the average stay is 1.5 nights (Associação Geoparque Arouca, 2021). The annual number of visitors to the Paiva Passage is above 100,000 since its opening. It should be noted there are improvements in the accessibility of the park, through the creation of parking lots and complementary services, as well as the accessibility between the main entrances of the park. The tourism product is an example that tourism is fundamental for local development as it has boosted trade in the region, enhanced the development of new infrastructures, and improved the quality of life of residents through economic circulation (Oliveira, Tavares, & Pacheco, 2019).

It is also crucial to prepare destinations with potential for economic growth, as the case of Arouca, so that antitourism sentiment by communities does not grow and for that it is a priority to ensure their quality of life (Sheivachman, 2017). For this reason, several authors consider that for the tourism industry to limit, anticipate, and plan the various effects of tourism, it is important to include local stakeholders such as companies directly linked to tourism, without ever forgetting the community as an important stakeholder of the destination. Taking also into account the community in which the tourism product is inserted (destinations with low population density), the impacts generated by tourism will be felt more immediately by communities and may generate feelings of revulsion toward tourists and the negative externalities generated by them. It is in the interest of the destination regulators to make sure the social sustainability of the territory, so that the community is one of the pillars of growth of the tourism product. In this perspective, the municipality of Arouca and the geopark product, meets the challenges proposed in the Tourism Strategy 2027, since the tourist destination in which it is inserted belongs to a community with reduced population density, integrated into a territorial strategic plan to "Extend the tourist activity to the whole territory and promote tourism as a factor of social cohesion" (Turismo de Portugal, 2017). Another objective proposed in the Tourism Strategy 2027 that can be framed in this context is "To ensure the preservation and sustainable economic enhancement of cultural and natural heritage and local identity, as a strategic asset, as well as the compatibility of this activity with the permanence of the local community," so that the receiving community feels less strongly the tourism growth.

As suggested by the UNESCO National Community (2014), it is relevant that management entities implement information systems that allow them to permanently monitor and evaluate the property, and the territory, as a fundamental instrument of tourism destination management, considering a crucial element for monitoring the sustainability of the territory (Table 2).

Surveys were applied to residents to analyze their perception of the impacts that tourism brought after the opening of the Paiva Walkways (Question 11.1–11.10) as well as their perception of spatial planning (Question 12.1–12.6) (Table 3).

This work highlights the importance of the existence of measures for monitoring the economic, social, economic, and environmental development without forgetting the economic indicators capable of ensuring effective planning according to the collection of information obtained by the stakeholders and local community. To trace the sociodemographic profile of the respondents, it is possible to verify the frequency and percentage of response of the total sample of 259 individuals. The respondents, mostly female (52.5%), are concentrated in an age bracket between 41 and 64 years (40.43%) and with educational attainment between high school and college degree (79.2%). Since the survey was aimed at residents of the municipality of Arouca and workers in the municipality with a perception of the impacts of tourism (business establishment owners and employees), it was found that 84.6% (219 people) of the respondents reside in the municipality of Arouca; 63.7% (165 people) work in the municipality of Arouca;

Table 2. Arouca Geopark and Paiva Walkways.

Strengths	Aspects to Consider
Preponderant for the economic-social development of the region (Liberato, Bernardo, & Liberato, 2019). It demonstrates that tourism is fundamental to local development and boosting trade; it has enhanced the development of new infrastructure and improved the quality of life of residents through economic circulation (Oliveira, Tavares, & 2019).	Prepare these destinations so that anti tourism sentiment by communities does not grow (Sheivachman, 2017). Lack of tourism specialization, can result in the loss of autonomy and capital (Scholz et al., 2012, p. 356).

Source: Own preparation based on the authors presented.

Table 3. Residents' Perception After the Opening of the Paiva Walkway.

Q.11.1	**I saw more tourists traveling through the region**	**Sheivachman (2017)**
Q.11.2	I felt that the daily commutes became longer	Michael (2003)
Q.11.3	There have been improvements in public spaces and access roads	Oliveira et al. (2019)
Q.11.4	Tourists respect the locals in the city and the residents	
Q.11.5	Public transportation has improved its frequency	Michael (2003)
Q.11.6	I feel safer	Sheivachman (2017)
Q.11.7	I consider tourism beneficial for Arouca	Oliveira et al. (2019)
Q.11.8	Jobs increased	
Q.11.9	In my professional activity, I received more clients from outside the region	
Q.11.10	The City Council takes into consideration my opinion about Tourism and its impacts	Tanguay et al. (2013)
Q.12.1	The monitoring of the social impacts of Tourism in the county	Brito (2012) and Lima et al. (2017)
Q.12.2	Periodic meetings between residents, businesses and the City Council on strategies for tourism	Tanguay et al. (2013)
Q.12.3	Up-to-date information on tourism decisions	Tanguay et al. (2013)
Q.12.4	Cleaning of public spaces	
Q.12.5	Cultural exchange between tourists and locals	Torabi Farsani et al. (2012)
Q.12.6	Awareness workshops for residents about the geopark	UN

Source: Own elaboration based on several authors.

only 21.2% (55 people) are owners of a commercial establishment; the respondents either have long-lasting jobs (over 16 years old—25.9%) or relatively recent ones (up to 2 years—21.6%). As the Geopark of Arouca and the Passadiços do Paiva are the drivers of tourism sustainability in Arouca, it was verified the monitoring by the respondents of the life cycle of this tourism product, through their presence in the highlighted dates (Table 4).

It is relevant the presence of respondents at the time of the UNESCO classification of Arouca Geopark in 2009 as well as at the time of the opening of the Arouca walkways in 2015 (81.5%).

Table 4. Relationship With Geopark and Paiva Walkways.

Were you living in Arouca before the UNESCO classification of Arouca Geopark in 2009?	F	%
Yes	211	81.5%
No	48	18.5%
What about during the opening of the Arouca walkways in 2015?		
Yes	202	81.5%
No	211	18.5%

Source: Own elaboration based on the data obtained.

The values concerning the territory and the impacts felt by residents since the opening of the Paiva Walkways and their perception regarding land management and sustainable tourism planning are analyzed. Additionally, it analyzed the perspective of residents regarding spatial planning, positive and negative factors associated with tourism since the opening of the Paiva Walkways. It is thus relevant the analysis of the sample of this study, having as population the residents of Arouca. The data will be analyzed and interpreted by calculating the mode (presenting the value of the variable with the highest frequency); the mean (average value of responses); median (value that divides the data set into two parts with the same number of observations); standard deviation (calculation of the sample dispersion), and variance (value of the deviation that varies from the mean). To allow a descriptive analysis of the variables under study, a five-point Likert scale was used to measure total disagreement or agreement with the statements presented: 1—I totally disagree; 2—I disagree; 3—I neither disagree nor agree; 4—I agree; 5—I totally agree. In this group of questions, the perception of residents after the opening of the Paiva Walkway was measured (Table 5).

With regard to the residents' perception of the impacts of tourism, the median and mode measures of central tendency have the same values in 6 of the 10 items. While the median and mode of the residents' perception of the increase in tourists is 5 (Strongly Agree), the perception of the positive impacts associated with tourism such as the improvement of public spaces, the feeling of safety, the beneficial component of tourism, the increase of external customers from the region in jobs, and the inclusion of the residents' opinion on the impacts of tourism is equal to 3 (Neither Agree nor Disagree). However, the perception about tourists' respect for the city and integrity of residents, increased frequency of public transport and increased jobs is equal to 4 (Agree). The sample under study presents a more neutral position regarding the perception of the impacts of tourists. Although the presence of tourists in the region is perceptible (Strongly Agree), the average sample of the population under study does not have an opinion about the impacts on the region, allowing us to assess the low perception of the negative impacts that infrastructures and services have on the territory, which reflects an overall positive balance (Table 6).

Table 5. Residents' Perception of Tourism Impacts on the Territory.

		N/ Valid	Average	Median	Mode	Standard Deviation	Variance
Q.11.1	I saw more tourists traveling through the region	259	4.66	5	5	0.62	0.39
Q.11.2	I felt that the daily commute became longer	258	2.85	3	3	1.29	1.67
Q.11.3	There have been improvements in public spaces and access roads	259	3.01	3	4	1.34	1.78
Q.11.4	Tourists respect city sites and residents	259	3.75	4	4	0.97	0.95
Q.11.5	Public transportation has improved its frequency	259	3.86	4	5	1.17	1.37
Q.11.6	I feel safer	258	3.13	3	3	1.01	1.01
Q.11.7	I consider tourism beneficial for Arouca	259	2.9	3	3	1.44	2.09
Q.11.8	Jobs increased	257	3.62	4	4	1.11	1.24
Q.11.9	In my professional activity, I received more clients from outside the region	253	3.25	3	3	1.19	1.41
Q.11.10	The City Council takes into consideration my opinion about Tourism and its impacts	259	2.93	3	3	1.19	1.41

Source: Own elaboration based on SPSS outputs.

Table 6. Residents' Perception of Tourism Impacts on the Territory.

	N/ Valid	Average	Median	Mode	Standard Deviation	Variance
Q.12.1 The monitoring of the social impacts of tourism in the county	258	4.25	4.5	5	0.89	0.079
Q.12.2 Periodic meetings between residents, businesses, and the City Council on strategies for tourism	258	4	4	5	1	0.99
Q.12.3 Up-to-date information on tourism decisions	258	4.07	4	5	0.88	0.78
Q.12.4 Cleaning of public spaces	258	4.62	5	5	0.72	0.52
Q.12.5 Cultural exchange between tourists and locals	258	4.22	4	5	0.88	0.78
Q.12.6 Awareness workshops for residents about the geopark	258	3.91	4	4	0.98	0.97

To enable the descriptive analysis of the variables under study, a five-point Likert scale was used to measure total disagreement or agreement with the statements presented: 1—Not important; 2—Not very important; 3—Important; 4—Very important; 5—Extremely important. In this group of questions, the perception of residents regarding sustainable tourism management and planning was measured. In this scope, the measures of central tendency median and mode present the same values in five of the six items. In most of the planning proposals presented in the survey, the measures of central tendency of the mode and median are equal to 4 (Very Important), demonstrating the concern that residents have with the sustainable planning of the destination, monitoring and sharing of updated information. Regarding information about the geopark, the measures of central tendency median and mode are equal to 3 (Important), giving no relevance of response from residents regarding this item.

In the last question, the resident had the opportunity to expose their perception about the impacts of tourism, generated after the opening of the Paiva Walkways in the municipality of Arouca. Of the 259 respondents, 172 people answered that improvements were observed. However, respondents show special concern around the social dimension (23 answers), environmental dimension (22 answers), and lastly the economic dimension (10 answers). In order to categorize the answers obtained, we used the European indicator system for tourism (European Commission: Luxembourg, 2013) which presents several subindicators of the three main dimensions of sustainability and which was addressed as one of the main concerns by the residents (Table 7).

It is important to constantly monitor the territory, through indicators adapted to its characteristics, with the participation of all stakeholders. Considering the literature review, around low population density territories and the growth of tourism in Arouca, provided since the opening of the Geopark of Arouca and the Paiva Walkways, the following micro cluster is suggested for the destination (Fig. 1).

The management and planning of a territory endowed with a geological heritage as is the case of Arouca should be transversal. The greater the number of stakeholders involved and dedicated to the monitoring and enhancement of heritage, the better the results obtained (Lima, Machado, Guerreiro, Nunes, & Costa, 2018).

Table 7. Impacts Felt With the Opening of the Walkways.

Subindicators Environmental Dimension	No. of Answers	Total
Solid waste management	6	
Landscape and biodiversity protection	8	
Reducing the impact of transportation	7	
Sewage treatment	1	22
Social Dimension		
Social/community impact	7	
Protecting and strengthening local resources	13	
Quantity and quality of employment	2	
Reducing the impact of transportation	1	
		23
Economic Dimension		
Tourism supply chain	8	
Quantity and quality of employment	2	10

Source: Own preparation based on European Commission's Tourism Indicators System (European Commission, 2013).

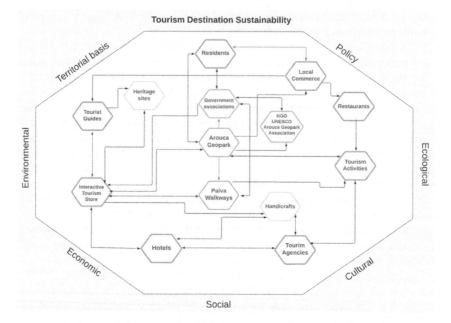

Fig. 1.   Arouca Tourism Sustainability *Cluster. Source:* Own
elaboration | Adapted source according to Michael (2003), Sigurðardóttir and
Steinthorsson (2018), Agyeiwaah et al. (2017), and Marujo and Carvalho
(2010).

Conclusion

The measurement of the tourism sustainability of a territory is a complex analysis
that must take into account the limitations of each territory such as the size of the
tourism activity and the existing resources according to this activity (Blancas,
Lozano-Oyola, González, & Caballero, 2018). In this perspective, it was observed
that the analysis of the territory in cluster generates several benefits such as
reduction of costs related to its management through network cooperation, creation of opportunities for the destination as a single and holistic promotion of the
territory (Nowaczyk, 2019). When analyzing the reality of a smaller scale territory
(SST), it is even more evident the need for cooperation between all stakeholders of
the destination, given the reduced capital available for promotion and tourism
innovation of these destinations, the lack of specialized tourism knowledge, and
lack of infrastructure (Nowaczyk, 2019; The Metropolitan Policy Program at
Brookings: Washington, D.C., 2018). However, when we are facing a territorial
reality of networking, knowledge-sharing, highlighting the attributes of the
destination, with economic activity, tourism, leisure, culture, and science, it

becomes easier to enhance the territories, making them more attractive (Covas, 2007) (Table 8).

When analyzing the development of a small territory with rural characteristics associated with depopulation and strong involvement with the territory as a physical and environmental space, the relationship with sustainable development applied to this reality is preponderant. Being the concept of sustainable development strongly linked to the promotion of a territory by its current characteristics without compromising the viability of the destination for future generations, it is important to make a management directed to the specificities of the destination, considering the cultural heritage, optimizing natural resources, and conserving the heritage and biodiversity (Turismo de Portugal, 2017; UNWTO, 2013; Vehbi, 2012; World Economic Forum's Switzerland, 2019). It is also one of the objectives of sustainable development, to mitigate the socioeconomic differences of the residents, through guidelines that encourage sustainable practices in the daily operations of the intuitions, enabling the equitable distribution of their economic benefits through stable employment and profitable economic opportunities, always based on intercultural tolerance and preservation of cultural authenticity. Most rural areas are rich in natural resources, resources that are owned by local communities and used as the main tourism activity of a destination (Matiku, Zuwarimwe, & Tshipala, 2021).

To verify whether the destination is following the guidelines of tourism sustainability, it is important to have metrics that allow the destination to be evaluated according to indicators that are appropriate to the characteristics of the territory. In this way, all the destination stakeholders should be involved in sharing updated information around the destination, so that it is possible to plan in the short, medium, and long term sustainable guidelines for a tourism destination (Agyeiwaah et al., 2017; Matiku et al., 2021; Ocampo et al., 2018; Turismo de Portugal, 2017; Vehbi, 2012). As local communities are the main holders of knowledge of a tourist destination (Ginting et al., 2020; Matiku et al., 2021;

Table 8. Benefits of a *Cluster*.

Communication and sharing of networked information for the benefit of the destination
Cost reduction
Infrastructure sharing
Specialization in the territory
Increased tourism competitiveness
Employability
Enhancement of the authenticity and exclusivity of the tourist experience
Reducing the negative impacts of seasonality

Source: Own elaboration based on the authors Mascarenhas et al. (2010), Tapachai (2019), Nowaczyk (2019), and The Metropolitan Policy Program at Brookings: Washington, D.C. (2018).

ONU, 2017), it is crucial to involve them in decision-making processes, territory conservation, and planning, becoming active agents of tourism activity and reducing the sense of tourist repulsion often felt due to negative externalities generated by tourism (Sánchez del Río-Vázquez et al., 2019; Sheivachman, 2017).

Geoparks are grounded in sustainable development and respect for rurality. The communities that integrate them absorb the spirit of networking and sharing of knowledge and mutual aid. The practice of geotourism allows the tourist to know the geological, cultural, and heritage context taking into consideration the natural, regional resources and the communities where the geopark is inserted (Pereira, 2019). For a tourist destination to be part of the GGN, it must present territorial characteristics of international geological relevance, having as a basic holistic concept the protection, education, research, and sustainable development.

Portugal is an example in the integration of the geoparks network of international geological relevance, counting already five examples of the 169 that make up the network of geoparks of UNESCO. Through the analysis of the five geoparks existing in Portugal, it is possible to verify the cooperation and synergy between the local community and associative in the community, through the efforts made to promote the tourism product and the destination as one. Each geopark becomes a unique and differentiating tourist destination, since the environmental context of each geopark is specific to that place, as well as the traditions, customs, heritage, and local and gastronomic products associated with it. The cultural identity present in each geopark and the network cooperation with the various stakeholders in the region give the tourist a unique experience with a varied tourism supply.

The municipality of Arouca and the Arouca Geopark Association ensure a high community participation in the promotional and cooperation dimension around the geopark and the endogenous resources of the destination. Since it is a territory of low population density, one of the strongest concerns is the carrying capacity and saturation of the destination, existing metrics already implemented in the territory, namely through the access to the Paiva Walkways and associated infrastructures/equipment. The information about the number of people visiting a geosite is important from the perspective of implementing a correct planning. According to the number of visitors, considering the fragility and vulnerability of geological elements, the specific number of visitors should be adapted, allowing safe conditions for the tourist experience and the preservation of the geosite (Lima, Nunes, & Brilha, 2017).

In line with other authors, the municipality and the Arouca Geopark Association believe that the sustainable growth of the region will only be possible when all *stakeholders of the* territory are involved in the form of a cluster, enabling the emergence of business opportunities and sustainable development of the region. It is notable the perception of increased tourists by residents as well as the associated economic and social aspects, such as the increase in tourism-related jobs. Regarding residents' perception of tourism planning in the region, it is noteworthy the concern about monitoring and sustainable planning as well as their participation in regular meetings with other stakeholders, and knowledge of the decision-making around tourism. Although most of the residents surveyed pointed out the improvements in the region, the concern about the negative externalities caused by rapid tourism growth regarding environmental and social dimensions was noticeable.

References

Agyeiwaah, E., McKercher, B., & Suntikul, W. (2017). Identifying core indicators of sustainable tourism: A path forward? *Tourism Management Perspectives, 24,* 26–33.

Ambiente Italia Research Institute, C. E.: B. (2003). European common indicators—towards a local sustainability profile.

Arouca Geopark Association (AGA). (2021). *Relatório de Atividades & Contas* 2020. Retrieved from http://aroucageopark.pt/pt/documentacao/

Blancas, F. J., Lozano-Oyola, M., González, M., & Caballero, R. (2018). A dynamic sustainable tourism evaluation using multiple benchmarks. *Journal of Cleaner Production, 174,* 1190–1203. doi:10.1016/j.jclepro.2017.10.295

Brito, M. B. M. de. (2012). Monitorização dos impactos turísticos: Uma proposta de modelo aplicável a territórios em mudança. *Cadernos de Geografia, 30–31,* 249–256. doi:10.14195/0871-1623_31_23

Comissão Europeia: Luxemburgo. (2013). *Caixa de ferramentas do Sistema Europeu de Indicadores de Turismo para Destinos Sustentáveis.* Comissão Europeia.

Covas, A. (2007). *Ruralidades I: Temas e Problemas do mundo Rural.* Universidade do Algarve. Retrieved from http://id.bnportugal.gov.pt/bib/bibnacional/1707609

Farsani, N. T., Coelho, C., & Costa, C. (2011). Geotourism and geoparks as novel strategies for socio-economic development in rural areas. *International Journal of Tourism Research, 13*(1), 68–81. doi:10.1002/jtr.800

Feil, A. A., & Schreiber, D. (2017). Análise da estrutura e dos critérios na elaboração do índice de Sustentabilidade. *Sustentabilidade em Debate—Brasília, 8*(2), 30–43.

Ginting, N., Marpaung, B. O. Y., Sinaga, F. A., Narisa, N., & Siregar, N. (2020). Geotourism and stakeholders: An approach to enhance geoconservation. *IOP Conference Series: Earth and Environmental Science, 452,* 012156. doi:10.1088/1755-1315/452/1/012156

Government of the Portuguese Republic: Lisboa. (2018). Programa Nacional para a Coesão Territorial República Portuguesa. Retrieved from https://www.portugal.gov.pt/pt/gc21/governo/programa/programa-nacional-para-a-coesao-territorial-/ficheiros-coesao-territorial/programa-nacional-para-a-coesao-territorial-pdf.aspx

Henriques, M., Castro, A., Félix, Y., & Carvalho, I. (2020). Promoting sustainability in a low density territory through heritage: Casa da Pedra case-study (Araripe Geopark, NE Brazil). *Resources Policy, 67.* doi:10.1016/j.resourpol.2020.101684

Heslinga, J., Groote, P., & Vanclay, F. (2019). Strengthening governance processes to improve benefit-sharing from tourism in protected areas by using stakeholder analysis. *Journal of Sustainable Tourism, 27*(6), 773–787. doi:10.1080/09669582.2017.1408635

Ketels, C. H. M., & Memedovic, O. (2008). From clusters to cluster-based economic development. *International Journal of Technological Learning, Innovation and Development, 1*(3), 375. doi:10.1504/IJTLID.2008.019979

Kunasekaran, P., Gill, S., Ramachandran, S., Shuib, A., Baum, T., & Herman Mohammad Afandi, S. (2017). Measuring sustainable indigenous tourism indicators: A case of Mah Meri ethnic group in Carey Island, Malaysia. *Sustainability*, *9*(7), 1256. doi:10.3390/su9071256

Liberato, D., Bernardo, V., & Liberato, P. (2019). Geotourism visitor's motivations: The case of Paiva walkways. In K. S. Soliman (Ed.), *Proceedings of the 33rd International Business Information Management Association Conference, IBIMA 2019: Education excellence and innovation management through vision 2020* (pp. 5192–5206). IBIMA.

Lima, E. A., Machado, M., Guerreiro, M., Nunes, J. C., & Costa, M. P. (2018). Geological heritage management in small Islands: The example of the Azores UNESCO global geopark (Portugal). *Geoheritage*, *10*(4), 659–671. doi:10.1007/s12371-018-0328-6

Lima, A., Nunes, J. C., & Brilha, J. (2017). Monitoring of the visitors impact at "Ponta da Ferraria e Pico das Camarinhas" Geosite [São Miguel Island, Azores UNESCO Global Geopark, Portugal]. *Geoheritage*, *9*(4), 495–503. doi:10.1007/s12371-016-0203-2

Marujo, N., & Carvalho, P. (2010). Turismo, planeamento e desenvolvimento sustentável. *Turismo e Sociedade*, *3*. doi:10.5380/tes.v3i2.19635

Mascarenhas, A., Coelho, P., & Subtil, E. (2010). The role of common local indicators in regional sustainability assessment. *Ecological Indicators*, *10*, 646–656.

Matiku, S. M., Zuwarimwe, J., & Tshipala, N. (2021). Sustainable tourism planning and management for sustainable livelihoods. *Development Southern Africa*, *38*(4), 524–538. doi:10.1080/0376835X.2020.1801386

Michael, E. J. (2003). Tourism micro-clusters. *Tourism Economics*, *9*(2), 133–145. doi:10.5367/000000003101298312

Nowaczyk, P. (2019). Tourism cluster in the sailing operations of small seaports in Poland. *Klaster Turystyczny W Działalności Żeglarskiej Małych Portów Morskich W Polsce*, *18*(2), 69–77. doi:10.22630/ASPE.2019.18.2.20

Ocampo, L., Ebisa, J. A., Ombe, J., & Geen Escoto, M. (2018). Sustainable ecotourism indicators with fuzzy Delphi method—A Philippine perspective. *Ecological Indicators*, *93*, 874–888. doi:10.1016/j.ecolind.2018.05.060

Oliveira, D., Tavares, F., & Pacheco, L. (2019). Os Passadiços do Paiva: Estudo Exploratório do seu Impacto Económico e Social. *Fronteiras: Journal of Social, Technological and Environmental Science*, *8*(1), 242–264. doi:10.21664/2238-8869.2019v8i1.p242-264

ONU. (2017). *Sustainable tourism: Sustainable development knowledge platform*. Retrieved from https://sustainabledevelopment.un.org/index.php?menu=243

Pereira, A. R. (2019). *Água e território: Um tributo a Catarina Ramos*. Centro de Estudos Geográficos da Universidade de Lisboa. doi:10.33787/CEG20190005

PORDATA. (2019). PORDATA—Densidade populacional. Retrieved from https://www.pordata.pt/Municipios/Densidade+populacional-452

Porter, M. (1998). Clusters and the new economics of competition. Reprint 98609. *Harvard Business Review*, 78–81.

Qiu Zhang, H., Fan, D. X. F., Tse, T. S. M., & King, B. (2017). Creating a scale for assessing socially sustainable tourism. *Journal of Sustainable Tourism*, *25*(1), 61–78. doi:10.1080/09669582.2016.1173044

Ramos, G., & Fernandes, J. (2016). Tourism territories in low density areas: The case of Naturtejo geopark in Portugal. *Journal of Tourism, Heritage & Services Marketing, 2*(1), 14–21. doi:10.5281/zenodo.376330

Remoaldo, P., Freitas, I., Matos, O., Lopes, H., Silva, S., Sánchez Fernández, M. D., ... Ribeiro, V. (2017). The planning of tourism on rural Areas: The stakeholders' perceptions of the Boticas municipality (Northeastern Portugal). *European Countryside, 9*(3), 504–525. doi:10.1515/euco-2017-0030

Sánchez del Río-Vázquez, M.-E., Rodríguez-Rad, C. J., & Revilla-Camacho, M.-Á. (2019). Relevance of social, economic, and environmental impacts on residents' satisfaction with the public administration of tourism. *Sustainability, 11*(22), 6380. doi:10.3390/su11226380

Scholz, W., Breuste, J., Bourlon, F., Rojas, J., & Torres Salinas, R. (2012). Tourism and microcluster in Aysés, Chile. *Tourism Review International, 15*, 355–361.

Sheivachman, A. (2017). Proposing solutions to overtourism in popular destinations: A skift framework. Retrieved from https://skift.com/2017/10/23/proposing-solutions-to-overtourism-in-popular-destinations-a-skift-framework/

Sigurðardóttir, I., & Steinthorsson, R. S. (2018). Development of micro-clusters in tourism: A case of equestrian tourism in northwest Iceland. *Scandinavian Journal of Hospitality and Tourism, 18*(3), 261–277. doi:10.1080/15022250.2018.1497286

Tanguay, G. A., Rajaonson, J., & Therrien, M.-C. (2013). Sustainable tourism indicators: Selection criteria for policy implementation and scientific recognition. *Journal of Sustainable Tourism, 21*(6), 862–879. doi:10.1080/09669582.2012.742531

Tapachai, N. (2019). Applying a tourism micro cluster model to rural development planning: A case study of Kaeng Ruang village in Thailand. *Human Geography Journal, 26*, 45–54. doi:10.26565/2076-1333-2019-26-05

The Metropolitan Policy Program at Brookings: Washington, D.C. (2018). *Rethinking cluster initiatives* (pp. 52).

Torabi Farsani, N., Coelho, C., & Costa, C. (2012). Geotourism and geoparks as gateways to socio-cultural sustainability in Qeshm rural areas, Iran. *Asia Pacific Journal of Tourism Research, 17*(1), 30–48. doi:10.1080/10941665.2011.610145

Turismo de Portugal. (2017). Estratégia de Turismo: Liderar o Turismo do futuro 2027. Retrieved from https://www.turismodeportugal.pt/pt/Turismo_Portugal/Estrategia/Estrategia_2027/Paginas/default.aspx

UNESCO Portugal. (2014). Geoparques Mundiais da UNESCO. Retrieved from https://unescoportugal.mne.gov.pt/images/Ci%C3%AAncia/desdobravel_geoparques.pdf

United Nations Organization. (2017). Sustainable tourism: Sustainable development knowledge platform. Retrieved from https://sustainabledevelopment.un.org/index.php?menu=243

UNWTO. (2013). Sustainable tourism for development guidebook—Enhancing capacities for sustainable tourism for development in developing countries. UNWTO. doi:10.18111/9789284415496

UNWTO. (2020). UNWTO recommendations on tourism and rural development—A guide to making tourism an effective tool for rural development. Retrieved from https://www.e-unwto.org/doi/epdf/10.18111/9789284422173

Vehbi, B. O. (2012). A model for assessing the level of tourism impacts and sustainability of coastal cities. In *Strategies for tourism industry—Micro and macro perspectives*. IntechOpen. doi:10.5772/38549

WCDE. (1987). Report of the world commission on environment and development: Our common future. United Nations Digital Library. Retrieved from https://sustainabledevelopment.un.org/content/documents/5987our-common-future.pdf

World Economic Forum's Switzerland. (2019). The travel & tourism competitiveness report 2019. Retrieved from https://www3.weforum.org/docs/WEF_TTCR_2019.pdf

Building Positive Zimbabwean Tourism Festival and Event Destination Brand Image and Equity

Farai Chigora, Brighton Nyagadza, Chipo Katsande and Promise Zvavahera

Abstract

Globalization has intensified marketing pressures for tourism destinations in their operations at a national, regional, and international level. The dynamics of the twenty-first century have resulted in immense competition, causing organizations in the tourism and hospitality business to adopt new strategic management and operational marketing processes. Branding has become one of the important marketing strategies in withstanding the competitive nature of the tourism industry when offering products and services to tourists. Zimbabwe as a tourism destination has also experienced various changes due to globalization, induced by its socioeconomic and political state of affairs. In order to survive and adhere to the changing market demands, Zimbabwe as a tourism destination has also adopted branding as a marketing strategy, with the aim of holding a high-valued global market position through an extensive brand identity.

Keywords: Event destination brand image; event marketing; sustainable destinations brand image and equity; market share; resilience; Zimbabwean tourism festival

Introduction

The aim of this chapter is to explore the concept of tourism festival and event destination branding and relate to practices in Zimbabwean festival and event tourism destination. The chapter is therefore based on the following objectives:

Resilient and Sustainable Destinations After Disaster, 63–74
Copyright © 2023 Farai Chigora, Brighton Nyagadza, Chipo Katsande and Promise Zvavahera
Published under exclusive licence by Emerald Publishing Limited
doi:10.1108/978-1-80382-021-720231005

- to understand the concept of tourism festival and event destination brand image in Zimbabwe;
- to explain the essence of tourism festival and event destination branding and its importance in Zimbabwe;
- to explore the tourism festival and event brand process by mainly looking at market analysis, brand development, brand positioning, brand personality, brand implementation, brand communication, and brand tracking;
- to understand the critical success factors for a tourism festival and event destination brand;
- to explore the variables that constructs tourism festival and event destination brand equity; and
- to analyze previous models and discussion in tourism festival and event destination brand equity.

Tourism Festival and Event Destination Brand Image in Zimbabwe

Destination image is a concept which is based on understating the perceptions that potential tourists have about a destination (Kim & Perdue, 2011). It mainly involves managing perception of tourists toward a destination and its offerings (Nyagadza & Chigora, 2022; Pan & Li, 2011, p. 134). A tourism destination that is perceived to have a good image is more likely to attract more tourists (Martins, 2015, p. 4). The use of marketing communication is important in creating a positive image of a tourism destination, though it is not the only means. There is little research on the role of destination branding in destination marketing particularly in a Zimbabwean context. The discussions provided by various authors show that destination branding helps in improving marketing of tourism destinations through positioning and differentiating the destination from others. Therefore, destination branding is indispensable in contemporary competitive markets dominated by producers and suppliers of homogenous tourism products and services. There are many existing tourism destinations globally, offering sometimes similar products and services, which call for differentiation as a marketing strategy, to which branding is a key and promising ingredient. Destination branding also helps in destination marketing through promoting identity of a destination in a global market. Zimbabwe destination's marketing success can be measured by its brand performance. Destination marketers should be able to develop and apply the most effective type of media that helps improve a positive image of the tourism destination when they do their festivals as depicted in Table 1, the major festivals which help to boost the nation brand's equity. There is a limited contribution from various global researchers on the best media to use in order to improve destination image. According to perspectives, imagery is increasingly becoming important in promoting tourism destinations through expressions and messages (Molina et al., 2010; Nyagadza & Chigora, 2022).

Table 1. Major Festivals in Zimbabwe Which Promote the Nation's Brand.

Festival	Description
Harare International Food Festival	The purpose of the festival is to showcase the food and wine from the top industries in the country.
Shoko Festival	This is one of the most successful and longest running festivals in Zimbabwe, where artists from the urban genre freely share their music and new music in an artistic way, including comedians.
Jikinya Dance Festival	The Jikinya Dance Festival was founded by National Arts Council of Zimbabwe (NACZ), with an idea of giving young children the chance to perform and learn the Zimbabwean cultural dances with an aim to preserve their cultural legacy.
Harare International Festival of Arts	Commonly known as HIFA, it's an arts festival meant to brand Zimbabwe through performances such as funk, jazz, opera, Afrobeat, theater, dance, and other related acts.
Chibuku Neshamwari Dance Festival	It is a platform for showcasing emerging talent through celebrating traditional dance such as mhande, mbende jerusarema, dinhe, chioda, and setapa.
Bulawayo Cultural Festival	Bulawayo Cultural Festival is a world music and dance festival that happens every year in the month of April. The organizers of this event make it an outreach program that attracts local dance and music groups to showcase their talent to all kinds of audiences.
Midlands Arts and Culture Festival	Midlands Arts and Culture Festival is a national event that happens in the month of September. Some genres featured in the event include theater, music, visual arts, literal, and dance performances. The program also includes a workshop for school-goers and practical writers to expose them to the rich art and culture of Zimbabwe.
Zimbabwe International Film Festival	The Zimbabwe International Film Festival is a 10-day event that happens annually in the

Table 1. *(Continued)*

Festival	Description
	months of August and September. The festival is organized by a nonprofit organization to provide an unbiased platform to artists across the country and beyond to show feature films, documentaries, short films, and more. The cultural event also provides workshops to interested participants. The main aim of the event organizers is to provide a competitive, nonpolitical environment to celebrate the dynamic culture of filmmaking and viewing.
Intwasa Arts Festival koBulawayo	The Intwasa Arts Festival koBulawayo is a cultural event that celebrates the rich and diverse arts of Zimbabwe. The program features workshops, performances, music, theater, readings, literary events, discussions, visual arts, films, competitions, and more. The festival is hosted in various parts of Bulawayo. The event attracts not only local artists but also international ones. The event is specially curated to give its audiences a memorable experience that focuses on quality programs and not just quantity.
Chimanimani Arts Festival	Chimanimani Arts Festival is a two-day annual event that showcases the local art and performances of Zimbabwe. The free festival draws crowds from all parts of the country who seek to enjoy music, poetry sessions, acrobatics, and dancers. The local community participates in all earnestness to display their Zimbabwe arts and crafts for festival-goers. Each year, the festival generates interaction within the community and contributes to the region's economic growth.

Source: Kanika (2021).

Essence of Tourism Festival and Event Destination Branding

The intensification of competition in tourism markets globally has resulted in authorities recognizing destination branding as a tool to use in marketing promotion and management of tourism resources (Kim & Lehto, 2013, p. 117). Traditionally, brands have been used to identify general products mainly using names and symbols and now the concept is applied to marketing of services (Pike, 2010, p. 127). Even with minimal practice in other destinations, the advent of destination branding has resulted in many tourism marketers viewing destinations as brands, such that they have applied the concept from generic product branding theories to destinations (Kim & Lehto, 2013, p. 118). The discussions provided by various authors show that destination branding helps in improving marketing of tourism destinations through positioning and differentiating the destination from others. Therefore, destination branding is indispensable in contemporary competitive markets dominated by producers and suppliers of homogenous tourism products and services. There are many existing tourism destinations globally, offering sometimes similar products and services, which call for differentiation as a marketing strategy, to which branding is a key and promising ingredient. Destination branding also helps in destination marketing through promoting identity of a destination in a global market. Zimbabwe destination's marketing success can be measured by its brand performance. The current situation shows that the Zimbabwe as a destination brand is struggling to stand its market dominance reflected by the continuous rebranding exercises. According to Morrison (2012), a good tourism destination brand should be market-tested and well accepted by all stakeholders. The fact that Zimbabwe as a destination brand keeps on changing can be due to its failure to positively perform on the global market and not being accepted by pertinent stakeholders. Festival and event destination branding helps in understanding how and to what extent brands are relevant to consumers which provide assistance to destination managers in knowing how to design branding mechanisms that make them work closely with their customers (Florek & Kavaratzis, 2014, p. 103; Nyagadza, Chuchu, & Chigora, 2022). It acts as a tool that is used to position a destination brand such that a good destination brand should be able to effectively position a destination on the global market (Morrison, 2012).

Tourism Festival and Event Destination Branding Process

Morrison (2013) noted that destination branding is a comprehensive concept, since it calls for maximum stakeholder involvement and participation. Since there are diversified views and different perspectives with regards to destination branding, there is the need to understand and clarify what characterizes the tourism destination brand process which are as follows:

Tourism Festival and Event Destination Market Analysis

Haskova (2015) indicated that at the initial stage of branding, marketers ought to carry out a market analysis. This is a process that helps in understanding how a destination is performing in a market that is dominated by other destinations. Market analysis can be regarded as a strategic approach that helps marketers to position their destination among competitors. It also helps in understanding the behavior of potential tourists, so as to provide specific products and services needed by the potential tourists. To add to this, understanding the needs and wants of the potential tourists is important, as it helps in formulating and crafting an effective brand that is able to meet the expectations of the market at that point in time. As announced by Morrison (2012), an effective destination brand ought to be easily understood by potential tourists. It is only when an effective market analysis is done that destination marketers are able to formulate a brand that attracts tourists.

Tourism Festival and Event Brand Development

Brand development is also an important stage in the branding process of a tourism destination. It is a highly involving stage resulting in the crafting of a brand that should be positioned in highly competitive markets (Naidoo et al., 2010, p. 96; Nyagadza, Chigora, et al., 2022). First, it is important to know and understand the requirements of the core market or segment that is targeted by the brand, where it is ultimately important to craft and develop a brand that serves all potential markets. A specific segment will help in understanding the real gap that the brand is supposed to fill. As for Zimbabwe as a tourism destination brand, traditionally, its core market segments were Western markets, though with time, it refocused its efforts to the Eastern tourism markets. It is important to understand that the values and objectives of a destination brand changes from one type of a market to another. Potential tourists will resist a tourism destination brand if it does not align with their expectations. There is a need to understand where Zimbabwe as a tourism destination brand has been developed, after considering the specific needs and requirements of the targeted markets as this might be the reason for failing to perform over the years.

Tourism Festival and Event Destination Brand Positioning

Morrison (2012) argues that a good brand should be consistent with positioning through conveying the desired image. There is a need for marketers to position their brand clearly to the minds of targeted customers looking at the three levels of positioning which are positioning with product attributes, positioning by associating its name with desirable benefits, and positioning on strong beliefs and values (Nyagadza, Chigora, et al., 2022). The current Zimbabwe destination brand positions itself by means of product attributes, and the concern is in proving whether the wonders in Zimbabwe are attractive and unique, so as to use them in positioning the destination's brand. Morrison (2012) postulated that a good destination brand should be unique and outstanding in a competitive market.

Tourism Festival and Event Destination Personality

A good festival and event destination brand should be able to express the destination's personality (Morrison, 2012). Zimbabwe destination's previous and current brands projected a personality might not be corresponding to the one perceived by its potential customers. There is a direct relationship between the self-congruity of tourists and their revisit intentions, which impacts greatly on the way that tourists view themselves in a destination (Uşaklı & Baloglu, 2011). There is a need to understand the personality that is perceived by tourists to be representing Zimbabwe destination brand whether it is sincerity, excitement, or ruggedness so as to craft a corrective strategy that matches with the expectations of potential tourists.

Tourism Festival and Event Brand Implementation

The implementation of a brand refers to the launching and use of a brand in its target markets. This involves the launching of a brand so as to assess its performance in the market. Destination marketing organizations are responsible for implementing a destination brand (Morrison, 2012). It is important to note that brand implementation also involves coordination and participation of all relevant stakeholders (Nyagadza, Chigora, et al., 2022; Peric et al., 2014, p. 275). Also, successful implementation of a destination brand relates to market acceptance. There is a need to consider all aspects that make a tourism destination and involve all the players in the implementation. This includes the travel personnel, hotel employees, communities, government officials, and representative of all tourism sectors in the destination.

Tourism Festival and Event Brand Communication

Brand communication involves a process of making the brand known by the potential customers. A brand on its own should be able to communicate with its targeted markets through user-generated mechanisms (Nyagadza, Chuchu, & Chigora, 2022; Smith, Fischer, & Yongjian, 2012), expressing the offerings it represents. Communication is vital, as its helps in informing and raising awareness of the brand. However, it is important to understand that some brands fail because they lack an effective communication channel so as to reach its targeted markets. Brand communication can be enhanced through the use of symbols, colors, having a brand name, and other factors. Therefore, the meaning and perception of a brand can be improved through brand communication (Bruhn, Schoenmueller, & Schäfer, 2012; Nyagadza, Mazuruse, Muposhi, & Chigora, 2022). Media play an important role in improving brand communication in a tourism destination. There are various types of media mixes in every tourism destination. It is difficult to know a specific media that are effective in communicating a brand to its target markets. There is a need to frame a message effectively (Metila, 2013) about the meaning of a brand, so as to improve the communication of a brand to its intended audience.

Tourism Festival and Event Brand Tracking

At this stage, it is important to assess whether the destination brand is unique, such that it can be differentiated from other brands that exist on the market. Destination marketers should go into the market and sample some customers who they investigate for their opinions and views about the brand (Nyagadza, Chuchu, & Chigora, 2022; Ritson, 2011, p. 17). The brand should be different in its general and emotional appeal. It should be able to fight competition existing in the market (Pike & Page, 2014, p. 34). A tourism destination brand ought to have features that are distinctive from those of its competitors. Also, at this stage, destination marketers should be able to know how people perceive the brand on its own, with regards to its "personality" (Usaki & Baloglu, 2011) and in relation to others existing in the market. This will also help in measuring the level of commitment that people have on the destination and its brand. The emotional appeal of a destination brand (Nyagadza, Mazuruse, et al., 2022; Pike & Page, 2014, p. 25) ought to be measured, as it is more important than any other brand issues. Quantitative research can be done through presenting a set of questions that help in benchmarking and measuring the level of emotional appeal of a brand.

Zimbabwe Tourism Festival and Event Destination Brand Equity

Brand equity refers to a brand's worthiness, measured by a combination of variables, namely, brand loyalty, name awareness, perceived quality, and potency of brand association, together with other key assets such as trademarks, patents, distribution channels, and advertising (Kotler & Keller, 2012). The definition shows that the concept of brand equity is an amalgamation of brand awareness creation, image-building, and loyalty (Gartner & Ruzzier, 2011, p. 473). Festival and event destination managers should evaluate their brand equity elements against those of their competitors in order to strengthen their competitiveness in the market (Im, Kim, Elliot, & Han, 2012, p. 386). Several reports and studies have been done on Zimbabwe's destination brand, but without directly analyzing the most dominant variable(s) that can lead to high destination brand equity.

Tourism Festival and Event Destination Brand Awareness

The stage forms a foundation on which brand equity is constructed around a destination. Awareness is the first important step in creating brand equity of any organization (Im et al., 2012, p. 389). Creation of awareness is essential because a place must be known by the potential tourists before regarding it as a destination to visit (Gartner & Ruzzier, 2011, p. 473). Marketers ought to improve visibility of symbols or visual imagery attached to a destination brand name (Im et al., 2012, p. 390). Gartner and Ruzzier have argued, "the idea is to understand that focal point of extensive coverage has led to social conflict which does not translate into increased travel inflows meaning that some dominant awareness of a place are of negative value to building brand equity" (2011, p. 473). Therefore, it does not follow that every awareness results in the profitability of a destination and its brand ascendancy. Rather, it depends on the type of construct informing the awareness, whether positive or negative.

Tourism Festival and Event Destination Brand Image

Branding has become a vital tool that helps a destination compete for visitors more effectively through enhancing its overall image (Nyagadza, Chuchu, & Chigora, 2022; Yusof, Ismail, & Omar, 2014, p. 1). The meaning of a brand is built on the image it portrays to the world. Brand image is directed at the perception that resides in the memory of the customer regarding the existing brand (Im et al., 2012; Pike et al., 2010). A festival and event destination brand that possesses excellence image provides memorable thoughts, such that tourists favor it anytime when they need a holiday. There is no consensus on the mechanism(s) that completely spreads negative or positive image of destination brand, or even highlighting the most probable type of media affecting destination brand image. Image in a destination is built from various aspects, both controllable and uncontrollable, by the destination marketers.

Perceived Tourism Festival and Event Destination Brand Quality

Brand quality is the perception given to a brand regarding its ability to add value. It is highly subjective (Nyagadza, 2021; Nyagadza et al., 2020a; Pike, 2005). There is a problem when trying to define and measure quality of a destination brand. Since quality is highly subjective and is related to emotions that are not tangible. There is a need for physical experience and interaction with the offerings of a destination before a tourist regards a destination brand to be of high quality. Im et al. (2012, p. 390) have postulated that quality is related to consumer's judgment on a product's overall superiority. One's judgment differs from that of the other party, such that a consensus on the quality of a destination brand would be hard to reach. In addition, the multidimensional nature and variety of stakeholders' involvement makes it difficult to relentlessly provide quality in a destination, where likewise, quality becomes a prerequisite for brand equity (Gartner & Ruzzier, 2011, p. 474; Nyagadza, Mazuruse, et al., 2022).

Tourism Festival and Event Destination Brand Loyalty

This is the highest level in destination brand equity building, whereby tourists develop an attachment and lasting relationship with a destination brand. According to Im et al. (2012, p. 391), brand loyalty comprises both the attitudinal and behavioral loyalty, with the former concentrating on consumer's repurchase intentions and the latter emphasizing the repeat purchasing of a brand. In a destination, loyalty is seen from repeat visits of tourists, which is triggered by past travel experiences and attachment to tradition (Gartner & Ruzzier, 2011, p. 474; Nyagadza, Chuchu, & Chigora, 2022). Tourists' destination brand loyalty therefore can be assessed according to two main perspectives, namely, attitudinal and behavioral loyalty. When there is a frequent repeat visitation and positive word-of-mouth recommendations, brand loyalty is established (Pike, 2010, p. 129). The situation in Zimbabwe as a destination shows that there is negative tourist loyalty to the destination brand. Tourists' inflows have reduced over the years, which constitute a sign that both behavioral and attitudinal loyalty in consumption have become negative.

Conclusion

The main focus of this study is to improve Zimbabwe tourism brand image and equity. This helped in understanding how destination branding developed through various stages. Due to the fact that the main thrust was on brand performance measured by brand equity variables, the chapter also reviewed literature for each selected brand equity variable, namely brand awareness, brand image, perceived brand quality, brand loyalty, and brand association. The aim was to understand how each variable affects overall brand equity. Lastly, the chapter analyzed contributions of various authors in the area of tourism destination branding. This helped to determine similarities of this study to other studies that have been made in the same area. It also helped to expose the gaps that have been discovered and filled by this study.

References

Bruhn, M., Schoenmueller, V., & Schäfer, D. B. (2012). Are social media replacing traditional media in terms of brand equity creation? *Management Research Review*, *35*(9), 770–790.

Florek, M., & Kavaratzis, M. (2014). From brand equity to place brand equity and from there to the place brand. *Place Branding and Public Diplomacy*, *10*, 103-107

Gartner, W. C., & Ruzzier, M. K. (2011). Tourism destination brand equity dimensions: Renewal versus repeat market. *Journal of Travel Research*, *50*(5), 471–481.

Haskova, K. (2015). Starbucks marketing analysis. *Bulletin of the Centre for Research and Interdisciplinary Study*, *1*(11), 11–29.

Im, H. H., Kim, S. S., Elliot, S., & Han, H. (2012). Conceptualising destination brand equity dimensions from a consumer-based brand equity perspective. *Journal of Travel & Tourism Marketing*, *29*, 385–403.

Kanika. (2021). 10 popular festivals in Zimbabwe. Retrieved from https://trip101.com/article/festivals-in-zimbabwe

Kim, S., & Lehto, X. Y. (2013). Projected and perceived destination brand personalities: The case of South Korea. *Journal of Travel Research*, *52*(1), 117–130.

Kim, D., & Perdue, R. R. (2011). The influence of image on destination attractiveness. *Journal of Travel & Tourism Marketing*, *28*, 225–239.

Kotler, P., & Keller, K. L. (2012). *Marketing management* (14th ed.). Upper Saddle River, NJ: Prentice-Hall International.

Martins, M. (2015). The tourist imagery, the destination image and the brand image. *Journal of Tourism and Hospitality Management*, *3*(2), 1–14.

Metila, R. A. (2013). A discourse analysis of news headlines: Diverse framings for a hostage-taking event. *Asian Journal of Social Sciences & Humanities*, 2(2), 71–77.

Molina, A., Gomez, M., & Martin-Consuegra, D. (2010). Tourism marketing Information and destination image management. *African Journal of Business Management*, 4(5), 22–728.

Morrison, A. M. (2012). *Marketing and managing tourism destinations*. London: Routledge.

Morrison, A. (2013). Destination positioning and branding: Still on the slow boat to China. *Tourism Tribune*, 28(2), 1–9.

Naidoo, P., Ramseook-Munhurrun, P., & Ladsawut, J. (2010). Tourist satisfaction with Mauritius as a holiday destination. Global *Journal of Business Research*, 4(2), 113–123.

Nyagadza, B. (2021). Futurology reorientation nexus: Fourth industrial revolution. Chapter 3. In H. Kazeroony & D. Tsang (Eds.), *Management education & automation*. Abingdon: Routledge, Taylor & Francis. ISBN: 9780367861117. Retrieved from https://www.routledge.com/Management-Education-and-Automation/Kazeroony-Tsang/p/book/9780367861117

Nyagadza, B., & Chigora, F. (2022). Futurology of ethical tourism digital & social media marketing post COVID-19. Chapter 6. In P. Mohanty, A. Sharma, & A. Hassan (Eds.), *COVID-19 and tourism sustainability: Ethics, responsibilities, challenges and new directions*. Abingdon: Routledge, Taylor & Francis. eBook ISBN: 9781003207467.

Nyagadza, B., Chigora, F., Pashapa, R., Chuchu, T., Maeeresa, W., & Katsande, C. (2022). Effects of COVID-19 on tourism and hospitality. Book Chapter. In P. Mohanty, A. Sharma, J. Kennell, & A. Hassan (Eds.), *The handbook of destination recovery in tourism and hospitality*. Bingley: Emerald Insight Publishers.

Nyagadza, B., Chuchu, T., & Chigora, F. (2022). Technology application in tourism events: Case of Africa. Chapter 9. In A. Hassan (Ed.), *Digital transformation and innovation in tourism events*. Abingdon: United Kingdom Tourism Society, Routledge, Taylor & Francis. eBook ISBN: 9781032220963.

Nyagadza, B., Kadembo, E. M. & Makasi, A. (2020a). Exploring internal stakeholders' emotional attachment & corporate brand perceptions through corporate storytelling for branding, *Cogent Business & Management*, 7(1), 1–22

Nyagadza, B., Mazuruse, G., Muposhi, A., & Chigora, F. (2022). Effect of hotel overall service quality on customers' attitudinal and behavioural loyalty: Perspectives from Zimbabwe. In *Tourism critiques: Practice and theory (TCPT)*. Bingley: Emerald Insight. doi:10.1108/TRC-12-2021-0026

Pan, B., & Li, X. (2011). The long tail of destination image and online marketing. *Annals of Tourism Research*, 38(1), 132–152.

Perić, M., Đurkin, J., & Lamot, I. (2014). Importance of stakeholder management in tourism projects: Case study of the Istra Inspirit Project. In *Tourism and Hospitality Industry, Congress Proceedings*, Opatija, Croatia. Trends in Tourism and Hospitality Industry.

Pike, S. (2005). Tourism destination branding complexity. *The Journal of Product and Brand Management*, 14(4), 258–259.

Pike, S. (2010). Destination branding case study: Tracking brand equity for an emerging destination between 2003 and 2007. *Journal of Hospitality & Tourism Research*, 34(1), 124–139.

Pike, S., Bianchi, C., Kerr, G., & Patti, C. (2010). Consumer-based brand equity for Australia as a long haul tourism destination in an emerging market. *International Marketing Review, 27*(4), 434–449.

Pike, S., & Page, S. (2014). Destination marketing organisations and destination marketing: A narrative analysis of the literature. *Tourism Management, 41*, 1–26.

Ritson, M. (2011, July to September). Keepin track of your brand. The challenge of brand tracking remains one of the most urgent and potentially rewarding for Australian marketers, pp. 16–19.

Smith, A. N., Fischer, E., & Yongjian, C. (2012). How does brand-related user-generated content differ across YouTube, Facebook, and Twitter? *Journal of Interactive Marketing, 26*(2), 102–113.

Usakli, A., & Baloglu, S. (2011). Brand personality of tourist destinations: An application of self-congruity theory. *Tourism Management, 32*, 114–127.

Yusof, M. F., Ismail, H. N., & Omar, R. N. (2014). A critical analysis on evolution of branding destination in Langkawi Island. In *SHS Web of Conferences* (Vol. 12, pp. 01002).

Destination Marketing as an Orienting Tool in Zimbabwe's Tourism Image and Publicity Crisis

Farai Chigora, Brighton Nyagadza, Chipo Katsande and Promise Zvavahera

Abstract

The immense returns generated from tourist destinations have caused govern-ments to invest to a greater extent in developing the tourism industry, with the aim of improving its market share. Scholars and policy makers for tourism destinations are not simply focusing on attracting more tourists but also on improving the competitive position of their destinations. For this reason, destination marketing has become a fountain for future growth and sustain-ability of tourism destinations in an increasingly globalized and competitive tourist market. The need to maintain a steady growth in tourism gains has increased pressure on marketers and promoters of Zimbabwe as a destination as they strive to attract and convince current and prospective tourists to partake in their tourism offerings. However, the efforts of various destination marketers in Zimbabwe have been undercut by the hyperinflation and unemployment of the country, which have destroyed both the supply and demand of tourism in Zimbabwe, as it became increasingly expensive, and where social unrest has grown. From a political perspective, the country witnessed fights and other forms of mayhem, which labeled the tourism destination unsafe for tourists' visits.

Keywords: Destination marketing; sustainable destinations; market share; resilience; publicity crisis; Zimbabwe tourism image

Introduction

For the past three decades, Tourism Area Life Cycle (TALC) introduced by Butler in 1980 is still mostly cited and used in a variety of tourism research

Resilient and Sustainable Destinations After Disaster, 75–85
Copyright © 2023 Farai Chigora, Brighton Nyagadza, Chipo Katsande and Promise Zvavahera
Published under exclusive licence by Emerald Publishing Limited
doi:10.1108/978-1-80382-021-720231006

(Butler, 2011, p. 3). Even with rapid changes in tourism destinations, the continued testing and application of Tourism Life Cycle (TLC) in resorts means that the model is still relevant, especially to highly dynamic situations (Pechlaner et al., 2007). A tourism destination follows a life cycle that defines stages in its development from the time it was not known to popularity (Hunt & Stronza, 2014; Nyagadza & Chigora, 2022). Every stage in the development has factors that either positively or negatively affect the growth of the tourism industry. Similar to the life of a generic product, Butler in 1980 developed a model that clearly shows the stages involved in the life cycle of a tourism destination (Nyagadza, Mazuruse, Muposhi, & Chigora, 2022; Zmyślony, 2011). As argued by Kamat (2010, p. 140), in the 1980s, Butler introduced a life cycle specifically for the tourism industry known as the TALC, and the model has six stages, namely exploration, investment, development, consolidation, stagnation, decline, and rejuvenation. The model is crucial in explaining the research and development of tourism resorts (Butler, 2011, p. 3).

This chapter explores the destination marketing position of the Zimbabwe tourism industry. The following objectives are addressed in this chapter:

- to explain on the marketing strategies used in Zimbabwe tourism destination;
- to establish the main tourism sectors involved in tourism destination marketing;
- to explain factors that affects the image of a tourism destination;
- to establish the competitive environment in tourism destination;
- to outline the stages in Zimbabwe tourism destination area life cycle;
- to inform on the marketing efforts that have been practiced in Zimbabwe tourism destination; and
- to evaluate the marketing mixes for Zimbabwe tourism destination success.

Exploring Tourism Globally

Globally, all tourism destinations, including Zimbabwe, have gone through some of these stages in their life cycle. Even with various world changes such as the Great Depression, the end of Apartheid, or the Oil Crisis of the 1970s, the model has remained a viable tool in understanding tourism development in various destinations (Butler, 2011; Butler & Suntiku, 2010). Zimbabwe as a tourist destination has witnessed a demise in its socioeconomic and political state, where reference to the TALC used to explain circumstances elsewhere might yield a conclusive analysis for Zimbabwe tourism destinations in crisis. According to United States Agency for International Development (USAID, 2013, p. 15), Zimbabwean tourism marketing can be classified into four main phases, namely, immediate after independence (1980–1984); stable growth (1985–1999); stagnation and decline (2000–2008); and recovery (2009–2012). The phases can be assessed in relation to the TALC, though there is little information on the pre-independence trends for Zimbabwe tourism destination and its marketing performance. From the statistics archived by Zimbabwe Tourism Authority (ZTA) as the leading marketer for Zimbabwe tourism as a destination, the year 1964 marks the earliest period with recorded and published figures of tourists' arrivals.

At the exploration stage, Zimbabwe discovered various areas for touristic activities, mainly driven by the esthetic scenic landforms, flora and fauna. There were a low number of tourists' arrivals compared to other stages in the destination's life cycle. According to the Zimbabwean Tourism Authority (2010), in 1964 the country had 198,121 tourists' arrivals, compared to the year 2011 some four decades later, when the number of arrivals increased to 2,423,280. The early stage is characterized by low development in accommodation and other tourism infrastructure development and neglecting locals benefiting from tourism activities carried out in their communities (Nyagadza, Chuchu, & Chigora, 2022; Zmyślony, 2011, p. 869). European "explorers" were the first to discover the attractiveness of Zimbabwe as a tourism destination. The discovery was achieved in their subsequent dominance over political and economic affairs of the country. The main popular tourist sites explored in the 1800s and beyond include the majestic Victoria Falls, which are reported to have been "discovered" by the European scout David Livingstone, who then named the falls after the British Queen Victoria from its Indigenous name, Mosi-oa-Tunya which means "The Smoke That Thunders." Also at the exploration stage of Zimbabwe as a tourists' destination was the discovery of wildlife, since the country is endowed with a variety range of wildlife, including the globally renowned "big five" animals, which refer to the (sighting of) lion, elephant, rhinoceros, leopard, and buffalo. Man-made structures and heritage became visible in their uniqueness at the exploration stage. These include traditional villages, ruins, and rock paintings. Great Zimbabwe is one of the ancient discoveries that has grown in its recognition and popularity over the years.

The exploration of various attractions in Zimbabwe as a tourism destination transformed to involvement and development stages. This relates to take-off, describing the point at which the numbers of tourists start to increase, number of day trippers decline, massive investment in infrastructure, and local direct and indirect tourism benefits start to increase (Zmyślony, 2011, p. 3). The involvement and development stages arose in Zimbabwe as a result of increased Western influences, development of jet aircraft, decreased travel restrictions, and travel, which developed beyond a mere privilege of a small elite, and was followed by the development of mass tourism (Butler, 2011, p. 5). Although the TALC has separated out involvement and development stages, this study has resorted to an analysis that either development should come first in order to attract involvement or having the two stages evolving concurrently. These stages witnessed the demarcation of land to build hotels, roads, railways, airports, resorts, and game parks in Zimbabwe as a tourism destination. Tourism resorts and holiday places are essentially a product, and their development follows the development of a generic product, starting with acceptance or rejection in a market and ending with becoming outmoded or unattractive (Butler, 2011, p. 4). Foreign tourists, especially from Europe, started to patronize Zimbabwe in sizable numbers in the 1980s.

Consolidation and stagnation can be combined, informing a period where the tourism destination is no longer growing, requiring strategies to be implemented in order to return to a vibrant status quo (Hussin, 2014, p. 161). These stages can be referred to as the critical range of elements of capacity (Butler, 2011, p. 6). According to Garay and Cànoves (2011, p. 625), this is when the area reaches the highest number in tourist inflows, becoming unattractive and no longer fashionable. The tourism destination at this point has exceeded its carrying capacity, with intense expansion into peripherals, day trippers increase, and tourists' inflows dramatically fall (Zmyślony, 2011, p. 3). This is a critical stage, where numbers of tourists start to decline and unsustainable practices, together with exceeding carrying capacity prevail. The decline in the tourism destination's attractiveness is characterized by diminishing demand, loss in attractiveness, high tourism costs, exorbitant prices, and loss of city's identity (Zmyślony, 2011, p. 3). Resorts will face decline if there is a lack of management intervention keeping them competitive in the tourism markets and where the intervention is not a biological evolution, but comes from the interested parties (Butler, 2011, p. 5). According to ZTA (2010, p. 1), tourists' arrivals declined to 1,966,582 in the year 2000 from 2,249,615 in the year 1999. The main contributor to this rapid decline was the chaotic political situation that took precedence from the year 2000 onwards (Chibaya, 2013; Ndlovu & Heath, 2013).

For Zimbabwe as a tourism destination, the usefulness of the TLC can be justified by the current state where the destination has reached stagnation, and rejuvenation strategies are needed. One of the main values of TALC is that it integrates an economic and territorial interpretation of tourism (Garay & Cànoves, 2011, p. 653). Much of the research and published literature on tourism destinations using the TALC has been descriptive and based on case studies, such as that done by Gilbert in 1939 in England (Butler, 2011, p. 3), and little discussion has been undertaken with reference to Zimbabwe TLC development. Therefore, there was a need to establish a framework for Zimbabwean tourism development, especially with regards to destination marketing.

Destination Marketing in Zimbabwe

Destination marketing is now acknowledged as a pillar of the future growth and sustainability of tourism destinations in an increasingly globalized and competitive market for tourists (UNWTO, 2011). The concept of destination marketing has been undertaken mainly by academics in applied studies, rather than pure research (Pike & Page, 2014, p. 4). On the other hand, destinations are unique and cannot be addressed by simply converting generic products and services marketing theories (Richards & Palmer, 2010). Undoubtedly, there is a lack of established concepts, frameworks, and theories in destination marketing by means of which to provide testing and retesting platforms for this field (Pike & Page, 2014, p. 5). In Zimbabwe, few studies have been done in destination marketing theories and models. Ndlovu and Heath (2013) explored the rebranding of Zimbabwe in relation to sustainable development. Ndlovu, in 2009, examined branding in order to position Zimbabwe tourism destination through a stake-holder survey, Chibaya in 2013 focused on the move from Zimbabwe's "Africa Paradise" to "A World of Wonders," and Vutete and Chigora (2013) investigated the role of tourism variables in rebranding Zimbabwe. While these studies have in common a focus on branding as a marketing concept, there is still limited liter-ature with regards to the evolution of destination marketing in Zimbabwe.

Tourism destination marketing literature has evolved from what it was in the 1970s (Pike & Page, 2014, p. 5). A destination represents an amalgam of a diverse and eclectic range of businesses and people, who might have a vested interest in the prosperity of their destination community (Thomas, Shaw, & Page, 2011). According to Kotler and Armstrong (2011, p. 4), marketing is the ability to manage a profitable customer relationship, with the objective of attracting new customers promising superior value, and to keep and grow current customers by delivering satisfaction. Destination marketing refers to the application of mar-keting tools in promoting tourism products so as to maximize associated benefits for the destination (Campelo, Aitken, & Gnoth, 2011, p. 4). Marketing can also be regarded as a social and managerial process that stimulates exchange between individuals and organizations, with the aim to improve customer satisfaction and maximizing high returns for the providers of goods and services (SANIB et al., 2013, p. 301).

Increased growth in the Zimbabwe tourism industry realized the need for intensive place marketing. The marketing of Zimbabwe as a place to visit with its tourism destinations became a responsibility of the Destination Marketing Organizations (DMOs). The main tourism marketing body that committed efforts and resources to create awareness informed and persuade tourists in Zimbabwe since independence was the Zimbabwe Tourism Development Corporation (ZTDC), which was then transformed to ZTA in the year 1996 (Chibaya, 2013, p. 85). The marketing of the tourism destinations by this body is enhanced through tourism brand promotion, tourism directories, destination magazines, indabas, expos, carnivals, and deployment of tourism marketers to other countries. Place marketing is concerned with achieving economic growth through enhancing industries, promoting the expansion of exports markets and attracting outside investment (Campelo et al., 2011, p. 4). Zimbabwe as a place has focused on the development of its industries and export markets, of which tourism proves to be one of the pillars for economic growth. However, at the center of place marketing is place image (Elliot et al., 2011, p. 520). Zimbabwe tourism marketing efforts have been disturbed by a negative image, caused by perceived socioeconomic and political upheavals in the country (Ndlovu & Heath, 2013; Nyagadza & Chigora, 2022). Image is a critical variable that can either positively or negatively affect the marketing performance of a place and its tourism destinations. Zimbabwe, with its multiple destinations, has seen its image negatively affect the tourism desti-nation's marketing efforts due to political conflict, a high inflation rate, soaring levels of unemployment, and associated social unrest, which caused the country to appear poverty-stricken and economically insolvent, and the marketing of Zim-babwe's tourism destinations became difficult. However, even with high recog-nition, place image is complex and lacks theoretical development (Elliot et al.,

2011, p. 520). Also, tourism destinations are difficult to market due to their complex nature, and the involvement of many stakeholders (Zehrera & Raichb, 2010). This shows that there is a research gap in the area of place marketing associated with images, complexity, the multiplicity of destinations in a given country, and diversified stakeholders. This study therefore focused on managing the marketing and image of Zimbabwe as a multifaceted place to visit. There is little relevant literature in relation to Zimbabwe tourism destination marketing. This study produced concepts, theories, and frameworks with regards to Zimbabwe's tourism destination marketing, focusing on branding as a marketing concept. This is because the tourism products being offered across the globe are increasingly becoming similar from general nature-seeking to more specific types of tourism such as adventure tourism. It is within the same perspective that this model helps in constructing a viable marketing strategy to overcome competition from the surrounding global environments (Nyagadza, Mazuruse et al., 2022).

These are crucial variables that have helped in establishing a gap for this study. It has been mentioned how the political economy of Zimbabwe affects its tourism. Tourism destination marketing should take into consideration legal and geophysical environment. The legal environment is pertinent to policy makers in tourism destination marketing with regards to preservation of the geophysical environment for posterity. Zimbabwean tourism destination marketing has been enhanced mainly by the geographical attractions like Victoria Falls, Hwange National Park, and other natural attractions. However, even with a rich geophysical environment, the marketing of Zimbabwe tourism destination is not providing expected returns.

Accommodation Sector

The accommodation sector makes the basis of any tourism destination. It is responsible for providing shelter, relaxation, and comfort to tourists during their stay in a tourism destination. Marketing of accommodation is important, since quality of the accommodation differs from one establishment to another (Nyagadza, Chuchu, & Chigora, 2022; Seyed, 2011). This results in various accommodations being evaluated and accredited using star ratings. Leading DMOs are responsible for the standardization and star rating of the accommodation, and for this study the ZTA is considered. The prime rating of these accommodations is the five stars (Karppinen, 2011, p. 13) and it is the desire of any marketers in this sector to have this ranking in order to attract the most tourists (Kamau et al., 2015, p. 32). Therefore, there is a need to charge a price that can match with the value of the product in accommodation (Markgraf, 2015). In addition, there are various types of accommodation ranging from lodges, motels, and hotels. In the accommodation provided, there are other facilities that directly influence marketing strategies of a given kind of accommodation through their tangibility (Rodriguez, 2013).

Globally, there has been a significant evolution and improvement in the marketing of accommodation in tourism destinations. Accommodation establishments have increasingly become a platform to sale brands as they make them more visible when they are displayed on the buildings in the form of logos, designs, and colors, such that tourists now visit them to stay for their holidays guided by popularity of the brand (Kamau et al., 2015, p. 33; Karppinen, 2011, p. 21). This has resulted in various operators working with the world's most powerful franchises in branding their businesses. The development has helped in creating and adhering to high global standards. However, the Zimbabwean accommodation sector requires further branding improvement. Despite the presence of other international brands such as Holiday Inn and Cresta, many establishments in Zimbabwe do not have international franchising such as the hotel Rainbow Towers, in the capital city of Harare, has moved out of the Sheraton franchise. There has been a reduction in occupancy rate for Zimbabwe accommodation sector (Sibanda & Muzapu, 2016, p. 60). The use of international brands in the marketing of accommodation has an advantage of attracting modern global tourists, who expect conformity in standards and quality. This might be the same reason why Zimbabwe as a tourism destination brand has failed to perform, where it can be found that the accommodation industry has failed to attract more tourists.

Green tourism is another concept that has influenced the marketing strategies of various accommodation establishments around the world (Mahika, 2011, p. 5). This includes conservation of natural resources, use of natural energy, and recycling of waste (Sibanda & Muzapu, 2016, p. 56). Those establishments that have managed to follow the green guidelines and standards have received recognition in the form of certification by international boards of standards, which they are able to display on their premises. This becomes a strong marketing concept, where tourists can be found to value such accreditation and will only patronize a tourism establishment that has been certified. Accreditation is still only practiced minimally in Zimbabwe. Many establishments in the Zimbabwean accommodation sector have not yet engaged in the certification program, which might destroy the marketing strategy of a tourism destination.

Travel Sector

This sector is responsible for enhancing the movement of tourists from one sector to another. It links a tourism destination with the world. Evolution of the travel sector shows the development of the modes of transportation from the basic to technologically advanced means of transportation. It used to take days to travel some longest journeys across the globe, but with the advancement in technology and development of most efficient airplanes, it is now taking mere hours. Therefore, a tourism destination can be marketed from the availability of transportation (Geza & Lorant, 2010). A tourism destination that enjoys various modes of advanced transport is likely to attract more tourists, since it will be easier to connect all the areas of touristic activities within the destination. It also helps in improving the links between the tourism destination and other existing destinations in the world. Marketing of Zimbabwe as a tourism destination has faced challenges with regards to air travel, where various international airlines have withdrawn their airbus services to the country. This has resulted in more connections required in order to reach Zimbabwe as a tourism destination. Even with some efforts to revamp the inflow of new and traditional airlines in Zimbabwe, there remain a low number when compared to the previous years (Sibanda & Muzapu, 2016, p. 58). Another advantage of having diverse airlines coming into the tourism destination is brand following. There are certain leading airline brands that are globally renowned for best quality in their comfort and service provision. These help in selling a tourism destination when a partnership is done with the local airliner. Air Zimbabwe is failing to form such partnerships, making it difficult to achieve this advantage. Also, the partnerships can help in achieving marketing economies of scale, which lead to a reduction in the marketing and promotion costs of the leading airliner in a given tourism destination. Air Zimbabwe is currently facing a budget deficit to develop and market its activities. This has even tarnished its reputation as a provider of excellence and quality services. In line with an increase in plane crashes globally, Air Zimbabwe is likely to suffer from negative perceptions regarding its safety, as there are many administrative and technical problems at the institution. For these various reasons, the Air Zimbabwe brand might be failing to attract potential tourists.

Traveling within Zimbabwe as a tourism destination has improved over the years, due to the availability of cars and buses. The number of vehicles in Zimbabwe has increased, especially because it has become cheaper to acquire second-hand cars from Japan. Road transport is important for the movement of tourists across a given tourism destination. This means that a tourism destination can also be marketed using its road transport. The challenge for Zimbabwe as a tourism destination is that, due to lack of financial capital, roads have deteriorated without being repaired, making tourism access difficult. In some areas there are no roads at all. Use of road transport in a tourism destination is needed as it is cheap and gives tourists more time to explore and view areas of scenic interest. The poor state of affairs of Zimbabwean roads might be also another reason for failure to attract more tourists.

The Role of Destination Marketing Organizations

DMOss is a coalition of many organizations with an interest of working together toward a mutual goal to market the country's tourism offerings (Klimek, 2013, p. 30). Their overall goal is to coordinate and integrate destination marketing elements so as to achieve effective and holistic destination marketing (Morrison, 2012). They work as the main vehicle that is used to compete and attract visitors to their distinctive place or visitor space (Nyagadza, Chigora, et al., 2022; Pike & Page, 2014, p. 2). DMOss conduct extensive destination marketing plans and communicate with the most crucial target markets (Morrison, 2012). They mostly focus on the marketing, selling and promotion of a tourism destination, redesigning, revaluating, reengineering, and repositioning the tourism destination in a highly competitive global tourism market (Klimek, 2013, p. 30). Their mandate ought to focus on harmonizing the development of destinations, with coherent use of their assets, especially to differentiate and attract visitors (Klimek et al., 2011). The Destination Consultancy Group (2012) summarized the critical roles of DMOs in destination management such as leadership and coordination, planning and research, product development, marketing and promotion, community relations, and partnerships and team-building. The Zimbabwean Tourism Authority is the chief destination marketer in the country. While the roles and discussions have been clearly spelled out, and align with the roles of ZTA, there is little literature from the available studies regarding how Zimbabwe as a tourism destination has adopted and contextualized these specific roles in line with its ever-changing negative socioeconomic and political operating environment, which sits in contrast with other relatively stable destinations around the world.

Conclusion

This chapter examined the power of destination marketing in Zimbabwe's tourism publicity. The main thrust of the chapter was to understand how the concept of marketing has evolved in tourism destination development and management. Survival of all the sectors of a tourism industry, viz., accommodation, travel, and resorts has been proved to be based on the ability to market and promote tourism destination offerings effectively. Therefore, this chapter explored the evolution of destination marketing from an international to a Zimbabwe tourism destination perspective. In line with the destination marketing evolution concept, the chapter then reviewed literature on the evolution of destination marketing, dwelling on the accommodation sector, travel sector, and resorts. Also, the chapter examined the effects of images on tourism destination marketing, with the aim to understand how images have affected the efforts of tourism destination marketers through perception and publicity management. Tourism destinations have gone through various stages in their development. This chapter also explored the Tourism Destination Life Cycle, particularly in relation to Zimbabwe as a tourism destination. This was achieved by looking at the generic Tourism Development Life Cycle, thereafter analyzing each stage in comparison to Zimbabwean tourism destination development. Lastly, the chapter explored the marketing mixes that affect performance of a tourism destination. In this regard, the chapter examined the so-called "Seven Ps" in relation to Zimbabwe tourism destination.

References

Butler, R. W. (2011). Tourism area life cycle. *Contemporary tourism reviews* (pp. 1–33). Woodeaton, Oxford: Goodfellow Publishers Limited.

Butler, R. W., & Suntiku, W. (2010). *Tourism and political changes* (pp. 2–6). Woodeaton, Oxford: Goodfellow Publishers Limited.

Campelo, A., Aitken, R., & Gnoth, J. (2011). Visual rhetoric and ethics in marketing of destinations. *Journal of Travel Research, 50*(1), 3–14.

Chibaya, T. (2013). From "Zimbabwe Africa's Paradise to Zimbabwe a world of wonders": Benefits and challenges of rebranding Zimbabwe as a tourist destination. *Developing Country Studies*, *13*(5), 84–91.

Elliott, R., Percy, L., & Pervan, S. (2011). *Strategic brand management* (2nd ed.). Oxford: Oxford University Press.

Garay, L., & Cànoves, G. (2011). Life cycles, stages and tourism history: The catalonia (Spain) experience. *Pergamon*, *38*(2), 651–671.

Geza, T., & Lorant, D. (2010). The connection between accessibility and tourism. *Delhi Business Review*, *11*(1), 1–18.

Hunt, C., & Stronza, A. (2014). Stage-based tourism models and resident attitudes towards tourism in an emerging destination in the developing world. *Journal of Sustainable Tourism*, *22*(2), 279–298.

Hussin, N. Z. (2014). Tracing the Malaysia tourism lifecycle and strategy assessment from the first Malaysia plan to ninth Malaysia plan. *International Journal of Business and Social Science*, *5*(3), 161–168.

Kamat, S. B. (2010). Destination life cycle and assessment—A study of Goa tourism industry. *South Asian Journal of Tourism and Heritage*, *3*(2), 139–148.

Kamau, F., Waweru, F. W., Lewa, P., & Misiko, A. J. (2015). The effects of the marketing mix on choice of tourist accommodation by domestic tourists in Kenya.

Karppinen, M. (2011). Strategic marketing plan for a hotel. Vaasa University of Applied Sciences.

Klimek, K. (2013). Destination management organisations and their shift to sustainable tourism development. *European Journal of Tourism, Hospitality and Recreation*, *4*(2), 27–47.

Kotler, P., & Armstrong, G. (2011). *Principles of marketing* (14th ed.). New York, NY: Pearson Prentice-Hall.

Mahika, E. C. (2011). Current trends in tourist motivation. *Cactus Tourism Journal*, *2*(2), 15–24.

Markgraf, B. (2015). *Eight P's in marketing tourism*. Texas: Hearst Newspapers, LLC. Retrieved from http://smallbusiness.chron.com/eight-ps-marketing-tourism-42140.html

Morrison, A. M. (2012). *Marketing and managing tourism destinations*. London: Routledge.

Muzapu, R., & Sibanda, M., (2016). Tourism development strategies in Zimbabwe, management, *6*(3), 55–63. doi:10.5923/j.mm.20160603.01

Ndlovu, J., & Heath, E. (2013). Re-branding of Zimbabwe to enhance sustainable tourism development: Panacea or villain. *Academic Journals*, *1*(12), 947–955.

Nyagadza, B., & Chigora, F. (2022). Futurology of ethical tourism digital & social media marketing post COVID-19, Chapter 6. In P. Mohanty, A. Sharma, & A. Hassan (Eds.), *COVID-19 and tourism sustainability: Ethics, responsibilities, challenges and new directions*. Abingdon: Routledge, Taylor & Francis. eBook ISBN: 9781003207467.

Nyagadza, B., Chigora, F., Pashapa, R., Chuchu, T., Maeeresa, W., & Katsande, C. (2022). Effects of COVID-19 on tourism and hospitality. In P. Mohanty, A. Sharma, J. Kennell, & A. Hassan (Eds.), *The handbook of destination recovery in tourism and hospitality*. Bingley: Emerald Insight Publishers.

Nyagadza, B., Chuchu, T., & Chigora, F. (2022). Technology application in tourism events: Case of Africa, Chapter 9. In A. Hassan (Ed.), *Digital transformation and innovation in tourism events*. Abingdon: United Kingdom Tourism Society, Routledge, Taylor & Francis. eBook ISBN: 9781032220963.

Nyagadza, B., Mazuruse, G., Muposhi, A., & Chigora, F. (2022). Effect of hotel overall service quality on customers' attitudinal and behavioural loyalty: Perspectives from Zimbabwe. *Tourism Critiques: Practice and Theory (TCPT)*. doi: 10.1108/TRC-12-2021-0026. Bingley: Emerald Insight Publishers.

Pechlaner, H., Raich, F., & Zehrer, A. (2007). The Alps: Challenges and potentials of a brand management. *Tourism Analysis*, *12*(5/6), 359–370.

Pike, S., & Page, S. (2014). Destination marketing organisations and destination marketing: A narrative analysis of the literature. *Tourism Management*, *41*, 1–26.

Richards, G. & Palmer, R. (2010). *Eventful cities: Cultural management and urban revitalisation*. Oxford: Elsevier.

Rodriguez, A. (2013). Tourism and the marketing mix. Retrieved from http://www.freenomads.com/ blog/? p=296#sthash.MyMLkbAk.dpbs

Sanib, N. I., Aziz, Y. A., Samdin, Z., & Rahim, K. A. (2013). Comparison of marketing mix dimensions between local and international hotel customers in Malaysia. *International Journal of Economics and Management*, *7*(2), 297–313.

Seyed, M. (2011). Marketing mix from the viewpoint of Zanjan Grand Hotel customers. *South Asian Journal of Tourism and Heritage*, *4*(1), 12–18.

Tasci, A. D. A. (2011). Destination branding and positioning. In Y. Wang, & A. Pizam (Eds.), *Destination marketing and management theories and applications*. Oxfordshire: CABI.

Thomas, R., Shaw, G., & Page, S. J. (2011). Understanding small firms in tourism: A perspective on research trends and challenges. *Tourism Management*, *32*(5), 963–976.

UNWTO. (2011). Tourism highlights. Retrieved from www.unwto.org/pub//. Accessed on May 11, 2016.

USAID. (2013). *Positioning the Zimbabwe tourism sector for growth: Issues and challenges*. USAID strategic economic research and analysis: Zimbabwe SERA program (pp. 1–26).

Vutete, C., & Chigora, F. (2013). Rebranding Zimbabwe through tourism and hospitality variables: The reality of nation branding. *International Open and Distance Learning*, *1*(3), 18–32.

Zehrera, A., & Raichb, F. (2010). Applying a lifecycle perspective to explain tourism network development. *Service Industries Journal*, *30*(10), 1683–1705.

Zmyślony, P. (2011). Application of the destination life cycle concept in managing urban tourism: Case of Poznan, Poland. Tourism in an era of uncertainty. In *International Conference on Tourism*, Rhodes Island, Greece (pp. 867–878).

Pandemic and Tourism: From Health Emergency to Standard Operating Procedures (SOPs) Adherence—Insights of Novel Adaptations in the New Normal

Farhad Nazir, Norberto Santos and Luis Avila Silveira

Abstract

Tourism and health outbreaks share a symbiotic history (Hall, Scott, & Gössling, 2020; Ozbay, Sariisik, Ceylan, & Çakmak, 2021). Pandemics, epidemics, and endemics have transformed the perception of tourists. Previous outbreaks were geographically limited, resulting in the substitution effect (Prideaux, 2005; van der Veen, 2014). However, the COVID-19 pandemic urged the authorities to cease mobility worldwide. Evidently, mobility-oriented businesses like tourism have received immediate impacts from the pandemic. From shutdown to the minimum clearances, under strict restrictions, the tourism industry suffered atypical outcomes. Heat check-meters, contactless check-ins and check-outs, automotive service trays and counters, and reduced carrying capacity have been introduced to curb the impact of the pandemic on tourism. Tourism requires, throughout its cycle—before, during, and after the trip—the use of artificial intelligence, virtual reality, augmented reality, the internet of things, and geotargeting (Buhalis & Amaranggana, 2015). The usage of technology has been assured to be compatible with the prerequisites of restrictive and compliance measures (Lau, 2020). Moreover, in the supply sector, a competitive environment has also been created to market these new modified products and services. This chapter pursues the investigation of new offerings in a different normal, concerned with health issues, ethical behaviors, and trips with a social purpose to contribute to local development. Secondary data analysis has been performed to achieve this goal. This study implicates the new offerings duly implemented during the new normal.

Resilient and Sustainable Destinations After Disaster, 87–95
doi:10.1108/978-1-80382-021-720231007

Keywords: Post-COVID-19 tourism; tourism new technologies; competitive tourism destinations; tourism new normal; new offerings

Introduction

Tourism and turbulent circumstances (natural or human-induced) share a protracted historical conduit, having history of severe economic, social, and environmental ramifications (Çetinsöz & Ege, 2013; Fuchs, 2013; Harrington, 2021; Wilks, 2006). Primarily, the health emergencies in the form of plaques, famines, and viral outbreaks have catastrophically impacted the tourism sector both in demand- and supply-side facets. Concomitantly, the interminable international scenario amid the COVID-19 pandemic is unpredictable and uncertain predominantly in the context of tourism (Gössling, Scott, & Hall, 2021; Ioannides & Gyimóthy, 2020; Santos & Oliveira Moreira, 2021; Sigala, 2020). Exceeding from almost all the previous health emergencies, in the trilateral line of impact on physical, psychological, and financial, COVID-19 has proved to be more impactful, triggering risks in the most diverse socioeconomic areas and with major repercussions on the world tourism system. While encapsulating the entire world in its sphere of influence for more than 2 years, this outbreak has remained a driving force for each typology of tourism business because of the page left blank in the immediate past.

It is imperative to understand the consequences of this disease outbreak on the social, cultural, financial, and psychological segments of society (Adom, 2020; Bukuluki, Mwenyango, Katongole, Sidhva, & Palattiyil, 2020; Craig, 2020; Renzaho, 2020), creating worldwide new cultural settings, filtered social relationships, and fears and deviations to the pathways, previously taken for granted. Above all, the financial element (Jackson et al., 2021), having a direct and indirect association with the remaining three (social, cultural, and psychological) and an economic (domestic and regional) significance have been a subject of emphasis in academic and industrial discourse (Mtimet, Wanyoike, Rich, & Baltenweck, 2021). However, other segments have suffered equally. For instance, this long period of restrictions on mobility has resulted in the closure of cultural exchange (Swaikoski, 2020), psychological and ancillary health issues (Chua, Al-Ansi, Lee, & Han, 2021), and caused employment insecurity for human resources (Mao, He, Morrison, & Andres Coca-Stefaniak, 2020). In fact, as stated by Salinas Fernández, Guaita Martínez, and Martín Martín (2022), the return of the destinations toward the normal situation has been conditional to the performance of these destinations on competitive grounds.

An enormous number of studies have asserted the intervention of this pandemic and resulted impacts on the tourism industry (Assaf, Kock, & Tsionas, 2022; Ateljevic, 2020; Filep, King, & McKercher, 2022; Fotiadis, Polyzos, & Huan, 2021; Spalding, Burke, & Fyall, 2021). Such a commitment on the bestowed qualities—changing the existing perception of almost all tourism forecasting models (Dragan, Keshavarzsaleh, Kramberger, Jereb, & Rosi, 2019; Witt & Witt, 1995), adjustment of statistical calculation of tourist's inflow (Dragan et al., 2019, p. 11), and looking carefully to multiplier effect of tourism (Tiku, Shimizu, & Hartono, 2022)—has become fundamental in any destination. In addition to the immense mobility control orders/measures necessarily introduced to curb the impacts of this health pandemic and their resultant impacts (Latif, Dominick, Hawari, Mohtar, & Othman, 2021; Sulaiman, Ibrahim, Motevalli, Wong, & Hakim, 2021; Wong et al., 2021), the frequent mutated layers of pandemic evidently obligated the countries to a close monitoring in reshaping and modifying the managerial dimensions of the tourism and travel sectors (Awan, Shamim, & Ahn, 2021; Hall et al., 2020; Kaushal & Srivastava, 2021; Ntounis, Parker, Skinner, Steadman, & Warnaby, 2021; Robina-Ramírez, Sánchez, Jiménez-Naranjo, & Castro-Serrano, 2021; Vărzaru, Bocean, & Cazacu, 2021). Concomitantly, national differentiated approach of many world countries to have protection from variants of this pandemic, looking out to weather conditions, impacts of main events or festivities, has further intensified the repercussions on the tourism sector. Resultantly, developing countries struggled and are, yet, with the ongoing pandemic, and only now they are seeing the light at the end of the tunnel. Certain financial relief packages from states have also been allocated for the sustenance of the tourism sector; however, again, the countries with low economic surplus could not keep up with such strategy and pace.

Comparative Analysis of Old and New Offerings

Prior to intervention of the pandemic, the tourism business was undergoing a transformation from conventional, sun seekers, less involved with local community, cautious, unsustainable behavior (Poon, 1993) to more environment-friendly, informed, smart, cultural seekers, with a digital literacy, which allows them to have customized, augmented, and virtually oriented experiences, that could reach transformative ways in everyone's life (Joseph Pine & Gilmore, 2014). Such a change has obliged the supply and demand sectors to introduce and apply the latest tech gadgets and software/s app/s and service/s as facilitators to the inbound tourists, on the one hand, and to the marketers and destination reputation in the promotion of their products and services, on the other.

Tourists being the central (demand determinant) entity experienced a divide amid this adaptation. However, simultaneously, the alternatives for conventional practices had been duly adopted and accepted. In fact, we must stress that the same visitor or tourist can be, in different destinations or/and influenced by specific motivations, a new or an old tourist (Poon, 1993). Predominantly, in the developing and underdeveloped countries, in acquiescence to lack of technology and digital gadgets, the tourism activity was on the classical pathways offering voluntary or involuntary digital-free products and services, usually with reduced coverage. Nevertheless, even in countries with advanced digital technologies in the scope of tourism, a segment of tourists highlighted the less satisfactory experience due to the bombardment of social media updates and commented on the digital freeness stage as a possible path to an authentic tourism experience (Cai & McKenna, 2021; Egger, Lei, & Wassler, 2020).

The abrupt disruption caused by pandemic and its different pathways up until now have been a notable reason for transforming the conventional tourism system into more contactless but still an immersive and intense experience: a phygital[1] approach (Andrade & Dias, 2020; Ballina, 2019; Nofal, Reffat, & Vande Moere, 2017). Moreover, every significant development amid current outbreak has a direct or indirect influence on the tourism business. To cite a few, pretesting requirements for potential travelers, quarantine obligations, air-bubble system, country-specific travel restrictions (implementation, updating, and lifting), vaccinated passports, traveler locator's forms/passenger locator forms (TLFs/ PLFs), sanitization gates and ancillary sprays, contact-free portals and machines, face masks, hand gloves, temporary dismissal of face-to-face interactions, movement control orders (MCO), regional movement control orders (RMCO), central movement control orders (CMCO), etc.

All such novel practices have been duly adopted and implemented in the demand and supply activities of tourism. The public and private sectors of tourism have also been frequently changing these compulsions as per the directives and orders of state's administrative authorities and regional and international organizations. The massive human-loss oriented factor of this health outbreak acted as a yardstick for both the state and complying sectors. In addition, classical narrative of free mobility and eased travel options have been replaced by controlled, monitored, and mitigated mobility, depending on conditional travel permissions. In accommodation sector, the personalized service has been substituted by contactless and online services, distanced seating, sanitized sitting, and bedding arrangements. On destinations, specifically, the first development came in the shape of total closure for visitors to the second phase of controlled opening for limited personals who already met the predescribed criteria of vaccination, testing, and recovery stages.

The dynamic influence of pandemic on the national, regional, and international destination management organizations resulted in the creation of an adjusted competitive milieu appropriately dictated by the sanitation and hygienic practices. In addition, particularly in the weak postpandemic scenario, despite of the fact that health protocols may not be adopted as they are in the last 2 years, the tourist's decision-making would be conditional-oriented to the new health mantras in the tourist destinations. It can be argued that the episodes of pandemic are expected to have visible and invisible consequences in the coming era. However, apart from devastating impacts the pandemic has introduced on the tourism sector, it has extended a time-period to rethink, reconsider, and revamp the conventional tourism practices, operational and safety procedures, and guiding policies. Table 1 narrates the comparative context of pre- and postpandemic measures taken by the relevant authorities globally.

Conclusion

The impact of the pandemic on the happenings of tourism has been evident and impressive. Reflecting on number of measures taken to curb and mitigate this

Table 1. Comparative Measures in Pre- and Post-COVID-19 Phases.

Pre-COVID-19 Measures	Amid/Post-COVID-19 Measures
Personalized products and services:	Touchless services:
• Physical greetings.	• Virtual greetings.
• Presential check-ins.	• Digital check-ins.
• Escort service.	• Online transactions.
Security features:	Safety features:
• Security check gates.	• Temperature checks.
• Body scanners.	• Sanitizer gates.
Mobility system:	Controlled mobility:
• Free movement.	• Movement control orders.
• Equal access land, air, and marine transport.	• Limited seated transports.
	• Limited seated dining.
• Indiscriminate behavior.	• Proximity reduction rules.
Free admission and entry:	Conditional admission and entry:
• Unmasked entry.	• Mandatory mask wearing.
• No vaccination conditions.	• Vaccination passport.
• No health pre-conditions.	• Compulsory vaccination.
Human resource:	Human resource:
• Hiring of contractual and daily wages staff in addition to regular employees.	• Firing of nearly all the contractual and daily wages staff.
• Fringe benefits for employees.	• Forced leaves for cost-cutting.

Source: Authors work.

viral outbreak, and the colossal damage this health emergency has caused on the tourism market, demand and supply sides, numberless adjustments and standard operating procedures (SOPs) have been introduced, implemented, and adjusted, nowadays with the relaxation of many of the restrictions. To this end, pertinently in the initial phases of the pandemic, with the total absence of mobilities, it was expected that this outbreak will entirely transform the tourism sector and these SOPs be an integral part of each of the segments of tourism. Of course, the digital smartification was and, in our view, will continue to be the most profound transformation in tourism activities. Thus, with the quest for new territories, those less associated with mass tourism, the increase in supply segmentation, the redoubled attention to local places/attractions, with the phygital-oriented always present, we identify the main novel introductions that may drive the tourism activities. However, certain phases amid the pandemic pointed toward the scenarios having little or no influence of pandemic on the tourism sector. Assuming this, over the last pandemic year, the signs for the postpandemic were associated with a forecast of intense tourist activity supplanting the prepandemic values, something that can already be witnessed. Despite these, the pandemic has highlighted many fragilities of tourism sector and invited the stakeholders to rethink about the potential same case situations in coming times.

Recommendations and Future Avenues

This study underpins certain recommendations and take-outs for various stakeholders directly or indirectly associated with the tourism business. For instance, for academia, this study paves the methodological pathway to contemplate the impacts of the pandemic on the tourism and imprints of this viral outbreak on the hustling happenings of tourism. For tourism stakeholders, this study sketches the fundamental touchpoints deemed compulsory in the duality of tourism and health emergencies as evident from the issue under probe. For health officials and institutions, this study identifies the market potential the tourism industry holds amid such health outbreaks. For governing institutions, the take-aways from this study comprised of authoritative issues in introducing and implementing the Do's and Don'ts in the attempts to contain the pandemic. This study, moreover, lays general implications as well. It provides comparative overview between the pre-pandemic practices of tourism and postpandemic tourism transformations. Specifically narrating, this study while based on existing academic and industrial endeavors highlighted the classical and modern fragments of tourism. Pertinently, the sudden paradigm shifts the tourism industry has experienced amid the novel COVID-19.

Note

1. Phygital (physical plus digital) is a neologism that refers to the blending of digital experiences with physical ones.

References

Adom, D. (2020). The COVID-19 global pandemic: Socio-cultural, economic and educational implications from Ghana. *International and Multidisciplinary Journal of Social Sciences, 9*(3), 202–229. doi:10.17583/rimcis.2020.5416

Andrade, J. G., & Dias, P. (2020). A phygital approach to cultural heritage: Augmented reality at Regaleira. *Virtual Archaeology Review, 11*(22), 15–25.

Assaf, A. G., Kock, F., & Tsionas, M. (2022). Tourism during and after COVID-19: An expert-informed agenda for future research. *Journal of Travel Research, 61*(2), 454–457. doi:10.1177/00472875211017237

Ateljevic, I. (2020). Transforming the (tourism) world for good and (re)generating the potential "new normal". *Tourism Geographies, 22*(3), 467–475. doi:10.1080/14616688.2020.1759134

Awan, M. I., Shamim, A., & Ahn, J. (2021). Implementing "cleanliness is half of faith" in re-designing tourists, experiences and salvaging the hotel industry in Malaysia during COVID-19 pandemic. *Journal of Islamic Marketing, 12*(3), 543–557. doi:10.1108/JIMA-08-2020-0229

Ballina, F. J. B. (2019). Smart tourism destination, experiencia phygital y turismo rural. *International Journal of Information Systems and Tourism (IJIST)*, *4*(1), 41–52.

Buhalis, D., & Amaranggana, A. (2015). Smart tourism destinations enhancing tourism experience through personalisation of services. In I. Tussyadiah & A. Inversini (Eds.), *Information and communication technologies in tourism 2015* (pp. 377–389). Cham: Springer International Publishing. doi:10.1007/978-3-319-14343-9_28

Bukuluki, P., Mwenyango, H., Katongole, S. P., Sidhva, D., & Palattiyil, G. (2020). The socio-economic and psychosocial impact of COVID-19 pandemic on urban refugees in Uganda. *Social Sciences & Humanities Open*, *2*(1), 100045. doi:10.1016/j.ssaho.2020.100045

Cai, W., & McKenna, B. (2021). Power and resistance: Digital-free tourism in a connected world. *Journal of Travel Research*. 00472875211061208. doi:10.1177/00472875211061208

Çetinsöz, B. C., & Ege, Z. (2013). Impacts of perceived risks on tourists' revisit intentions. *Anatolia*, *24*(2), 173–187. doi:10.1080/13032917.2012.743921

Chua, B.-L., Al-Ansi, A., Lee, M. J., & Han, H. (2021). Impact of health risk perception on avoidance of international travel in the wake of a pandemic. *Current Issues in Tourism*, *24*(7), 985–1002. doi:10.1080/13683500.2020.1829570

Craig, D. (2020). Pandemic and its metaphors: Sontag revisited in the COVID-19 era. *European Journal of Cultural Studies*, *23*(6), 1025–1032. doi:10.1177/1367549420938403

Dragan, D., Keshavarzsaleh, A., Kramberger, T., Jereb, B., & Rosi, M. (2019). Forecasting us tourists' inflow to Slovenia by modified Holt-Winters Damped model: A case in the tourism industry logistics and supply chains. *Logistics & Sustainable Transport*, *10*(1), 11–30.

Egger, I., Lei, S. I., & Wassler, P. (2020). Digital free tourism—An exploratory study of tourist motivations. *Tourism Management*, *79*, 104098. doi:10.1016/j.tourman.2020.104098

Filep, S., King, B., & McKercher, B. (2022). Reflecting on tourism and COVID-19 research. *Tourism Recreation Research*, 1–5. doi:10.1080/02508281.2021.2023839

Fotiadis, A., Polyzos, S., & Huan, T.-C. (2021). The good, the bad and the ugly on COVID-19 tourism recovery. *Annals of Tourism Research*, *87*, 103117. doi:10.1016/j.annals.2020.103117

Fuchs, G. (2013). Low versus high sensation-seeking tourists: A study of backpackers' experience risk perception. *International Journal of Tourism Research*, *15*(1), 81–92. doi:10.1002/jtr.878

Gössling, S., Scott, D., & Hall, C. M. (2021). Pandemics, tourism and global change: A rapid assessment of COVID-19. *Journal of Sustainable Tourism*, *29*(1), 1–20. doi:10.1080/09669582.2020.1758708

Hall, C. M., Scott, D., & Gössling, S. (2020). Pandemics, transformations and tourism: Be careful what you wish for. *Tourism Geographies*, *22*(3), 577–598. doi:10.1080/14616688.2020.1759131

Harrington, R. D. (2021). Natural disasters, terrorism, and civil unrest: Crises that disrupt the tourism and travel industry-a brief overview. *Worldwide Hospitality and Tourism Themes*, *13*(3), 392–396. doi:10.1108/WHATT-01-2021-0008

Ioannides, D., & Gyimóthy, S. (2020). The COVID-19 crisis as an opportunity for escaping the unsustainable global tourism path. *Tourism Geographies, 22*(3), 624–632. doi:10.1080/14616688.2020.1763445

Jackson, J., Weiss, M., Schwarzenberg, A., Nelson, R., Sutter, K., & Sutherland, M. (2021). Global economic effects of COVID-19. In *The effects of COVID-19 on the global and domestic economy* (pp. 1–221). Washington, DC: Congressional Research Service. Retrieved from https://crsreports.congress.gov/product/pdf/R/R46270/67

Joseph Pine, B., II, & Gilmore, J. H. (2014). A leader's guide to innovation in the experience economy. *Strategy & Leadership, 42*(1), 24–29. doi:10.1108/SL-09-2013-0073

Kaushal, V., & Srivastava, S. (2021). Hospitality and tourism industry amid COVID-19 pandemic: Perspectives on challenges and learnings from India. *International Journal of Hospitality Management, 92,* 102707. doi:10.1016/j.ijhm.2020.102707

Latif, M. T., Dominick, D., Hawari, N. S. S. L., Mohtar, A. A. A., & Othman, M. (2021). The concentration of major air pollutants during the movement control order due to the COVID-19 pandemic in the Klang Valley, Malaysia. *Sustainable Cities and Society, 66,* 102660. doi:10.1016/j.scs.2020.102660

Lau, A. (2020). New technologies used in COVID-19 for business survival: Insights from the Hotel Sector in China. *Information Technology & Tourism, 22*(4), 497–504. doi:10.1007/s40558-020-00193-z

Mao, Y., He, J., Morrison, A. M., & Andres Coca-Stefaniak, J. (2020). Effects of tourism CSR on employee psychological capital in the COVID-19 crisis: From the perspective of conservation of resources theory. *Current Issues in Tourism,* 1–19. doi:10.1080/13683500.2020.1770706

Mtimet, N., Wanyoike, F., Rich, K. M., & Baltenweck, I. (2021). Zoonotic diseases and the COVID-19 pandemic: Economic impacts on Somaliland's livestock exports to Saudi Arabia. *Global Food Security, 28,* 100512. doi:10.1016/j.gfs.2021.100512

Nofal, E., Reffat, R., & Vande Moere, A. (2017). *Phygital heritage: An approach for heritage communication.* doi:10.3217/978-3-85125-530-0-36

Ntounis, N., Parker, C., Skinner, H., Steadman, C., & Warnaby, G. (2021). Tourism and Hospitality industry resilience during the COVID-19 pandemic: Evidence from England. *Current Issues in Tourism,* 1–14. doi:10.1080/13683500.2021.1883556

Ozbay, G., Sariisik, M., Ceylan, V., & Çakmak, M. (2021). A comparative evaluation between the impact of previous outbreaks and COVID-19 on the tourism industry. *International Hospitality Review* (ahead-of-print). doi:10.1108/IHR-05-2020-0015

Poon, A. (1993). *Tourism, technology and competitive strategies.* Wallingford: CAB International.

Prideaux, B. (2005). Factors affecting bilateral tourism flows. *Annals of Tourism Research, 32*(3), 780–801. doi:10.1016/j.annals.2004.04.008

Renzaho, A. M. N. (2020). The need for the right socio-economic and cultural fit in the COVID-19 response in Sub-Saharan Africa: Examining demographic, economic political, health, and socio-cultural differentials in COVID-19 morbidity and mortality. *International Journal of Environmental Research and Public Health, 17*(10). doi:10.3390/ijerph17103445

Robina-Ramírez, R., Sánchez, M. S.-O., Jiménez-Naranjo, H. V., & Castro-Serrano, J. (2021). Tourism governance during the COVID-19 pandemic crisis: A proposal for a sustainable model to restore the tourism industry. *Environment, Development and Sustainability.* doi:10.1007/s10668-021-01707-3

Salinas Fernández, J. A., Guaita Martínez, J. M., & Martín Martín, J. M. (2022). An analysis of the competitiveness of the tourism industry in a context of economic recovery following the COVID-19 pandemic. *Technological Forecasting and Social Change, 174*, 121301. doi:10.1016/j.techfore.2021.121301

Santos, N., & Oliveira Moreira, C. (2021). Uncertainty and expectations in Portugal's tourism activities. Impacts of COVID-19. *Research in Globalization, 3*, 100071. doi:10.1016/j.resglo.2021.100071

Sigala, M. (2020). Tourism and COVID-19: Impacts and implications for advancing and resetting industry and research. *Journal of Business Research, 117*, 312–321. doi:10.1016/j.jbusres.2020.06.015

Spalding, M., Burke, L., & Fyall, A. (2021). COVID-19: Implications for nature and tourism. *Anatolia, 32*(1), 126–127. doi:10.1080/13032917.2020.1791524

Sulaiman, T., Ibrahim, A., Motevalli, S., Wong, K. Y., & Hakim, M. N. (2021). Effect of e-evaluation on work motivation among teachers during the movement control order in COVID-19: The mediating role of stress. *Interactive Technology and Smart Education, 18*(3), 435–449. doi:10.1108/ITSE-05-2020-0066

Swaikoski, D. (2020). Leisure in the time of coronavirus: Indigenous tourism in Canada and the impacts of COVID-19. *World Leisure Journal, 62*(4), 311–314. doi:10.1080/16078055.2020.1825266

Tiku, O., Shimizu, T., & Hartono, D. (2022). Tourism's income distribution in West Papua Province. *Annals of Tourism Research Empirical Insights, 3*(1), 100038. doi:10.1016/j.annale.2022.100038

Vărzaru, A. A., Bocean, C. G., & Cazacu, M. (2021). Rethinking tourism industry in pandemic COVID-19 period. *Sustainability, 13*(12). doi:10.3390/su13126956

van der Veen, R. (2014). Substitution, tourism. In J. Jafari & H. Xiao (Eds.), *Encyclopedia of tourism* (pp. 1–2). Springer International Publishing. doi:10.1007/978-3-319-01669-6_341-1

Wilks, J. (2006). Current issues in tourist health, safety and security. In J. Wilks (Ed.), *Tourism in turbulent times* (pp. 3–18). New York, NY: Routledge.

Witt, S. F., & Witt, C. A. (1995). Forecasting tourism demand: A review of empirical research. *International Journal of Forecasting, 11*(3), 447–475. doi:10.1016/0169-2070(95)00591-7

Wong, L. P., Lai, L. L., See, M. H., Alias, H., Danaee, M., Ting, C. Y., & Tok, P. S. K. (2021). Psychological distress among cancer survivors during implementation of a nationwide Movement Control Order over the COVID-19 pandemic. *Supportive Care in Cancer, 29*(10), 6087–6097. doi:10.1007/s00520-021-06182-0

Post-disaster Tourism: Building Resilient and Sustainable Communities

Gina B. Alcoriza and John Ericson A. Policarpio

Abstract

Tourism sites around the world which are often hit by calamities caused by climate change normally affect extremely the regions and economies. Disasters affect directly or indirectly the number of tourist arrival, the hotel industry, tourism receipts, employment, and the overall economy of a region (Naeem, Bhatti, & Khan, 2021). To thrive or adapt in this novel and rapidly changing environment, tourism communities need to be resilient in order to maintain the economic benefits (Wu, Chiu, & Chen, 2019). This requires strategic approach in local tourism development with strong public private partnership and collaboration. Economy, environment, emergency management and response, disaster risk management, community-based participation, post-disaster tourism recovery management, psychological behavior of people, nature-based tourism, dark tourism, responsive consumer behavior, and transportation are the key areas to focus on. Developing resilient and sustainable local tourism communities must be guided by the carefully defined goals and objectives depending on the dynamics and resources of the communities, and anchored of guidelines, pertinent laws and policies implemented by the local, national, and international governing and regulatory bodies.

Keywords: Post-disaster tourism; resilient communities; sustainable communities; dark tourism; tourism recovery; local resiliency

The concept of post-disaster tourism has been integrated with the developments of certain special-interest or niche tourism activities such as dark tourism, doom tourism, and black tourism. The said tourism activity follows that notion of visitation on a destination or site that is considered the epicenter of a natural or man-made catastrophe that built a strong narrative about the site. Destination management has gone a long way from its inception in the tourism development

Resilient and Sustainable Destinations After Disaster, 97–107
Copyright © 2023 Gina B. Alcoriza and John Ericson A. Policarpio
Published under exclusive licence by Emerald Publishing Limited
doi:10.1108/978-1-80382-021-720231008

practice to the present-day thrust of destination sustainability and resiliency. This chapter will uncover the concept of creating a resilient and sustainable tourism communities in the context of post-disaster tourism through a comprehensive review of different challenges, solutions, and best practices of disaster-hit desti-nations toward their way to bounce back and further move forward. Thus, this defines and introduces the concepts of post-disaster tourism, its parameters and the framework in developing a resilient local community.

Definition and Concepts of Post-disaster Tourism

Disaster seems to be a negative terminology and often regarded as a counteracting force toward development of a certain nation. It is true on destinations that had experienced abrupt and drastic changes brought by a disaster, may it be a natural catastrophe or a man-made disaster. Disasters are difficult to predict and control, and in the recent years, occurrences has grown, affecting the tourism industry around the globe. These can happen anytime to more destinations and the possible damage cannot be avoided. Destinations learned to be more resilient and innovative in coping up with the situations, especially when the area is more dependent on tourism as a major economic driver. Many theoretical arguments came out since more disasters happened that affect tourist destinations along tourist arrivals, infrastructure, destination image and reputation, and tourist behavior on destination choices. Destination managers normally make critical decisions in relation to recovery, reconstruction, and marketing of destination after the disaster (Rosselló, Becken, & Santana-Gallego, 2020). They tend to employ post-disaster response and recovery, in relations to rural livelihoods of tourism communities as per economic aspects is greatly affected (Neef, 2021). Destinations significantly offering tourism services while responding and recov-ering from the aftermath of disaster. The post disaster tourism has become a tourism product that significantly brings to light the relationship of disaster tourism and dark tourism.

Post-disaster tourism is an activity often spurred out of the niche dark tourism at which the purpose of travelers constitutes visitation of places associated with death, sufferings, destruction, and loss (Lin, Kelemen, & Tresidder, 2018). On a lighter note, risk reduction responses and recovery plans are the usual solution for any types of disaster. As seen, nations with a strong tourism recovery plan and high rebuilding initiatives are deemed catalysts of economic and social recovery (Li et al., 2012). Disasters, particularly natural ones, can be classified as a low-probability high-impact event wherein it puts strong pressure to an affected community that needs to be acted upon fast in order to recover (World Travel and Tourism Council, 2019).

Tourism as more exposed to danger than other industries is often difficult to initiate and respond to immediately address the massive damages to tourism assets. Restoring destination image is significantly essential since it plays a critical role for tourists in selecting their vacation destination. Kaur (2015) cited that tourism is especially vulnerable due to the following reasons: (1) tourism is highly people-oriented, (2) unpredictable behavior of tourists, (3) language barrier in chaotic situations, (4) unfamiliarity to local hazards of tourists, and (5) Many of the tourism destinations are located in areas of natural beauty, coastlines, mountains, rivers, and lakes with greater risks.

Parameters of Post-disaster Tourism

Tourism industry is considered as especially vulnerable to disasters that basically includes physical infrastructure and more intangible elements like destination image and reputation. Local tourism managers that are greatly affected by disasters essentially introduced strategies to recover and regain the economic impact of tourism to local communities thru disaster response and sustainable recovery plans that feature different types of assets, including human, social, natural, and economic resources, and further proposed sustainable livelihood framework for tourism (Yan et al., 2017). The keys areas are the following: (1) Economic capital that refers to the economic benefits resulting from the development of post-disaster tourism that basic infrastructure, produced goods, and financial resources that people use to realize their aimed livelihoods, (2) Human capital that involves local residents' improvement in skills, knowledge, ability, and experiences which can help residents to pursue livelihood strategies and achieve livelihood objectives as a result of the post-disaster tourism development, (3) Social capital that focuses on the residents' shared sense of identity, notions, norms, and values related with the post-disaster tourism development like their networks and bonding, and (4) Institutional capital that speaks on the local people's access to the tourism market, the sharing benefits they have associated with post-disaster tourism, and their participation in the development process of post-disaster tourism. These plans had essentially provided a holistic approach to the effects of post-disaster tourism on local communities from multiple perspectives.

Post-disaster Tourism in the Asian Pacific Context

The Asia-Pacific region is known to be the most affected of natural disasters in the last three decades with 29% of global statistics, and major increase in water stress over the next 20 years is expected, according to the 2020 Ecological Threat Register (ETR). Floods and storms are considered the largest share made of the total natural disasters in the Asia-Pacific at more than two-thirds (2/3) of the total. The region was exposed to the largest number of natural disasters with 2,845 events in the last 30 years, and with the highest prevalence of food insecurity with 48% of the population deemed food insecure. The most affected countries are China, Philippines, Indonesia, Japan, and Vietnam. These severely affecting more than 57 million people by climate-related disasters during the peak of the global pandemic (Balmain, 2022).

The devastating earthquake and tsunami that struck Indonesia in September 2018, the earthquake that hit Nepal in April 2015, the strong typhoon in the

Philippines in 2020, and the increasingly frequent natural disasters throughout Asia and the Pacific are reminders of the urgency of building and maintaining resiliency plans against future catastrophes to minimize the damages to the local communities and to immensely recover on the economic losses. It is known that Asia-Pacific nations experience more natural disasters than any regions around the globe. Nations share common characteristics such as large growing populations with high poverty incidence, inadequate sea defenses as poor villages and coastal farms are vulnerable to monsoon rains and storms that caused flooding that destroys hoes, livestock, and crops, pollutes fresh water supplies, and cuts off food and medicine supply access. In addition, industrialization is driving high focus of people to live in crowded cities that are more vulnerable, particularly near coastal regions and large rivers. Thus, high rates of environmental degradation and the effects of climate change are greatly felt. Many of these areas are tourist sites normally with panoramic views, dive spots, surfing areas, alluring mountains and volcanoes, and magnificent seascapes and landscapes that are all attractive to tourists.

In 2015, Vanuatu in Oceania was struck by Tropical Cyclone Pam, an extremely destructive cyclone of category five with wind speeds of about 250 km/h, recorded an estimated damage of 17,000 buildings, displaced around 65,000 people with livelihood greatly affected of at least 80% of the rural population's crops and livestock (Government of Vanuatu, 2015). Weeks after, the Vanuatu Tourism Office (VTO) started to launch a campaign on social media platforms to regain potential visitors' confidence in Vanuatu as a tourist destination under the slogan #VanuatuStillSmiles. VTO wanted to assure people specially tourist in the major source countries Australia and New Zealand that Vanuatu was still open for travelers. The country slightly felt the recovery in 2016 (Neef, 2021).

Philippines experienced an earthquake of 7.2 magnitude in Bohol province and the Super Typhoon Haiyan occurred successively in October and November of the year 2013. The reboot of tourism has been closely managed by the collaborative efforts of the government and private sectors. The optimism to recover and reach the greater heights again of the local government officials and the entire business community resulted in the fast recovery of tourism by repositioning the place focused on environmental and cultural heritage (Chen, 2014) with fast-paced infrastructure rehabilitation. Bohol is known for the tarsiers, chocolate hills, dive spot in Balicasag, resorts in Panglao, and old churches. The province scaled on about one million tourist arrival in 2016 (Provincial Planning Development Office Bohol). In 2020, Super Typhoon Rolly devastated the Bicol Region at the Central Philippines by heavy flooding, lahar-carrying boulders from Mayon Volcano came down the villages that damaged bridges and houses, and the strong winds that caused the shutdown of power and communication lines (PNA, 2020). Amid the COVID-19 pandemic, local people affected by the super typhoon tried to initiate fast recovery from both unexpected phenomena thru the help of the local interagency task force and the local disaster risk reduction management office. Rehabilitating the tourism infrastructure, swift restoration of power supply and communication lines, government supports to the small and medium tourism establishments or known as SMEs (Small and Medium Enterprises) are some of the immediate actions to regain the good status of tourist sites and to reopen to local tourism. There are local tourists have to visit the areas with greater damages brought by the super typhoon.

The Indian Ocean earthquake and tsunami hit Aceh, Indonesia, in December 2004, killing over 160,000 people and destroying the coastal infrastructure. This resulted in the decrease of tourist arrival, years after the incident. The place recovered from the effects of tsunami through government's collaboration with various humanitarian organizations and foreign countries and focused on the reconstruction of the damaged infrastructure and tourism development was notably highlighted. This collaboration efforts resulted in several prominent tsunami-related sites, such as the Aceh Tsunami Museum, the Tsunami Educational Park, the Tsunami Inundation Monuments, and the "Aceh Thanks the World" Memorial Park, and these became tourist attractions and inspired the further development of post-disaster tourism in Aceh, or known as "tsunami tourism" (Liu-Lastres, Mariska, Tan, & Ying, 2020).

Looking back at the 2011 Great East Japan earthquake and tsunami, Japan has witnessed an increased fascination with post-disaster tourism or dark tourism, wherein visitors' pilgrimages to landmark disaster sites in tsunami-hit areas were stimulated. In addition, blue tourism was launched in the coastal area of Minamisanriku, Japan, in the aftermath of the 2011 tsunami and considered as a community-led transformative tourism initiative (Lin et al., 2018). On the other hand, the eruption of Mount Agung on November 21st, 2017 (bbc.com) and December 23rd, 2017 (regional.kompas.com) in Indonesia brought great impact in the tourist arrival in Bali. The earthquake of seven Richter Magnitude Scale on August 5th, 2018, which happened in Lombok, Nusa Tenggara Barat, and surrounding areas, damaged the infrastructure and facilities of the many tourism establishments (Kurniasari et al., 2019). The government focused on trauma healing for people living in the tourist area, promotion and publication in social media, digital marketing trainings and campaigns to promote meetings and events. These are some of the immediate actions done by tourism stakeholders in the area. In China, there has been a growth of initiatives and movements toward preserving the damage caused by earthquakes, marketing the as "earthquake ruins," and turning them into viable tourist destinations. This is considered as an alternative form of disaster resilience strategy by creating new heritage and tourism opportunities after disaster rather than restoring the structures to their original state (Tanaka, 2020). Jiuzhaigou National Scenic Spot in China is considered as a disaster-prone destination with rapid tourism development (Zhang, Seyler, Di, Wang, & Tang, 2021) in the country through their successful tourism recovery strategies which domestic tourism plays a very important role achieving resilience and rejuvenating local economic activities. Although Asia-Pacific region is prone to disaster, the local governments and private sectors continuously learn the strategies in coping with the disasters and in regaining the economic success through their well-established local recovery plans and highly spirited collaborations of tourism stakeholders.

Framework Development on Resilient and Sustainable Communities

Basically, after every disaster, many aspects of tourism demand are truly affected negatively, such as fall of visitor arrivals, decrease in employment levels, decline in private sector profits that result in reduction of government revenues, and eventually the cessation of further business involvement and investment (Kaur & Mehta, 2022). These mostly felt by nations frequently suffered from the aftermath of disasters. Many approaches were strategically defined and eventually implemented in order to achieve the aimed tourism recovery.

Community-led approaches in rebuilding disaster-hit destinations have been an integral way to consolidate efforts toward tourism resilience development. In this relation, the voice of the host community really matters and has a huge involvement in the planning, implementation, and monitoring phase. Communities severely hit by a disaster, regardless if its natural or man-made, require enough time to recover and rebuild their community. Though post-disaster tourism is commonly associated with dark tourism in most narratives, a number of evidences suggest that communities responding to a post-disaster development may sometimes discard the idea of being tagged as a "dark tourism" site (Lin et al., 2018). For instance, in the town of Minamisanriku, Japan, the entire community rejected the idea to be associated as a dark tourism site though their place is the epicenter of the 9.0 magnitude earthquake followed by a gigantic tsunami that reached almost 40 meters, also known as the 2011 Great Eastern Japan earthquake and tsunami. Looking at this case, even though the community has suffered immensely on the said disaster, the host community is still strong with their belief that tourism recovery can only be achieved if positive narratives about the place is incorporated in the story-telling component instead of dwelling with the remembrance of death, suffering, and loss. Thus, post-disaster tourism contributes greatly to the development of new concepts in tourism studies such as blue tourism which focuses on the environmental, political, social, and economic planning of coastal areas for tourism located along the shores of major seas (Lin et al., 2018). Through blue tourism, the rehabilitation process of Minamisanriku has been included in the resilience narrative of the place and thus, shun away the negative interpretivist image brought by dark tourism.

Community participation goes beyond the context of helping out disaster-hit communities when we are speaking of post-disaster tourism. Multisectoral cooperation and large-scale enterprise involvement are indeed necessary toward such progress (Wu et al., 2019). Social capitalism is a prerequisite of large-scale enterprise involvement toward tourism development of disaster sites. We have to accept the fact that areas that have undergone a catastrophe require more than just doling out from their stakeholders but rather they need a sustainable program toward recuperating from their losses, assisting them to regain their way of living, and further improve their status as a community.

Speaking of community participation, social capitalism plays a big role in adaptive capacity of a community to withstand the challenges of destination management in disaster-prone sites (Hovelsrud, Karlsson, & Olsen, 2018). Social capital is identified as a collective element of social network, place attachment, experiential knowledge, trust, risk perception, and engagement of individuals toward their community for development. When these elements are at play, communities tend to increase their adaptive capacity to easily respond, recover, and rebuild disaster-hit tourism destinations. Take in the case of Northern Norway where tourism to the Alps is frequented by risk of avalanche. Locals who took part in this social cohesion phenomenon have greater chances to take in greater challenges and recover faster compared to communities which are loosely connected. Social capitalism exists as a foundational collective behavioral response but the "way of responding" is a different story. Thus, it is also noted that adaptive capacity of disaster-hit tourism destination varies from destination characteristics, culture of the community, and openness in accepting external assistance.

Apart from strengthening community participation and social capitalism in the destination, it is also viable for the tourism suppliers to establish a system of identifying early risks to avoid further concerns in the tourism supply chain. Fu (2020) termed it as a risk-warning mechanism which entails early detection of an impending catastrophic event through crisis awareness training of tourism players as well as the organization of the crisis management agency or division whose main task is to identify, monitor, and rectify strategic execution and management of tourism enterprise.

A more resilient economy depends on a shift to sustainable practices (OECD, 2020) especially after the disaster. The economic consequences of a disaster in a particular tourist destination generally affect international tourist arrival and receipts due to infrastructure and tourist sites damages that caused wider

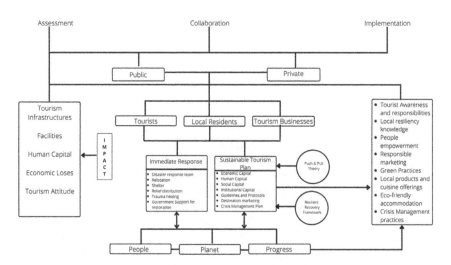

Fig. 1.   Post-disaster Tourism Resiliency Development Framework
for Local Communities.

weakening of the local economy. The government and the other tourism stake-holders are indeed in need to develop a post-disaster tourism framework to achieve the aimed tourism and local economic recovery. The tourism development or tourism recovery after disaster may be done considering the suggested provisions of the post-disaster tourism resiliency development framework for local communities illustrated in Fig. 1.

The post-disaster tourism development may be developed focusing on most resilient way through the proposed approach of coming into three important phases – assessment, collaboration, and implementation. The recovery efforts must be a collaborative work of the public sector that consists of the government agencies and the private sectors that involves tourism businesses, nongovernmental organizations, academe, research organizations, etc. The first step is the assessment of the impact of the disaster such as the damages on tourism infrastructures and facilities, the effects on human capital, the local economic losses, and tourist attitude toward the destination as a result of the disaster. Considering that the recovery approach depends on many aspects including the scale of the damage, the destination's financial resources, the government's planning, the involvement of the private sector, and people's awareness (Moshakova, 2021). The assessment of the effects of a hazard event should include both the physical and socioeconomic assessment of the impacts of the disaster. Secondly, the collaboration phase where in all tourism stakeholders are involved follow the sequence from the immediate response to sustainable tourism plan which will be anchored with the two theories, the push and pull theory of Crimpton and the resilient recovery theory as a guide in formulating plans for recovery and sustainable tourism way forward focusing on people (social), planet (environment), and progress (economy). Collaboration efforts by stakeholders must be manifested in the immediate response such as creating disaster response team, relocating affected tourists and local residents, providing shelters to affected families, conducting relief distributions containing basic goods, conducting trauma healing, and coordinating with the government support to affected tourism stakeholders. The sustainable development plan should greatly include the strategies for economic capital, human capital, social capital, and institutional capital as pointed out by Liu-Lastres et al. (2020). In addition, guidelines and protocols, as a result of the impact of the disaster, destination marketing and crisis management plan must be incorporated in the sustainable tourism plan. Marketing a destination right after a disaster is a complex task due to the bad media publicity associated with the destruction; thus, crisis communication is a key role of Destination Management Organizations (DMOs) to minimize the negativities and bring the private together with the public sector to implement consistent messages on destination updates and some recovery marketing methodologies. Crisis management is indeed significant in the collaborative recovery phase which involves the planning for, responding to, and recovering from a crisis and aiming to restore a positive image and impede the decrease of perceived tourist arrivals; hence, potential crises or disasters could be avoided to come their way again with the use of active crisis management plans of the government and private sectors

(Niyaz, 2015). The strategies shall be consistent with the guiding principles for the recovery and rehabilitation efforts.

Lastly, the implementation phase must ensure that the stakeholders are aware about the situation of the destination and so with their responsibilities in the process of recovery. Disaster knowledge can significantly contribute to the full understanding of stakeholders of their roles and responsibilities. The chain of tourists' roles in the recovery stage of affected areas are considered strategies to the social networks in order to increase the number of tourists visiting the recovering local communities. Local resiliency knowledge is also taken into account to further understand the situation and stakeholders can go along with the implementation. Good communication is important to be viewed as contributing to other goals of the rehabilitation and recovery program, including transparency, accountability, and good governance. The communication strategy should consider the following components: (1) key principles; (2) core messages; (3) spokesperson; (4) forms of communication materials; and (5) communication channels. Here are the key principles presented in the Philippine Disaster Rehabilitation and Recovery Framework: (1) Establish communication protocols that would serve as a primary guide between national and local governments, and other relevant stakeholders in implementing communication-related activities such as regular updating and reporting, (2) Identify focal person/spokesperson who is well versed on addressing the media and the public, (3) Manage people's expectations by providing proactive messages to address or clarify recovery issues like possible delays in the implementation of programs and projects, and issues on beneficiaries' selection process (4) Establish a feedback mechanism at the national and local level that allows the affected communities to be heard and be responded to. (5) Promote transparency and accountability throughout the recovery process, (6) Involve the public and affected communities in the recovery process through the regular reporting of progress, responding to issues raised, and updating on the plans and timeframes of program implementation, (7) Establish the regularity of releases of information and consistency of data provided to the public.

Community-based recovery can be in the form of financial or material assistance that is channeled through people and community organizations to be actively involved in making decisions, developing management, and intensifying people empowerment (Rahmatika, Sakti, & Boediarto, 2021) in the recovery process. Community participation in tourism development is important for several reasons such as it helps design better tourism plans, contributes to equitable distribution of costs and benefits among community members, and helps satisfy locally identified need (Cruz, 2019). Empowering local people, normally evident in recognizing the rights and beliefs of local people, supports human rights and democratic movement, partnership with local tour operators and other service providers, gender equality, and inclusivity. Furthermore, more initiatives in offering locally produced products and cuisines and by patronizing them by the residents are a great help to boost local economy. Responsible marketing of the destination is an impressive move by creating social media content that may attract more viewers and turn them to be tourists. Promotional contents/ messages may have the power to relieve some affected people as well as the tourists of this anxiety by sharing an uplifting story that has come out of the event or what you may be experiencing as a business right at the moment. Green practices in all the sectors of tourism industry is a very impressive move to manifest the inclusions of sustainable tourism in recovery process by employing environmentally friendly practices (reduce, reuse, and recycle), using energy efficient light bulbs and eco-friendly cleaning products, etc. These apparently contribute in mitigating the effects of climate change. The crisis management plan must be carefully practiced to avoid greater disaster impact to the community. These things are to be considered in the implementation phase in the journey of the aimed post-disaster tourism recovery.

The occurrence of disasters is indeed unpredictable and uncontrollable, it is in the hands of the people on how to accept, cope up, and manage the recovery from the aftermath of the disasters. Proper planning, collaboration, team work, and consistencies in implementation are essential factors to be considered. It is indeed important that the responsibilities of each of the tourism stakeholders be properly identified in order for each sector to be able to participate and contribute to the attainment of tourism recovery and a more resilient post-disaster sustainable tourism development for local communities.

References

Balmain, A. (2022). Over 57 million affected by climate disasters across Asia Pacific in 2021. International Federation of Red Cross and Crescent Societies Press Release. Kuala Lumpur, Malaysia.

Chen, C. C. (2014). Tourism experiences as a stress reliever: Examining the effects of tourism recovery experiences on life satisfaction. *Journal of Travel Research*, *55*(2).

Cruz, R. (2019). *Sustainable tourism* (1st ed.). Philippines: Rex Publishing Inc.

Fu, Y. K. (2020). The impact and recovering strategies of the COVID-19 pandemic: Lessons from Taiwan's hospitality industry. *Cogent Social Sciences*, *6*(1). doi:10.1080/23311886.2020.1829806

Global Rescue and World Travel & Tourism Council: Crisis Readiness - Crisis readiness are you prepared and resilient to safeguard your people & destinations, World Travel and Tourism Council. (2019). United Kingdom.

Hovelsrud, G. K., Karlsson, M., & Olsen, J. (2018). Prepared and flexible: Local adaptation strategies for avalanche risk. *Cogent Social Sciences*, *4*(1). doi:10.1080/23311886.2018.1460899

Kaur, S., & Mehta, S. (2022). Liberalisation and technological accumulation strategy in industries from developing economies: An analysis of Indian capital goods manufacturing firms. *Millennial Asia*. doi:10.1177/09763996221092243. SAGE Journal.

Kaur, V. (2015). Restoring tourism in the Paradise lost in floods restoring tourism in the Paradise lost in floods knowledge-based dynamic capabilities: The road Ahead in gaining organizational competitiveness view project knowledge-based dynamic capabilities and competitive Advantage: A study of MNCs in IT sector view project. Retrieved from https://www.researchgate.net/publication/358575765

Kurniasari, N., Haloho, H. N., & Christian, A. E. (2019). Tourism image recovery strategy post-natural disasters in Indonesia. *Jurnal IPTA p-ISSN, 7*(2), 2019.

Lin, Y., Kelemen, M., & Tresidder, R. (2018). Post-disaster tourism: Building resilience through community-led approaches in the aftermath of the 2011 disasters in Japan. *Journal of Sustainable Tourism, 26*(10), 1766–1783. doi:10.1080/09669582.2018.1511720

Li, M., Zhang, J., Luo, H., Dong, X.-W., Shangguan, X.-Y., & Cai, Y.-S. (2012). *The study of post-disaster tourism recovery and reconstruction based on tourist motivations. The case of Jiuzhaigou after "5·12" Wenchuan.* Retrieved from https://web.p.ebscohost.com/ehost/delivery?sid=3ca1af80-4042-46d6-87ce-29d52669d1e2%40redis&vid=20&ReturnUrl=https%3a%2f%2fweb.p.ebscohost.com%2f...

Liu-Lastres, B., Mariska, D., Tan, X., & Ying, T. (2020). Can post-disaster tourism development improve destination livelihoods? A case study of Aceh, Indonesia. *Journal of Destination Marketing and Management, 18.* 100510.

Moshakova, E. (2021). *The recovery of a tourist destination after a natural disaster.* Auckland University of Technology, TUWHERA.

Naeem, S. B., Bhatti, R., & Khan, A. (2021). An exploration of how fake news is taking over social media and putting public health at risk. *Health Information and Libraries Journal, 38,* 143–149. Blackwell Publishing Ltd. doi:10.1111/hir.12320

Neef, A. (2021). The contentious role of tourism in disaster response and recovery in Vanuatu. *Frontiers of Earth Science, 9.* doi:10.3389/feart.2021.771345

Niyaz, A. (2015). *Post disaster tourism crisis recovery in SIDS: Development and testing of an integrated approach.* Lincoln University, USA.

OECD. (2020). Building back better: A sustainable, resilient recovery after COVID-19. Organisation for Economic Co-operation and Development.

Philippines: Mayon Volcano Eruption - DREF Final Report. International Federation of Red Cross and Philippines News Agency. (2020).

Post-Disaster Needs Assessment Tropical Cyclone Pam, Government of Vanuatu. (2015).

Rahmatika, N. I., Sakti, S. K., & Boediarto, A. (2021). Women empowerment in postdisaster recovery after 2018 tsunami in Sumur Regency Pandeglang District. *IOP Conference Series: Earth and Environmental Science, 708*(1). doi:10.1088/1755-1315/708/1/012072

Rosselló, J., Becken, S., & Santana-Gallego, M. (2020). The effects of natural disasters on international tourism: A global analysis. *Tourism Management, 79.* doi:10.1016/j.tourman.2020.104080

Tanaka, M. (2020). *Resilient policies in Asian cities: Adaptation to climate change and natural disasters.* Singapore: Springer Book.

Wu, S. T., Chiu, C. H., & Chen, Y. S. (2019). An evaluation of recreational benefits and tribal tourism development for aboriginal villages after post-disaster reconstruction - a case study of Taiwan. *Asia Pacific Journal of Tourism Research, 24*(2), 136–149. doi:10.1080/10941665.2018.1556710

Yan, Y., Eckle, M., Kuo, C. L., Herfort, B., Fan, H., & Zipf, A. (2017). Monitoring and assessing postdisaster tourism recovery using geotagged social media data. *ISPRS International Journal of Geo-Information, 6*(5). doi:10.3390/ijgi6050144

Zhang, M., Seyler, B. C., Di, B., Wang, Y., & Tang, Y. (2021). Impact of earthquakes on natural area-driven tourism: Case study of China's Jiuzhaigou National Scenic Spot. *International Journal of Disaster Risk Reduction, 58.*

Rebuilding Tourism in Asia for Future (Post-COVID-19)

Syed Haider Ali Shah, Kamran Jamshed, Sharjeel Saleem, Basheer M. Al-Ghazali and Ozair Ijaz Kiani

Abstract

This chapter is about how the tourism is revived and how it can be rebuilt in Asian and Pacific countries after the deadliest COVID-19 pandemic with facts and stats of prepandemic and postpandemic impacts on economies of Europe and Asia due to COVID-19. The pandemics are not new to the hospitality industry but this COVID-19 pandemic has changed the whole industry concepts, and several hotels have revived their products and protocols and redesigned them to cope with any pandemic in future. Family businesses hotels are the most affected stakeholders in the hospitality industry of Asia where the governments of different countries have provided the financial support to them to revive back. The purpose of this chapter is to provide the readers with the facts about the current scenario of the hospitality and tourism industry in Asian tourist destinations and how these countries have taken proper measures to face the future (Pandemic situations). The literature is based on prepandemic stats and the effects of COVID-19 on tourism industry during the existing phases of COVID-19 including the facts and available stats of Asia which will help in the understanding of how these countries are rebuilding the tourism industry in postpandemic situation.

Keywords: Tourism; pandemic; COVID-19; rebuilding; monkeypox; hospitality; Asia

Introduction

Tourism is an empirical part of the economy of any country, it employs one out of 10 people in the world according to UN, and it is world's largest and profitable

Resilient and Sustainable Destinations After Disaster, 109–119
doi:10.1108/978-1-80382-021-720231009

industry with 10.4% (8.8$ trillion dollars) of world's total GDP and it provides about 319 million jobs worldwide (WTTC, 2022). Some countries like Macau, Maldives, Aruba, and Seychelles are depending on the economy raised through tourism; on the other hand, some countries have taken the initiative to develop themselves in a way to attract the tourists (such as United Arab Emirates (UAE) and Saudi Arabia). The Middle East has received around 60 million tourists in 2018 with a 73 billion USD, and since we are talking about rebuilding the tourism for future, we have seen these countries are bringing changes to attract the tourists and to sustain in the tourism industry. Due to the strong and growing middle class in the emerging economies, advance technologies, reconstructed business models, economical travel costs, and ease in visa facilitation made international tourist arrivals grew 5% in 2018 to reach the 1.4 billion mark, and this figure was reached two years ahead of UNWTO forecast and at the same time, export earnings generated by tourism have grown to USD 1.7 trillion. After the deadliest World War I and II which killed millions of people worldwide, COVID-19 has killed millions of people worldwide and brought several days lockdown due to which the people have faced a lot of damage. Now after COVID-19 the sustainability of the tourism industry is challenging for some countries, but despite it can provide opportunity to rebuild tourism in postpandemic situation to maintain good mental health and quality of life. Losing your loved one because of COVID-19 created trauma overall the globe where rethinking their death reasons caused anxiety and stress which results in poor mental health (Jamshaid, Malik, Haider, Jamshed, & Jamshad, 2020). We are still not out of the COVID-19 era as the fourth wave is hitting globally and now it is a new normal to live with it or to face any kind of same happening in the future. Moreover, now monkeypox is a new viral disease which is taking over the world and spreading but it is not as dangerous as the COVID-19 was.

Background

Throughout the history, some of the greatest plagues and pandemics have wiped out entire civilizations and brought powerful nations to their knees and killed millions of people. While these awful disease epidemics continue to menace humanity, we no longer suffer the same devastating repercussions as our fore-fathers did due to breakthroughs in epidemiology. Cholera, bubonic plague, smallpox, and influenza are among the world's deadliest diseases, and outbreaks of these diseases across international borders are appropriately referred to as pandemics, particularly smallpox, which has killed between 300 and 500 million people over the course of its 12,000-year life. The first outbreak of COVID-19 was in the end of October 2019 in Chinese city Wuhan and then it gets out of control and by the end of February 2020, it was declared a pandemic by the World Health Organization (WHO). It spread from China to Europe where the most fatalities were recorded in Italy in March 2020, then it spread to United States in April 2020 after that in India, Brazil, and the rest of Asia with record infections and deaths. The scholars narrated this new normal due to COVID-19 has impacted the tourism industry with the same force and huge depression as it was after the World War I and II (Bisby, Burgess, & Brewin, 2020). The mental health and worriedness were the outcomes due to COVID-19 in China (Jamshaid & Others, 2022) so the tourists were also afraid to travel abroad or domestically. This pandemic has given an opportunity to people so that they can find hope and consider the destruction in tourism industry by COVID-19 as an error and now we have to work on the present and future of the tourism industry with more socially and environmentally sustainable community. The governments have to work with their tourism and travel sectors on recovery plans and travel bubbles can be the opportunity to a fully open regime, and during this recovery phase the governments have to work on rebuilding the confidence of the tourists and should encourage them for a sustainable tourism sector (Helble & Fink, 2020). In most of the countries, the focus is on the domestic tourism after COVID-19 and this step is helping in recovery whereas the international travel ban has categorized the tourist destinations. According to IATA it will take time to be back on pre-COVID-19 levels until 2024. Some countries are working on domestic tourism while some are offering travel bubbles for neighboring countries and some countries in the Middle East like Saudi Arabia (Aswani & Aswani, 2021) and UAE (EXPO-2020) are bringing the entertainment events to attract the international tourists.

Change in GDP Due to COVID-19

The rapid increase in cases all over the world with a panic and causalities and the worst thing was the fear of death and then a substantial impact on worldwide economic, political, and sociocultural systems, health communication strategies and measures, and it halted global travel, tourism, and leisure (Sigala, 2020). With almost 4 billion people, Asia and the Pacific is the world's most populous region which covers almost 59.76% of the global population where mostly to China (1.4 billion) and India (1.2 billion). The region's GDP (US$ 23 trillion) accounts for 31% of global output and has grown rapidly in recent decades, with an average annual growth rate of 5.5% between 1995 and 2019. The initial days of this pandemic halted almost all business activities in this region where the death rate in India was unstoppable while China has imposed strict ban on traveling and lockdown of the entire cities with ban on any kind of intercity trades. India is the biggest economy with millions of products exported to entire world and not just products but the manpower and technical support, the hospitality industry of India faced closure with ban on inbound flights and no arrival of domestic tourists, and same happened in all tourist destinations of Asia and over all the world. COVID-19 influenced several countries at different times and in various ways and to diverse degrees but efforts to contain the epidemic on the other hand have resulted in national lockdowns, extensive travel restrictions, and border closures which made tourism one of the worst-affected businesses. Tourism is a very important industry for any country because it helps the economy and demands significant national and international aid through competent organisations, which was affected very badly due to COVID-19. Unemployment increased in hospitality sector after implication of measures against the COVID-19 spread and to avoid social contact (Jackson, 2021). COVID-19 has showed that how much lacks we are having even after so much advancements in our life; humans are so fragile that we were not prepared for any kind of such pandemics which has covered the whole world in days. In this digital world where the economy and algorithms were the prophets through the knowledge and information gathered by big data where the hotels can predict and forecast the coming years plans, but a small virus has changed everything (Del Valle, 2020).

The deaths counted globally due to COVID-19 till May 2022 was about six million and the overall infected cases were 527 million which are the registered cases, and according to WHO, a more number of people died and infected from these numbers.

Europe and Asian Hospitality Industry Economical Stats

The hospitality sector is the backbone of economy and supports the economy and millions of people worldwide are attached to this sector and that is why it is counted one of the biggest industries. Travel and tourism contributed an estimated 2,191 billion euros to European GDP in 2019, accounting for close to 10% of the EU's total GDP (GDP). Tourism accounts for more than 6% of total employment in the EU, with some countries, such as Greece, Italy, and Croatia, accounting for more than 30% of total employment. It is intertwined with many other industries, such as food, transportation, and lodging, and has an impact on the GDP generated by other industries. It also influences the appeal of places, not just as tourist destinations, but as places to live, work, invest, and study. In 2019, the hospitality sector in Europe employed approximately 38 million people, with 281.3 million international tourists visiting Europe, with 65 million visiting Italy, and 55 million visiting Turkey. The tourism industry has been heavily damaged by the coronavirus outbreak and the impact on different tourist destinations in the EU has been asymmetrical and highly localized, reflecting differences in the types of tourism on offer, varying travel restrictions, the size of domestic tourism markets, exposure to international tourism, and the importance of tourism in the local economy.

Travel and Tourism Share Regionwise (2019)

The number of nights spent in EU tourist lodging establishments fell by 61% (1.1 billion) between April 2020 and March 2021 and the same in Asian countries. As a countrywise comparison of tourists arrival in 2019 prior to COVID-19, the top tourist destinations of Europe have faced the fall in arrival of tourists such as in Malta (-80%) and Spain (-78%) which was the largest declines among EU Member States with accessible data and then in Greece (-74%), Portugal (-70%), and Hungary (-66%).

Forecast by ADB

Economic growth fell to -3.2% in 2020 globally where the forecasted recovery is 5.9% for 2021 and 4.9% for 2022 (IMF, 2022). The GDP in Asia as per the ADB (Asian Development Bank) will rise up to 5.3% in 2023 which was 5.2% in 2022 and 6.9% in 2021; however, it was -0.8% in 2020.

Overcrowding perception, xenophobia, and ethnocentrism caused the spread of coronavirus during the epidemic; hence, the tourism industry in China is adversely affected by COVID-19 (Ma & Others, 2022). Prior to COVID-19, tourism in Asia and the Pacific was thriving and an increase in international tourists' arrival from 208 million to 360 million from 2010 to 2019. Millions of jobs created due to this rapid growth which made this industry as an important aspect of the region's development. The pandemic, on the other hand, interrupted international travel and wreaked havoc on tourism locations, businesses, and communities. Before the pandemic of COVID-19, tourist markets were influenced by market dynamics and consumer behavior, travel priorities, and advancements in tourism technology. The People's Republic of China (PRC), South Korea, Japan, Singapore, Maldives, Pakistan, and India are the top tourist-visiting countries in Asia and the Pacific. Before this pandemic the consumers were aware from the patterns; therefore, the hospitality industries focused on top destinations and their marketing and their products development efforts on increasing visitor numbers, contributing to "over tourism" sometimes. As an estimation, around 56% tourists traveled to Asia for pleasure, recreation, or vacation in 2018, and about 27% traveled for family, friends, religion, or health, and around 13% tourists traveled for job. From January to July 2021, travel restrictions contributed to a 95.3% reduction in international visitors to Asia and the Pacific, the world's greatest drop since the same time in 2019. Advancement in communications, transportation, automation, and finance helped to build and popularize low-cost airlines and alternative accommodation booking systems. The traveling to Asian countries was banned and restricted till July 2021 and for some areas it is still not opened and will maybe opened till 2023 and these areas are still under the radar due to the phases of COVID-19, Ebola, Omicron, and monkeypox. Some locations have begun to experiment and open their borders for domestic and international tourists with fewer quarantine procedures, especially for vaccinated visitors. Due to concerns about new phases of COVID-19 or any other infectious diseases in destinations and the potential of returning travelers will may take these infections home, the region's resumption of abroad travel has been fragile and inconsistent. The impact of travel restrictions on tourism and the economy as a whole has been significant.

In Asia and the Pacific (excluding China, Hong Kong, South Korea, and Singapore) the average GDP growth due to tourism fall from 5.5% to 0% in 2020 and the countries which were depending on tourism economy are suffering the outcomes which will last for long. Half of the world's heritage sites were closed in March 2021 which highlighted the extent to which tourism sustains the preservation of cultural heritage in the region. There were many tour cancellations in 2020 and 2021, with some asking for updated items in response to changing conditions, while others were forced to close (temporarily or permanently). Some began offering outdoor activities to domestic visitors, while others began offering digital tours or online experiences. There are various countries in Asia that are rich in natural beauty and have top attraction sites, ranging from the Himalayas to the beaches of the Philippines. Tourists from all over the world visit Asian countries throughout the year. Thailand (Phuket) is the most visited destination in Asia which is liked by the tourists due to its beaches, night life, and the food while China and India are the runner-up choices for tourists. Japan, Malaysia, Pakistan, Indonesia, Vietnam, South Korea, Maldives, Philippines, and Singapore are the main places which attracts millions of the tourists, and the tourism is the main player for the GDP of these countries.

Strategies Opted for Rebuilding Tourism After COVID-19 Pandemic in Asia

The reduction in visitor numbers highlighted the extent to which tourism underpins the preservation of cultural heritage in the region, as many sites suddenly lacked essential earnings for site upkeep and improvement. Operators have begun to provide digital tours in the hopes of reviving tourism. Travel is beneficial for self-improvement, education, and wellness. In 2017, the wellness industry generated $639 billion in revenue and employed over 18 million people, with Asia accounting for six of the top 10 wellness destinations. Nature-based travel has increased dramatically during the pandemic, notably among domestic tourists throughout in Asia and PRC especially. Furthermore, travel restrictions lowered air pollution emissions and cleaner air increased tourist appreciation for outdoor activities, emphasizing the significance of environmental protection once tourism returns. Theme parks have to implement strict social distancing and hygiene restrictions that have harmed earnings, such as partial closures and improved health measures. Major operators, on the other hand, opened new parks in 2021, and financial analysts predicted a record year for parks in 2022 in 2020 and early 2021. Park attendance in the China is restricted to domestic visitors due to COVID-19 laws while in other Asian and Pacific countries they have similar restrictions, but there are still some international visitors who are vaccinated and demonstrating that the region has potential. In Maldives and other tropical island countries, the beach locations were closed too while several remained open to domestic visitors and experimented with innovative techniques to draw visitors, such as customized digital packages and long-term stay discounts. Several cruise industry outbreaks grabbed international headlines and caused widespread concern. Ports refused entrance, and the United States slapped a no-sail order, effectively halting cruises in the region. Despite the fact that some operators have begun resuming services, passenger traffic remains low. Industrywide health guidelines are being developed to expedite the safe return of cruise tourism. By 2019, domestic travelers accounted for 80% of visitor arrivals in Asia and the Pacific, making urban travel one of the engines fueling tourism growth. However, every major city in the region has suffered considerable casualties. Bangkok was formerly one of the world's most visited cities, but it lost 14.5 million visitors in 2020 compared to 2019. During travel limitations, the PRC is working to promote home markets. In the PRC, tax-free shopping malls were constructed for domestic travelers who had returned from abroad or had made arrangements to travel in the future. The capacity of localities to keep visitors and inhabitants distinct will play a role in the success of reintroducing luxury travel. Business travel and the "meetings, incentives, conventions, and exhibitions" category were significant revenue drivers for the travel industry prior to COVID-19. The shape and timing of recovery is highly complex, given that the pandemic has resulted in a considerable increase in remote work and videoconferencing, and many organizations are paying increased attention to the environmental impact of business travel. Small businesses were the hardest hit, with many unable to cover fixed operational costs due to a lack of funds. Hotels, on the other hand, have begun to adapt their business models by offering specialized services and quarantine facilities away from other guests, or by starting new businesses such as food delivery or donating land to community gardens. The tourism industry is facing an unprecedented confluence of threats, including a global health alert, a plane shortage due to the Boeing 737 Max crisis, social demonization of travel, exaggerated and even false media offensives, climate catastrophes, sector taxes, operator and airline bankruptcies, and political instability and economic slowdown in large markets. All Asian countries were put under lockdown during the COVID-19 epidemic, with complete bans on travel and even domestic tourism. Due to the Corona phases, some countries have taken efforts to open their borders, while others have yet to do so. International tourist visits fell by 74% in 2020 compared to the previous year, resulting in economic losses of $1.7 trillion to $2.4 trillion in 2021, according to the United Nations Conference on Trade and Development. Governmental backing and appropriate measures have resurrected tourism in Asian countries, resulting in the creation of millions of jobs, and additional initiatives can aid in the long-term viability of tourism following COVID-19. During the COVID-19 outbreak, most countries enforced travel bans, affecting visitor movement, and as a result, every country's hospitality business has survived. After a year of COVID-19, several countries provided sufficient vaccination to their personnel and permitted tourists who had received vaccine to stay in their hotels, but tourist arrivals were still low. Different hotels in Europe offered different discounts and offers to attract tourists, such as some hotels offering significant discounts on group bookings for business meetings or stays, some hotels offering free extra nights, and some hotels offering discounts and awards to the first tourists who booked their hotels after the first wave of COVID-19. Free breakfast and discounted or free amenities or services, lower rates, work from home offers for employees working in MNCs abroad, free dinners, and lavish and luxury hotels offered affordable prices that drew a large number of tourists. Because most of Asia's countries are still developing, yet they do offer tourist attractions, hotels in these locations are mainly operated by family companies. The proprietors of these family-owned hotels have largely survived the initial wave of COVID-19 owing to closures, although some have reopened with sufficient sanitary standards. Without ongoing government support, the continued existence of businesses across the tourism ecosystem is in jeopardy, and while governments have taken impressive steps to cushion the blow to tourism, minimize job losses, and build recovery in 2021 and beyond, more needs to be done, and in a more coordinated manner, increasing the resiliency and sustainability of tourism. Due to COVID-19, the abrupt drop in tourist arrivals and resulting demand in the tourism sector has resulted in millions of job losses and economic hardships, as well as the extinction of many businesses, particularly micro, small, and medium-sized businesses that catered to tourists or worked in related industries. This section briefly looks at the main trends in tourism in Asia before COVID-19 to demonstrate the sector's dynamic development, on which many economies around the region were pinning hopes (Helble & Fink, 2020).

COVID-19 has altered the globe in every way imaginable and has had a tremendous influence on international travel, tourism demand, and the hospitality industry, which is one of the world's greatest jobs and is extremely vulnerable to significant shocks like as the COVID-19 pandemic (Chang & Others, 2020). In a "6 foot-tourism world," where sanitary safety would be at the core of a closed and restricted tourism development, there is a prospect of a reinforcement of the alternative and a greater delinking of tourism (Lapointe, 2020). Consumer behavior, demand and performance modeling, forecasting, destination and facilities administration, information systems, and quality of life would all receive more effort as the hospitality business positions itself post-COVID-19 (Assaf, Kock, & Tsionas, 2022). The COVID-19 pandemic serves as a wake-up call and an opportunity for the tourism industry to embrace mindfulness, trusting in its ability to reflect on current issues and pave a new path toward more compassionate and meaningful tourism for both hosts and guests (Stankov, Filimonau, & Vujii, 2020). More conscious consumers, who are more aware of their unconscious actions, purchase patterns, and enhanced ability to refuse the promise of false happiness, could help a postpandemic tourism economy. The new COVID-19 variant known as B.1.1.529 or Omicron began to spread in several nations at the end of 2021, prompting many governments to re-implement the COVID-19 preventive strategy (Saengtabtim, Leelawat, Tang, Suppasri, & Imamura, 2022). Consumerism and tourism should not be viewed as the exclusive means of achieving enjoyment, soul, and (economic) progress. COVID-19 tourism research should inspire tourists, companies, and destinations to reimagine and reset new mindsets, frontiers, and behaviors, such as how to use and develop tourism to valorize rather than consume tourism resources, to generate well-being, sustainability, and transformational learning (Gordon & Doraiswamy, 2020). Fear of COVID-19 has a good and large impact on work instability, job loss insecurity, and a negative and significant impact on job performance (Sun, Sarfraz, Khawaja, Ozturk, & Raza, 2022). The poverty rate has risen in the last half-year of the pandemic, creating a troubling situation and a hazy picture of shared associates. It is recommended that for a sustainable tourist industry, a quick response be implemented as a recovery initiative, assisting in the development of consensus and the formulation of guiding principles for small tourism businesses (Kalsoom & Alam, 2022). At the moment, each country's government is dealing with and mitigating the COVID-19 crisis by declaring suitable answers and steps. The majority of these solutions and measures entail collaboration among several stakeholders, including citizens, governments, and businesses. Despite Social isolation and a state of lockdown in 2019, the tourism sector in South Asia generated USD 234 billion, or 6.6% of the region's GDP. Countries like the Maldives and Mauritius have had major problems since the COVID-19 pandemic shut down their tourism businesses completely. Tourism must be revived in these counties; else, their postpandemic economic recovery would be severely hampered (Gadkari, 2022). Hotels in the United States, like those in Europe, have used a variety of techniques to attract travelers.

Recommendations and Discussions

The travel and tourism sector were one of the world's largest and fastest-growing industries until the end of 2019, with about 1.47 billion international tourists earning $1.7 trillion in international tourism profits. International tourist arrivals climbed in every region, with Asia and the Pacific seeing a 7% increase in 2018 and a 4% increase in 2019. Asia and the Pacific accounted for around 26% of global growth in 2019, with the Southeast Asia subregion accounting for over 70% of the region's growth. Traditional business models of hotels need to be revised where all the catering and accommodation services protocols will have new norms to cope the pandemics in future. The products, supply chain networks, distribution system, marketing, consumption, and most importantly the sustainable goals of hospitality industry will be reconstructed. Another thing is the customers behavior which is changed now due to this pandemic and hotels should develop the products and strategies by keeping the customers demand in view and hygiene products, health, and sustainability should be focused (Del Valle, 2020). Government involvement can help in bringing the tourists back with an ease in visa processes and provision of health facilities like insurance at the government level with minimum prices. The fear of pandemic is also stopping tourists which need to be handled, and if the hotels are taking proper safety measures which can prevent these kind of infectious diseases, then tourists can plan for their trips. Most of the hotels are family businesses hotels and all of them have gone through the worst days of pandemic and they are not financially stable and government should either provide the loans with no mark up or lower mark up or these hotels should get foreign aid. Travel bubbles are helping where the neighbor countries are offering special discounts for each other to promote the tourism and the hotels are offering special discounted packages for the tourists of each other. The closure of borders is impacting the tourism industry as we can see that China has closed its borders again which is bringing down the confidence of tourists and now the planned trips to China are diverted by tourists to other countries. Hotels can work with the online traveling agencies and platforms like OYO, Booking.com, Kayak, Qunar, and TripAdvisor to provide guaranteed hygiene rooms for any kind of bookings with discounted meals. Some of the big chain hotels are using technologies to provide contactless services for the visitors with self check-in, virtual reality, artificial intelligence, robots for room service, and voice-controlled services are being provided. Such services will help in future against any kind of pandemic like nowadays the monkeypox is spreading but these humanless services will help the tourists. Another thing is about using artificial intelligence and big data in family business hotels which are larger in number around the globe, but the management or the owners of these hotels are not well informed about the usage of modern technologies. Most of the domestic tourists and some of international tourists prefer to stay in these economical hotels, and due to COVID-19, the adoption of hygiene protocols, sanitizing the rooms and utensils, and usage of disposable products are basic requirements which these hotels need to provide.

References

Assaf, A. G., Kock, F., & Tsionas, M. (2022). Tourism during and after COVID-19: An expert-informed agenda for future research. *Journal of Travel Research*, *61*(2), 454–457.

Aswani, N., & Aswani, B. (2021, December 1). Riyadh Season 2021: Everything You Need to Know About. Travelwings. Travelwings.com. Retrieved from https://journal.travelwings.com/everything-you-need-to-know-about-saudi-arabia-riyadh-season-2021/

Bisby, J. A., Burgess, N., & Brewin, C. R. (2020). Reduced memory coherence for negative events and its relationship to posttraumatic stress disorder. *Current Directions in Psychological Science*, *29*(3), 269–272.

Chang, C. L., McAleer, M., & Ramos, V. (2020). A charter for sustainable tourism after COVID-19. *Sustainability*, *12*(9), 3671.

Del Valle, A. S. (2020). *The tourism industry and the impact of Covid-19, scenarios and proposals*. Madrid: Global Journey Consulting.

Gadkari, A. (2022). Resetting tourism after COVID-19 with particular emphasis on South Asia. *Environmental Sciences Proceedings*, *15*(1), 39.

Gordon, J., & Doraiswamy, P. M. (2020). High anxiety calls for innovation in digital mental health. In *World Economic Forum*.

Helble, M., & Fink, A. (2020). Reviving tourism amid the COVID-19 Pandemic1. Retrieved from

https://ec.europa.eu/eurostat/web/products-eurostat-news/-/ddn-20210625-2

https://www.europarl.europa.eu/RegData/etudes/BRIE/2021/696166/EPRS_BRI(2021)696166_EN.pdf

https://www.qs.com/revival-of-the-tourism-industry-in-2021/

IMF. (2022). *World economic outlook*. [online] Retrieved from https://www.imf.org/en/Publications/WEO#:~:text=Description%3A%20The%20global%20economy%20is

Jackson, J. K. (2021). *Global economic effects of COVID-19*. Congressional Research Service.

Jamshaid, S., Malik, N. I., Haider, A. A., Jamshed, K., & Jamshad, S. (2020, December). Overthinking hurts: rumination, worry and mental health of international students in China during Covid-19 pandemic. In *International Joint Conference on Arts and Humanities (IJCAH 2020)* (pp. 17–24). Atlantis Press.

Jamshaid, S., Olorundare, A., Wang, L., Lo-Ngoen, N., Afzal, M. I., & Bibi, M. (2022). Global pandemic fear and international students: Negative thoughts, mental and physical well-being. In *Innovation on education and social sciences* (pp. 111–120). London: Taylor & Francis Group.

Kalsoom, B., & Alam, M. (2022). The impact of COVID-19 pandemic on small tourism enterprises in Pakistan. In *COVID-19 and the tourism industry* (pp. 252–266). Taylor & Francis Group.

Lapointe, D. (2020). Reconnecting tourism after COVID-19: The paradox of alterity in tourism areas. *Tourism Geographies, 22*(3), 633–638.

Ma, Z., Wahid, F., Baseer, S., AlZubi, A. A., & Khattak, H. (2022). Influence of COVID-19 on the tourism industry in China: An artificial neural networks approach. *Journal of Healthcare Engineering, 2022*.

Saengtabtim, K., Leelawat, N., Tang, J., Suppasri, A., & Imamura, F. (2022). Consequences of COVID-19 on health, economy, and tourism in Asia: A systematic review. *Sustainability, 14*(8), 4624.

Sigala, M. (2020). Tourism and COVID-19: Impacts and implications for advancing and resetting industry and research. *Journal of Business Research, 117*, 312–321.

Stankov, U., Filimonau, V., & Vujičić, M. D. (2020). A mindful shift: An opportunity for mindfulness-driven tourism in a post-pandemic world. *Tourism Geographies, 22*(3), 703–712.

Sun, J., Sarfraz, M., Khawaja, K. F., Ozturk, I., & Raza, M. A. (2022). The perils of the pandemic for the tourism and hospitality industries: Envisaging the combined effect of COVID-19 fear and job insecurity on employees' job performance in Pakistan. *Psychology Research and Behavior Management, 15*, 1325.

World Travel, & Tourism Council (WTTC). (2022, February 2). News Article | World Travel & Tourism Council (WTTC). https://wttc.org/news-article/travel-and-tourism-could-grow-to-8-point-6-trillion-usd-in-2022-say-wttc

Synthesizing Theories for Resilient Medical Tourism

Kasturi Shukla and Avadhut Patwardhan

Abstract

Medical tourism demands tremendous responsiveness and accountability. The *triple bottom line* in medical tourism indicates that these organizations must emphasize on economic profits, environmental protection, and conservation of social resources. Developing a resilient medical tourism ecosystem is another critical necessity after the COVID-19 pandemic. The present study attempts to study the various aspects of medical tourism while synthesizing the relevant theories. This synthesis was used to propose a framework for developing a resilient medical tourism system. The outcomes of the chapter also propose the long, medium, and short-term goals. These goals focus on relevant stakeholders for developing highly integrated and resilient medical-tourism destinations.

Keywords: Medical tourism; resilience; destination; model; healthcare; wellness

Introduction

The COVID-19 pandemic has significantly impacted at individual and business levels. The pandemic not only eroded the bottom lines (financial losses) but also challenged the strategic and operational efficiencies of the businesses. The impact was at social levels (unmeasurable human loss), economic levels (huge amount of losses), and individual levels (psychological) (Partington & Inman, 2020). Service sector industries like travel, tourism and healthcare were deeply affected due to the pandemic and the resultant shrinkage of supply and demand due to lockdown (Seetharaman, 2020; Rishe, 2020).

These actions like lock-down have impacted the tourism industry which was predicted to see a massive decline (20%–30%) in international travel movements (Liu, Wen, Kozak, Jiang, & Li, 2022). Majority of the countries have imposed

Resilient and Sustainable Destinations After Disaster, 121–137
Copyright © 2023 Kasturi Shukla and Avadhut Patwardhan
Published under exclusive licence by Emerald Publishing Limited
doi:10.1108/978-1-80382-021-720231010

travel bans, canceled visa on arrival and ensured an almost complete entry and exit ban through air including other routes. Pandemic led to grounding of airplanes and closing down of hotels. This decline was predicted to result into a huge economic loss of 300–450 Billion US$ (Liu et al., 2022). These travel bans affected the medical tourism sector and there is still a sustained impact on prospective medical tourists due to multiple factors.

The challenge to revamp medical tourism indicates a lack of resilience and a need to build sustainable and resilient medical tourism destinations. In light of these happenings the researchers opined that the revamping exercise necessitates the participation and involvement of various stakeholders including government, public administration, travel facilitators, academicians, and researchers working in tourism sectors (Kamassi, Abd Manaf, & Omar, 2020; Liu et al., 2022). Therefore, this chapter aims to fulfill two key objectives related to resilient medical tourism.

(1) To understand the aspects associated with the resilient medical tourism ecosystem.
(2) To synthesize the theories for redesigning the resilient medical tourism ecosystem.

The chapter is written systematically in four sections as shown in Fig. 1. The *introduction* section discussed the preamble and aims of the study. The second section informs about the *aspects* related to medical tourism. The third section highlights the *relevance of key theories* considered. The last section details about the *outcomes of synthesis* and recommendations.

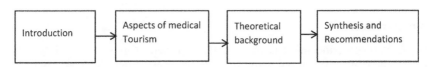

Fig. 1.   Structure of the Chapter. *Source:* Author Contribution.

Aspects of Medical Tourism

This section discusses various aspects like concept of and the push and pull factors relevant with the medical tourism.

Concept of Medical Tourism

Any travel aimed toward improving one's health status is known as medical tourism (Wong, Velasamy, & Arshad, 2014). Medical Tourism is classified into two broad categories – *therapeutic* (for surgical treatment, cosmetic surgery, and alternative therapies) and *nontherapeutic or wellness* (health promotion, recreation, and leisure) (Gautam & Bhatta, 2020). These travel plans are known as Medical Value Travel (MVT) and the tour service providers are the MVT facilitators (Global Wellness Institute [GWI], 2018). Further, the consumption behaviors for these two categories are different. The medical tourists demand strong therapeutic services like, surgical services, organ transplant, dental procedures, fertility treatments including many others (Liu et al., 2022). Wellness tourists are consumers demand for spas, lifestyle resorts, spiritual retreats, and Indigenous medicine like Ayurveda, Yoga, and naturopathy to maintain/promote health by staying at the facilities particularly designed for holistic enhancement of well-being (Sharafuddin & Madhavan, 2020; Voigt, 2013).

The Pull and Push Factors Relevant With Medical Tourism

From the marketing perspective, the pull factors are those that attract the customers to a tourism destination and push factors *push away* and force the customers to look for other *options*. Psychological aspects like needs, wants, and benefits act as motives for medical tourism (Crouch, Perdue, Timmermans, & Uysal, 2004; Pizam, Mansfeld, & Chon, 1999). Further, factors like affordability, availability of advanced technology, and better quality of care provided influence the medical tourism decision (Sharma, Vishraj, Ahlawat, Mittal, & Mittal, 2020). The factors like waiting time, unavailability of medical insurance, and legal factors, rendering some procedures as illegal in any country, act as strong push factors. The demand–supply cycle is strengthened by the low-cost high-quality luxurious treatment facilities enabling even the most budget conscious traveler to get services from highly talented and skilled healthcare workers (HCWs) (Reddy, 2022). The critical push factors for many patients of Western countries is the lack of insurance and lack of surgeons and long waiting times (Brown, Johnson, Ozan-Rafferty, Sharma, & Barbera, 2020). The affordable high quality medical services in the Asian countries combined with well-known tourism opportunities create a strong *pull* for all such patients (De Zordo et al., 2021; Wong et al., 2014). It is a well known fact that perceived service quality, satisfaction, trust, and perceived reasonableness of price are the critical pull factors for spreading a positive word of mouth, especially, in the postpurchase stage (Han & Hyun, 2015). This makes hospitality, recreation and leisure relevant in the context of medical tourism (GWI, 2018). However, these studies have explored medical tourism, either from the supply-side or the demand-side perspective. In order to build a resilient medical tourism ecosystem, application of various theories and analysis from multiple stakeholder perspectives is required. The upcoming sections present a synthesis of such relevant theories and propose an action plan for developing a resilient medical tourism ecosystem.

Theoretical Background

The medical tourism ecosystem consisted of multiple stakeholders. These stakeholders are medical tourists, healthcare providers, government agencies, facilitators, accrediting bodies, marketers, insurance providers, and infrastructure (Kamassi et al., 2020). Therefore, to create resilient medical tourism ecosystem, it is inevitable to enhance the degree of integration among the various stakeholders. Primarily, the healthcare tourists visit a destination for enhancing wellness or for availing medical/surgical treatment. Hence, integrating these organizations seamlessly in the tourism value chain is the key for developing marketable destinations by bringing together accommodation, health and tourism infrastructure, various service providers, air and ground transport, and government support (Dash & Sharma, 2021). A comprehensive package with all pre-booked services that ensures a hassle-free and seamless medical tourism experience that attracts the tourists (Liu et al., 2022). The next section discusses the role and relevance of various stakeholders.

Role and Relevance of Various Stakeholders

This section has broadly covered the role and relevance of infrastructure, providers and government. In addition to government support (for foreign travel), service providers like hospitals, diagnostic and surgical facilities, hotels and restaurants, mind body studios, natural and recreational amenities, spiritual organizations are the main attractions. The process of value chain creation involves various health resorts, spa, wellness retreats, thermal and mineral springs, and Indigenous wellness and medical centers and other integrative health centers that provide leisure and rejuvenation (Liu et al., 2022). Airport facilities like concierge services, pick and drop, multilingual support staff (drivers, attendants), and providing safety measures especially for solo and female travelers are value additions (Dash & Sharma, 2021; Wong et al., 2014). Internationally, quality accredited hospitals are treated as a promising destination in the post-crisis era. Further, linking technology (e.g., telemedicine) for reaching out to foreign patients is a tool that can be used to create resilient systems (Liu et al., 2022). Infrastructural differentiators combined with multilingual trained staff like doctors, nurses, and healthcare professionals create a smooth communication system with foreign nationals (Wong et al., 2014).

Government is a key stakeholder for promoting medical tourism, healthcare, and investment through integration of ministries like tourism, external affairs, health and family welfare, and finance. For instance, in March 2022, Ministry of Tourism, Government of India, has started "Medical Visa," "e− Medical Visa," and "e-Medical Attendant Visa" for specific purposes to foreign medical travelers from 156 countries (Reddy, 2022). A strong support from the government to standardize healthcare services and extending support in the form of grants, subsidies, and incentives are required to enhance the reliability among international patients for the developments of tourism infrastructure (Sharma et al., 2020). These initiatives will also support the small and medium-sized companies whose working capital has fallen by almost 60%–80% (Dash & Sharma, 2021). The government interventions are also required for addressing the increased hygiene, sanitation, and safety-related measures (Liu et al., 2022). One of the major supports required from external affairs and foreign ministries is to devise policies for smooth visa issue, visa on arrival, and hassle-free visa extension as per medical recommendation. Beyond the external stakeholders, the emphasis of internal capabilities cannot be undermined. The service triangle model is the appropriate framework to identify strategies for developing resilient medical tourism destinations which is elaborated in the next section.

Appropriateness of Service Triangle Model

The healthcare sector follows the unique characteristics of services. Therefore, the service marketing concepts, frameworks, models, and theories become imperative to medical tourism (Yadav & Dabhade, 2013). The *Service Triangle Model* (introduced in 1970's) emphasizes on the three prominent dimensions, namely, internal, external, and interactive marketing (Kotler & Keller, 2009). The *external marketing* explores the interactions between the service provider and customers. The *interactive marketing* deals with the interactions between the employees of the service organization and customers. The *internal marketing* deals with the inter-actions between employees (treated as "internal" customers) and the organizations. The effectiveness of interactive marketing majorly depends on the efficiency of the employees. Further, the efficiency of the employees is a result of internal marketing of the organization (Malhotra, Uslay, & Bayraktar, 2007).

According to the internal marketing process flow, the employees are the first set of customers (Bose & Pillai, 2019) who understand the core idea, attributes and aspects, and the delivery process of the service product. The effectiveness of the organization is dependent on the effectiveness of internal customers. There-fore, the healthcare services researchers (Tsai, 2014) reported that the satisfied employees lead to satisfied customers. This requires strengthened internal mar-keting efforts by providing financial and nonfinancial recognition to employees to build resilient healthcare systems.

It was experienced that the healthcare system was unprepared for the COVID-19 pandemic disaster which impacted the frontline health workers drastically. Furthermore, the multitude of factors (like shortage of Personal Protective Equipment (PPEs), high levels of stress, anxiety and burnout, extended working hours, isolation from home, risk of catching infection, fear of carrying the infection back to their homes and family members, fear of death, and physical and mental exhaustion due to high patient load) contributed to the decline in health status in all dimensions (Chakraborty & Chakraborty, 2015). Since the pandemic began, almost half of the HCWs continue to report serious psychiatric symptoms, including suicidal ideation. This impact indicated the importance of assessment and maintenance of Work-Related Quality of Life (WRQoL) of health professionals. Hence, integrating the WRQoL perspectives with previously discussed theories and models may help in establishing the resilient medical tourism ecosystem. The rationale and relevance of WRQoL are reported in the next section.

Rationale and Relevance of Work-Related Quality of Life

WRQoL is an evidence-based outcome measure of quality of work life. It examines employee contentment for intervention planning, workforce monitoring, and helps in introducing organizational change and resilience (Easton & Van Laar, 2018). It is a relevant measure for the sectors where employees work under sustained stress like healthcare (Van et al., 2007). WRQoL is measured across six factors, namely: Job and Career Satisfaction, General Well-Being, Home–Work Interface, Stress at Work, Control at Work, and Working Conditions.

Recent literature suggested that COVID-19 pandemic has distressed the already burdened healthcare systems which has a direct impact on the WRQoL of HCWs (Suryavanshi et al., 2020). WRQoL assessment is viewed as a reflection of the internal marketing practices in healthcare organizations. If the WRQoL of healthcare professionals is low, it is likely to affect their interactions with tourists (Customers). Research has showed the importance of measures taken by hospitals, support from the hospital toward employees and organizational preparedness (Creese et al., 2021; Hynes, Trump, Love, & Linkov, 2020). Similarly, loneliness and neighborhood perception toward HCWs have a tremendous impact on their mental health and QoL (Saltzman, Hansel, & Bordnick, 2020). The social stigma, financial loss, and job insecurity among health professionals demand recovery strategies that can help the employees and organization bounce back to regular functioning (Hamouche, 2020).

Recent studies have shown that almost half of the health professionals have reported serious psychiatric symptoms, including suicidal ideation (Saltzman et al., 2020). Resilience is a strong determinant of WRQoL and those with higher resilience are known to be better able to adapt to changes and unforeseen challenges (Keener, Hall, Wang, Hulsey, & Piamjariyakul, 2021; Young et al., 2021). The synthesis of perspectives indicates that a resilient ecosystem suitable for medical tourism demands integration of individuals (Healthcare and non-healthcare professionals), organizations (Both healthcare and nonhealthcare service providers) and other environmental aspects. The interrelation between these aspects is presented as Fig. 2. The synthesis and other discussions are detailed in the next section.

Synthesis and Recommendations

Resilience at individual, organizational and social level is "Cumulative Resilience" which has been an essential dimension for creating resilient ecosystem for medical tourism. The employees with better WRQoL ensure higher resilience which may lay the foundation of organizational resilience. The organizational resilience intern would help in establishing resilient environment effectively. This logic is supported by the studies which reported that enterprise-based and human-centered categories aid in finer understanding of the elements that drive resilience (Moti, 2020). In addition to individual resilience, organizational resilience has been identified as a strong contributor to WRQoL of employees by

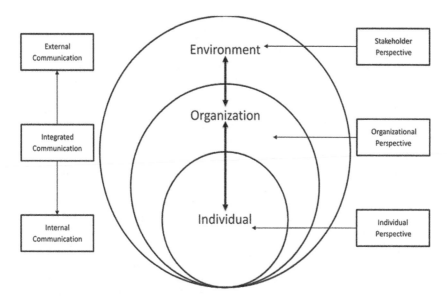

Fig. 2.   Conceptual Framework for Resilient Medical Tourism
Ecosystems. *Source:* Author Contribution.

achieving timely and flexible behavioral responses to a crisis which was much
needed during COVID-19 pandemic (Zhang, Dong, & Yi, 2020). Past research
has highlighted the various foundations of organizational resilience and
capability-based conceptualization of organizational resilience (Moti, 2020).
These conceptualizations included synergy cocreation with various stakeholders,
transforming and transformational catalysts, resource planning and protection,
leadership, culture and communication, monitoring and review, and learning and
change (Chhabra, 2020). Considering these researches, the further synthesis is
presented.

Synthesis

In case of resilient ecosystem for medical tourism, it is essential to view the
components of communication. While planning for medical tourism, a large
number of people are apprehensive to travel to a new place. Lack of awareness
about the local culture, dialects, and fear of being left alone in the host country
are few of the reasons behind these apprehensions. In case of such situation the
relevant reference groups help the medical tourism organizations. Therefore,
understanding the aspects related to reference group becomes crucial.

A person's reference membership group consists of all the groups (like family,
friends, and office colleagues) that have a direct or indirect influence on his/her
attitude, behavior, and decisions (Kotler & Keller, 2009). The members of

reference group experience more frequent and largely informal interaction. Primary reference groups usually consist of the health-conscious family members or friends, particularly someone who has availed these services and returned to home country. The secondary reference groups require a closer integration with stakeholders like, doctors, health professionals, and MVT companies for attracting patients for medical tourism. Reference groups help in managing the follow-up care and minimizing the strong positive opinion for the host country (Brown et al., 2020). These interactions result in word-of-mouth which has a substantial impact on the consumption (Liu et al., 2022). Therefore, these group members are crucial considering the external marketing communications (Kotler & Keller, 2009). Hence, the medical tourism organizations and stakeholders need to identify the relevant reference groups and members.

The three essential objectives for any medical tourism destination are: tourist satisfaction, economic development, and tourists' health and well-being. This indicates that medical tourism organizations need to respond to the environment by creating relevant value propositions. The value proposition needs to be reinforced combined with COVID-safety compliant services and hygienic spaces. The COVID appropriate behavior (CAB) compliance is the most crucial ingredient for completing the value chain of medical tourism (MOHFW, 2020). The advancements in the environment are demanding establishment of value networks. This concept focuses on identifying target markets and designing the supply chain to address the customer's demands on priority basis (Kotler & Keller, 2009). This is done through the *SIVA* model that involves: *Solutions, Information, Value, and Access.* The sequence is essentially important as solutions are the critical component based on the needs, wants, and demands of the target markets (Liu et al., 2022).

Solutions offered need to focus on domestic population, safety and hygiene protocols, creating spaces for healthy lifestyle and exercise, advanced health centers, ethical systems, and ensure safety for solo/women travellers. Highly integrated value chain of all stakeholders, and establishing foreign connection through telemedicine or offshore centers is also critical. Disseminating information about all such initiatives, quality systems and benefits, government rules, and value-added services have to be communicated to the target market. Further, addressing feedback, support systems for the postpurchase stage and reinforcement through media goes a long way in creating positive image and customer loyalty.

Information. Spreading information, through promotions and digital marketing, is inevitable to reinstate medical tourism. The essential information that needs to be rigorously disseminated is government initiatives, visa support, availability of high quality and accredited services, safety and hygiene assurance, and personalized tourism and leisure activities.

Value creation is the need of the hour with tourists being spoilt for choices due to multiple substitutesdue to multiple substitutes (Rosenbusch, Ismail, & Ringle, 2018). Therefore, introducing highly integrated medical value travel chain with comprehensive and attractively priced packages covering end-to-end services has becomes a critical aspect for medical tourism organizations. Some of the components that are considered in such packages could be air and ground transport, accommodation and airport concierge services, meal choices, treatment packages, hospital and hotels accommodations, tourism options, and posttreatment follow-up care after the return to the home country. Asian countries are known to provide best quality treatments with authentic tourism experiences for which Thailand, Malaysia, Singapore, and India are best known (Wong et al., 2014) out of which India has a unique cost advantage in addition to having a strong heritage of alternative medicine and wellness care (Hafizan et al., 2018).

Finally, ensuring *Access* through supportive government policies, medical visa, and smooth transportation chain at all stages of travel, high "digital" visibility through interactive websites, online customer support in their mother tongue, and closely integrated services by medical value travel aggregators.

The proposed framework ensures fulfillment of the four factors (SIVA) and hence could be considered as useful framework for establishing resilient medical tourism ecosystem. Along with the logical representations the authors have also done the underpinning for determining the factors which may impact the framework. The post-COVID era has seen booming opportunities for alternative medicines and wellness tourism due to the lockdown, sustained stress, and mental exhaustion (Gautam & Bhatta, 2020; Sharafuddin & Madhavan, 2020). It was reported that the avenues and modalities which provide wellness are searched frequently for mental relaxation and emotional healing (Maitra & Joseph, 2022). The medical tourism can be *inbound* (within one's own country) or *outbound* (visiting a foreign country). In terms of locations considered, the medical tourists visit destinations like India for well-developed alternative medicine systems such as Ayurveda (Gautam & Bhatta, 2020). In the post-COVID times, most of the Asian destinations have marketed themselves as COVID-safety compliant, vaccinated staff, and abiding by the protocols (Dash & Sharma, 2021). These aspects indicate that medical tourists have preferences related to the location.

These deliberations indicate that one of the factors which could influence the medical tourism is the country-of-origin effect/perceptions toward host country. This factor looks relevant because the countries have differences in terms environment, organizations, and individuals. Therefore, different countries would have different effects on the perceptions of medical tourists.

Country-of-origin effect is the perceptions, mental associations, and beliefs that are triggered by the image of a country in the minds of customers (Kotler & Keller, 2009). The stakeholders are integral in developing and disseminating country-of-origin effects. In the postpandemic and recovery era, these effects and perceptions have a tremendous effect on the decisions made by the tourists for finalizing the destination. Before the COVID-19 pandemic, India earned US$2.3 billion yearly from its health and medical tourism sector (Maitra & Joseph, 2022) which demands serious efforts for image building post-COVID-19 pandemic. Majority of the countries are experiencing the challenge of recreating image – the image that could assure the medical tourists about safety and hygiene. Managing country-of-origin effect is necessary for long-term associations and engagements with present and potential customers.

Research studies have reinforced that providing a strong structural support and including the best compliance practices and safety protocols could help in re-building both tourist confidence, and organizational resilience. Such initiatives would also help managing country-of-origin perceptions (Dash & Sharma, 2021). In 2017–2018, India, Thailand, and Turkey were among the top five destinations for medical tourism out of which India and Thailand have the advantage of widely spoken English language (Hafizan et al., 2018). Further, both countries have well-developed medical services and a rich heritage of traditional Indigenous alternative medicine systems like Thai medicine and Thai herbs for physical and mind therapy (Thailand), Malaysia (spa industry), and Ayurveda and yoga in India (Brown et al., 2020; Sopha, Jittithavorn, & Lee, 2019). However, there are many challenges to create a positive perception like poor visitor experiences (expressed in negative online reviews), travel logistics (long flights, having to get passports, cumbersome visa process for medical travel), lack of capital compared with other countries, poor or unsafe country image, and negative feedback of healthcare infrastructure. Unavailability of trustworthy or verifiable information online poses a major drawback (Brown et al., 2020). The proposed framework indicates integration of policies, practices, and performances for cumulative resilience.

Implications

Interdisciplinary research approaches and online promotions can bring out the theoretical frameworks to build sustainable and resilient medical tourism ecosystem (Liu et al., 2022). However, the research recommends to address the treatment and wellness offerings separately. Even though these offerings offer different outcomes, the dependence on hospitality infrastructure is common (GWI, 2018). Hence, it is recommended that a general attention to basic tourism infrastructure is inevitable to benefit both the sectors (GWI, 2018). The proposed framework introduced the logical linkages between the relevant stakeholders and defined the importance of cumulative resilience. This framework would help the organizations in addressing the differences and leveraging the commonalities.

As an importance aspect of the proposed framework, the role and relevance of internal, integrated, and external communication is underlined. Therefore, destination marketing (external marketing) is a key component of resilient medical tourism ecosystem. The evolving medical tourism industry is combining the travel, treatment, and wellness. In the post-pandemic era, healthcare quality assurance will be an even more essential factor to create trust and credibility in the minds of international patients (Sharma et al., 2020). This unique combination is enabling an experience of coworking, coliving, and travel while promoting exposure to other countries and cultures (GWI, 2018). Many companies provide on-site wellness/fitness amenities, yoga classes, meditation, and other community events. This can also be one of the strategies to promote and market the destinations.

Along with the communication, it is essential to fulfill the promise made. Availability of well-defined medical and wellness services has transformed the tourism destinations into state-of-the-art treatment destinations (Wong et al.,

2014). Majority of marketing efforts for medical tourism are emphasizing on assurance of amenities and access to state-of-the-art treatment infrastructure. The nations (like Thailand, Malaysia, Singapore, Argentina, Brazil, Turkey, Mexico, Costa Rica, and India) have implemented travel policies and developed and promoted infrastructural aspects to increase the medical tourism (Brown et al., 2020; Warangkana & Supawat, 2020; Wong et al., 2014). The countries like Sri Lanka, Nepal, and Bhutan have linked the medical tourism experiences with yoga, meditation, spirituality, pilgrimage, Indigenous medicine, faith healing, and happiness (e.g., Costa Rica's "Wellness Pura Vida" tourism campaign, Source: GWI, 2018). Further, these targeted and authentic initiatives are acting as a *pull* for the customers (GWI, 2018; Zolfagharian, Rajamma, Naderi, & Torkzadeh, 2018). Besides the above strategies, countries like Thailand have developed offshore medical centers in various countries (Wong et al., 2014). These centers refer the patients and the people seeking wellness services to Thailand hospitals thus creating an inflow of patients. The unique specialties like yoga, Naturopathy and Ayurveda for India and similar such treatments which are the forte of the destination must be highlighted and exploited as opportunities. Many patients have stated the benefits they received by following alternative medicine like Ayurveda (Brown et al., 2020).

These aspects indicate the relevance of SIVA model and also produce the evidence for the proposed framework. Corroborating previous research, we propose that tourism management and destination marketing are usually done at geographic level (macro), community level (meso), and enterprise (micro) levels (Mtapuri, Giampiccoli, & Jugmohan, 2021; Sigala, 2020). As an implication, the authors propose that the stakeholders may use the proposed framework to set the short-, medium-, and long-term targets. The details are presented in Table 1.

Table 1. Implications of the Proposed Framework.

	Micro-Environment (Organizational Level)	Meso-Environment (Community Level)	Macro-Environment (Policy Level)
Short-term focus	• *Research* – Identify the market demand through online surveys, media reports, and available literature. • *Internal marketing* – Hospitals, hotels, and service organizations to provide financial and nonfinancial	• *Focus on Local* - Don't lose focus on domestic population for better local support. • Emphasize on the unique services available for medical and wellness tourists. • Reinforce [a]CABs and COVID-safety protocols locally	• Ministries and government departments need to strengthen digital marketing for global connect. • Intensify the communication about COVID-safety compliant destinations.

Table 1. *(Continued)*

	Micro-Environment (Organizational Level)	Meso-Environment (Community Level)	Macro-Environment (Policy Level)
	"recovery" boosters to employees for improving their WRQoL.	among all social systems for better country image among foreigners.	
Medium-term focus	• Develop *attractive all-inclusive packages* for medical and Wellness tourism. • *Strong stakeholder integration* – Medical Value Travel (MVT) facilitators to create a hassle-free value chain of all service providers. • Create *offshore centre network* for increased patient referrals units in target countries. • Identify *Primary and secondary reference groups* of target customers and apply targeted marketing strategies.	• Develop COVID-safety compliant hospitality, recreation, and leisure centers. • Creating *Safe and secure destinations* especially for solo or female travelers or those traveling with kids. • Complete *vaccination* of staff members, hospitals, and all service providers to medical tourists. • Promote inbound tourism among domestic population. • Focus on WRQoL of HCWs. • Promote "*Vaccine Tourism*" (TOI, 2021).	• Create *interactive platforms* on government websites with live chatting facility in multiple languages. • Smooth Visa facility, transport, and concierge services at airport and multilingual staff. • Strengthening technological support for better *Telemedicine* and online counselling and consultation during prepurchase and postpurchase (recovery) stages. • *Grants and subsidies* and incentivizing investments in tourism infrastructure.
Long-term focus	• Identify past beneficiaries and integrate them for	• General social compliance of safety and	• Exploiting the potential of traditional alternative medical

Table 1. *(Continued)*

Micro-Environment (Organizational Level)	Meso-Environment (Community Level)	Macro-Environment (Policy Level)
feedbacks and testimonials. • Word-of-mouth marketing and testimonials should always be in focus. • Promoting *international accreditations* for better global visibility and credibility. • Through necessary support to employees, build employee and organizational resilience.	hygienic practices. • Promote local handicrafts, heritage, culture, artifacts, and traditional medicine. • Focus on *cumulative resilience* through top-down and bottom-up approach.	systems through *package pricing and promoting the same.* • Developing and marketing "*Onsite" tourism destinations for professionals* posted in the host country for co-working and travel combined with tourism. • Curbing and *responsively handling any spread of negativity* by news and media for the host country. • Reduce the number of licenses to start a business and lower tax deductions on CSR expenses.

Source: Author Contribution.

[a]Covid Appropriate Behavior (CAB).

Many regions are developing a truly authentic and place-based medical tourism product (like the state of Kerala, India, is branded as the "Land of Ayurveda"). This is a useful strategy to loop in the potential customers for healthcare tourism considering the post-pandemic situations.

Unlike other tourism sectors, healthcare tourism is unique and demands a lot more responsiveness and accountability. The "triple bottom line" in healthcare tourism indicates that the organizations working in this industry must emphasize on economic profits, protection of the environment, and conservation of social resources (Liu et al., 2022). Hence, a stronger focus on "triple bottom line" combined with highly integrated stakeholders can go a long way in building and marketing a well-developed and resilient medical tourism ecosystem.

References

Bose, G. P., & Pillai, P. R. (2019). Differentiating the concept of internal marketing and human resource management-a comparative study on the existing literature. *International Journal of Applied Engineering Research, 14*(8), 1917–1922.

Brown, J., Johnson, J., Ozan-Rafferty, M. E., Sharma, M., & Barbera, S. (2020). Internet narratives focused on health Travelers' experiences in India: Qualitative analysis. *Journal of Medical Internet Research, 22*(5). doi:10.2196/15665

Chakraborty, R., & Chakraborty, C. (2015). Pandemic influenza planning and response in India, 1949–2009. *Eubios Journal of Asian and International Bioethics, 25*(1), 7–13.

Chhabra, D. (2020). Transformational wellness tourism system model in the pandemic era. *International Journal of Heat and Mass Transfer, 5*(2), 76–101.

Creese, J., Byrne, J. P., Conway, E., Barrett, E., Prihodova, L., & Humphries, N. (2021). We all really need to just take a breath: Composite narratives of hospital doctors' well-being during the COVID-19 pandemic. *International Journal of Environmental Research and Public Health, 18*. doi:10.3390/ijerph18042051

Crouch, G. I., Perdue, R. R., Timmermans, H. J. P., & Uysal, M. (2004). Building foundations for understanding consumer psychology of tourism, hospitality and leisure. In G. I. Crouch, R. R. Perdue, H. J. P. Timmermans, & M. Uysal (Eds.), *Consumer psychology of tourism, hospitality and leisure* (Vol. 3, pp. 1–5). Wallingford: CABI Publishing.

Dash, S. B., & Sharma, P. (2021). Reviving Indian tourism amid the Covid-19 pandemic: Challenges and workable solutions. *Journal of Destination Marketing & Management, 22*. doi:10.1016/j.jdmm.2021.100648

De Zordo, S., Zanini, G., Mishtal, J., Garnsey, C., Ziegler, A. K., & Gerdts, C. (2021). Gestational age limits for abortion and cross-border reproductive care in Europe: A mixed-methods study. *BJOG: An International Journal of Obstetrics and Gynaecology, 128*(5), 838–845. doi:10.1111/1471-0528.16534

Easton, S., & Van Laar, D. (2018). *User manual for the Work-Related Quality of Life (WRQoL) Scale: A measure of quality of working life* (2nd ed.). University of Portsmouth. doi:10.17029/EASTON2018

Gautam, P., & Bhatta, K. (2020). Medical tourism in India: Possibilities and problems of alternative medical treatment. *International Journal of Health Management and Tourism, 5*(3), 181–207.

Global Wellness Institute (GWI). (2018). *Global wellness tourism economy report.* Retrieved from https://globalwellnessinstitute.org/wp-content/uploads/2018/11/GWI_GlobalWellnessTourismEconomyReport.pdf

Hafizan, A. H., Mardiana, O., Syafiq, S. S., Jacinta, M. R., Sahar, B., Juni, M. H., & Rosliza, A. M. (2018). Analysis of medical tourism policy: A case study of Thailand, Turkey and India. *International Journal of Public Health and Clinical Sciences, 5*(3), 17–31.

Hamouche, S. (2020). COVID-19 and employees' mental health: Stressors, moderators and agenda for organizational actions. *Emerald Open Research, 2*, 15. doi:10. 35241/emeraldopenres.13550.1

Han, H., & Hyun, S. S. (2015). Customer retention in the medical tourism industry: Impact of quality, satisfaction, trust, and price reasonableness. *Tourism Management, 46*, 20–29.

Hynes, W., Trump, B., Love, P., & Linkov, I. (2020). Bouncing forward: A resilience approach to dealing with COVID 19 and future systemic shocks. *Environment Systems & Decisions, 40*(2), 174–184. doi:10.1007/s10669-020-09776-x

Kamassi, A., Abd Manaf, N. H., & Omar, A. (2020). The identity and role of stakeholders in the medical tourism industry: State of the art. *Tourism Review, 75*(3), 559–574. doi:10.1108/TR-01-2019-0031

Keener, T. A., Hall, K., Wang, K., Hulsey, T., & Piamjariyakul, U. (2021). Relationship of quality of life, resilience, and associated factors among nursing faculty during COVID-19. *Nurse Educator, 46*(1), 17–22. doi:10.1097/NNE. 0000000000000926

Kotler, P., & Keller, K. L. (2009). *Marketing management.* Upper Saddle River, NJ: Pearson Prentice Hall.

Liu, X., Wen, J., Kozak, M., Jiang, Y., & Li, Z. (2022). Negotiating interdisciplinary practice under the COVID-19 crisis: Opportunities and challenges for tourism research. *Tourism Review, 77*(2), 484–502. doi:10.1108/TR-01-2021-0034

Maitra, R., & Joseph, M. A. (2022). New avenues of wellness tourism in untouched aspects of healing in India. *International Journal of Research in Tourism and Hospitality, 8*(1), 1–8. doi:10.20431/2455-0043.0801001

Malhotra, N. K., Uslay, C., & Bayraktar, A. (2007). Internal relationship marketing. In *Relationship marketing re-imagined.* Brighton, MA: Business Expert Press, LLC: Harvard Business Publishing.

Ministry of Health and Family Welfare (MOHFW). (2020). *An illustrated guide on COVID appropriate behaviour (CAB).* MOHFW, Government of India. Retrieved from https://www.mohfw.gov.in/pdf/Illustrativeguidelineupdate.pdf

Moti, S. (2020, December). Building organisational resilience for pandemic preparedness. Retrieved from https://www.researchgate.net/publication/346890876

Mtapuri, O., Giampiccoli, A., & Jugmohan, S. (2021). Impact of COVID-19 on small community-based tourism businesses: Diversification of opportunities and threats in modern Africa. *Economic Annals-XXI, 192*(7–8(2)), 177–187. doi:10.21003/ea. V192-15

Partington, R., & Inman, P. (2020, March 2). Coronavirus escalation could cut global economic growth in half – OECD. Retrieved from https://www.theguardian.com/business/2020/mar/02/coronavirus-escalation-could-cut-global-economic-growth-in-half-oecd

Pizam, A., Mansfeld, Y., & Chon, K. S. (1999). *Consumer behavior in travel and tourism.* London: Psychology Press.

Reddy, G. K. (2022, March). *Ministry of tourism has formulated a national strategy and roadmap for medical and wellness tourism.* Retrieved from https://pib.gov.in/PressReleaseIframePage.aspx?PRID=1805825

Rishe, P. (2020, March 12). Coronavirus impact upon sports industry most felt by hotel, restaurant industries and sports venue service workers. Retrieved from https://www.forbes.com/sites/prishe/2020/03/12/coronavirus-impact-upon-sports-

industry-most-felt-by-hotel-restaurant-industries-and-in-venue-service-workers/#
15cf9a1f5bc6

Rosenbusch, J., Ismail, I. R., & Ringle, C. M. (2018). The agony of choice for medical tourists: A patient satisfaction index model. *Journal of Hospitality and Tourism Technology*, *9*(3), 267–279. doi:10.1108/JHTT-10-2017-0107

Saltzman, L. Y., Hansel, T. C., & Bordnick, P. S. (2020). Loneliness, isolation, and social support factors in post-COVID-19 mental health. *American Psychological Association*, *22*(S1), S55–S57. doi:10.1037/tra0000703

Seetharaman, G. (2020, March 14). How different sectors of the economy are bearing the brunt of the coronavirus outbreak. *The Economic Times*. Retrieved from https://economictimes.indiatimes.com/news/economy/policy/how-different-sectors-of-the-economy-are-bearing-the-brunt-of-the-coronavirus-outbreak/articleshow/74630297.cms?from=mdr

Sharafuddin, M. A., & Madhavan, M. (2020). Measurement model for assessing community based wellness tourism needs. *e-Review of Tourism Research*, *18*(2), 311–336. Retrieved from https://ertr-ojs-tamu.tdl.org/ertr/index.php/ertr/article/view/459/227

Sharma, A., Vishraj, B., Ahlawat, J., Mittal, T., & Mittal, M. (2020). Impact of COVID-19 outbreak over medical tourism. *IOSR Journal of Dental and Medical Science*, *19*(5), 56–58.

Sigala, M. (2020). Tourism and COVID-19: Impacts and implications for advancing and resetting industry and research. *Journal of Business Research*, *117*, 312–321.

Sopha, C., Jittithavorn, C., & Lee, T. J. (2019). Cooperation in health and wellness tourism connectivity between Thailand and Malaysia. *International Journal of Tourism Sciences*, *19*(4), 248–257.

Suryavanshi, N., Kadam, A., Dhumal, G., Nimkar, S., Mave, V., Gupta, A., ... Gupte, N. (2020). Mental health and quality of life among healthcare professionals during the COVID-19 pandemic in India. *Brain and behavior*, *10*(11). doi:10.1002/brb3.1837

Times of India [TOI]. (2021, May 19). Vaccine tourism takes off with no-quarantine Moscow package. *The Times of India*. Retrieved from https://timesofindia.indiatimes.com/city/mumbai/mumbai-vaccine-tourism-takes-off-with-no-quarantine-moscow-package/articleshow/82746668.cms#:~:text=A%20Delhi%2Dbased%20travel%20agency,21%2Dday%20interval%20between%20jabs

Tsai, Y. (2014). Learning organizations, internal marketing, and organizational commitment in hospitals. *BMC Health Services Research*, *14*(1), 1–8. doi:10.1186/1472-6963-14-152

Van Laar, D., Edwards, J. A., & Easton, S. (2007). The work-related quality of life scale for healthcare workers. *Journal of Advanced Nursing*, *60*(3), 325–333. doi:10.1111/j.1365-2648.2007.04409.x

Voigt, C. (2013). Wellness tourism: A critical overview. Retrieved from http://www.tobewell.eu/media/universityofexeter/businessschool/documents/research/tobewell/Wellness_Tourism_-_Cornelia_Voigt.pdf

Warangkana, T., & Supawat, M. (2020). Antecedents of tourist loyalty in health and wellness tourism: The impact of travel motives, perceived service quality, and satisfaction. *International Journal of Innovation, Creativity and Change*, *11*(10), 300–315.

Wong, K. M., Velasamy, P., & Arshad, T. N. T. (2014). Medical tourism destination SWOT analysis: A case study of Malaysia, Thailand, Singapore and India. In *SHS Web of Conferences*. doi:10.1051/shsconf/20141201037

Yadav, R. K., & Dabhade, N. (2013). Service marketing triangle and GAP model in hospital industry. *International Letters of Social and Humanistic Sciences, 8*(2), 77–85.

Young, K. P., Kolcz, D. L., O'Sullivan, D. M., Ferrand, J., Fried, J., & Robinson, K. (2021). Health care workers' mental health and quality of life during COVID-19: Results from a mid-pandemic, national survey. *Psychiatric Services, 72*(2), 122–128. doi:10.1176/appi.ps.202000424

Zhang, Z., Dong, Y., & Yi, X. (2020). Building resilience via cognitive preparedness, behavioral reconfigurations, and iterative learning: The case of YunKang. *Management and Organization Review, 16*(5), 981–985. doi:10.1017/mor.2020.60

Zolfagharian, M., Rajamma, R. K., Naderi, I., & Torkzadeh, S. (2018). Determinants of medical tourism destination selection process. *Journal of Hospitality Marketing & Management, 27*(7), 775–794.

Tourists' Harassment During Pilgrimage: A Case Study of TripAdvisor's Review for the Hindu Pilgrim Centers in India

Debasish Batabyal, Nilanjan Ray, Sudin Bag and Kaustav Nag

Abstract

India is the birthplace of four major religions which are Hinduism, Jainism, Buddhism, and Sikhism. It is a country where people of all religions live in peace and harmony. Many tourists experience different forms of harassment during their pilgrimage journey, for example, fleecing, extortion of money, harassment by beggars, persistence by vendors and priests, fraud, sexual harassment, and other unacceptable behaviors. In order to appreciate the extent of harassment encountered by tourists, an in-depth study was conducted on the reviews provided by tourists on TripAdvisor's (Indian) website. This study characterizes harassments through ethnographic research approach of published reviews. A total of 260 reviews of 28 top Hindu temples are considered for all the states and union territories where the top Hindu pilgrim centers are located, (excluding Nagaland) according to TripAdvisor. The concerned reviews are categorized and further investigated through a primary data collection in proportion with the reviews received in respective temple sites in the study. through structural equation modeling (SEM). Important factors have been identified for future policy issues and recommendations in these most crowded places with unique mass tourism practices.

Keywords: Pilgrimage tourism; tourists harassment; TripAdvisor's review; Hindu pilgrim destinations; ethnographic research approach; structural equation modeling (SEM)

Introduction

Worldwide there are numerous places with various holy locations where tourists gather in great numbers every year. Forty percent of the approximated 600

Resilient and Sustainable Destinations After Disaster, 139–156
Copyright © 2023 Debasish Batabyal, Nilanjan Ray, Sudin Bag and Kaustav Nag
Published under exclusive licence by Emerald Publishing Limited
doi:10.1108/978-1-80382-021-720231011

million national/international religious/spiritual journeys are organized in Europe and over half in Asia (Rifai, 2011). India, with its population of over 135 billion in 2018 and home to some of the most exotic and oldest extant religions, witnesses over 2.3 billion domestic tourist arrivals across the country in 2019. A large amount of these domestic tourist arrivals are for pilgrimages in this country (966 million Hindus 2019). These holy locations relate to history and mythology of the four religions noted above. As religion plays an important role in a person's life, it supports the person to be more righteous and guides the person to follow a better path and live a better life. According to Alliance of Religion Conservation, nearly 155 million people opt for pilgrimage tourism all over the world, and India is no different with every religion having its own important search of moral and/or spiritual significance. Throughout the year, various festivals take place in India which increases the inflow of tourists in those regions. Pilgrimage sometimes is referred to a journey or search of moral or spiritual significance. Typically, it is a journey to a shrine or other location of importance to a person's beliefs and faith, although sometimes it can be a metaphorical journey into someone's own beliefs. In this context, very few studies have been conducted in the past to elicit socio-cultural issues, crises, and challenges of pilgrimages in the Hindu pilgrim centers in India with new attributes, traits, and characteristics as unholy practices in the holy places undermine community culture and prestige with a lot of adverse and unsustainable consequences. Again, this study will further provide new inputs during and after post-COVID-temple/shrine management and pilgrimage handling anywhere in the world.

Review of Literatures

Tourism is a social phenomenon in which the quality of service depends on the degree of the interaction between service providers and consumers or end-users (Johns, 1999). Religious tourism, spiritual tourism, sacred tourism, or faith tourism has different forms of rituals involved and activities associated. Pilgrimage often brings about mass tourism practices, sometimes overtourism with a number of unique issues, perspectives to be studied and managed for the essential sustainable pilgrim tourism practices without undermining faith and public sentiments. Understanding pilgrim–host interactions are largely religion-specific, activity-specific, and site-specific in nature. Hinduism and *Sanatana Dharma* are believed to have been the oldest extant religion in the world and as such offers different spiritual thoughts and perspectives. Every person can find their own space in it. Traditionally, Hindu temples are not only considered as a prayer hall but also an auspicious place where the presiding deity dwells. Since time immemorial, these places were also a courtyard for performing and patronizing culture, heritage, traditions, and several performing arts unlike prayer halls in other religions. Sometimes, these places converted into secret treasures of kingdom. Therefore, presiding deities, sites, and religious practices are varied, transformed, and unique practices. From orthodox schools of thoughts to secu-laristic and casteless practices are quite evident in modern Hindu pilgrim centers, and noncore pilgrims have been coming into being who travel for nonreligious or other purposes. Two distinct aspects to religious tourism came into being in recent times in India with dedicated and novel pilgrims (Strategic Initiatives & Government Advisory (SIGA) Team, 2012). Singh (2005) described the proto-typical pilgrim from among the wide array of contemporary religious and secular tourists through two approaches, viz., pilgrimage as a distinctive activity and the quest for geopiety. The later was mostly associated with the exploration of the Himalayan pilgrimage. This has been achieved with a discussion of the emerging practices and recent trends in Himalayan pilgrimology. This appraisal alluded to Cohen's quest for a Theology of Tourism also. This wide array of contemporary religious tourism exhibited and reoriented again in the research study of Srivastava (2019). He assessed the relationship among pilgrimage, tourism, and leisure, and commented on nonsecular and secular practices in pilgrimage with the most modern trend of just tourism for leisure in Indian pilgrim centers, undermining the basics of religious tourism with more noncore pilgrims and reasons for some nonreligious sociocultural and economic practices. Vijayanand (2014) investigated the issues and challenges of pilgrimage tourism in an Indian pilgrim center, Thanjavur. The socioeconomic perspectives are addressed along with the involvement of pilgrimage tourists. The levels of inspiration and prospect of religious tourists are recognized as type factors in the emergent pilgrimage tourism in his study. On the other hand, Khajuria and Khanna (2014) opined that tourism demand is very sensitive to safety concern, particularly in pilgrim centers like Shri Mata Vaishno Devi Shrine, Jammu, India, attracting approximately 10 million pilgrims annually. The same concern is equally true for all major Hindu pilgrim centers from *Char Dham, Twelve Jyotirlingas, Fifty Shakti Pithas*, to all other places of huge religious gatherings. Their empirical study exhibited and recorded experiences of tourists or pilgrims as to how they feel while they travel to these destinations vis-à-vis various safety concerns in the terms of tourist risks and crimes.

Now, one can raise reassessment of planning and policy issues involved. Shinde (2012) highlighted how most religious tourism activities take place outside the state's framework of policies and institutions with quasireligious entrepreneurship, minimum civic responsibility, and institutional vacuum. This related fragmentation resulted in a free-market situation and in the absence of regulation and lack of infrastructural support leading to a condition where a high influx of religious tourists threatens and get threatened. Whereas, Dasgupta, Mondal, and Basu (2006) focused on impacts of an event-based pilgrimage called Ganga Sagar Mela in West Bengal and recommended heritage conservation and sustainable orientation. This study is found to have been dealing with a market-led approach for the future of tourism rather than actual problems and practices of the event and unsustainable issues involved. Another significant approach adopted was structural equation modeling (SEM) for identifying significant attributes responsible for satisfaction in a grand religious event, *Kumbhmela* at Ujjain in 2016 (Verma & Sarangi, 2019, p. 2). Pure human interaction and human harassment separately were almost absent in Indian perspectives. The other approach that is often cited in relation to managing this type of religious tourism is the Hajj to Mecca in Saudi Arabia (Din, 1989; Henderson,

2011; Woodward, 2004). In an international perspective, this market-led approach brings about malpractices by local businessmen as Kozak (2007) explored in his study at Marmaris in Turkey. He found that the primary driving force of harassment was the intention of local businesses for more profits mostly in the streets, the beach area, and the least occurring at hotel properties. In another study on pilgrimage in the central Himalaya, Nepal, Bleie (2000) incorporated impacts and quality of some sacred religious journey and sociocultural, economic, and environmental risks involved in the opening of cable car service to a famed pilgrimage site. Interestingly, another truly global sociocultural issue addressed by Moufakkir (2015) while discussing on Arab Muslim tourists going abroad with the ethnic identity. Also, Khairat (2016) intended to classify the types of harassment in the city of Sadat varying from verbal harassment, misguiding information, and monetary losses to physical harassment. Therefore, sustainable socioeconomic and cultural issues have been essential and imperative in this study. These innovative destination systems have been varying from one destination to another because a destination itself is resource-specific, political philosophy–oriented, community-oriented, and deeply influenced by suppliers and intermediaries (Batabyal, 2010). This is more important in a place of intensive mass tourism distinctively different from leisure and recreation.

Objectives of the Study

Toward sustainable pilgrimages in some of the world's most populous pilgrim centers and events, following objectives are studied keeping in view the most urgent sociocultural practices often complained by pilgrims and tourists in India.

a. To understand the types of harassments common in the most-rated Hindu pilgrim centers in India.
b. To measure how various forms of harassments resulting in the service dimensions of temples or shrines in the Hindu pilgrims
c. To contribute to the major policy issues and recommendations for temple or shrine authorities and tourism departments at state and central levels in India.

Methodology

For a tourism business, access to big data like solicited or unsolicited feedback of tourists, information access patterns, and mobility behavior forms a base for developing customer profiles, service, or product recommendation accuracy. The ethnographic data distinguish face-to-face cultural data in terms of the ongoing development of new adaptations of ethnographic procedures. This study considered 260 reviews, comprising of 328 feedback statements in word sample texts that are drawn from a discussion about the Hindu pilgrim harassment in the Indian platform of TripAdvisor. Such temples are considered as found to have been top-rated for each state or union territories in India, as far as the TripAdvisor is concerned. Utmost care was taken in selecting the reviews from the website, TripAdvisor while selecting the reviews for this study on tourist harassment. A set of all possible worlds synonymous with major and minor degree of harassment were chosen beforehand. The time period considered for the review was all reviews from 2016 to 2019. To harness the associated terms, two semantic search engines named "Social Mention" and "wordle.com" were used. Since harassment-related reviews are found to be superseding by COVID-19 pandemic, new issues and challenges exhibited through COVID-19 pandemic have not been incorporated in this study. Jagannath, Kashi Biswanath, Brihadeswara, Kantakeswara, Venkateswara, Siddhivinayak, Chilkur Balaji, Dakshineshwar, Mahakaleshwar, Somnath, Karni Mata, Vaishno Devi, Jwalamukhi, Kedarnath, Durgaina, Rajiv Lochan Vishnu Mandir, Padmanabaswamy, Mangeshi, Ganesh tok, Kamakhya, Shiv Mandir in Aziwal, Shiv Linga in Ziro, Tripura Sundari, Sri Govindji, Nartiang Durga, Baba Baidyanathdham, Vishnupada Mandir, Maa Bhadrakali temples are considered for this study based on TripAdvisor's ratings. A total of 260 reviews of 28 top Hindu temples are considered for all the states and union territories where the top Hindu pilgrim centers are located, (excluding Nagaland) according to TripAdvisor. Following are the chronological steps taken for retrieving the reviews during 2016 to 2019 as shown in Fig. 1.

After categorizing harassments during pilgrimages in Hindu pilgrim centers, a total of 3,850 responses were surveyed through a structured questionnaire through a stratified random sampling. Each pilgrim center represents responses in proportion to the reviews received in the TripAdvisor. Finally, a total of 355 questionnaires are found suitable for further investigation of the most important ones to be contributing to the planning and policy issue. Scale techniques comprising of

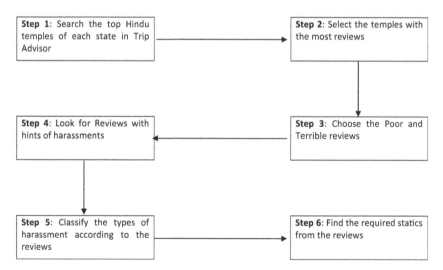

Fig. 1. Basic Steps for Collecting Temple Reviews From the Website of the TripAdvisor.

five-point Likert scale (Strongly Agree, Agree, Undecided, Disagree, and Strongly Disagree) and semantic scale (extremely important – absolutely unimportant) were used to elicit opinion of the respondents. The types of harassments are grouped into five components (as shown in Table 1) considering the similar characteristic features and represent the important area of designing blue print for temple services (Nag, 2020; Batabyal, Rawal, Chatterjee, Goswami, 2023). Based on the reviews of the TripAdvisor, types of harassments have been categorized into five service dimensions, viz., behavioral, information, infrastructure, monetary, and security and safety dimensions respectively. In Table 2 these five dimensions are classified with more number of items evident in the pilgrim centers that are being observed in the study.

Table 1. TripAdvisor's Review-Based Destination-Specific Harassment in Hindu Temples and Shrines.

Harassment	Places of Harassment
Fleecing	Kashi Vishwanath, Jagannath temple, and Dakshineshwar
Extortion	Jagannath Temple, Dakshineshwar, Kashi Vishwanath, Padmanabaswamy temple, Venkateshwara temple, and is evident in many more
Harassment by beggars	Dakshineshwar and Jagannath temple mainly
Vendor's persistence	Dakshineshwar, Puri, Kashi Vishwanath, and Siddhivinayak temple
Priest persistence	Kashi Vishwanath, Jagannathtemple, Dakshineshwar, Venkateshwara temple, and Baidyanath temple
Lack of proper information, direction, and poor facilities and management	Dakshineswar and Jagannath temple
Verbal and physical abuse	Padmanabaswamy temple, Siddhivinayak temple, Jagannath temple, and is evident in many more
Fraud and rowdy behavior	Kashi Biswanath temple
Sexual harassment	Vaishno Devi

Source: Author's own review from TripAdvisor during the study period (2019–2020).

Table 2. Five Service Dimensions of Harassment Study in Hindu Pilgrim Sites in India.

Service Dimensions	Items (Forms of Harassment Resulting in Negative Experience/Service Failure, etc.)
Behavioral (BI)	Copilgrims (BI1)
	Pandas/Purohits/Priests (BI2)
	Restaurants, coffee-shop, tea-stall owners in adjacent pilgrim sites (BI3)
	Souvenir sellers (BI4)
	Shrine/temple officials (BI5)
	Local transport providers (BI6)
	Local police, security, etc. (BI7)
	Lock-and-key service providers (BI8)
	Sweepers, shrine-cleaning personnel (BI9)
	Beggars, trespassers (BI10)
Information-oriented (IO)	Road, street, and lane-related information (IO1)
	Time required for temple/shrine activities, prayers, night prayers, etc. (IO2)
	Local sight-seeing related (IO3)
	History, mythological, religious information (IO4)
	Discrimination to pilgrims associated with caste, race, etc.(IO5)
	Special dress code or such other ritualistic information (IO6)
Infrastructural (INI)	Space to manage daily crowd (INI1)
	Facility to access to the presiding deity without discrimination, i.e., VIP pass etc. (INI2)
	Cleanliness (1 being highly disagreed to 5 being strongly agreed) (INI3)
	Facility for elderly persons, old timers, etc. (INI4)
	Facility for prayer, evening prayer, special prayer, distribution or availability of *prasadam* (special food offered to deity), etc. (INI5)
	Arrangement for keeping pilgrims' possessions safe (INI6)
Monetary (MI)	Rich–poor discrimination by temple staff, etc. (MI1)
	Discrimination through VIP ticket, pass, etc. (MI2)

Table 2. *(Continued)*

Service Dimensions	Items (Forms of Harassment Resulting in Negative Experience/Service Failure, etc.)
	Undue collection of gems and jewelry, etc. through emotional religious black-mailing by priests, pandas, etc. (MI3)
	Improper/without billing of donations, worthy gifts to gods, etc. (MI4)
	Defalcation of donation, etc. for related welfare activities (MI5)
	Undue collection of money, donation, etc. by priests, pandas, *goswamis*, etc. (MI6)
	Inflated price of essential goods, *prasadam*, etc.(MI7)
Security and safety (SS)	Inactiveness of security on fleecing money, jewelry, etc. (SS1)
	Threats from trespassers, beggars in the temples/ shrine (SS2)
	Inactiveness of security in conflict with local vendors, priests, pandas, etc. (SS3)
	Late or no actions of the local police on loss of possessions of pilgrims (SS4)
	Almost inactive 24 hours emergency number (SS5)
	Ineffective complaint cell or grievance cell (SS6)
	Safety and security on queue to reach the presiding deity (SS7)

Source: TripAdvisors reviews, 2016–2019.

With reference to Table 2, the important items have been extracted using principal component factor analysis. The result of rotated components has been presented in Table 3. The result reveals that five factors mostly affected in the tourist harassment in Hindu pilgrims namely "Behavioral issue," "Infrastructure issue," "Information orientation," "Security and safety" and "Monetary issue" respectively.

From Table 3, it is found that the construct behavioral issue comprises seven items out of total 10 items. The remaining three items have been excluded from the further study due to the low loadings. Similarly, infrastructure, information orientation, "security and safety," and monetary issues comprises equal number of items, which is five.

Table 3. Rotated Components Matrix.

Items	Factor 1	Factor 2	Factor 3	Factor 4	Factor 5
BI1	0.796				
BI2	0.831				
BI3	0.812				
BI4	0.831				
BI6	0.848				
BI7	0.829				
INI1		0.881			
INI2		0.885			
INI3		0.821			
INI4		0.760			
INI5		0.733			
IO1			0.814		
IO2			0.823		
IO3			0.764		
IO4			0.771		
IO5			0.826		
MI2				0.795	
MI3				0.782	
MI4				0.834	
MI5				0.839	
MI6				0.845	
SS1					0.860
SS2					0.856
SS3					0.913
SS4					0.823
SS5					0.830

After identifying the important dimensions of Hindu tourist harassment, the researchers have used SEM to measure the relationship between the constructs. The initial requirement in SEM is to test for reliability and validity (Chin, 2010).

Table 4 presents the score of Cronbach's alpha, composite reliability, and average variance extracted. It is noted that the alpha value exceeds the value of 0.70 (Bag, Ray, & Banerjee, 2021; Nunnally & Bernstein, 1994). The convergent validity is tested with the help of Fornell and Larcker (1981) criterion in which the average variance extracted (AVE) should exceed 0.5 (Bag, Aich, & Islam, 2020;

Table 4. Scale Reliability for Five Dimension Model of Harassment During Pilgrimage.

	Cronbach's Alpha	Composite Reliability	Average Variance Extracted (AVE)
Behavioral (BI)	0.906	0.927	0.680
Infrastructure (IO)	0.875	0.910	0.670
Information (INI)	0.861	0.899	0.640
Monetary (MI)	0.879	0.911	0.671
Security & safety (SS)	0.909	0.932	0.735
Tourist harassment	0.887	0.916	0.686

Source: Primary data collection, 2020, Statistical package used is Stata.

Götz, Liehr-Gobbers, & Krafft, 2009). As shown in the table, the AVE values lie between 0.640 and 0.735. Thus, the convergent validity is established for this study.

Apart from the covergent validity, the divergent validity was also studied employing two measures such as "Fornell–Larcker Criterion," and "Heterotrait–Monotrait Ratio (HTMT)." Firstly, according to the Fornell–Larcker criterion (Fornell & Larcker, 1981), the square root of AVE of the each latent constructs should be greater than the construct's highest correlation value with any other construct. As shown in Table 5, all correlations values were lower than the square root of AVE; hence, discriminant validity was established for the constructs. Secondly, the HTMT ratio should be significantly lower than the threshold level of 0.85 for establishing the discrimination between two factors

Table 5. Discriminant Validity (1) Fornell–Larcker Criterion.

	BI	INI	IO	MI	SS	TH
Behavioral (BI)	0.825					
Infrastructural (INI)	0.771	0.819				
Information (IO)	0.766	0.822	0.800			
Monetary (MI)	0.758	0.751	0.799	0.819		
Security and safety (SS)	0.729	0.826	0.814	0.743	0.857	
Tourist harassment (TH)	0.765	0.827	0.826	0.776	0.823	0.828

Table 6. Discriminant Validity (2) Heterotrait–Monotrait Ratio (HTMT).

	BI	**INI**	**IO**	**MI**	**SS**	**TH**
Behavioral (BI)						
Infrastructural (INI)	0.848					
Information (IO)	0.848	0.832				
Monetary (MI)	0.827	0.837	0.893			
Security and safety (SS)	0.797	0.825	0.898	0.809		
Tourist harassment (TH)	0.835	0.830	0.807	0.835	0.803	

(Bag & Omrane, 2020; Henseler, Ringle, & Sarstedt, 2016). Table 6 shows that the HTMT ratio for all correlation values was significantly less than the conservative level, which indicates that the discriminant validity was also established.

Data Analysis and Discussion

Following selection and reviewing of 260 reviews of 28 top Hindu temples from TripAdvisor, 12 types of pilgrimage tourist ill treatment and harassment have been drawn following the review process. There are 328 statements taken from the 260 reviews which are falling under the categories noted in Table 7.

Location of the place of worship is extremely important while studying this type of harassments in any pilgrim center as evident in the study of Kozak (2007) in Turkey. It is found that the maximum types of harassment that the pilgrimage tourists experience is the persistence by priests which is 92 statements (28.03%) under which we can see the tourists are mostly harassed for forced donations which is 65 statements of the 92 statements (70.65%) followed by special offerings which is 17 statements (18.48%) and money for special benefits which is 10 statements (10.87%). It is followed by extortion which is 67 statements (20.44%) under which we can see touting by guides which is 37 statements (55.22%) and overpricing by guides which is 30 statements (44.78%), bad and disorderly behavior by local authorities, official police, and civic police which is 49 statements (14.93%), lack of information and direction which is 26 statements (7.93%), vendor's persistence which is 25 statements (7.63%) which includes charging high price for keeping accessories which is 13 statements (52%) and forcing to buy expensive offerings which is 12 statements (48%). The minimum types of harassments are fraud which is 12 statements (3.65%), poor facilities and management which is 14 statements (4.217%), harassment by beggars which is 5 statements (1.53%), defrauding which is 13 statements (3.96%), physical abuse which is 15 statements (4.57%), verbal abuse which is 9 statements (2.74%), and sexual harassment which is 1 statement (0.30%).

Therefore, Hindu pilgrim sites in India lack quality interaction between copilgrims and priests at the time of actual prayer or performing rituals. It is also a

Table 7. Table Showing the Ill Treatment and Persecution in the Number of
Statements Reviewed.

Ill Treatments in Temple Complex	No. of Statements	Percentage of Statements (%)
Defrauding due to lack of stringent pricing policy	13	3.96%
Extortion of money	67	20.44%
(a) Overpricing by guides and priests	30	44.78%
(b) Touting by guides	37	52.22
Harassment by beggars	*5*	*1.53*
Persistence by vendors	*25*	*7.63%*
(a) Charging visitors inflated prices for storing personal property (i.e., shoes, etc.)	13	52%
(b) Forcing visitors to buy expensive items to secure greater worship offerings	12	48%
Persistence by priests	*92*	*28.03%*
(a) Forced donations	65	70.65%
(b) Special offering	17	18.48%
(c) Money for special benefits	10	10.87%
Lack of proper direction and information	*26*	*7.93%*
Poor facilities and management	*14*	*4.217%*
Verbal abuse	*9*	*2.74%*
Physical abuse	*15*	*4.57%*
Fraud	*12*	*3.65%*
Sexual harassment	*1*	*0.30%*
Disorderly and bad behavior of the local authorities, official police, and civic police	*49*	*14.93%*

Source: Author's own review from TripAdvisor during the study period (2019–2020).

noticeable point that copilgrims lack good interpersonal relationship and a feeling of religious brotherhood among themselves. Based on the evaluation of outer model, i.e., establishment of convergent and divergent validity, the inner model was evaluated to examine the power of explanatory variables and also predicted relevance of the proposed model. Moreover, the size of the path coefficients and significance of the hypothesized relationships were estimated. The main criterion for evaluating the structural model in PLS is the variance explained ($R2$).

According to Chin (1998), the $R2$ values of 0.67, 0.33, or 0.19 imply substantial, moderate, or weak for endogenous latent variables in the inner path model. The result of the path model is presented in Fig. 2 and Table 8.

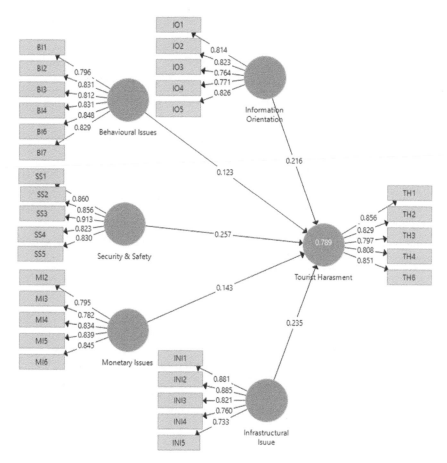

Fig. 2. The Path Model of Service Dimensions in the Hindu Pilgrim Sites in India.

The behavioral dimension is unique in the study as it represents pilgrimage with poor interpersonal relationship with copilgrims, priests, local shopkeepers, souvenir sellers, local transport operators, and local security as well.

The infrastructural dimension emphasizes crowd management in temple, accessibility to the presiding deity without discrimination, e.g., VIP pass, special donation pass, etc., cleanliness, arrangement for elderly people and specially abled persons, and facility for customized special rituals, prayers, etc.

Information dimension incorporated racial and caste-based discriminations, allocated time to each pilgrim on queue, correct signage, and history or mythological and local sight-seeing related information in the study.

Monetary dimension incorporates undue collection of cash, undue collection of gems, jewelry with religious fear, etc., defalcation of donation for welfare

Table 8. The Values of Path Model of Service Dimensions in the Hindu Pilgrim Sites in India.

Paths	Path Loadings	T Statistics	P Values	Remarks
Information orientation → Tourist harassment	0.216	2.297	0.022	Supported
Behavioral Issue → Tourist harassment	0.123	3.250	0.001	Supported
Security and Safety → Tourist harassment	0.257	3.827	0.000	Supported
Monetary issue → Tourist harassment	0.143	2.760	0.006	Supported
Infrastructural issue → Tourist harassment	0.235	3.577	0.000	*Supported*

Source: Primary data collection, 2020, Statistical package used is Stata.

activity, improper donation process, and provision for economic discrimination in the Hindu pilgrim centers.

Out of seven items in the safety and security dimension, five uploaded items are inactiveness of local security officials, threats from trespassers, beggars in the temples/shrines, inactiveness of security in conflict with local vendors, priests, pandas, etc., late or no actions of the local police on loss of possessions of pilgrims.

Outcomes of the Study

Following the review of statements retrieved from TripAdvisor, an interesting result was found in the study which highlighted a lack of reliability of pilgrims on law and order and their experiences of a very poor interaction with the priests, pandas, and goswamis. As these priests are very respectable to the Hindu society, 73.47% pilgrims do not report the statements of harassment or lodge any complaints to the policing authorities. Only 17.69% pilgrims reported incidents to the local authorities of temples whereas 7.69% went to the police station nearby. Only 1.15% statements are intervened and resolved by local police, according to this review. This study is found to be impactful as it can question many policy issues and temple management procedures. It raises and highlights many illegitimate and unsustainable practices that need to be investigated further for policies and procedures to be reviewed and updated accordingly. As the Hindu temples are mirrors to the society, these are not only representing heritage grandeur but also today's society with all odds and evils. Despite all these, it is observed that many pilgrim sites are restricted sites with high security alert.

Suggestions, Recommendations, and Future Scope of the Study

As the temple and pilgrimage economy relies on the mutual relationships established between four sets of senior individuals, viz., leaders of religious sects (*goswamis*), ritual priests (*pandas*), auxiliary service providers, and devotees, this relationship has to be redefined, though religious barriers and sentiments are to be understood well in advance. A classification of day-to-day management and policy issues needs to be reviewed, which are varying from one another depending upon community culture and location.

The most weighted malpractices are interestingly found in front of the presiding deity by the priests in the form of forced donations, special offering, and money for special benefits. Again, this is very difficult to investigate as you are directly dealing with faith and certain age-old rituals. Therefore, the rule of humanity, may be through extensive awareness, is recommended which supersedes such gray areas. Respective temple trustees and crowd managers may seriously think over it, mostly in populous destinations. Managing precious gems and jewelry in the forms of daily offerings is another important factor that requires immediate attention from the most populous centers to lesser known temples.

The Ministry of Tourism (MoT), in consultation with the state governments/ union territory administrations had proposed to set up Tourist Police at prominent tourist spots around the country which mainly consists of the most visited states of India. Destination or pilgrim center specific tourist police and/or civic volunteers can be given responsibility for "hassle-free" worshiping, fair trade practices, neonormal formalities, and safe crowd management.

Training for hospitable and tourist-friendly behavior, dealing with foreign nationals, and knowledge in foreign languages are among the most important areas to be seriously taken care of as disorderly behavior of official police, civic police, and other local authorities itself is a major problem exhibited in the study.

Tour guides are expected to be more sincere about the adverse effect of touting, extra brokerage, and irresponsible behaviors. Open air stall owners and small local entrepreneurs are expected to be more hospitable and refrain from extra pricing charged upon pilgrims. Overall awareness campaign and community responsibility to be promoted for sustainable practices in pilgrimages.

The MoT, Govt. of India, has already adopted "Code of Conduct for Safe &Honorable Tourism." This code of conduct is yet to be successfully implemented in all centers with neonormal measures. It must be the prerequisite for opening new popular pilgrim centers in the future.

Serious and more extensive research and investigation for assessing the future effects of a pilgrim's ill treatments and harassment need immediate attention in India's tourism with a distinctive orientation; therefore, the study is a highly recommending source of sustainable pilgrimages, following the COVID-19 pandemic.

Through this study, many important sociological problems can be addressed and managed varying from shrine authority to the respective tourism departments of the states or union territories. Previous crowd management techniques will be beneficial for the new COVID-19 era, as the central government plays a cartelistic role, they can rank the managerial efficiency of temple authorities or trustees for safe tourism in all aspects. Unique best practices, managerial strengths of temples regarding day-to-day operation must be encouraged. In continuation with various expert recommendations, crowd categorization and management, mandatory requirements for the crowd, certain norms and practices for tourists, temple staff, local entrepreneurs, beggars, etc. have become the important aspects for pilgrimages in India without delay.

References

Bag, S., Aich, P., & Islam, M. A. (2020). Behavioral intention of "digital natives" toward adapting the online education system in higher education. *Journal of Applied Research in Higher Education*. doi:10.1108/JARHE-08-2020-0278

Bag, S., & Omrane, A. (2020). Corporate social responsibility and its overall effects on financial performance: Empirical evidence from Indian companies. *Journal of African Business*. doi:10.1080/15228916.2020.1826884

Bag, S., Ray, N., & Banerjee, B. (2021). Assessing the effects of experiential quality on behavioural intention of customers in banking services: The moderating role of experiential satisfaction. *FIIB Business Review*, 1–14. doi:10.1177/23197145211052817

Batabyal, D. (2010). Implication of a scientific destination study in tourism product management: A case study in Sikkim. In *Article presented and published in a National Conference "Science and Technology Applications in Tourism Sector focusing on Uttarakhand Opportunities"*.

Batabyal, D., Rawal, Y. S., Chatterjee, P., Goswami, S. (2023). Temple service quality model for future pilgrimages in Indian sub-continent through user generated contents (UGC) in trip advisor. *International Journal of Tourism Anthropology*, *10*(1). doi:10.1504/IJTA.2022.10054798

Bleie, T. (2000). Pilgrim tourism in the Central Himalayas. *Mountain Research and Development*, *23*(2), 177–184. doi:10.1659/0276-4741(2003)023[0177:PTITCH]2.0. CO;2

Chin, W. W. (1998). The partial least squares approach to structural equation modeling. *Modern Methods for Business Research*, *295*(2), 295–336.

Chin, W. W. (2010). How to write up and report PLS analyses. In V. E. Vinzi, W. W. Chin, J. Henseler, & H. Wang (Eds.), *Handbook of partial least squares: Concepts, methods and applications in marketing and related fields* (pp. 655–690). Berlin: Springer.

Dasgupta, S., Mondal, K., & Basu, K. (2006). Dissemination of cultural heritage and impact of pilgrim tourism at Gangasagar Island. *The Anthropologist*, *8*(1), 11–15. doi:10.1080/09720073.2006.11890928.

Din, K. H. (1989). Islam and tourism: Patterns, issues, and options. *Annals of Tourism Research*, *16*(4), 542–563.

Fornell, C., & Larcker, D. F. (1981). Structural equation models with unobservable variables and measurement error: Algebra and statistics. *Journal of Marketing Research*, *18*(3), 382–388.

Götz, O., Liehr-Gobbers, K., & Krafft, M. (2009). Evaluation of structural equation models using the partial least squares (PLS) approach. In *Handbook of partial least squares: Concepts, methods and applications* (pp. 691–711). Berlin, Heidelberg: Springer Berlin Heidelberg.

Henderson, J. C. (2011). Religious tourism and its management: The Hajj in Saudi Arabia. *International Journal of Tourism Research, 13*(6), 541–552.

Henseler, J., Ringle, C. M., & Sarstedt, M. (2016). Testing measurement invariance of composites using partial least squares. *International Marketing Review, 23*(3), 406–431.

Johns, N. (1999). What is this thing called service? *European Journal of Marketing, 33*(9/10), 958–973.

Khairat, G. M. (2016). Investigating the tourists' harassment effect on the destination choice (a case study: Egypt). *Journal of Association of Arab Universities for Tourism and Hospitality, 13*(1), 91–102.

Khajuria, S., & Khanna, S. (2014). Tourism risks and crimes at pilgrimage destinations – A case study of shri Mata Vaishno Devi. *International Journal of Event Management Research, 8*(1), 77–93.

Kozak, M. (2007). Tourist harassment: A marketing perspective. *Annals of Tourism Research, 34*(2), 384–399.

Moufakkir, O. (2015). The stigmatized tourist. *Annals of Tourism Research, 53,* 17–30.

Nag, K. (2020). *Developing a typology of pilgrimage tourist harassment in Indian temples: A netnographic approach.* Unpublished master dissertation. Amity University, Kolkata.

Nunnally, J. C., & Bernstein, I. H. (1994). *Psychometric theory.* New York: McGraw.

Rifai, T. (2011). *Religious tourism in Asia & Pacific* (Vol. 398). Madrid: World Tourism Organization. doi:978-92-844-1380-5

Shinde, K. (2012). Policy, planning, and management for religious tourism in Indian pilgrimage sites. *Journal of Policy Research in Tourism, Leisure and Events, 4*(3), 277–301.

Singh, S. (2005). Secular pilgrimages and sacred tourism in the Indian Himalayas. *GeoJournal, 64*(3), 215–223.

Srivastava, V. K. (2019). Pilgrimage, tourism and leisure: A tribute to Ishwar Modi. *Journal of the Anthropological Survey of India, 68*(1), 95–113.

Strategic Initiatives & Government Advisory (SIGA) Team. (2012). *Diverse beliefs: Tourism of faith religious tourism gains ground* (pp. 2–11). Yes Bank Ltd and FICCI.

Verma, M., & Sarangi, P. (2019). Modeling attributes of religious tourism: A study of Kumbh Mela, India. *Journal of Convention & Event Tourism,* 1–29. doi:10.1080/15470148.2019.1652124

Vijayanand, S. (2014). The issues and perspectives of pilgrimage tourism development in Thanjavur. *International Journal of Tourism & Hospitality Review (IJTHR), 1*(1), 45–51. doi:10.18510/ijthr.2014.117

Woodward, S. C. (2004). Faith and tourism: Planning tourism in relation to places of worship. *Tourism and Hospitality Planning & Development, 1*(2), 173–186.

Web Link of Reviews

https://pib.gov.in/newsite/PrintRelease.aspx?relid=103654

https://www.india-tourism.net/pilgrimage.htm

https://www.researchgate.net/publication/283538128_The_Issues_and_Perspectives_of_Pilgrimage_Tourism_Development_in_Thanjavur

https://www.researchgate.net/publication/235315884_Tourist_harassment_Review_
of_the_literature_and_destination_responses
https://www.exeter.ac.uk/staff/equality/dignity/examples/
https://www.researchgate.net/publication/283538128_The_Issues_and_Perspectives_
of_Pilgrimage_Tourism_Development_in_Thanjavur/citation/download
http://www.arcworld.org/downloads/ARC%20pilgrimage%20statistics%20155m%
2011-12-19.pdf
https://www.ukessays.com/essays/tourism/pilgrimage-tourism-and-its-economic-
dimensions-tourism-essay.php
http://www.ijemr.org/wp-content/uploads/2014/10/Khajuria.pdf
https://www.tripadvisor.in/Attraction_Review-g424926-d1837966-Reviews-Brihadees
hwara_Temple-Thanjavur_Thanjavur_District_Tamil_Nadu.html
https://www.tripadvisor.in/Attraction_Review-g297685-d320084-Reviews-Shri_
Kashi_Vishwanath_Temple_Golden_Temple-Varanasi_Varanasi_District_Uttar_
Prades.html
https://www.tripadvisor.in/Attraction_Review-g304553-d3705352-Reviews-Srikantesh
wara_Temple-Mysuru_Mysore_Mysore_District_Karnataka.html
https://www.tripadvisor.in/Attraction_Review-g297587-d1220147-Reviews-Tirumala_
Temple-Tirupati_Chittoor_District_Andhra_Pradesh.html

Communication Effectiveness in Rebuilding and Raising Awareness for Safe and Innovative Future Tourism in Oman

Sangeeta Tripathi and Muna Al Shahri

Abstract

Purpose: The main objective of this chapter is to examine the country's internal communication environment that helps create community awareness and improve public–private tourism partnerships to achieve Oman Vision 2040. This chapter also attempts to understand the efforts of the National Tourism Organization (NTO) in building community relationships and empowering them by capitalizing on available resources within the community.

Methedology: The study is based on qualitative and quantitative methods. A purposive sampling technique has been applied, and the data collection has been done through surveys and interviews from the Ministry of Heritage and Tourism, Salalah, Oman, to reach out to the findings.

Keyswords: Innovative tourism; communication; awareness; community relationships; public–private partnerships; tourism stakeholders

Introduction

The COVID-19 pandemic has profoundly impacted tourism sectors across the world regions. According to the World Tourism Organization, UNWTO World Tourism Barometer (May 2020), a sharp decline in tourists' arrivals had been recorded by -22% in the first four months of 2020. This scenario pointed out a possible annual decline between 60 and 80% (UNWTO BRIEFING, 2020). The COVID-19 outbreak has impacted several countries with different intensities at different times. Like other countries, Oman's tourism industry was the hardest hit by the pandemic, and a direct loss of half-billion Omani Rials was recorded at the end of September 2020 (Al-Nassriya, 2020). Due to the increasing infection of

Resilient and Sustainable Destinations After Disaster, 157–178
Copyright © 2023 Sangeeta Tripathi and Muna Al Shahri
Published under exclusive licence by Emerald Publishing Limited
doi:10.1108/978-1-80382-021-720231012

COVID-19 worldwide, a 53.9% drop-down had been registered in the number of visiting guests in Omani hotels. At the first 10 months of 2020, 646,841 guests visited the Omani hotels, 1.40 million less than in 2019. Among 646,841, 50% of guests (337,687) were Omani nationals. At the same time, 47,643 were Asian, 164,873 European, 34,349 GCC and Arabs, 18,335 other non-Gulf Arab countries, 17,919 Americans, 5,302 from Oceania, 3,391 from Africa, and 17,342 from visitors from different nationalities (National Centre for Science Information, 2020). It is worth noting that 3- to 5-star hotels' revenue dropped by 60.2%. Their occupancy rates had declined by 50.1%. Limited operation of the flights made a calamitous impact on associated business activities such as tour operators, travel booking agents, event management companies, restaurants, and other tourism-related services (Al-Mughairi, Bhaskar, & Alazri, 2021).

The ease of COVID restrictions and reopening of international borders brought a glimmer of hope to boost Oman tourism. With the rebounding of domestic activities, Oman tourism is witnessing a recovery as the revenue of 3- to 5-star Omani hotels recorded an increase of 135% with a rise in guest numbers by 79.1%. As a result, Omani hotel occupancy increased by 39.1% in February 2022 (ONA, 2022). Along with this, the Sultanate has a vast recovery plan to mitigate the impact of COVID-19 on Oman tourism. The Ministry of Heritage and Tourism has unveiled a comprehensive tourism plan that aims to bring tourism back to its previous status. The estimated revival plan is 6 billion Omani Rials, mainly focused on developing divergent tourist destinations in Dhofar region (Oman News Agency, 2021). The tourism industry is multistakeholder, including travel, food, tourist services, leisure/entertainment, and tourism agents/organizers (Mason, 2020). Due to digital communication, the competition is now more extensive than before. Potential tourists have become more critical and conscious about their value for money. They seek more adventure and new experiences with leisure (Liu, 2003). The Oman government is now emphasizing all tourism sectors after the crisis; therefore, it becomes significant to assess the country's internal communication environment for sustainable tourism, dynamic capability building, and creating awareness on two layers – (1) making the host community aware about the country's tourism and their role in promoting several innovative projects and (2) destination image building among national and international communities to achieve long-term goals.

Image Building – Oman as a Spectacular Tourist Destination

Oman's tourism industry was a significant contributor to the Sultanate's GDP by 2.8% in 2019, before COVID-19. Under the new tourism strategy, the tourism sector is aimed to boost a 6% contribution to the country's GDP by 2040. This strategic plan has been divided into three stages to achieve the tourism goal – 2016–2020: preparation phase; 2021–2030: growth phase; and 2031–2040: stability phase. The new tourism strategy aims to create over 545,000 job opportunities through potential investment valued at 20 billion Omani Rial (Oxford Business Group, 2020). Under the new tourism policy, natural aesthetic tourism has been identified as a potential section of tourism. That is why new investment and recreational projects focus on enhancing beaches, mountains, valleys, and deserts to serve marvelous experiences to visitors (Oxford Business Group, 2020). Several promotional campaigns have started to achieve 3 billion Omani Rial by 2023 (Nair, 2022). In this series, the Ministry of Heritage and Tourism adopted an innovative marketing strategy and launched a transit advertising campaign in the French Capital, Paris, in February 2022. It aimed at reenhancing the Sultanate as an exotic destination to attract European tourists (Muscat Daily, 2022). Another campaign has been launched at the 59th edition of the Venice International Biennale. This campaign has also used transit advertising on the transport buses, airports, and water buses (ONA, Tourism campaign launched in Venice to promote Oman, 2022). The Ministry of Heritage and Tourism aims to showcase natural aesthetic beauty, forts, castles, and archeological and religious sites (ÇETİN & AL-Alwi, 2018). There are several places to visit and experience the essences of Oman, such as Muscat, Nizwa, Al Wahiba Sands, Musandam, Ras Al Jinz, turtle reserve, Jabal Al Akhdar, Mirbat, Salalah, Hasik, Hoota Cave, etc. According to the Government Communication Centre, Oman is the seventh tourist destination due to the variety of wildlife and marine life (Oman Observer, 2022). The Oman government is emphasizing more on Dhofar tourism due to its unique kind of monsoon, green mountain, waterfall, beaches, and Dhofar culture. However, Salalah tourism is seasonal and mainly focused on Khareef (monsoon season). Therefore, the Ministry of Heritage and Tourism prepared a whole year plan of different adventurous and entertainment tourism activities to attract national and international tourists in the whole year (Ministry of Heritage and Tourism, Salalah) (Table 1).

Table 1. Year-Based Event Planning for Dhofar Tourism.

Event List for Dhofar Region	Date	Location
Empty Quarter Festival	December 23, 2021, to January 8, 2022	Thumrait State
Archaeological discoveries exhibition	January 17 to February 15, 2022	Frankincense Land Museum, Salalah
Tour guide workshop	6th to 15th March	Plaza Crown Hotel
International Museums Day	May 18, 2022	Frankincense Land Museum
Meteorites Gallery	July to August 2022	Media
Man competition – iron man	September 23	Hawana Salalah – Taqa – Mirbat
Celebrating World Tourism Day	September 27, 2022	Salalah
Heritage Symposium	October 2022	Directorate Theater

Table 1. *(Continued)*

Event List for Dhofar Region	Date	Location
Authentic and insightful An event for people with storage, a session	October 15, 2022	Frankincense Land Museum
Discover the beauty of the East	National Day holiday 24th and November 25, 2022	Sadah State
Mountain Marathon (Gulf Compass)	2 and December 3, 2022	Mirbat Province
Wildlife exhibition in Fakhor Rory	November 13 to December 10, 2022	Samharam Archaeological Park
Inclusion of the Land of Frankincense Sites in the World Heritage List	December 2, 2022	-
Job fair for the tourism sector in Dhofar Governorate	End of December 2022	Directorate building

Source: Ministry of Heritage and Tourism, Oman.

In addition, Oman tourism development company "Omran" and Dhofar Municipality have also signed an agreement to develop tourist sites available throughout the year. These projects are Harmgeer Talalat, the Ayn Garziz development project, the Attin Garden project, and the Mughsail beach project (Times of Oman, 2022).

The success of Oman Tourism can be estimated by inbound and outbound tourism from 2010 to 2018. However, data from 2019 to 2022 are not mentioned here due to the massive impact of COVID-19 on the tourism sector worldwide.

Overall Sultanate Tourists' Data From 2010 to 2018

Table 2 shows a continuous growth in inbound tourism from overseas coming to Oman to experience spectacular sightseeing, cultural heritage, and tradition.

Table 3 displays a compressive view of outbound tourism which is lower than the average inbound tourism spending.

Table 4 shows the growth of hotel establishment in Oman. It improved from 229 to 412 from 2010 to 2018. The number of workers has just got doubled, and revenue has also increased from 156,730 OMR to 259,638 OMR.

Table 2. Yearly Statistics of Inbound Tourism.

Items	2010	2011	2012	2013	2014	2015	2016	2017	2018
Visitors Arrivals	1,500	1,393	1,714	1,923	2,225	2,634	3,207	3,178	3,242
Tourists (Overnight Stay)	1,441	1,018	1,241	1,392	1,611	1,909	2,335	2,316	2,301
Day Visitors	59	375	473	531	614	725	872	863	941
Tourists Nights	6,137	6,495	8,575	9,569	11,086	13,139	16,357	17,480	20,344
Average stay	4.3	6.4	6.9	6.9	6.9	6.9	7.0	7.5	8.8
Inbound Tourists spending (OMR)	140,548	158,614	192,993	238,473	306,489	364,753	427,341	532,264	679,175
Average spends (OMR)	93.7	113.9	112.6	124.0	137.7	138.5	133.3	167.5	209.5

Source: Ministry of Heritage and Tourism, Oman.

Table 3. Yearly Statistics of Outbound Tourism.

Items	2010	2011	2012	2013	2014	2015	2016	2017	2018
Departing visitors	2,829	3,341	3,972	4,301	4,727	5,424	5,902	6,368	5,975
Tourists (Overnight Stay)	1,873	2,446	2,888	3,103	3,358	3,838	4,167	4,473	3,350
Day Visitors	956	895	1,084	1,198	1,369	1,586	1,735	1,895	2,625
Tourists Nights	43,100	50,563	56,659	59,214	60,290	65,332	67,622	77,970	80,297
average stay	23.0	20.7	19.6	19.1	18.0	17.0	16.2	17.4	24.0
Outbound Tourism Expenditure (O.M.R.)	262,971	285,811	364,697	397,311	435,192	481,242	542,530	642,969	955,278
Average spends (O.M.R.)	93.0	85.5	91.8	92.4	92.1	88.7	91.9	101.0	159.9

Source: Ministry of Heritage and Tourism, Oman.

Table 4. Growth in Hotel Establishment in the Sultanate.

Items	2010	2011	2012	2013	2014	2015	2016	2017	2018
No. of hotels	229	248	258	282	297	318	337	367	412
No. of rooms	11,037	12,195	12,792	14,369	15,424	16,691	18,825	20,105	22,182
No. of workers	9,142	9,481	9,557	9,893	10,763	11,053	12,381	14,050	18,627
revenue (1,000)	156,730	153,881	179,103	198,835	216,898	226,965	230,332	236,136	259,638
Guests (A)	1,631	1,678	1,890	2,048	2,409	2,735	3,324	3,313	3,560
No. of room nights (1,000)	1,664	1,808	2,207	2,518	2,678	2,975	3,425	3,293	3,544
Room occupancy (%)	51.1	43.4	45.8	47.7	49.2	46.9	47.3	45.2	38.4

Source: Ministry of Heritage and Tourism, Oman.

Tables 5 and 6 are mainly based on tourist statistics for Dhofar tourism. It becomes essential to mention Dhofar tourism statistics because it is a great tourist destination in Oman for European, American, Australian, Arab, and GCC tourists. Table 6 indicates that the tourists' number has increased year-wise. The number of cruise passengers increased in 2016. Again, it recorded a fall but improved further in 2018 and 2019 (Table 7).

Table 5. Year-Wise Statistics of Dhofar Tourists in Different Seasons.

Year	No. of Visitors in Autumn	Difference
Statistics of Autumn for Dhofar Region		
2015	514,046	+
2016	652,986	+
2017	644,931	−
2018	826,376	+
2019	766,772	−
2020	COVID-19	
2021	COVID-19	
Statistics – Winter Tourism for Dhofar Region		
2016–2015	35,674	
2017–2016	40,748	+5,074
2018–2017	44,420	+3,672
2019–2018	40,161	−4,259
2020–2019	52,798	+12,637
2021–2020	COVID-19	

Source: Ministry of Heritage and Tourism, Oman.

Table 6. Year-Wise Cruise Ship Statistics.

Year	Number of Cruises	Number of Passengers
2015	25	28,295
2016	34	35,524
2017	26	25,630
2018	35	37,901
2019	45	69,060
2020	COVID-19	COVID-19

Source: Ministry of Heritage and Tourism, Oman.

Table 7. Statistics for Communication.

Descriptive Statistics

	N	Minimum	Maximum	Mean	Std. Deviation
COM1	19	1	3	2.37	0.831
COM2	19	1	3	1.68	0.885
COM3	19	1	3	1.53	0.772
COM4	19	1	3	2.16	0.688
COM5	19	1	5	2.63	1.012
COM6	19	1	5	2.79	1.182
COM7	19	1	5	2.79	1.273
COM8	19	1	3	2.16	0.834
COM9	19	1	5	3.21	1.134
COM10	19	1	5	2.53	0.905
COM11	19	1	5	2.79	0.918
COM	19	1.45	3.45	2.4211	0.57112
Valid N (listwise)	19				

Significance of Communication in Community Engagement

The above data show that due to government efforts, the number of tourists is increasing year by year. Oman's government is working hard to fast-track infrastructure development and the country's hospitality industry to facilitate better national and international tourists; as a result, Muscat and Salalah got their new International Airports. The Oman government is also making several significant efforts to ensure equal development in the villages. However, a research work by Mershen claimed that most locals still do not receive feasible benefits from tourists' activities (Mershen, 2006).

Research by Buerkertet al. (2010) claimed that ecotourism arguably faces the challenge of overcoming the conflicts in Oman that often exist within small towns. Al Shabiba mentioned an example regarding Ayn Al Kasfa. It is a hot water spring in the governorate of Al Batinah South. It was stopped because conflicts occurred between local people and government representatives in the area. There were disagreements concerning the water source and how it could be shared and disseminated among the locals and the project (Al-Balushi, 2015). Another community concern and resistance have been seen in Ain Al Hamran, Dhofar region when hotel projects started in 2022.

However, some projects have succeeded due to involving local people in tourism services' decision-making, planning, and development. For example, Khasab Castle in the governorate of Musandam received a UK-based "Museums and Heritage Awards for Excellence" (Eturbonews, 2010).

Nevertheless, as Raisanen (2018) stated, local communities do not consider tourism as a high prestige job. On the contrary, they feel that tourism and hospitality sector jobs are inferior and a reflection of the low salaries. This seems to be a cultural stigma associated with tourism jobs, as conservative families glare upon family members working in tourism. For example, they do not consider a hotel job suitable for women (Raisanen, 2018). How local communities react to tourism can come in different forms, such as resistance, retreatism, boundary maintenance, revitalization, and adoption (Doğan, 1989). For example, Gutberlet's (2016) research on the sociocultural impacts of large-scale cruise tourism in Mutrah Souq (Oman) found that the local community has fears and concerns about the loss of Omani identity for most of the local community. It is because the old town transferred to be a tourist destination that tourists overcrowd (Gutberlet, 2016).

Local community consensus, acceptability, and participation have become essential requirements for any economic development initiative (Muganda, Sirima, & Ezra, 2013). When the Government is highly focused on innovative tourism to diversify the country's economy, it becomes more significant to gain full community support. A strategic communication plan is a prerequisite to securing the top global tourist destination. Without strategic communication, no success can be ensured. However, sustainable tourism practices have become rampant in the last decade in the Sultanate, emphasizing the development of institutional entrepreneurship and social innovation. The country is trying to create a brand image to attract mass tourism by using visuals through different media platforms. In the series of these efforts, the communication emphasis is laid on image building rather than community communication (Al-Riyami, Scott, Ragab, & Jafar, 2017). It has been observed that many research works have been done on Oman Tourism. However, all research works have mainly addressed the multidisciplinary variables linked to an emerging trend in tourism and community-based tourism. Therefore, there has been a relatively minor realization of communication significance in creating consensus and acceptability for innovative tourism to support a diversified economy drive 2040 in the Sultanate. In tourism, communication strategies have been used to invite tourists and visitors to the country to access their country's land and scenic beauty. While communicating for community participation and contributing to facilitating visitors with an open-heart warm welcome still requires a considerable response at the local level. A single resentment of the local community to a recreational adventurous tourism idea can get a big jolt and discourage its whole development process.

Mainly when the country is focusing on a mass tourism drive, at the same time, it manifests many concerns to the local community (Baporikar, 2011). In some cases, it has been noticed that local communities have turned dissident against these visitors. Due to the influx of tourists, traffic jams, and accidents problems have become common. The food prices used to also push up high during tourist seasons. Such annoyance can be seen in small places and towns where the resources are limited, and demands get higher for daily needs. When the communities get affected because of the high influx of tourists, they raise their voices and displeasure at the ubiquitous development of innovative tourism (Mershen, 2006).

The Oman government is investing considerable money to develop world-class facilities in hospitality/accommodation, transportation, the recreation of adventurous exotic tourism attractions, and restoring cultural monuments and cultural heritage (Zyl, 2005). However, this whole drive cannot be successful without community participation and contribution. Along with the investment, understanding is also an essential requirement for developing innovative tourism enterprises. Here, communication plays a vital role. In some tourism-based European countries, national and state governments focus on community partnerships. They insist that tourism activities will take place in the public interest to achieve booming tourism and high revenue (AL-Mawali, AL-lawati, & Anandas, 2019; Al-Riyami et al., 2017).

This perception is supported by Robert Christie Mill (1990). He mentioned in his book *Tourism: The International Business* that tourism is considered an industry but cannot be treated like other technological and production unit industries. He said that it supports a variety of industries and promotes a diversified economy (Mill, 1990). Van Harssel (1993) supported Robert Christie's (1990) statement and added that the tourism industry is a composite of accommodation/hospitality, the recreation of adventure, transportation, food/beverages, and facilitating other travel comforts to the tourists to make them feel fantastic (Harssel, 1993).

According to Stephen L. J. Smith (1995), the tourism industry can be defined as those organizations and enterprises involved in facilitating tour and travel activities for tourism. It requires tourists' temporary movement from their routine life to places where they can experience stress-free time to fulfill their dream leisure. At the same time, it requires understanding, acceptance, and contribution of the locals and natives of the host country to facilitate a warm welcome to the tourists/visitors (Smith, 1995).

Graham Dann (2002) described tourism as a sociological process. Through strategic communication, its value can be enhanced. The tourists get inspired to visit a place due to mental needs, entertainment, adventure, esteem, self-actualization of nature, to explore another country's culture, religious reason, or aesthetic need (Dann, 2002). Oman has much more to offer its tourists as the country has spectacular mountain ranges, sea beaches, islands, scenic wadis, castles, forts, etc. (AL-Mawali, Al Lawati, & Anandas, 2019; Buerkert et al., 2010). In Oman, the Ministry of Heritage and Tourism is the focal point for planning, developing, managing, and interpreting tourist activities. In addition, they are responsible for maintaining communication with other stakeholders of country tourism. As Dann mentioned, tourism is a sociological process; communication becomes crucial for success. Hence, it becomes compulsory to understand the communication flow in the tourism sector.

How Communication Information Flow Works

Communication plays a significant role in sustainable tourism as it supports multiple dimensions of managing and marketing a business, an essential element for business survival (Dileep, 2014). A comprehensive communication strategy helps to create awareness, inform, advocate and build a network for tourism (McCabe, 2008). In the time of new media and communication exposure, information and dialogue-sharing can support different tourism industry stakeholders. It works in two layers – available information helps tourists search for destinations, book flights, accommodation, transportation, tourist guide, and adventurous activities for different types of tourism. In addition, it plays a determinant role in image building, while the host community and other stakeholders need the information to facilitate better to the tourists (Dileep, 2014). Therefore, a proper communication flow is essential as it connects government agencies, tourists, tourism stakeholders, and the host community. The communication flow is apparent in the below graph (Graph 1).

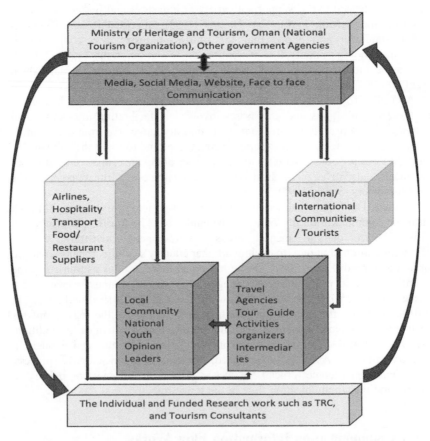

Graph 1.   Communication Flow in Tourism. *Source:* Adapted Model (Benckendorff, Xiang, & Sheldon, 2019; Dileep, 2014).

CARE Model and Its Relevance to the Oman Tourism

Tourism is a multistakeholder industry, so each stakeholder has a significant role in its sustainable growth. In this series, the host community plays a vital role in creating the country's image for safe and innovative tourism at the "world" level. The country's tourism can boom and score high revenue (AL-Mawali, Al Lawati, & Anandas, 2019; Al-Riyami et al., 2017) if the local community is aware of tourism benefits and encourages public–private partnerships. The C.A.R.E. model seems relevant here to create consensus and acceptability for innovative tourism. This model has been used for medical studies but its four variables: Communication, Awareness, Relationship, and Empowerment appear very significant in understanding the communication environment within the Ministry of Heritage and Tourism (Graph 2).

C.A.R.E. RESEARCH MODEL	
COMMUNICATION	Form a diverse research team that is relatable to community Establish focal point of communication in the beginning stage of innovative tourism Engage in active listening Share significant knowledge and information to the community regarding innovative tourism Encourage participation in country tourism and investment frequently
AWARENESS	Cultivate a visible and accessible presence in the community Educate community about innovative tourism and its benefits Review purpose of research partnership in creating awareness among the community. Discuss current Innovative tourism project and call for active participation of the community Disseminate research findings and potential of country tourisms among community members
RELATIONSHIPS	Build a collaborative coalition with tourism stakeholders and participants Identify opportunities for mutual benefits Explain the role of the community members in promoting country tourism Provide transparency to the tourism stakeholders throughout initiative Meet and collaborate community in all phases
EMPOWERMENT	Establish Trust with community members regarding new innovative tourism projects. Capitalize on available resources within community and intrinsic community capability Ensure confidence of the community in tourism investments. Provide Accessibility and openness to answers- questions Disseminate information about ongoing innovative project success to motivate more investment opportunities from the community
Build Trust	

Graph 2.   Adapted CARE Model. *Source:* Ceasar, Peters-Lawrence, Mitchell, and Powell-Wiley (2017).

Methodology

This chapter is based on qualitative and quantitative research methods. First, the purposive sampling technique is applied as the respondents are targeted from the

Ministry of Heritage and Tourism, Salalah. A survey questionnaire has been devised in Arabic, and an online questionnaire link has been created through Google Docs. Nineteen responses have been collected. Under the qualitative method, a semistructured interview has been conducted with senior specialists – geographic information system, A.D. tourism promotion, and tourism officer to understand the ministry communication flow to promote public–private partnership.

Discussion

The present discussion is based on 19 responses from the Ministry of Heritage and Tourism, Salalah, Dhofar. Communication is identified as an independent variable, while awareness, relationship, and empowerment have been devised as dependent variables. The items have been coded and analyzed by using IBM SPSS statistics 25.

After analyzing the Ministry of Heritage and Tourism's responses, the authors found that Oman tourism is characterized by participation with a mean score of 1.68 (SD = 0.885). However, a substantial lack of research relatable to the community is found with a mean score of 2.27 (SD = 0.831). The interview responses have also confirmed the quantitative responses. The Ministry of Heritage and Tourism employees agreed that they could submit their points of view related to tourism to their management and heads. As a result, they receive all relevant information and significant changes that occur several times. Still, 2.63 mean scores with (SD = 1.012) indicate that they all do not access information about current events in their local areas events and happening. With a mean score of 2.79 (SD = 1.182), it can be predicted that the idea of innovative tourism is yet to be explained among the different levels of employees within the ministry. The Oman Ministry of Heritage and Tourism is the focal point for planning, developing, managing, and interpreting tourism activities. If the ministry employees are clear about all aspects of innovative tourism, they can explain it better to other tourism stakeholders. Although different levels of employees do not know the innovative tourism idea, even then, they are trying to manage communication between different tourism institutions. It has been achieved more than 60%, yet 100% needs to be achieved. The interview responses have also supported this result. To achieve 100%, it needs to establish proper communication channels and a focal point of communication in all stages of innovative tourism. As 2.16 mean score (SD = 0.834) predicts that the communication channel lacks a focal point of communication strongly. A mean score of 3.21 (SD = 1.134) inclines toward neutral and disagreement; it predicts that due to a lack of communication channels and focal points of communication, there is a lack of sharing significant knowledge and information to the community regarding innovative tourism. However, the ministry employees at different levels are enthusiastic about encouraging the community to participate in country tourism and investment.

The interviewees stated that some local tourism facilitators were resistant and reluctant to adopt the new and innovative tourism approach when the empty quarters festival was organized between December 2021 and January 2022. Because they were accustomed to old tourism patterns. However, after understanding its benefits, they became encouraged to participate. The credit goes to the Ministry of Heritage and Tourism employees. Even though they do not have a suitable communication strategy to engage community members in innovative tourism, they are working harder to achieve their goal (Table 8).

Table 8. Statistics for Awareness.

Descriptive Statistics

	N	Minimum	Maximum	Mean	Std. Deviation
Aware1	19	1	5	3.26	1.284
Aware2	19	1	5	1.89	0.937
Aware3	19	1	5	2.16	0.958
Aware4	19	2	5	3.21	0.976
Aware5	19	1	3	2.42	0.838
Aware6	19	1	5	2.74	1.046
Aware7	19	1	3	2.26	0.872
Aware	19	1.57	3.43	2.5639	0.52267
Valid N (listwise)	19				

The awareness table shows a cumulative mean score of 2.5639 (SD = 0.52267), showing that communication affects the employees' awareness. It shows that innovative tourism is still in its very early stage. A mean score in the table for Aware 2 shows that social media is the most used channel to create awareness among community members. In contrast, other media channels are less utilized for awareness. The awareness program is getting done off and on during different span years, and the community later connects to different tourism activities to the ministry themselves. The review purpose of a research partnership in creating awareness among the community is still shallow as the responses of the ministry employees display a mean score of 2.42 (SD = 0.838). The responses about awareness of innovative tourism projects and the call for active community participation still need to be achieved as the mean score indicated in the table for Aware 6. Only 26.3% of the respondents are optimistic about disseminating research findings on awareness about potential country tourism. In comparison, 73.7% of respondents are unaware of disseminating any research and findings related to tourism (Table 9).

Table 9. Statistics for Relationships.

Descriptive Statistics

	N	Minimum	Maximum	Mean	Std. Deviation
Rel1	19	1	5	2.68	1.157
Rel2	19	1	5	2.63	1.065
Rel3	19	1	5	2.95	1.177
Rel4	19	1	5	2.84	1.015
Rel5	19	1	3	1.89	0.875
Rel	19	1.00	4.40	2.6000	0.83799
Valid N (listwise)	19				

52.6% of the ministry employees agreed that they built a collaborative coalition with tourism stakeholders and participants. At the same time, 47.4% of the respondents do not agree with this statement. With a mean score of 2.63 (SD = 1.065), the respondents agreed that different opportunities must be identified to build a mutual benefit. 42.2% of the respondents agreed that a strong relationship and trust can be built by explaining the role of the community members in promoting country tourism. 36.9% of respondents agreed that transparency to tourism stakeholders throughout the initiative works well, while 63.1% either disagreed or were neutral. 42.1% of respondents said they meet and collaborate with the community in all phases of tourism activities (Table 10).

Table 10. Statistics for Empowerment.

Descriptive Statistics

	N	Minimum	Maximum	Mean	Std. Deviation
EMP1	19	1	5	2.58	0.961
EMP2	19	1	5	2.74	1.098
EMP3	19	1	5	2.63	1.012
EMP4	19	1	5	2.53	1.073
EMP5	19	1	5	2.63	1.342
EMP6	19	1	5	3.00	1.374
EMP	19	1.33	4.33	2.6842	0.89735
Valid N (listwise)	19				

The mean score for Emp1 shows that most respondents agreed to establish trust among the community members regarding new innovative tourism projects. Because trust empowers and encourages them to participate actively. The respondents believe that empowerment can be done by capitalizing on available resources within the community and intrinsic community capability. It can also be done by ensuring community confidence in the tourism investment. As the country's tourism is characterized by participation, more than 63.2% of respondents agreed that empowerment of the community in the tourism sector can be achieved by openness – question and answer. In addition, 68.4% of respondents agreed that investment opportunities in tourism could be enhanced by disseminating information about ongoing innovative tourism projects. Finally, 52.7% of the respondents agreed that training could play a significant role in community engagement (Table 11).

Table 11. Correlations Between all Four Variables.

Correlations

		C.O.M.	Aware	Rel	E.M.P.	C.O.M.
C.O.M.	Pearson Correlation					
Aware	Pearson Correlation	0.507				
Rel	Pearson Correlation	0.715	0.786			
EMP	Pearson Correlation	0.703	0.494	0.692		

According to the received responses, a significant strong correlation appears in all four variables in positive trends. The data show that communication influences awareness, community relationships, and empowerment, whether it is in organizations or the community at large.

Findings and Results

- In the last decade, the Ministry of Heritage and Tourism's efforts has become successful nationally and internationally in building the image of Oman as an exotic tourist destination.
- The findings indicate that the existing communication mechanism lacks research relatable to the community.
- Innovative tourism idea is still in the early stage in Oman. It needs to be explained among different levels of employees within the Ministry of Heritage and Tourism, especially in the Dhofar region, where the vast opportunities for innovative tourism can create a massive difference in attracting national and international tourists to contribute to the country's GDP.

- There is no focal point of communication. Due to this, a communication gap persists between local communities and NTO. A suitable communication strategy must be adopted to ensure communication effectiveness among tourism stakeholders. A focal point of communication must be designated in all stages of innovative tourism.
- There is a lack of insufficient significant knowledge and information with the community regarding innovative tourism.
- Different communication opportunities must be identified, and community benefits must be explained to the community members.
- The community can be empowered by capitalizing on available resources and opening easy access to communication and information. In addition, training and workshops for national youth can play a significant role in community engagement and enhance investment opportunities.

Implications and Future Direction

In the digital era, when global societies and virtual tourists are accessing information about a country and its culture for their destination search, it becomes significant to emphasize the image-building of a country for sustainable tourism. That is why, most of the time, the communication plan is centered on attracting national and international tourists. Community communication becomes secondary. In the image-building process, the tourism countries target their audience by communicating USP, which makes them different from their competitors. However, when it comes to community communication to create a mutually beneficial relationship for public and private partnerships, the RACE Model can be applied to develop strategic public relations communication as it includes four phases: research, action planning, communication to build relationships, and evaluation. Here, the authors suggest that research relatable to the community needs to be emphasized, and an active research center can be established. The research center aims to connect directly with the community for feedback, concerns, ideas, and suggestions to help policymakers and communication strategists to enhance public and private partnerships and accelerate investment in-country tourism.

A communication center must be established within the ministry as a focal point of communication for the community. It needs to be responsible for facilitating information and creating awareness among the community about innovative tourism and its benefits in enhancing their living standards. It also needs to create suitable communication strategies to meet the international communication standard and promote different countries' tourism levels. The center can invite queries and provide relatable information to ensure the community's confidence in tourism investment and encourage risk-taking. It will work as a two-way communication flow, providing information and ensuring communication effectiveness. This will help enhance the community relationship with the Ministry of Heritage and Tourism and empower the community with confidence. A communication strategy power-packed with research can serve the essential elements for the success of the country's tourism and help in achieving the vision of 2040 for tourism.

Yearly basis, community tourism awareness campaigns can be conducted, and youth risk-takers and opinion leaders can be kept a focal point to influence the community at large.

Workshops and training programs need to be arranged for the different levels of employees in the ministry to communicate about innovative tourism, new market strategies, and strong partnership with the community.

Limitations and Directions for Future Studies

- The present research has some limitations, such as accessing the data, which are more centralized in Muscat, the capital city.
- The authors faced challenges in collecting the data in the Ministry of Heritage and Tourism, Dhofar region. Only 19 survey responses and 3 interviews could be conducted because the Dhofar region has Khareef season (Monsoon season) during July and August, and the ministry employees were busy preparing for Khareef activities which is the measure tourists' destination in monsoon season.
- The present study can be considered as pilot research and a foundation stone to understanding the communication role in creating consensus and acceptability for innovative tourism to support diversified economic drive in the Sultanate.
- The Ministry of Heritage and Tourism in Muscat is the main center where the planning and other decisions related to country tourism take place. The present study data have been collected from the Ministry of Heritage and Tourism, Salalah, Dhofar region. So, the findings can be confirmed with the main center in Muscat.
- The present study focused on the data from the Ministry of Heritage and Tourism; another study can be done with different stakeholders of tourism from the community to understand the effectiveness of communication in promoting country tourism. This will facilitate a comprehensive understanding of communication effectiveness in rebuilding and raising awareness for Oman's safe and innovative future tourism.

Conclusion

Oman tourism is on the path of recovery postpandemic. In this series, the Government focuses on Khareef season tourism in the Dhofar region as it has always been a divergent tourist destination for Omanis and other Arabs, GCC countries, the United States, Australia, and European countries. The Government has made all efforts to achieve prepandemic tourism status of Oman. Several research projects are going on under the Research Council, the Ministry of Higher Education, Research and Innovation, to promote country tourism and achieve Oman Vision 2040. Previous studies in the tourism discipline are more focused on sustainable tourism, while communication significance in sustainable growth in Oman tourism is less addressed. When the country emphasizes achieving its previous status after the pandemic, this chapter is a must-read as it fills the gap in communication significance in achieving tourism plans with community participation. The study reflects a comprehensive understanding of the development drive of Oman tourism, its challenges, and their efforts to engage the community in-country tourism to achieve Oman Vision 2040.

References

Al-Balushi, Y. (2015, March 23). The people of Ain al-Kasfa in Rustaq refuse to develop it! What.

AL-Mawali, N. R., AL-lawati, A. M., & Anandas, S. (2019). *Diversification of Oman economy for sustainable development: Strategic issues and imperatives.* Oman: College of banking and financial studies, Muscat.

Al-Mughairi, H. M., Bhaskar, P., & Alazri, A. k. (2021, November 9). The economic and social impact of COVID-19 on tourism and hospitality industry: A case study from Oman. *Wiley.* doi:10.1002/pa.2786

Al-Nassriya, Z. (2020, December 13). The tourism sector in Oman has lost half a billion rials due to the impact of Coronavirus. Zawya. Retrieved from https://www.zawya.com/en/business/tourism-sector-in-oman-loses-half-a-billion-rials-due-to-impact-of-coronavirus-go37cawq

Al-Riyami, H., Scott, N., Ragab, A. M., & Jafar, v. (2017). Evaluating ecotourism challenges in Oman. In M. L. Stephenson & A. Al-Hamarneh (Eds.), *International tourism development and the Gulf cooperation Council states: Challenges and opportunities* (pp. 156–168). London, essay: Routledge, Taylor & Francis Group.

Baporikar, N. (2011). Emerging trends in tourism industry in Oman. In P. O. Pablos, O. P. Pablos, R. Tennyson, & J. Zhao (Eds.), *Global hospitality and tourism management technologies* (p. 20). I.G.I. Global. Retrieved from https://www.researchgate.net/publication/288753624_Emerging_Trends_in_Tourism_Industry_in_Oman

Benckendorff, P. J., Xiang, Z., & Sheldon, P. J. (2019). *Tourism information technology* (3rd ed.). Boston, MA: CABI.

Buerkert, A., Luedeling, E., Dickhoefer, U., Lohrer, K., Mershen, B., Schaeper, W., Nagieb, M., & Schlecht, E. (2010). Prospects of mountain ecotourism in Oman: The example of As Sawjarah on Al Jabal al Akhdar. *Journal of Ecotourism, 9*(2), 104–116. doi:10.1080/14724040902803404

Ceasar, J., Peters-Lawrence, M. H., Mitchell, V., & Powell-Wiley, T. M. (2017). The communication, awareness, relationships and empowerment (CARE) model: An effective tool for engaging urban communities in community-based participatory research. *International Journal of Environmental Research and Public Health, 14*(11), 1422.

ÇETİN, İ., & AL-Alwi, A. N. (2018). Economic diversity and contribution of tourism to an economy. *International Journal of Tourism, Economic and Business Sciences, 2*(2). Retrieved from https://dergipark.org.tr/tr/download/article-file/619724

Dann, G. (2002). *Tourist as a metaphor of the social world* (1st ed.). New York, NY: CABI Publishing.

Dileep, M. R. (2014, July). Sustainable tourism development: An explorative study of inter-stakeholder communication in the sultanate of Oman. *Tourism Dimensions*, 39–48. Retrieved from https://www.researchgate.net/profile/Adarsh-Batra/publication/325822883_The_Role_of_Airport_Servicescape_The_Transient_Community_Perspective/links/5cef555b4585153c3da54eda/The-Role-of-Airport-Servicescape-The-Transient-Community-Perspective.pdf#page=45

Doğan, H. Z. (1989). Forms of adjustment: Socio-cultural impacts of tourism. *Annals of Tourism Research*, *16*(2), 216–236. Retrieved from https://www.sciencedirect.com/science/article/abs/pii/0160738389900698

Eturbonews. (2010). The Khasab Castle is spectacularly-mountainous. e Turbo News. Retrieved from http://www.eturbonews.com/16213/khasab-castle-oman-bagsinter national-award. Accessed on February 1, 2015.

Gutberlet, M. (2016). Sociocultural impacts of large-scale cruise tourism in Souq Mutrah, Sultanate of Oman. *Fennia*, *194*(1), 46–63.

Harssel, J. V. (1993). *Tourism: An exploration* (3rd ed.). Prentice-Hall.

Liu, Z. (2003, March 29). Sustainable tourism development: A critique. *Journal of Sustainable Tourism*, *11*(6), 459–475. doi:10.1080/09669580308667216

Mason, P. (2020). *Tourism impacts, planning and management* (4th ed.). London: Routledge.

McCabe, S. (2008). *Marketing communications in tourism and hospitality: Concepts, strategies and cases* (1st ed.). London: Routledge.

Mershen, B. (2006). Development of community-based tourism in Oman: Challenges and opportunities. In R. F. Daher (Ed.), *Tourism in the Middle East*. Channel View Publications.

Mill, R. C. (1990). *Tourism: The international business*. Englewood Cliffs, NJ: Prentice Hall.

Muganda, M., Sirima, A., & Ezra, P. M. (2013). The role of local communities in tourism development: Grassroots perspectives from Tanzania. *Journal of Human Ecology*, *41*(1), 53–66.

Muscat Daily. (2022, February 27). Tourism promotion in Paris. Muscat Daily. Retrieved from https://www.muscatdaily.com/2022/02/27/oman-moving-around-paris-mht-launches-tourism-promotional-campaign-in-france/

Nair, V. (2022, February 27). R.O. 3 Billion investment in tourism sector by 2023. Oman Observer. Retrieved from https://www.omanobserver.om/article/1115312/oman/tourism/ro-3-billion-investment-in-tourism-sector-by-2023

National Centre for Science Information. (2020). 53.9% decrease in guests of hotels rated (3–5) stars by the end of October 2020. Retrieved from https://www.ncsi.gov.om/News/Pages/NewsCT_20201130120332490.aspx

Oman News Agency. (2021, August 17). Oman to unveil R.O. 6 bn tourism revival plan. Oman Observer. Retrieved from https://www.omanobserver.om/article/1105537/oman/tourism/oman-to-unveil-ro-6-bn-tourism-revival-plan

Oman Observer. (2022, March 8). Oman is the seventh-best tourist destination in the world. Retrieved from https://www.omanobserver.om/article/1115825/oman/tourism/oman-7th-best-tourist-destination-in-world

ONA. (2022, June 14). 3–5 star hotels see a remarkable revenue increase. *Times of Oman*. News. writecaliber. Retrieved from https://news.writecaliber.com/tourism-oman-3-5-star-hotels-see-remarkable-increase-in-revenues-i-times-of-oman/

ONA. (2022, April 23). A tourism campaign was launched in Venice to promote Oman. Times of Oman. Retrieved from https://timesofoman.com/article/115918-tourism-campaign-launched-in-venice-to-promote-oman

Oxford Business Group. (2020). *The report: Oman 2020.* Oxford Business Group. Retrieved from https://oxfordbusinessgroup.com/news/report-what-extent-has-covid-19-pandemic- accelerated-economic-diversification-oman

Raisanen, J. (2018). *Changing perceptions of tourism as a respectable career choice for Omani women.* Hämeenlinna: H.A.M.K. Häme University of Applied Sciences, Business Management and Entrepreneurship.

Smith, S. L. (1995). The tourism satellite account: Perspectives of Canadian tourism associations and organizations. *Tourism Economics, 1*(3), 225–244. doi:10.1177/135481669500100302

Times of Oman. (2022, June 6). Six tourist sites to be developed in Dhofar. Times of Oman. Retrieved from https://timesofoman.com/article/117716-6-tourist-sites-to-be-developed-in-dhofar

UNWTO BRIEFING. (2020, June). How are countries supporting tourism recovery? U.N.W.T.O. Retrieved from https://webunwto.s3.eu-west-1.amazonaws.com/s3fs-public/2020-06/BFN_V4.pdf

Zyl, C. J. (2005, April). The role of tourism in the conservation of cultural heritage with particular relevance for South Africa. The University of Stellenbosch, Department of History. Retrieved from https://core.ac.uk/download/pdf/37318992.pdf

Responsible Sustainable Tourism Product Planning and Design for Recovery

Sweety Jamgade and Puja Mondal

Abstract

Tourism product designing is a process of integrating all the components of a tourism product, i.e., the 5 A's: Attraction, Accommodation, Accessibility, Amenities, and Activities. The lack of awareness and unaccountability of mass tourism has demanded the need for "Responsible and Accountable Tourism, calling for better places to live and visit." However, due to the COVID-19 pandemic restrictions on mass travel, "Mother Earth" got the opportunity of environmental restoration. The tourism business was badly hit by the pandemic and created an introspection phase for the tourism stakeholders to control and check their activities for a better global recovery. The responsible tourism product development in this VUCA (volatile, uncertain, complex, ambiguous) world needs controlled planning and a duty-bound PPP (Public–Private Partnership) model. A scoping review was done to analyze the planning process of the responsible sustainable tourism product. It was observed that all the stakeholders involved in tourism product development need to understand their accountability. Local host communities and tourists visiting the destinations should be culturally and environmentally sensitive. They should be involved in decision-making during the tourism product development and be pride bearers. The responsibility of the various tourism agencies, organizations, and individuals toward minimizing the impact of carbon footprints is evident from various research.

Keywords: Product planning; product design; sustainability framework; tourist responsibility; tourist behavior; stakeholders

Resilient and Sustainable Destinations After Disaster, 179–193
Copyright © 2023 Sweety Jamgade and Puja Mondal
Published under exclusive licence by Emerald Publishing Limited
doi:10.1108/978-1-80382-021-720231013

Introduction

According to UNWTO "Tourism is a series of activities, facilities, and industries that provide a travel experience for persons traveling away from home, including transport, lodging, retail shops, businesses, and other hospitality services." The tourism industry is a significant contributor to the global economy (Haid & Albrecht, 2021). Tourism is a large industry worldwide, as well as a key economic sector in many countries (Vu, Tran, Nguyen, & Nguyen, 2020). At the moment, tourism development occurs in a very dynamic and competitive atmosphere. Tourist stakeholders must decide on how to perform in the growing and transforming conditions pertaining to the market supply and demand (Eckert & Pechlaner, 2019). In the real market condition, the demand for sustainable tourism development methods can improve the role of the customers, only when market participants are involved in tourism planning (Lorincz, Banász, & Csapó, 2020).

Due to the growing competitiveness, tourism planning must be reconsidered. Previously, places used to compete on an individual basis in the global market, but now there is a need for more cooperation, new planning methods, and contemporary organizations. It is necessary that planners and managers comprehend sustainability and incorporate it into tourism planning and practices because it is essential to a destination's capacity to compete. Additionally, a number of strategies and guiding principles for the development and promotion of sustainable tourism are based on tourism industry planning (Fernandes, Brandão, & Costa, 2017). Forecasts indicate that the global tourism industry will continue to experience significant growth in terms of both visitor numbers and spending well into the future. The evidence that tourism's continued growth is now generating decreasing returns for suppliers and host populations that rely on volume growth to offset yield declines is mounting, even as business owners and destination managers look for ways to promote tourism. Additionally, there is growing evidence that tourism's expansion is creating more negative social and environmental costs (Dwyer, 2016).

Responsible tourism has emerged as an important tool for implementing a pro-poor, pro-community, and long-term program. Because the concept is new, it is gaining a lot of interest around the world (Mathew & Thankachan, 2019). Application of sustainability refers to responsible tourism. History has shown the significance of sustainable tourism, and accountability as the foundation of its complete implementation (Mihalic, Mohamadi, Abbasi, & David, 2021).

The concept of responsible tourism is "Tourism which does the following":

- reduces adverse societal, economic, and environmental effects;
- increases the wellness of host communities and brings about higher local economic benefits;
- enhances employment opportunities and industry access;
- offers travelers more pleasurable encounters through deeper ties with locals, and a better comprehension of their cultural, socioeconomic, and environmental concerns
- engages locals in decisions that influence their quality of life and chances for the future (Idahosa, 2019).

Sustainable tourism maintains an equilibrium between the pros and cons of tourism development by focusing on the important pillars of economic, social, and environmental sustainability (Nigg & Eichelberger, 2021). While responsible tourism refers to the concept of sustainability and its causes, environmental sustainability refers to the concept of sustainable tourism, and its pillars and impacts. History has shown the value of sustainable tourism, but accountability is the foundation of its complete implementation (Mihalic et al., 2021). As applied technology and consumption patterns change, sustainable tourism development is a dynamic process that is continuously facing new problems (Streimikiene, Svagzdiene, Jasinskas, & Simanavicius, 2020).

The term "sustainable tourism product" refers to a broad concept of the use of resources that are limited in a way that is socially acceptable, environmentally responsible, and economically viable, allowing users to fulfill their current necessities without jeopardizing the facility of future generations to use the same resources. Therefore, greater practical improvements to cater to the next generation are through the goal of sustainable tourism products. Tourism products that are sustainable require the assurance of all the stakeholders in addition to a strong commitment by the governing body to ensure to accomplish their objectives in terms of economic, sociocultural, and environmental factors (Global Sustainable Tourism Council, n.d.). Also, every stakeholder must ensure that tourism-related goods improve the life standards of local people who have lived in tourist areas for a long time sustainably (Argon, Daragmeh, & Oshora, 2021). The number of people traveling to places that are part of protected areas continues to rise. A clear trend of general interest in traveling off the beaten path can be seen in the growing number of tourism products, including leisure travel to secluded Black Sea beaches, skiing, adventure, gastronomy, and other types of tourism to eco-friendly rural regions and maintained cultural heritage sites (Karolev & Ohridska-olson, 2017). Therefore, the creation of marketable and appealing products can be seen as the foundation for the long-term growth of tourism in any location (Acha-Anyi, 2016). Recent advancements in the tourist sector have reignited interest in rural tourism as a driver of socioeconomic renewal and development of rural areas, particularly sensitive areas with declining agricultural or soft industrial activity (Ibănescu, Stoleriu, Munteanu, & Iatu, 2018).

Niche tourism is a form of specialty tourism and has emerged as contradictory to mass tourism. Niche tourism product identification is a powerful task to the tourism organization (Bandaru & Kumar, 2021). In addition to transforming tourist places into "green destinations" by protecting these locations' environments from deterioration, "green innovation" has emerged as one of the most crucial strategic tools for sustaining tourism resources and making tourism environmentally friendly (Elzek, Gaafar, & Abdulsamie, 2021).

The United Nations highlighted the importance of meeting Sustainable Development Goals (SDGs) through tourism by declaring the "International Year of Sustainable Tourism for Development" in 2017 (Marin-Pantelescu, Tachiciu, Capusneanu, & Topor, 2019). Environmental protection, quality of life, social justice, cultural diversity, and a robust dynamic economy that creates employment and wealth for everyone should be taken into consideration when planning sustainable tourism products (Zeng, 2022). The notion of responsibility is well known, but it links to many areas of tourism, social and sustainable development, and tourist behavior, and provides a variety of research opportunities (State & Bulin, 2016). Sustainable development of tourism requires informed participation from all key stakeholders as well as strong governance in order to facilitate broad engagement and consensus building. Monitoring the impact continuously and adopting preventive measures are essential for sustainable tourism. Diverse stakeholders should be included in tourism planning. Due to the existence of several stakeholders with vast viewpoints, diverse visions, and varied interests, the process of developing a tourism destination is complex. High levels of stakeholder cooperation are one characteristic recognized for successful destination management planning, despite the complexity of the planning process (Pjerotic, 2017).

Reduced bad effects on the environment, and also the wellness of building inhabitants are the goals of sustainable design, which seeks to enhance building performance. Limiting the use of nonrenewable resources, eliminating waste, and establishing productive ecosystems are indeed the main objectives of sustainability (GSA, n.d).

Sustainable design concepts may be seen in all of these instances.

- Improve site ability;
- Lessen the use of nonrenewable energy;
- Utilize eco-friendly materials;
- Conserve and protect water;
- Improve the value of the environment; and
- Enhance operation and maintenance practices

Purpose of the Study

The primary goal of this chapter is to disseminate conceptual knowledge of sustainable and responsible tourist product planning in order to support the tourism industry in recover from the COVID-19 pandemic's devastating effects. The purpose of this study is to conduct an extensive literature search in order to learn more about responsible sustainable product planning. The current research looks at the case study of tourism in India and Belize after COVID-19.

Methodology

A systematic scoping review was utilized in this study to assess the literature review using four criteria: (1) sustainability; (2) product planning and development; (3) responsible tourist behavior; and (4) recovery. Scoping reviews are frequently used to give a general overview of a subject, and literature map, and recognize essential theories, conceptual, and sources of information. They work finest when a subject is difficult or hasn't been thoroughly studied (Rasoolimanesh, Hall, Ramakrishna, & Esfandiar, 2020). Systematic scoping reviews and comprehensive systematic reviews are distinct from one another due to the specificity of the research topic in the former, which is more focused and less exploratory, and the latter, which is typically confined to one suitable database in the latter (Rasoolimanesh et al., 2020). The social sciences, including tourism, are increasingly using scoping reviews (Rasoolimanesh et al., 2020). The current study analyzed journal papers published in Scopus-indexed publications and Google Scholar from 2016 to 2022 for responsible sustainable tourist product planning and design for recovery. Many of the information was also collected from website articles and newsletters. Major databases like the Web of Science, Scopus, and Google Scholar are typically used for large-scale bibliometric research. The authors identified the case study of India and Belize regarding sustainable tourism products planning post-COVID-19. The details of the systematic literature review are given in Table 1.

Table 1. Systematic Literature Review.

Data base	Scopus index
	Google Scholar
	Web of Science (WoS)
Number of papers and articles downloaded	64
Number of papers and articles included	42
Number of papers and articles excluded	22
Keywords searched	Sustainable tourism product planning
	Responsible design for recovery
	Responsible sustainable tourism
Total journal papers	25
Total website articles and news	17

Case Study

This pandemic, which has caused a global health disaster, has paralyzed the entire planet. Service businesses have suffered locally, nationally, and internationally as a result of prolonged lockdowns and social isolation (Hussain & Fusté-Forné, 2021).

The COVID-19 pandemic had a significant influence on the travel and tourist industry. In March 2020, lockdowns and quarantines were implemented to stop the virus's spread. During the spring coronavirus pandemics, popular tourist spots across the globe shut their borders (Golja, 2021).

However, there were few destinations across the globe that were resilient to attracting tourists and contributing to the tourism industry by incorporating various strategic practices. The case study considered for this chapter is of India and Belize shown in Tables 2 and 3.

India ranks second in the most populous country in the world, the seventh country in terms of land area, and the world's most populous democracy. The region is defined by the Indian Ocean to the south, the Arabian Sea to the southwest, and the Bay of Bengal to the southeast (India, n.d).

India's national and state governments, as well as the public and private sectors, have shown an interest in wide development plans in the social, clean technology (clean energy and water, and sustainable agriculture), and human resources sectors (IBEF, 2011). India is anticipated to start greening its national income accounting and include the wealth of depleting natural resources as a significant factor in measuring its gross domestic product (Ministry of External Affairs Government of India, 2021) (Table 2).

Table 2. Case Study of India.

Case 1: Himachal Pradesh	In the months following the state's relaxation of COVID-19 restrictions in June 2021, about 6–7 lakh tourists visited Himachal Pradesh. Atal Tunnel Rohtang (ATR), located in the Kullu area, is now a popular tourist destination (Mint, 2021). 18,500 tourists pass through Himachal each day, including 7,500 who visit the Rohtang Tunnel (Times of India, 2021).
Popular places and tourist footfall:	It is also famous for temples, parks, valleys and trekking trips. The number of tourists visiting the state has increased dramatically. Around 42 lakh visitors have visited the state this year (2022), with roughly 27 lakh arriving since March's commencement. In 2021, there was a 55 lakh tourists footfall. The prominent tourist destinations of Shimla, Manali, and Dharamsala attracts majority visitors. Lahaul & Spiti Valley, a tribal district in the Himalayas, has also become a popular tourist destination, particularly since the construction of the Atal Tunnel in 2020. Officials estimate that the number of visitors is from Delhi and Punjab (The New Indian Express, 2022).
Strategies:	To attract more visitors, the state administration is encouraging religious tourism and adventure sports.
Case 2: Kashmir	Around 1.8 lakh tourists visited the valley, the biggest number in a decade (India.com, 2022). In the year 2021, there was 65,814 tourists. There were 664,199 domestic visitors and 1,615 international visitors. In the month of March 2022, 179,970 tourists visited Kashmir.

Table 2. *(Continued)*

Popular places and tourist footfall:	With 3.5 million arrivals, Srinagar airport broke its previous record (2021). In December 2021 it recorded the highest visitor of 1.5 lakh the greatest monthly figure (Rashid, 2022). According to Dr. GN Itoo, Director of Tourism for Kashmir, the high footfall of tourists is the result of a number of initiatives, such as roadshows that promoted Kashmir tourism across the nation and other measures that helped draw visitors after the virus' second wave. The Kashmiri government has planned 21 roadshows around the nation (Times of India, 2022).
Strategies:	The first hot-air balloon ride has begun in Zabarwan Park in Srinagar, according to the tourism bureau. The department is also considering adventure sports like paragliding (India.com, 2022).
Case 3: Kerala	A remarkable increase of 72.48% of domestic ravellers, i.e., 3.8 million in the first quarter of 2022 when compared to 2.2 million footfalls during the same period of 2021 is seen in Kerala.
Popular places and tourist footfall:	With 811,426 visitors, the Ernakulam district had the most domestic tourists, followed by Thrissur (358,052), Idukki (511,947), Thiruvananthapuram (600,933), and Wayanad (310,322). Idukki, Malappuram, Kasaragod, Pathanamthitta, and Wayanad are the five districts with the most footfall since their creation.
Strategies:	The first three months of this year 2022 saw a considerable increase of 16 lakh tourists as compared to the previous year. This significant increase in the number of visitors within the country suggests that Kerala Tourism's domestic segment has recovered from the pandemic's effects. New tourist goods and activities, such as caravan travel, adventure travel, and the second Champions Boat League season (CBL), which will be hosted in 2022 as well as STREET Project and Responsible Tourism, will undoubtedly boost the domestic tourism sector (The Economics Times, 2022).

Table 2. *(Continued)*

Industry stakeholders launch "Keralam Kaanaam," a project to provide inexpensive lodging and activities to local tourists, in an effort to resume tourism following COVID-19. Kerala Tourism intends to introduce short-haul tours after COVID-19, with a focus on local tourism (The New Indian Express, 2020).

With just over 390,000 citizens, Belize is a tiny nation. It is dubbed "Mother Nature's Best Kept Secret," has one foot in the Central American tropical jungle tucked between Mexico (north) and Guatemala (southwest) and the other in the Caribbean Sea (east), with hundreds of islands ripe for exploration protected by the Western Hemisphere's longest living coral reef. The tourism business in Belize is still a developing industry, and its long-term viability is crucial. Belize's tourism offering is relatively diverse, despite its tiny size. It has a strong ecotourism, adventure, and cultural tourism industries, as well as some growth in sun and beach, maritime and cruise tourism. Belize has a lot of ecotourism assets, as well as cultural tourism assets. International tourism is attracted to a wide spectrum of these assets (Nuennunghoff, Lemay, Rogers, & Martin, 2015).

Table 3. Case Study of Belize.

Popular places and tourist footfall:	The lush jungle and breathtaking Mayan ruins experiences bring in roughly USD $15 million a year to Belize's economy. The Chiquibul-Mountain Pine Ridge-Caracol Complex is a nature-bound environment that offers the people and economy of Belize advantages like biodiverse forests, rivers, clean water, and food production. More than $15 million is brought in a year by 13 tourist attractions and 27 resorts because of the area's beautiful rainforests and Mayan ruins.
Strategies:	Prior to COVID-19 scuba diving, ziplining, and live-seeing of jaguars in the jungle habitat were all major tourist attractions in Belize. According to the research of the Stanford Natural Capital Project, the government of Belize announced in 2020, an ambitious plan to resuscitate its economy by capitalizing on its ecosystems to avoid the economic collapse.

Table 3. *(Continued)*

However, the sustainable development team of the Prime Minister was aware that Belize could no longer rely on it as a source of income when the COVID-19 hit. They then prepared strategies for these activities:

- sustainable forestry and agriculture
- safeguarding water resources; and
- greater emphasis on home tourism rather than an international tourist (Cafasso, 2020).

The development of the tourism industry for other Belizeans was part of the building of a more comprehensive plan. Belizeans could be drawn to ecotourism and Mayan cultural sites, but the government's tourism agency has hitherto prioritized the global market. Belizean visitors might take advantage of the existing ecotourism infrastructure while insulating the country from the cyclical nature of international tourism. Through the implementation of this audacious and cutting-edge master plan, Belize will be able to set the standard for landscape management in its protected areas (Cafasso, 2020).

Many nations that are heavily reliant on tourism (such as Mallorca, Belize, and Cuba) have implemented "safe corridors" plans in response to the tourism industry's rapid decline and travelers' dislike of solitude. Tourists can visit nations on the "safe corridor" list without being quarantined under the "safe corridor" system.

The Belizean government adopted a number of actions to lessen the outbreak's financial toll.

(1) A COVID-19 assistance program was established, providing unemployed people with payments of 150 Belize dollars (BZ$) every two weeks and BZ$2,500 to support MSMEs.

(2) In addition, according to Moloney (2020) native people in Belize, such as the Garifunas, have reverted to their traditional origins by rearing chickens and developing of herbal gardens to supplement their income (Cheng & Zetina, 2021).

Responsible Sustainable Tourism Product Planning and Design

The knowledge of the primary constituents of the tourism industry is necessary to understand tourism product planning and design. The constituents of the tourism industry refer to the basic services which are the core indispensable elements in the tourism industry. The secondary constituents are directly and indirectly linked to the tourism core services and generally in intangible form, for added services to the tourism industry. The tertiary constituents are linked indirectly to the tourism industry and are in tangible form, i.e., bodies with their contribution to the social and economic development of the tourism industry (Gupta, Singh, Kirar, & Bairwa, 2015). Table 4 indicates the various constituents of the tourism industry:

Table 4. Constituents of the Tourism Industry.

Primary/Major Constituents	Secondary Constituents	Tertiary Constituents
Transport industry – air, road, water and rail transport facility, local transport – auto, cabs, share ride, etc.	*Facilitation services* of passport, visa, customs, immigration, permit	Developers, real estate
Accommodation – hotel, lodges, home stay, etc.	*Retail* – Shops, handicrafts, and state emporiums, arts and crafts	Communication service providers
Food and Catering – restaurants, food joints, catering outlets, etc.	*Banking facilities* – ATM, Forex, etc.	Education and training Institutes
Intermediaries – Travel Agents, Tour Operators, OTA – Online Travel Agency, guides, escorts, translators, tourism organizations, tourist information and reception centers, and allied government departments, reservation systems	*Entertainment industry* – performing artists, films	Hygiene and sanitation control bodies
	Travel and health insurance companies, brokers	Automobiles
	Hawkers, coolies/porters	Distilleries
	Advertising agency, Publishers	Food and service quality assurance bodies
	Safety and security agencies	

Tourism product development means planning and designing a product that has all the components of a tourism product, viz. destination, tourist facilities, services, amenities, activities, etc. In tourism business management, it is a way of integrating all the components of tourism products, the 5 A's, i.e., Attraction, Accommodation, Accessibility, Amenities, and Activities. Due to the lack of awareness and unaccountability of mass tourism, it had created the demand for Responsible: "Accountable" Tourism- "Calling for better places to live and visit".

The responsible tourism product development in this era of pandemic disaster needs controlled planning and a duty-bound PPP (Public–Private Partnership) product model. All the stakeholders involved in tourism product development need to understand their accountability. Local host communities and tourists visiting the destinations should be culturally and environmentally sensitive. They should be involved in decision-making during tourism product development and be pride bearers. The process of any product development has a cycle of planning of the core product development, facilitated and augmented product development. Tourism product development requires the responsibility of public and private partnerships for effective functioning. Table 5 illustrates the components of a tourism product and its fundamental strategic responsible practices required for a "Responsible Sustainable Tourism Product Planning and Design for Recovery."

Table 5. Responsible Sustainable Tourism Product Planning and Design.

Product	Stakeholders	Responsible Practices
1. Core Product – "Attraction"	Governing bodies, authorities and stake holders	Amendment of socioeconomic, cultural, and economic ethics. Eco-conservation practices and education through Ecotourism
2. Facilitated Product – "Accommodation and Accessibility"	Hotel and Transport Industries	Voluntary act for eco-friendly practices, energy management, preservation through green practices. Corporate Social Responsibility.
3. Augmented Product – "Amenities and Activities"	Service consultants, Entertainment organizations, Academic institutes, host, local public, and tourists	Sustainable, social-cultural practices, responsible deeds toward economic and environmental development.

Each illustrated component has its key stakeholders who play a major role in developing the product. They have vital accountabilities and should efficiently and effectively practice them. This entire framework of the tourism system produces "Responsible Tourism Products." Hitherto, the responsible tourism system with product planning and development of each component of the tourism product, its responsible stakeholders, and their practices are shown in Table 5.

The responsibility followed by the various stakeholders – tourism agencies, organizations, and individuals contributes to minimizing the impact of carbon footprints, which is evident from various researches. The green practices adopted to counter the bad effects on nature and the environment such as voluntary tree plantation, using renewal energy, and avoiding deforestation are apparent. The other remedial solution to attract the tourists to revive the economy through various organizations is required. The responsibility taken together by participants like tour operators, destination management companies, and tourism organizations is evident in countries like France, Spain, China, the United Kingdom, the United States, Australia, Canada, Sri Lanka, Singapore, Malaysia, India, Belize, etc.

References

Acha-Anyi, P. N. (2016). Planning and development of sustainable tourism products in local communities. *African Journal of Hospitality Tourism and Leisure*, *5*(3), 1–20. Retrieved from https://fdocuments.in/document/planning-and-development-of-sustainable-tourism-products-in-2020-01-26-planning.html?page=10

Argon, N. Md., Daragmeh, A., & Oshora, B. (2021). Market design for sustainable tourism products and services. In A. Hassan (Ed.), *Tourism products and services in Bangladesh* (pp. 397–417). Singapore: Springer. doi:10.1007/978-981-33-4279-8_17

Bandaru, R., & Kumar, R. J. (2021). Tourism service in India: A model for identifying niche tourism products in view of foreign tourists. *International Journal of Hospitality and Tourism Systems*, *14*(1), 122–127. Retrieved from https://www.i-scholar.in/index.php/ijhts/article/view/206960

Cafasso, S. (2020). Stanford researchers help Belize plan for sustainable, nature-based development to create more economic resilience amid global pandemic. *Standard news*. Retrieved from https://news.stanford.edu/2020/10/15/belizes-economy-gets-boost-nature/

Cheng, J., & Zetina, Z. (2021). A study to investigate the impact of the COVID-19 pandemic on tourist arrivals in Belize. *Journal of Social Sciences*, *9*(7). doi:10.4236/jss.2021.97023

Dwyer, L. (2016). Planning for sustainable tourism: An alternative paradigm. *International Journal of Tourism and Spirituality*, *1*(1), 29–43. doi:10.22133/ijts.2016.43075

Eckert, C., & Pechlaner, H. (2019). Alternative product development as strategy towards sustainability in tourism: The case of Lanzarote. *Sustainability*, *11*(13), 3588. doi:10.3390/su11133588

Elzek, Y., Gaafar, H., & Abdelsamie, H. (2021). The impact of green innovation on sustainability performance in travel agencies and hotels: The moderating role of environmental commitment. *International Journal of Hospitality & Tourism*

Systems, *14*(2), 16–24. Retrieved from https://www.researchgate.net/publication/ 351515547_the_impact_of_green_innovation_on_sustainability_performance_in_ travel_agencies_and_hotels_the_moderating_role_of_environmental_commitment

Fernandes, S., Brandão, F., & Costa, C. (2017). Network-based planning for the sustainable development of tourism destinations: Conceptual approach. *Revista Turismo & Desenvolvimento*, *27*(28), 1719–1731. Retrieved from https://www. semanticscholar.org/paper/Network-based-planning-for-the-sustainable-of-Fernandes-Brandão/6f553167d1f237e35faa1eb28033a205843f8150

Global Sustainable Tourism Council. (n.d). What is sustainable tourism. Retrieved from https://www.gstcouncil.org/what-is-sustainable-tourism/

Golja, T. (2021). The behavior and response of regional destination management organizations in the two recovery phases of tourism destination amid covid-19 pandemic. The case of Croatia. *Turismo: Estudos & Práticas*, *10*(1), 1–18. Retrieved from https://geplat.com/rtep/index.php/tourism/article/view/553

GSA. (n.d). U.S.General service administration. Sustainable design. Retrieved from https://www.gsa.gov/real-estate/design-and-construction/design-excellence/ sustainability/sustainable-design

Gupta, R., Singh, N., Kirar, I., & Bairwa, K. M. (2015). Tourism as an industry. In *Hospitality and tourism management* (1st ed., pp. 14–29). Noida: Vikas Publishing House.

Haid, M., & Albrecht, J. N. (2021). Sustainable tourism product development: An application of product design concepts. *Sustainability*, *13*(14), 7957. doi:10.3390/ su13147957

Hussain, A., & Fusté-Forné, F. (2021). Post-pandemic recovery: A case of domestic tourism in Akaroa (South island, New Zealand). *World*, *2*(1), 127–138. Retrieved from https://www.mdpi.com/2673-4060/2/1/9. doi:10.3390/world2010009

Ibănescu, C. B., Stoleriu, M. O., Munteanu, A., & Latu, C. (2018). The impact of tourism on sustainable development of rural areas: Evidence from Romania. *Sustainability*, *10*(10), 3529. doi:10.3390/su10103529. Retrieved from https://www. mdpi.com/2071-1050/10/10/3529

Idahosa, L. O. (2019). Understanding environmental sustainability, corporate social responsibility and responsible tourism in literature vs practice. *GeoJournal of Tourism and Geosites*, *26*(3), 957–973. doi:10.30892/gtg.26322-410

India Brand Equality Foundation (IBEF). (2011). Sustainable development in India. Retrieved from https://www.ibef.org/pages/sustainabledevelopment

India. (n.d). India. Retrieved from https://en.wikipedia.org/wiki/India

India.com. (2022). Kashmir records footfall of 1.8 lakh tourists in March, highest in 10 years. Retrieved from https://www.india.com/travel/articles/kashmir-records-footfall-of-1-8-lakh-tourists-in-march-highest-in-10-years-5327748/

Karolev, V., & Ohridska-olson, R. (2017). The myth, reality and future of tourists' and travel industry responsibilities: A model for sustainable tourism in protected areas and its applications in Bulgaria. *Revista Turismo & Desenvolvimento*, *27*(28), 161–163. Retrieved from https://dialnet.unirioja.es/servlet/articulo?codigo =6968913

Lőrincz, K., Banász, Z., & Csapó, J. (2020). Customer involvement in sustainable tourism planning at Lake Balaton. Hungary—Analysis of the consumer prefer-ences of the active cycling tourists. *Sustainability*, *12*(12), 1–18. Retrieved from https://www.mdpi.com/2071-1050/12/12/5174/pdf

Marin-Pantelescu, A., Tachiciu, L., Capusneanu, S., & Topor, D. I. (2019). Role of tour operators and travel agencies in promoting sustainable tourism. *Amfiteatru Economic*, *21*(52), 654–669. doi:10.24818/ea/2019/52/654

Mathew, P. V., & Thankachan, S. S. (2019). Responsible and sustainable tourism: A comparison of community perceptions. *Journal of Tourism Management Research*, *6*(1), 82–92. doi:10.18488/journal.31.2019.61.82.92

Mihalic, T., Mohamadi, S., Abbasi, A., & David, D. L. (2021). Mapping a sustainable and responsible tourism paradigm: A bibliometric and citation network analysis. *Sustainability*, *13*(2), 853. doi:10.3390/su13020853

Ministry of External Affairs Government of India. (2021). India records significant progress on Sustainable Development Goals. Retrieved from https://indbiz.gov.in/india-records-significant-progress-on-sustainable-development-goals/

Mint. (2021). Tourists throng Himachal Pradesh's Manali after COVID 19. Retrieved from https://www.livemint.com/news/india/tourists-throng-himachal-pradesh-s-manali-after-covid-curbs-eased-see-pics-11625498441445.html

Moloney, A. (2020). Caribbean indigenous people return to roots as COVID-19 shrinks tourism. Thomson Reuters Foundation, US-Health-Coronavirus-Caribbean-Tourism.

Nigg, J. J., & Eichelberger, S. (2021). Sustainable product development for accessible tourism: Case studies demonstrating the need for stakeholder collaboration. *Sustainability*, *13*(20), 11142. Retrieved from https://www.mdpi.com/2071-1050/13/20/11142. doi:10.3390/su132011142

Nuenninghoff, S., Lemay, M., Rogers, C., & Martin, D. (2015). Inter-American Development Bank (IDB) sustainable tourism in Belize. Retrieved from http://www.iadb.org

Pjerotic, L. (2017). Stakeholder cooperation in implementation of the sustainable development concept: Montenegrin. *Journal of International Studies*, *10*(2), 148–157. doi:10.14254/2071-8330.2017/10-2/11. Retrieved from https://www.researchgate.net/publication/320233590_Stakeholder_cooperation_in_implementation_of_the_sustainable_development_concept_Montenegrin_tourist_destinations

Rashid, A. (2022). Kashmir's tourism sector sees steady increase in tourist footfall despite COVID-19. Retrieved from https://www.firstpost.com/india/kashmirs-fledgling-tourism-sector-sees-steady-rise-in-tourist-footfall-despite-covid-19-10329351.html

Rasoolimanesh, S. M., Hall, M. C., Ramakrishna, S., & Esfandiar, K. (2020). A systematic scoping review of sustainable tourism indicators in relation to the sustainable development goals. *Journal of Sustainable Tourism*. doi:10.1080/09669582.2020.1775621. Retrieved from https://www.tandfonline.com/doi/abs/10.1080/09669582.2020.1775621?journalCode5rsus20

State, O., & Bulin, D. (2016). Aspects of responsible tourism – A quantitative approach. *Amfiteatru Economic*, *18*(10), 781–797. Retrieved from https://docplayer.net/212196472-aspects-of-responsible-tourism-a-quantitative-approach.html

Streimikiene, D., Svagzdiene, B., Jasinskas, E., & Simanavicius, A. (2020). Sustainable tourism development and competitiveness: The systematic literature review. *Sustainable development*, *29*(1), 259–271. doi:10.1002/sd.2133

The Economics Times. (2022). Kerala attracts 3.8 million domestic tourists in Q-1 2022, registers 72.48 per cent growth. Retrieved from https://economictimes.indiatimes.com/

news/india/kerala-attracts-3-8-mn-domestic-tourists-in-q-1-2022-registers-72-48-per-cent-growth/articleshow/91793005.cms?utm_source=contentofinterest&utm_mediu m=text&utm_campaign=cppst

The New Indian Express. (2020). Post Covid, Kerala tourism is all set to go local. Retrieved from https://www.newindianexpress.com/states/kerala/2020/jul/15/post-covid-kerala-tourism-is-all-set-to-go-local-2169735.html

The New Indian Express. (2022). In search of cooler climes: Summer leads to rush of tourists in Himachal. Retrieved from https://www.newindianexpress.com/nation/2022/apr/21/in-search-of-cooler-climes-summer-leads-to-rush-of-tourists-in-himachal-2444556.html

Times of India. (2021). Himachal records a footfall of 18500 tourists daily; 7500 for Rohtang Tunnel. Retrieved from https://timesofindia.indiatimes.com/travel/travel-news/himachal-records-a-footfall-of-18500-tourists-daily-7500-for-rohtang-tunnel/articleshow/84633649.cms

Times of India. (2022). Kashmir witnesses highest tourist footfall in seven years. Retrieved from https://timesofindia.indiatimes.com/travel/travel-news/kashmir-witnesses-highest-tourist-footfall-in-seven-years/articleshow/88697404.cms

Vu, D. V., Tran, G. N., Nguyen, H. T. T., & Nguyen, C. V. (2020). Factors affecting sustainable tourism development in ba ria-vung tau, vietnam. *Journal of Asian Finance, Economics and Busines*, *7*(9), 561–572. doi:10.13106/jafeb.2020.vol7.no9. 561

Zeng, L. (2022). Economic development and mountain tourism research from 2010 to 2020: Bibliometric analysis and science mapping approach. *Sustainability*. doi:10. 3390/su14010562

Vulnerability and Resilience of Tourism: Recovery Plans and Strategies of Countries

Derya Toksoz and Ali Dalgic

Abstract

Negative issues in the world have increased in recent years. The continuing COVID-19 pandemic has forced the global tourism industry to take precautions against these disasters to be ready to respond. Given tourism's vulnerability to environmental and social changes, the pandemic has dramatically impacted tourism worldwide. Tourism enterprises have developed various strategies and approaches to eliminate vulnerabilities that negatively affect their structures. This chapter tries to measure and recover plans implemented by various countries to increase the tourism industry's resilience in the face of crises and disasters.

Keywords: Vulnerability; resilience; disaster in tourism; resilience of tourism; destination management; recovery plans

Introduction

Over the last 20 years, several disasters have severely affected the whole world, with the tourism industry being one of the most affected areas as tourists are particularly vulnerable to disasters (Bird, Gisladottir, & Dominey-Howes, 2010). In particular, the continuing COVID-19 pandemic has forced the global tourism industry to take precautions against these disasters to be ready to respond. Given tourism's vulnerability to environmental and social changes, the pandemic has dramatically impacted tourism worldwide, especially the hospitality and transportation sectors. This is critical because tourism constitutes an important part of many economies.

Vulnerability in tourism refers to the degree to which the industry is affected, distorted, and displaced by incidents related to risks (Buultjens, Ratnayake, & Gnanapala, 2014, p. 133). More specifically, Barbhuiya and Chatterjee (2020) define it as "the degree of being affected by negative situations such as a decrease

Resilient and Sustainable Destinations After Disaster, 195–211
Copyright © 2023 Derya Toksoz and Ali Dalgic
Published under exclusive licence by Emerald Publishing Limited
doi:10.1108/978-1-80382-021-720231014

in tourism demand, a crisis, a negative image and reputation, and even the inability of businesses to continue their normal activities as a result of the exposure of tourism enterprises/countries to some negative environmental changes and risks."

Considering that tourism is a composite product, tourism businesses cannot be considered independently of destinations, so any negative conditions affecting destinations directly or indirectly affect tourism businesses (Espiner & Becken, 2014). Tourism businesses are very vulnerable to all kinds of negative local, regional, or even global environmental conditions. These include natural factors like seasonality, climate change, natural disasters, and epidemics, business factors like legal regulations, energy costs, dependence on destination, high investment requirements for fixed production factors, and the carrying capacity of tourism enterprises, and more general factors like economic and political crises, war, terrorism, and security problems (Hystad & Keller, 2008; Le Masson & Kelman, 2011; Perles-Ribes, Ramón-Rodríguez, Rubia-Serrano, & Moreno-Izquierdo, 2016).

Tourism enterprises have developed various strategies and approaches to eliminate these vulnerabilities that negatively affect their structure and functioning and reduce their competitiveness. Some involve recognizing and preventing crises and adverse conditions; some involve solving a crisis after it occurs; some involve eliminating the negative effects of these conditions on society (Gönen, 2012, p. 128). Many countries have also begun assisting the tourism industry and building its resilience to cope with disasters (Larsen, Calgaro, & Thomalla, 2011; Rosselló, Becken, & Santana-Gallego, 2020). That is, disaster management has shifted from a reactive to a more inclusive approach that seeks to proactively minimize the negative consequences of disaster (Innocenti & Albrito, 2011). Many countries have been forced to take greater precautions against disasters, especially after COVID-19, including reaching a consensus regarding the most effective approach to strengthen the resilience of tourism in the face of disasters. Resilience is a key factor enabling a socioecological system to sustain itself over a long period (Cheer & Lew, 2017). It refers to the system's ability to regain its original shape or position after bending, stretching, or other deformations. For many years, the term was usually used to describe the ability of communities to survive difficult conditions. In recent years, however, it has been rediscovered and assigned new meanings, first in the natural sciences, then in the social sciences, and finally in tourism (Butler, 2017).

This chapter examines the measures and recovery plans implemented by various countries to increase the tourism industry's resilience in the face of crises and disasters. In particular, it identifies what can be done to prepare and fortify destinations against disasters and other risks. The first section discusses the issue of vulnerability in tourism while the following section considers resilience in tourism, which has become increasingly important due to the pandemic. The third section presents different countries' recovery plans and recovery policies before the final section draws some conclusions.

Vulnerability in Tourism

Vulnerability can be defined in various ways. From the perspective of disaster studies, Gabor and Griffith (1980) consider vulnerability as "a concept associated with a threat and risk to which systems are exposed" while Hogan and Marandola (2005) define vulnerability within environmental and development studies as "the capacity to be affected by adverse events." Finally, Adger (2006, p. 268) defines it as a lack of adaptive capacity "resulting from exposure to pressure created by environmental and social changes."

Although vulnerability is closely related to sensitivity, the two concepts are distinct. According to Çobanyılmaz (2011, p. 27), for example, sensitivity refers to the degree to which a system is affected by both the positive and/or negative effects of risks whereas vulnerability only refers to the negative effects. Hence, vulnerability can be considered a subset of sensitivity.

Tourism establishments are highly sensitive to the pressures created by crises and adverse environmental conditions as tourism destinations are becoming more vulnerable to environmental change. This vulnerability changes destinations' decision-making processes and recovery plans. However, in order to fully explain the concept of vulnerability in tourism, it is necessary to identify the factors causing vulnerabilities.

Researchers have identified various conditions affecting the tourism sector and creating vulnerabilities. These include seasonality, constantly changing tourist preferences, multiple substitute opportunities (competition), exceeding carrying capacity limits due to tourist density, degeneration of natural and cultural assets, and increased urban traffic density due to tourism. These vulnerabilities arise both from tourism's own dynamics and external developments, such as economic crises and natural disasters (Thomas, 2012).

Regarding the latter, Akıncı (2010, p. 216) argues that tourism is extremely vulnerable to unexpected incidents like war, terrorism, epidemics, life-threatening natural disasters, and economic crises that reduce available income for travel, and political and social developments that damage destination image. Similarly, Akar (2008, p. 41) identified seven types of external factors that can cause crises in tourism and thus vulnerabilities: economic factors, political and legal regulations, natural disasters, technological developments, sociocultural factors, physical environmental factors, and competition.

Resilience is frequently discussed alongside vulnerability due to their inverse relationship. As Proag (2014, p. 376) puts it, the more the resilience of a system increases, the more its vulnerability to intense dangers decreases. Thus, vulnerability is important in determining the level of resilience because resilience does not apply in cases where the system faces no problems. That is, a system is not vulnerable if there is no danger, risk, or uncertainty. In such cases, there will be no need for resilience capacity, so spending resources, effort, and time to develop it will be seen as wasteful. In short, resilience represents ways to prevent vulnerabilities while vulnerabilities change the resilience capacity of enterprises.

Resilience in Tourism

Davidson et al. (2005, p. 43) describe resilience as "healing power" or the process of "reversing adverse conditions." The concept first entered the ecology literature with the ecological system studies of C. S. Holling (1973). Environmental resilience focuses on showing "resistance" and "flexibility" against difficulties to maintain a system's integrity (Kantur & Say, 2013, p. 355). In the literature, vulnerability is discussed in relation to various other concepts apart from resilience, such as danger and risk, sensitivity, flexibility, and adaptation. That is, vulnerability is not only determined by the risk itself but also the capacity of enterprises to predict, prevent, reduce, and cope with risk (Shakya, 2009, p. 39).

In particular, resilience is especially related to flexibility and defined as the ability to keep up with rapid changes in the environment as opposed to stagnation (Tomer, 1995, p. 412). As a way for businesses to adapt to their environment, flexibility forms part of the repertoire of strategic capabilities that increase a business's mobility (Lengnick-Hall, Beck, & Lengnick-Hall, 2011, p. 244). Resilience and flexibility are distinct in several ways. First, businesses struggle to survive if they rely on their own internal dynamics rather than flexing by developing capacity. Secondly, following a positive or negative change in the environment, businesses develop their flexibility capabilities to adapt to it whereas resilience focuses not only on adapting to adverse environmental changes but also on understanding how to survive such conditions.

Cumming et al. (2005) define resilience as "the capacity to maintain the stability of the organization after unfavorable conditions or disruptions and to provide a state of equilibrium." Two elements draw attention. The first is facing a significant threat or difficulty while the second is the organization's ability to survive despite these threats or difficulties. As the subject of research in different disciplines, resilience is named in various ways. In engineering studies, flexibility and strength are often used rather than resilience to refer to a material's ability to return to its original state against force (Omurtag, 2007). In psychology, on the other hand, indomitableness and resilience are used to refer to the ability of individuals exposed to psychological pressure or difficulty to hold on to life (Bildirici, 2014). In this chapter, we adopt the following definition of resilience: the capacity of an enterprise to take action, maintain a state of balance, return to its former state, or turn threats into opportunities by becoming better than before in the face of disruptive incidents.

It is noteworthy that resilience is often discussed together with risk management, crisis management, and change management in the marketing literature. Crisis management is the process of examining and evaluating crisis signals, and taking and implementing the necessary measures to survive the crisis with the least damage (Haşit, 2000, p. 64). That is, crisis management involves predicting possible problems and preventing them from turning into a crisis. Risk management, on the other hand, is to be aware of and predict risks, and minimize the resulting losses or turn those risks into opportunities (İbiş, 2015). Resilience capacity differs from both crisis management and risk management because resilience depends on particular vulnerabilities rather than focusing on specific risks, and refers both to crises and the ability to protect and recover from situations that may adversely affect the business (Pettit, Croxton, & Fiksel, 2013).

Most resilience studies in the tourism literature have investigated destinations considered as socioecological systems. More specifically, they focus on the negative regional effects of disasters like epidemics, natural disasters, and terrorism, and assess the destination's vulnerabilities, adaptive capacity, and recovery power (Becken, 2013; Biggs, 2011; Calgaro, Lloyd, & Dominey-Howes, 2014; Lew, 2014; Orchiston, 2013; Orchiston, Prayag, & Brown, 2016).

Tourism enterprises like accommodation providers need to be particularly resilient against external problems, such as external economic and financial crises, terrorist attacks, and natural disasters. Zeng, Carter, and De Lacy (2005) also lists external incidents that force tourism enterprises to develop resilience, namely, human or animal epidemics, devastating weather conditions, natural disasters, civil conflicts, violence, war, and terrorism. However, their resilience can be impaired by their dependency on intermediaries and inability to predict approaching crises (Yılmaz, 2004, pp. 180–181).

Despite the importance of resilience for the tourism industry, however, very few studies have considered how to develop an effective resilience capacity (Orchiston et al., 2016; Stevenson, 2014). Moreover, these studies have only considered resilience capacity from an internal perspective, thereby neglecting the effects of threatening external environmental factors on resilience capacities. Accordingly, this chapter provides an important update regarding the plans and strategies that tourism enterprises in various countries have implemented in response to the crises they have faced.

Recovery Plans and Strategies of Countries

Institutions took various measures in response to the COVID-19 pandemic. While these responses were not very effective after the crisis first began, short-, medium-, and long-term strategies have been gradually developed. Regarding emergency response measures, tourism-related boards and destination management organizations (DMOs) are required to inform tourism sector stakeholders and local residents about any developments affecting the destination. National boards should be established to include both public and private sector members. Effective communication is one of the most important factors in this emergency response while another important issue is state grants. That is, it is important to use grants during the early stages of a crisis to support small and medium-sized enterprises (SMEs) with liquidity concerns. Another crucial short-term measure is the provision of training in health, hygiene, and emergency response for both local people and tourism workers and the prevention of layoffs. Since employees will be needed after the crisis, training is needed on retention, and skills development should be continued (World Bank, 2020, p. 30).

After taking emergency measures, short-term actions are needed to enable economic recovery and implement new business models. Accordingly, new regulations and incentives should be proposed for tourism sector enterprises like hotels, travel agencies, and tour guides, along with innovations that fit the destination's new postcrisis strategic identity. In addition, new target markets should be identified and studies (products, pricing, access, etc.) should be carried out. In order to stimulate tourism, the sector should primarily offer opportunities for the domestic market. During this period, recovery strategies should be established for both the sector and the destination. For example, the destination can increase its competitiveness by repositioning products and services, using technology, and promoting sustainability. As in the emergency phase, SMEs need to be supported for their financing needs while training for employees and local people should continue. Finally, recovery strategies should include technological advances for smart destinations and business digitalization (World Bank, 2020, pp. 31–32).

Following the short-term measures, medium-term recovery plans are also important. These have various aspects. First, as the tourism sector accelerates its recovery, it must implement policies and measures to increase destination competitiveness and strengthen resilience against future crises while public investment and conservation efforts for employment and sustainability should be accelerated. Second, tourism managers need to be trained in crisis management, and awareness should be raised about large-scale training and certification programs. In addition, crisis desks should be established that prioritize cooperation and coordination between the public and private sectors to enable rapid responses to future crises. Third, new zoning policies should ensure sustainable development in the destination's natural and cultural heritage areas. The sector's sustainability should be supported through greening policies while infrastructure and superstructure works should be carried out within the framework of sustainability. In addition, destinations and businesses should be oriented toward renewable energy sources. Finally, the target markets identified through the earlier short-term measures should be reviewed and work accelerated accordingly (World Bank, 2020, pp. 32–33).

Given the COVID-19 pandemic's severe economic, managerial, social, environmental, and climatic negative effects, the response requires both national and international efforts. Investments should be made to transform tourism value chains, with particular attention to issues like preventing economic leakage, promoting recycling, renovation, and repair in the tourism sector. The sector can also create economic value for customers and the local economy through efficient use of energy, water, and other resources. The sector also needs to adopt innovative and sustainable business models to gain a competitive advantage, for example, by reducing and managing food waste (European Commission, 2022).

During the COVID-19 crisis, information exchange at governmental, private-sector, and international levels has been crucial to decision-making and crisis management. Leveraging the lessons learned from this will be key to efficiently implementing recovery plans and increasing global resilience. By increasing sustainability, more inclusive and smarter destination management and partnerships can play a crucial role in tourism's revival. This requires regular and timely data and the implementation of measures on climate change and biodiversity to support sustainable decision-making in tourism. Management and finance should prioritize precautions to protect the health of local people, increase digitalization, and provide green incentives. The rescue funds for financing tourism's revival must encourage the survival of tourism enterprises by providing loans and grants for those businesses needing urgent support (European Commission, 2022).

As already indicated, these rescue measures should be taken in line with preventing climate change, particularly through improving the measurement and disclosure of CO_2 emissions from tourism, promoting science-based targets, and investing in climate-conscious tourism development to protect destinations. Resilience in the tourism sector depends on increasing mitigation efforts, including investing in low-carbon transport options, greener infrastructure development, and protecting biodiversity. In many destinations, tourism jobs are the main source of income for local communities, particularly youth, women, rural populations, Indigenous groups, and other vulnerable populations, including those in the informal economy. A more inclusive recovery in the sector therefore depends on providing targeted support that meets their needs. This should include principled measures to provide decent work, increase occupational safety, and ensure formal employment in tourism. The initial emergency measures will not be enough. Rather, targeted support will be needed to ensure that small and medium-sized businesses can survive while ensuring that destinations provide diverse and attractive offers. Adopting digital technologies can contribute to business continuity (One Planet Sustainable Tourism Programme, 2020).

The World Tourism Organization (UNWTO) has presented three main strategies and 23 criteria to deal with the crisis in the tourism sector. The three strategies are "crisis management and impact mitigation," "stimulus and recovery acceleration," and "preparing for tomorrow." The recovery criteria require the sector to "provide financial stimulus for tourism investment and operations," "review taxes, charges, and regulations impacting travel and tourism," "mainstream tourism in national, regional and international recovery programs and in development assistance," "promote new jobs" and skills development particularly in the digital realm," "advance travel facilitation," "boost marketing, events and meetings," "mainstream environmental sustainability in stimulus and recovery packages," "understand the market and act quickly to restore confidence and stimulate demand," and "invest in partnership" (Collins-Kreiner & Ram, 2020). These recovery strategies should be implemented at various levels, for example, nationally, by groups of countries, and on a continental basis.

A number of countries and regions have acted along these lines. For example, the Pacific region's tourism sector has taken several medium- and long-term measures to accelerate the region's attractiveness, accessibility, capacity, and recovery. Their approach highlights the need to act locally by thinking regionally. That is, improvements should be made through country interventions and programs as well as cooperation programs for regional efficiency. It is also important to identify opportunities to reduce costs, increase the ease of doing business, and strengthen regional cohesion and accessibility to increase the impact and relevance of the Pacific tourism destinations with their key markets. Pacific tourism destination marketing requires clear, targeted, and differentiated experiences across the region while all levels of its tourism industry can build overall capacity by developing industry skills and sharing best practices. Furthermore, to recover from the region's overall skill loss due to the pandemic, it is necessary to recruit skilled tourism industry workers (SPTO, 2020, pp. 16–17). Pacific tourism made the following specific recommendations (SPTO, 2020, p. 18).

(1) Promote job retention, sustain the self-employed, and protect the most vulnerable groups
(2) Support the liquidity of companies
(3) Review taxes, duties, charges, and regulations that affect transport and tourism
(4) Ensure consumer protection and trust
(5) Promote skill development, especially digital skills
(6) Include tourism in national, regional, and global economic contingency packages
(7) Establish crisis management mechanisms and strategies
(8) Provide financial incentives for tourism investments and operations
(9) Review taxes, fees, and regulations that affect travel and tourism
(10) Ease of travel ahead
(11) Promote the development of new jobs and skills, especially digital ones
(12) Mainstream environmental sustainability and sociocultural aspects in incentive and improvement packages
(13) Understand the market and act quickly to restore confidence and stimulate demand
(14) Increase marketing, events, and meetings
(15) Invest in partnerships
(16) Mainstream tourism in national, regional, and international recovery programs and development assistance

There have been similar calls to action in the OECD countries, where various policies have been proposed to support the tourism sector's recovery. The OECD reports have emphasized that countries should work together because actions taken by each government have global implications for travelers and businesses in other countries. In other words, strengthened multilateral cooperation and solid support are essential for reviving tourism. In addition, focused support is required to meet the specific needs of tourism workers, businesses, and destinations as well as to support the broader economic recovery. In particular, destinations and tourism businesses will need help to ensure their readiness to provide tourism services to meet rising demand when the recovery comes. However, they must also remain sustainable after this support ends. Additionally, taking steps to ensure policy clarity and limit uncertainty will be crucial to support tourism's recovery. Finally, policy and business decisions should become better informed through data collection, research, and analysis (OECD, 2020a, pp. 7–8).

Within the OECD, the UK government wants the United Kingdom to become one of the most desired destinations for post-COVID-19 tourists. Accordingly, it has prioritized marketing of tourism assets, sustainable and dynamic development, and large-scale employment creation. The primary short-term goal is to return to previous visitor numbers by the end of 2022 by stimulating domestic tourism. This entails attracting the attention of new audiences and improving visitor experiences by creating a structure that ensures a more productive, innovative, and resilient tourism industry. In addition, the government is prioritizing the development and protection of the UK's natural, cultural, and historical heritage while also ensuring the development of local people (Department for Digital, Culture, Media & Sport, 2021, p. 17). Accordingly, VisitBritain is currently working with the government to develop a rescue campaign to promote the UK tourism once the pandemic is over. The recovery packages aim to increase consumer awareness, provide business and product support, and strengthen marketing and industry coordination. During the pandemic, VisitEngland used a 1.3 million GBP fund to support DMOs and ensure that they can provide critical support and expert guidance to the many small and medium-sized businesses comprising the UK's tourism sector (OECD, 2020b, pp. 71–72).

Meanwhile, France has implemented effective emergency measures, including 20 reforms in its National Recovery and Resilience Plan. These address bottlenecks hindering sustainable growth, investments to accelerate the transition to a more sustainable, low-carbon, and climate-resilient economy, support for the digital transformation of all economic actors, including public authorities, and to make the French economy stronger. Among these reforms, the most important for resilience are the green transition, digital transition, and economic and social resilience (OECD, 2020b, pp. 48–49). The plan includes the following key components (Ragonnaud, 2022, pp. 3–4).

(1) Energy regeneration to improve energy efficiency in public and private buildings to reduce energy consumption and associated greenhouse gas emissions, and to improve the quality of life of households, especially lower income households, through energy renewal
(2) Ecology and biodiversity to reduce the ecological impact of production and consumption patterns by combating land use, conserving biodiversity, decarbonizing industrial production, promoting a more circular economy, and accelerating the agricultural transition
(3) Green energies and technologies to support their development to secure the green transition
(4) Infrastructure and green mobility to reduce the transport sector's environmental footprint by promoting the development of efficient alternatives to road transport and accelerate the automotive sector's transition to cleaner vehicle production
(5) Business support to strengthen the equity of SMEs by mobilizing financial savings
(6) Technological sovereignty and resilience to support investments that will help France achieve its economic and technological independence, and

support strategic sectors to ensure the future resilience of economic, social, and industrial models across the country
(7) Protecting jobs, youth, disability, vocational training to support employment, limit the impact of the economic crisis on the career paths of young people, and reduce the risks of unemployment

In Spain, the government has implemented a number of measures. First, it has encouraged businesses to continue their activities by postponing tax payments, reducing by 50% employer's social security contributions for employees with permanent or temporary contracts in the tourism sector and related activities. Second, it has provided 400 million Euros of liquidity to support tourism companies affected by the crisis and, depending on the region, postponed interest and/ or loan principal payments from companies affected by the crisis. Third, it has published guidance on best practices for those working in the tourism industry. Fourth, it has tried to prevent layoffs by promoting improved protection for tourism workers suffering from COVID-19, temporary unemployment (suspension of employment), or reduced working hours (OECD, 2020b, pp. 68–69). Fifth, it has taken decisions regarding digitalization, business establishment and growth laws, active labor market policies, action plans for youth unemployment, vocational training, the tax system, and pension funds. Spain's government allocated 3.4 billion Euros to increase digitalization in the tourism sector along with efforts to improve business environments and remove unnecessary regulatory barriers. Another 2.4 billion Euros was allocated to digitize public employment services, create training opportunities, and encourage recruitment. Finally, 765 million Euros was provided to improve vocational opportunities through work-based training and provincial professional experience (European Commission, 2021).

In Italy, another leading tourism destination, the Council of Ministers has introduced various measures. First, it prepared special allowances for tourism and cultural workers, including those lacking social security benefits. Second, it expanded the social safety net to include seasonal tourism and entertainment workers. Support was also increased for tourism enterprises through suspension of many debt repayments. To help the tourism sector survive and recover, the government allocated 130 million Euros for 2020. Coupons were issued that are valid for the coming years for tourists whose reservations in Italy were canceled due to COVID-19. Finally, extraordinary campaigns have been launched to reestablish Italy's image (OECD, 2020b, pp. 55–56).

Before the pandemic, Thailand had several comparative advantages. According to the World Economic Forum's Global Competitiveness Index, for example, Thailand has high-quality medical facilities and a good reputation for medical tourism, capacity for high-end tourists, and good ratings for infrastructure quality and usability. Thailand's tourism sector has also proven resilient in the past against political unrest and natural disasters. In addition, the industry is supported by long-standing visa policies, a well-connected airport hub, and strong strategic oversight through the Tourism Authority of Thailand under the Ministry of Tourism and Sports (IMF, 2021, pp. 58–59).

Nevertheless, Thailand's government had to take emergency financial measures in response to the pandemic, including three million dollars in funding for tour operators. Thailand has also started to focus primarily on promoting domestic tourism by subsidizing domestic tourists' spending on accommodation, food and beverages, and other travels. The Thailand Special Tourist Visa has been implemented to allow long stays for international tourists. In addition, the government has tried to transition from mass tourism to low-intensity quality tourism. Finally, investments have been made in digital/mobile resources and connections to support contactless service delivery (IMF, 2021, pp. 58–59).

Portugal's government has announced a 9.2 billion Euro recovery package for the COVID-19 pandemic. It includes government-backed loan guarantees of 3 billion Euros to provide liquidity to affected companies. Of this, 900 million Euros is for hotels and accommodation (including 75 million Euros for micro and small businesses) while 200 million Euros is for accommodation providers. In addition, 600 million Euros (including 270 million Euros for micro and small businesses) was announced for travel agencies, leisure services and event organizers, and restaurants. Turismo de Portugal has also introduced special measures to support the tourism industry and minimize the impact of the temporary drop in tourism due to the pandemic. These include the Hotline for Tourism Micro-Business Liquidity, support for reimbursing expenses incurred by organizers of postponed or canceled events in 2020, measures to postpone certain tax obligations, and updating the information and advisory team at Turismo de Portugal. Tourism schools have also acted by introducing online support for companies, updated data on International Source Markets for Portugal, and monitoring the flow of tourists to Portugal using mobile and airlines data (OECD, 2020b, pp. 64–65).

Greece has established a crisis management committee on COVID-19, which is responsible for providing the tourism market with up-to-date information on developments, preparing plans for the ministry, preparing a precautionary package to revive the market by considering suggestions from the tourism sector, preparing promotional programs, and cooperating both nationally and internationally. At a national level, Greece has highlighted protecting destination safety and supporting tourism businesses in terms of public health (OECD, 2020b, pp. 49–50).

The Hungarian government intends to provide 600 billion HUF support for priority intervention areas through investment subsidies, tax breaks, infrastructure development, soft and guaranteed loans, and capital programs while the Hungarian Central Bank also announced new monetary measures. The Hungarian Tourism Agency reports to the government every 48 hours on the state of the tourism industry and consults daily with the leaders of professional organizations. The agency also prepared a detailed COVID-19 handbook (one week before the EU protocols) containing essential public health information for travelers and accommodation providers. The handbook contains recommendations to help hotel managers and other tourism companies adapt to the current situation while ensuring the safety of guests and employees. Finally, it set up a task force to consult stakeholders and gather information. The agency has now created an action plan to support the industry's recovery (OECD, 2020b, pp. 51–52).

In New Zealand, the government implemented its COVID-19: Economic Response Package worth 12.1 billion NZD to support businesses from the global impacts and prepare the economy for recovery. It included important elements to mitigate the economic shock on businesses and employees and support confidence in the near term. More specifically, it provided a loan facility of 900 million NZD for Air New Zealand while the 2020 budget allocated 400 million NZD for the Tourism Improvement Fund. New Zealand also prepared a tourism transition program with advice and financial support for businesses. The program identifies the key tourism assets for New Zealand's domestic tourism offerings and for its international brand through its strategic tourism asset protection program. This will provide them with the protection and assistance they need. In addition, the government's tourism improvement ministers' group has overseen the sector's recovery. During the pandemic, various policies and regulatory reforms were implemented with the cooperation of both the public and private sectors to ensure the future of tourism. Meanwhile, a one-year interest-free loan was provided to small businesses to support their immediate cash flow needs and to cover their fixed costs (OECD, 2020b, pp. 61–62).

Costa Rica's tourism industry is well placed to adapt to new travel habits and protocols by attracting visitors through accommodation, outdoor activities, and social distancing preferences at its major natural attractions and resorts. The country has been able to create significant synergies between protecting forests and ecotourism to mitigate climate change and promote adaptation. Tourists are also particularly attracted to Costa Rica over other tropical destinations by its high-quality healthcare system, thereby partially reducing health problems during the pandemic. To reactivate the industry and adapt to the new normal, Costa Rica launched a roadmap with several initiatives to regain the trust of travelers and attract visitors. More specifically, the Costa Rica Tourism Institute, in collaboration with the private sector, has launched 16 health and hygiene protocols for tourism-related activities. Costa Rica has also provided attractive offers, discounts, and financing options, primarily in domestic tourism while also focusing on sustainable tourism with local guides rather than mass tourism (IMF, 2021, pp. 47–48).

In Jamaica, the authorities have aimed to limit the economic fallout and ensure that Jamaica remains a safe tourism destination. This has included taking advantage of fewer tourism arrivals to boost the skills and qualifications of the country's 10,000 tourism workers through free online training certification classes. In November 2020, the authorities also launched a unique traveler protection and emergency program called Jamaica Cases, which includes on-site rescue and repatriation for medical emergencies, including from COVID-19 or natural disasters. The authorities have also implemented policies to prevent bankruptcies and maintain employment in the tourism industry. Finally, the country has tried to attract North American tourists by upgrading infrastructure while maintaining low prices (IMF, 2021, pp. 50–52).

Conclusion

The COVID-19 pandemic demonstrated that the world is not fully prepared for such crises. Consequently, despite the measures taken worldwide, the pandemic's negative effects were felt severely in many sectors, particularly tourism. Furthermore, because tourism is so connected with other sectors, countries realized the sector's importance more than before. In the pandemic's initial stages, the measures taken were insufficient while the crisis demonstrated the importance of effective communication. That is, both national and international sector stakeholders have had to remain in constant communication throughout the pandemic and act together while making decisions. One of the most important reasons for the initial problems, such as regarding cleaning, hygiene, and social distancing, was the lack of awareness raising and education activities. Another reason was disruptions in production. In short, countries are unprepared for such crises (One Planet Sustainable Tourism Programme, 2020; World Bank, 2020).

During the pandemic, governments in many countries had to provide financial support, especially due to national and international restrictions. Larger states were able to sustain tourism businesses despite the uncertain environment. In particular, SMEs were supported financially, efforts were made to keep tourism employees at work, and opportunities were provided for them to develop their skills. Initial emergency measures included grants and credit support to businesses, deferral of taxes, and postponing debt repayments. Other focuses of short-term government actions included digitalization, sustainability, new products and services, and new markets. While these deficiencies were quickly detected worldwide, it has been almost impossible to rectify them in the short term, so actions have been implemented gradually over time (OECD, 2020b).

Countries have also focused their medium-term measures on correcting short-term shortcomings, for example, by increasing state support for tourism enterprises and their employees, and encouraging innovative and sustainable business models, especially the design of smart businesses. Other medium-term policies include increasing recovery funds, digitalization, and involving stakeholders in decision-making (World Bank, 2020). Governments have also focused on keeping businesses afloat, protecting jobs, supporting defense groups, providing liquidity, digitalization, specializing in crisis management, making arrangements regarding travel and tourism, and activities to revitalize the sector (Collins-Kreiner & Ram, 2020; SPTO, 2020). Finally, one of the important medium- and long-term issues is the need for better information collection, research, and data analysis to improve policies and measures to respond to future crises (European Commission, 2021; SPTO, 2020).

Regarding tourism specifically, various countries, such as France, Spain and the United Kingdom, have implemented effective recovery strategies. Of these countries, France stands out in terms of business support, infrastructure, green mobility, green energy and technologies, energy renewal, employment support, and vocational training (OECD, 2020b). Spain stands out for its measures regarding liquidity support and debt relief, employee retention, digitalization and training funding, improving business environments, and removing regulatory barriers (European Commission, 2021; OECD, 2020b). The United Kingdom has particularly emphasized sustainable and dynamic development and large-scale employment creation. In addition, measures have been taken to create a structure for a more productive, innovative, and resilient tourism industry, to develop and protect the UK's natural, cultural, and historical heritage, support businesses, develop products, and market and coordinate the sector through the Tourism Recovery Plan (Department for Digital, Culture, Media & Sport, 2021; OECD, 2020b).

References

Adger, W. N. (2006). Vulnerability. *Global Environmental Change, 16*(3), 268–281.
Akar, Z. E. (2008). *T.C. Kültür ve Turizm Bakanlığı'nın basına yönelik kriz yönetimi çalışmaları: Kuş gribi örnekleminde Hürriyet Gazetesi'nin incelenmesi.* Uzmanlık Tezi. Kültür ve Turizm Bakanlığı Araştırma ve Eğitim Genel Müdürlüğü, Ankara.
Akıncı, Z. (2010). *Konaklama işletmelerinde kriz yönetimi: Alanya bölgesindeki konaklama işletmelerinde kriz sürecinde karşılaşılan sorunların tespit ve çözümüne yönelik bir araştırma.* Yayımlanmamış Doktora Tezi. Süleyman Demirel Üniversitesi, Isparta.
Barbhuiya, M. R., & Chatterjee, D. (2020). Vulnerability and resilience of the tourism sector in India: Effects of natural disasters and internal conflict. *Tourism Management Perspectives, 33*, 100616.
Becken, S. (2013). Developing a framework for assessing resilience of tourism subsystems to climatic factors. *Annals of Tourism Research, 43*, 506–528.
Biggs, D. (2011). Understanding resilience in a vulnerable industry: The case of reef tourism in Australia. *Ecology and Society, 16*(1), 30.
Bildirici, F. (2014). *Özel eğitime gereksinimi olan çocuğa sahip ailelerde aile yükü ile psikolojik dayanıklılık arasındaki ilişki.* Yayımlanmamış Yüksek Lisans Tezi. Haliç Üniversitesi, İstanbul.
Bird, D., Gisladottir, G., & Dominey-Howes, D. (2010). Volcanic risk and tourism in southern Iceland: Implications for hazard, risk and emergency response education and training. *Journal of Volcanology and Geothermal Research, 189,* 33–48.
Butler, R. W. (Ed.). (2017). *Tourism and resilience.* Wallingford: CABI.
Buultjens, J., Ratnayake, I., & Gnanapala, A. C. (2014). Form tsunami to recovery: The resilience of the Sri Lankan tourism industry. In B. W. Ritchie & K. Campiranon (Eds.), *Tourism crisis and disaster management in the Asia-Pacific* (pp. 137–147). Wallingford: CABI.
Calgaro, E., Lloyd, K., & Dominey-Howes, D. (2014). From vulnerability to transformation: A framework for assessing the vulnerability and resilience of tourism destinations. *Journal of Sustainable Tourism, 22*(3), 341–360.
Cheer, J. M., & Lew, A. A. (Eds.) (2017). *Tourism, resilience and sustainability: Adapting to social, political and economic change.* Oxfordshire: Routledge.
Çobanyılmaz, P. (2011). *Kentlerin iklim değişikliğinden zarar görebilirliğinin belirlenmesi: Ankara örneği.* Yayımlanmamış Yüksek Lisans Tezi. Gazi Üniversitesi, Ankara.

Collins-Kreiner, N., & Ram, Y. (2020). National tourism strategies during the Covid-19 pandemic. *Annals of Tourism Research*, 103076. doi:10.1016/j.annals.2020.103076

Cumming, G. S., Barnes, G., Perz, S., Schmink, M., Sieving, K. E., Southworth, J., ... Van Holt, T. (2005). An exploratory framework for the empirical measurement of resilience. *Ecosystems*, *8*(8), 975–987.

Davidson, J. R. T., Payne, V. M., Connor, K. M., Foa, E. B., Rothbaum, O., Hertzberg, M. A., & Weisler, R. H. (2005). Trauma, resilience and saliostasis: Effects of treatment in post-traumatic stress disorder. *International Clinical Psychopharmacology*, 43–48.

Department for Digital, Culture, Media and Sport. (2021). The tourism recovery plan. Retrieved from https://assets.publishing.service.gov.uk/government/uploads/system/uploads/attachment_data/file/992974/Tourism_Recovery_Plan__Web_Accessible_.pdf. Accessed on May 01, 2022.

Espiner, S., & Becken, S. (2014). Tourist towns on the edge: Conceptualising vulnerability and resilience in a protected area tourism system. *Journal of Sustainable Tourism*, *22*(4), 646–665.

European Commission. (2021). Spain's recovery and resilience plan. Retrieved from https://ec.europa.eu/info/business-economy-euro/recovery-coronavirus/recovery-and-resilience-facility/spains-recovery-and-resilience-plan_en. Accessed on May 01, 2022.

European Commission. (2022). Transition pathway for tourism. Retrieved from https://ec.europa.eu/commission/presscorner/detail/en/ip_22_850. Accessed on April 29, 2023.

Gabor, T., & Griffith, T. K. (1980). The assessment of community vulnerability to acute hazardous materials incidents. *Journal of Hazardous*, *8*, 323–333.

Gönen, İ. (2012). *Konaklama işletmelerinde kriz yönetimi: Krizler ve stratejik yaklaşımlar*. İstanbul: Kriter Yayınevi.

Haşit, G. (2000). *İşletmelerde kriz yönetimi ve Türkiye'nin büyük sanayi işletmeleri üzerinde yapılan araştırma çalışması*. Eskişehir: Anadolu Üniversitesi Yayınları.

Hogan, D. J., & Marandola, E., Jr. (2005). Towards an interdisciplinary conceptualisation of vulnerability. *Population, Space and Place*, *11*(6), 455–547.

Holling, C. S. (1973). Resilience and stability of ecological systems. *Annual review of ecology and systematics*, *4*(1), 1–23.

Hystad, P. W., & Keller, P. C. (2008). Towards a destination tourism disaster management framework: Long-term lessons from a forest fire disaster. *Tourism Management*, *29*(1), 151–162.

İbiş, A. (2015). *İşletmelerde risk yönetimi ve türev ürünlerin kullanımı üzerine BİST'de bir uygulama*. Yayımlanmamış Yüksek Lisans Tezi. Balıkesir Üniversitesi, Balıkesir.

IMF. (2021). Economic challenges and opportunities for Asia-Pacific and the Western Hemisphere. | International Monetary Fund. Asia and Pacific Department (Series). | International Monetary Fund. Western Hemisphere Department (Series). Retrieved from https://www.imf.org/en/Publications/Departmental-Papers-Policy-Papers/Issues/2021/02/19/Tourism-in-the-Post-Pandemic-World-Economic-Challenges-and-Opportunities-for-Asia-Pacific-49915. Accessed on May 01, 2022.

Innocenti, D., & Albrito, P. (2011). Reducing the risks posed by natural hazards and climate change: The need for a participatory dialogue between the scientific community and policymakers. *Environmental Science & Policy*, *14*(7), 730–733.

Kantur, D., & Say, A. İ. (2013). Örgütsel dayanıklılık temasının kavramsallaştırılması ve ölçümü. In *21. Ulusal Yönetim ve Organizasyon Kongresi* (pp. 355–360). Kütahya: Dumlupınar Üniversitesi.

Larsen, R. L., Calgaro, E., & Thomalla, F. (2011). Governing resilience building in Thailand's tourism-dependent coastal communities: Conceptualizing stakeholder agency in social ecological systems. *Global Environmental Change, 21*(2), 481–491.

Le Masson, V., & Kelman, I. (2011). Disaster risk reduction on non-sovereign islands: La Réunion and Mayotte, France. *Natural Hazards, 56*(1), 251–273.

Lengnick-Hall, C. A., Beck, T. E., & Lengnick-Hall, M. L. (2011). Developing a capacity for organizational resilience through strategic human resource management. *Human Resource Management Review, 21*, 243–255.

Lew, A. A. (2014). Scale, change and resilience in community tourism planning. *Tourism Geographies, 16*(1), 14–22.

OECD. (2020a). Rebuilding tourism for the future: COVID-19 policy responses and recovery. Retrieved from https://www.oecd.org/coronavirus/policy-responses/ rebuilding-tourism-for-the-future-covid-19-policy-responses-and-recovery-bced9859/. Accessed on May 01, 2022.

OECD. (2020b). Tourism policy responses to the coronavirus (COVID-19). Retrieved from https://oecd.org/coronavirus/policy-responses/tourism-policy-responses-to-the-coronavirus-covid-19-6466aa20/. Accessed on May 01, 2022.

Omurtag, M. H. (2007). *Mühendisler için mekanik: Statik ve mukavemet* (2. Baskı). İstanbul: Nobel Yayın.

One Planet Sustainable Tourism Programme. (2020). One planet vision for a responsible recovery of the tourism sector. Retrieved from https://webunwto.s3.eu-west-1.amazonaws.com/s3fs-public/2020-06/one-planet-vision-responsible-recovery-of-the-tourism-sector.pdf. Accessed on May 01, 2022.

Orchiston, C. (2013). Tourism business preparedness, resilience and disaster planning in a region of high seismic risk: The case of the Southern Alps, New Zealand. *Current Issues in Tourism, 16*(5), 477–494.

Orchiston, C., Prayag, G., & Brown, C. (2016). Organizational resilience in the tourism sector. *Annals of Tourism Research, 56*, 145–148.

Perles-Ribes, J. F., Ramón-Rodríguez, A. B., Rubia-Serrano, A., & Moreno-Izquierdo, L. (2016). Economic crisis and tourism competitiveness in Spain: Permanent effects or transitory shocks? *Current Issues in Tourism, 19*(12), 1210–1234.

Pettit, T. J., Croxton, K. L., & Fiksel, J. (2013). Ensuring supply chain resilience: Development and implementation of an assessment tool. *Journal of Business Logistics, 34*(1), 46–76.

Proag, V. (2014). The concept of vulnerability and resilience. *Procedia Economics and Finance, 18*, 369–376.

Ragonnaud, G. (2022). France's national recovery and resilience plan. Retrieved from https://www.europarl.europa.eu/RegData/etudes/BRIE/2022/698929/EPRS_BRI(2022)698929_EN.pdf. Accessed on May 01, 2022.

Rosselló, J., Becken, S., & Santana-Gallego, M. (2020). The effects of natural disasters on international tourism: A global analysis. *Tourism Management, 79*, 104080.

Shakya, M. (2009). *Risk, vulnerability and tourism in developing countries: The case of Nepal*. Berlin: Logos Verlag Berlin GmbH.

SPTO. (2020). SPTO Covid19 recovery strategy. Retrieved from https://
southpacificislands.travel/wp-content/uploads/2021/07/Pacific-Tourism-COVID-
19-Recovery-Strategy.pdf. Accessed on May 01, 2022.

Stevenson, J. R. (2014). *Organizational resilience after Canterbury earthquakes: A
contextual approach.* Doctor of Philosophy in Geography. University of Canterbury, New Zealand.

Thomas, A. D. (2012). *An integrated view: Multiple stressors and small tourism
enterprises in the Bahamas.* Degree of Doctor of Philosophy New Brunswick
Rutgers. The State University of New Jersey, New Jersey.

Tomer, J. F. (1995). Strategy and structure in the human firm: Beyond hierarchy,
toward flexibility and integration. *The Journal of Socio-Economics, 24*(3), 411–431.

World Bank. (2020). Rebuilding tourism competitiveness: Tourism response, recovery
and resilience to the COVID-19 crisis. Retrieved from https://openknowledge.
worldbank.org/handle/10986/34348. Accessed on May 01, 2022.

Yılmaz, Ö. D. (2004). *Turizm işletmelerinde kriz yönetimi ve konaklama işletmeleri
yöneticilerinin krizlere yönelik yaklaşımlarına ilişkin bir araştırma.* Yayımlanmamış
Yüksek Lisans Tezi. Dokuz Eylül Üniversitesi, İzmir.

Zeng, B., Carter, R. W., & De Lacy, T. (2005). Short-term perturbations and tourism
effects: The case of SARS in China. *Current Issues in Tourism, 8*(4), 306–322.

Rebuilding Senior Tourism Destinations in the Post-COVID Era

Sultan Nazmiye Kılıç

Abstract

The environment of uncertainty that emerged due to COVID-19 brought the need for the creation of new policies and strategies. In this aspect, it has been observed that various recovery strategies have been adopted by policy-makers. Thus, this study aimed to investigate the efforts of destinations for senior tourism and to determine the development and change in the academic studies and related strategies. The methodology was based on a literature review and examining policy documents linking senior tourism, tourism destinations, and post-COVID-19 strategies. In this vein, this study is exploratory and displays a conceptual foundation for future research.

Keywords: Senior tourism; rebuilding tourism; post-COVID; tourism destinations; destination strategy; post-COVID destinations

Introduction

COVID-19 has affected the world as a crisis that generated a broad geographical impact and significantly changed the lives of individuals. With this crisis, a variety of new medical terms have been used in daily life, and the health sector has gained more importance, maybe more than ever. Various restrictions have been enforced, and an increase in social anxiety and stress has been observed. This period has also been challenging for the elderly group, one of the vulnerable special need groups of society. Thus, elderly individuals had to stay away from social interaction and other activities in order not to be affected by possible contamination. It would not be wrong to say that they could not get socially together enough, even with their relatives, and they were more alone than ever. Hence, they tried to learn and use remote communication opportunities. During this period, some chronic diseases have progressed due to the lack of physical activity, or hospital appointments have been postponed due to the fear of COVID-19.

Resilient and Sustainable Destinations After Disaster, 213–225
Copyright © 2023 Sultan Nazmiye Kılıç
Published under exclusive licence by Emerald Publishing Limited
doi:10.1108/978-1-80382-021-720231015

The effect of this epidemic, which changes daily life to such a degree, has also been reflected in varied sectors. As a collective traumatic event, COVID-19 has affected individual and collective behavior, including tourism (Zambianchi, 2020). In this period, the travel and tourism sector has been seriously affected (Orîndaru et al., 2021) as perceived health risk reduces tourists' future travel intentions (Hanafiah, Md Zain, Azinuddin, & Mior Shariffuddin, 2021). The impact of COVID-19 on global tourism was characterized as "overwhelming and immediate" (OECD, 2020). In this aspect, changes have also been observed in related studies. During the pandemic, the focus was shifted from overtourism to the industry's survival. In the chain reaction of the pandemic, a significant paradigm shift was required, and the survival of tourism stakeholders, maintenance of the workforce, and performance of DMOs became a priority (Guerreiro, 2022). When the scope of research on the subject is examined, especially the concepts of recovery and resiliency are encountered. For instance, Mensah and Boakye (2021) addressed the conceptualization of post-COVID-19 tourism recovery. Yeh's research (2021) had the theme of recovery strategy. On this spot, it was seen that concepts such as resilience (Adams, Choe, Mostafanezhad, & Phi, 2021; McCartney, Pinto, & Liu, 2021; Mittal & Sinha, 2021), re-building (Guerreiro, 2022), revival (McTeigue, Sanchez, Santos, Walter, & Au-Yong-Oliveira, 2021), and recovery (McCartney et al., 2021) were studied.

As various components of the tourism market, many tourism types have been affected by the crisis, and tourism development in emerging markets has experienced a period of temporary stagnation. Some countries have supported different areas of tourism. For example, in Korea, importance was given to the forest recreation or camping sector (OECD, 2020). In related studies, it was seen that different types of tourism were discussed within the scope of post-COVID revitalization of destinations. In their study, Spencer and Spencer (2022) explored strategies that were needed for the post-COVID period in cruise tourism. Chin (2021) examined the practical plan on the competitiveness of rural tourism destinations in the post-COVID period. Mittal and Sinha (2021) studied resilient religious tourism supply chain within the framework of postpandemic risk. Adams et al. (2021) stated that rural tourism areas could serve the socially distanced leisure needs of citizens in domestic tourism. Similarly, as an impact of COVID-19, the diversification of tourism products was expected to arise for countries such as Ghana. As indicated in the study of Mensah and Boakye (2021), recovery strategies were themed under two dimensions: revamping domestic tourism and rethinking relief. Expansion of tourism offerings by developing new attractions and events was a subdimension of revamping domestic tourism.

An escalation has been observed in the preferences of villa-type businesses that provide high-priced services and guarantee social distance for vacation. In all these conditions, elderly individuals could not participate sufficiently in activities such as recreation and tourism. However, due to the change in population, active aging is a phenomenon that has been supported and encouraged more nowadays. For this reason, it is essential to develop innovative tourism types and service technologies by also adapting to the changing demographic structure for the survival of the tourism sector (Taloş et al., 2021). Although the responses of countries to the elderly have been studied within the scope of COVID-19 (Daoust, 2020), the number of studies on this subject in the field of tourism is limited. Additionally, despite the significant appeal to tourism sector revival, very little academic attention has been given to senior tourism. Based on the gaps in the literature linking senior tourism, destinations, and COVID-19, this research aimed to provide a deeper understanding of strategies for the development of senior tourism and destinations in the post-COVID-19 era. This study was built on the following questions: (1) What have been the destination recovery strategies related to senior tourism? (2) What approaches were handled in academic studies regarding post-COVID senior tourism destinations? Hence, the remainder of the chapter is structured as follows. First, policy responses for the tourism sector under the conditions of COVID-19 were presented. Then, the changing characteristics of seniors and senior tourism were given. Finally, lessons to destinations for senior tourism post COVID-19 were examined.

Policy Implications for the Tourism Sector

The COVID-19 crisis has revealed a necessity to change policy and management practices in tourism. However, there has been uncertainty in the recovery process of tourism (Guerreiro, 2022). The sector presented various challenges and opportunities in postcrisis recovery (Adams et al., 2021). Governments have prepared different policies and strategies to take advantage of the economic opportunities that the tourism sector will provide, overcome uncertainties, and revitalize the tourism sector. Tourism policy responses developed against COVID-19 have been researched by international organizations such as the OECD and UNWTO. In this vein, the OECD (2020) has determined that policy responses are developed in three main areas: (1) visitors, (2) employees and businesses (especially SMEs), and (3) destinations. Governments and the industry have demonstrated efforts such as removing travel restrictions, implementing new health protocols for safe travel, diversifying the market, restoring tourist confidence, domestic tourism promotion campaigns, preparing comprehensive tourism plans, and promoting innovation and investments (OECD, 2020). In addition, governments have prepared various economic incentives in sectors such as tourism to reduce the adverse effects of the pandemic, and these incentives vary according to the size of the sector (Khalid, Okafor, & Burzynska, 2021). In order to overcome the problems caused by the closure, supportive policies such as bank loans and subsidies were implemented for the supply side (Orîndaru et al., 2021). European governments such as Spain, Ireland, Greece, and the Netherlands have also prepared tourism improvement plans for the post-COVID-19 period. Plans, initiatives, and strategies prepared to support the tourism sector due to the pandemic have attracted great interest in the relevant literature (Jones, 2022). Studies dealing with the response of countries such as Ghana have been prepared (Mensah & Boakye, 2021). In parallel with this, Khan, Nasir, and Saleem (2021) made a bibliometric analysis of the studies on post-COVID tourism management strategies and policies in their research. As a result of the research, it was understood that the most academic contribution in this field was made by China. The research themes related to the subject were defined as post-COVID recovery of the tourism sector, postpandemic risk factors of the tourism and hospitality industry, ecosystem and economic strategies, and crises and disaster management. The topic of resilient tourist destinations was one of the streams studied in tourism and hospitality-related research. Different destinations were examined in the literature. For example, Portugal (McTeigue et al., 2021), Southeast Asia (Adams et al., 2021), Macao (McCartney et al., 2021), Madeira Island (Franco & Mota, 2021), Guayaquil, Ecuador (Orden-Mejía et al., 2022), and Bali (Subadra, 2021). It is assumed that the issues related to the crisis will come to the fore more in the post-COVID-19 period (Xu, McKercher, & Ho, 2021).

Seniors and Senior Tourism

The increase in the elderly population has led to changes in many different sectors, including tourism. It is thought that it will be the target group with the fastest growing market potential in the global tourism market in the future (Stončikaitė, 2021). Senior tourism has the potential to support the tourism industry by providing demand in the off-season and reducing overtourism. For this reason, understanding the behavior of senior tourists is critical for market planning (Szromek, Pytel, Markiewicz-Patkowska, & Oleśniewicz, 2021). As a market segment, senior tourists have specific behavioral characteristics (Filipe, Barbosa, & Santos, 2021). Generally, research in this field is on European tourists and European destinations. The most critical factor affecting the tourism expenditures of senior European tourists is their income, which is mainly determined by the pension system (Taloş et al., 2021). Retirees are a considerable consumer segment for the tourism sector by minimizing the seasonal effect and increasing sustainability (Filipe et al., 2021). In the research conducted on retirees in Portugal, three tourist segments were identified: "the experts, the new tourists, and the nontourists." (Filipe et al., 2021). In another research conducted on senior tourists from remote regions of Europe, it was understood that seniors' holiday reasons were the possibility of rest and silence. Top attractions in destination selection were safety, nature, historical sites, service quality, and easiness of transportation services. Problems that negatively influence were difficulty in accessibility to tourism offers, lack of promotion, and lack of supportive financial resources for local projects relating to senior tourism development (Zielińska-Szczepkowska, 2021). Senior tourists have a heterogeneous feature within themselves. According to a study on senior Italian tourists, it was understood that senior tourists stayed 26% longer than young seniors (Campolo, De Pascale, Giannetto, & Lanfranchi, 2022). For the senior group, income level and health status are decisive levels of segmentation (Taloş et al., 2021). Today's senior tourists differ from previous generations as they participate more in overseas trips and travel for pleasure-related purposes (Patterson, Balderas-Cejudo, & Pegg, 2021). In the study conducted by Zielińska-Szczepkowska (2021), it was revealed that seniors were enthusiastic about traveling to small towns and rural areas. Thus, seniors have had the potential to move permanently to places where they visited before. The nonseasonality of senior travel is a considerable opportunity for the revitalization of the tourism industry (Szromek et al., 2021).

In another aspect, making tourism more accessible to the elderly can improve the quality of life for them together with providing economic benefits by expanding the potential market (Wan, Lo, & Eddy-U, 2022). However, according to Daoust (2020), governments' strategies for the elderly during the COVID-19 era were not successful enough.

The COVID-19 pandemic was a humanitarian crisis that affected the lives of individuals and caused a global economic crisis (OECD, 2020). In this period, there were practices such as social distancing, which were expected to be applied in the whole society, but could create mistrust, discrimination, and violence among people (Yeh, 2021). Various public health measures were implemented to minimize the impact of the pandemic. Since the elderly were the most vulnerable population group during this crisis, public authorities aimed to persuade the elderly to comply with the measures (Daoust, 2020). Some of these measures were lockdowns and limitations on using public transportation. Afterward, these were constrained to certain hours. However, due to all similar restrictions, individuals who were already physically, psychologically, and socially disadvantaged were further restricted. Although communication could be provided by technological means, elderly individuals who did not have sufficient knowledge and experience in this subject could not find enough opportunities to socialize. Therefore, loneliness and inactivity for the elderly led to the emergence and worsening of various health problems (Aydın & Tütüncü, 2021). The loneliness and isolation brought by the quarantine also caused significant mental health problems in the elderly (Shuja, Shahidullah, Aqeel, Khan, & Abbas, 2020).

The epidemic crisis has affected the participation of the elderly in travel (Szromek et al., 2021). After the pandemic, the demographic characteristics of tourists changed. Younger and nonfamily segments came to the fore (OECD, 2020). In the Northeast of England, an innovative and aggressive pricing strategy for the young segment was implemented due to a lack of business customers (Spanaki, Papatheodorou, & Pappas, 2021). In this vein, in order to stimulate domestic tourism in Chile, discounts and the provision of vouchers were provided to encourage the participation of lower-income families and the elderly group in tourism (Mulder, 2020). Due to COVID-19, before traveling, warnings have been made for elderly people. For example, examining the web pages of destinations, obtaining information about the requirements and health risks such as vaccines and medicines, informing their doctors about their travels, having the necessary vaccinations, and taking the medicines recommended by their doctors (CDC, 2022).

Due to its market size and growth potential, senior travelers and their behavior have become an important research area of interest (Filipe et al., 2021). Researchers such as Handler (2022) and Otoo, Kim, Agrusa, and Lema (2021) handled COVID-19 and senior travelers together in their studies. Research by Silva (2020) regarding Sri Lanka was prepared within the scope of senior tourism, destination resilience, and recovery of post-COVID. In a similar vein, Taloş et al. (2021) handled Romania, and Bizzarri, Buonincontri, and Micera (2022) studied Bibione, Italy. According to the results of the research conducted by Zambianchi (2020) on senior Italian tourists, the elderly thought that their travel patterns would change due to the pandemic. This idea was expressed more by women. The sudden return of the coronavirus, the lack of safety systems in tourism establishments, and the inadequate measures of the tour operators regarding the coronavirus in tourist destinations were the most feared obstacles (Zambianchi, 2020). In the study by Patterson et al. (2021), it was found that social interaction and networking with others are essential parts of travel as well as the visited destination. Although it is generally overlooked, perceived life quality is essential for seniors during their travels. For this reason, it may be beneficial to design the recreational activities in destinations in a way that eases and encourages the interaction of different age groups.

Lessons to Destinations for Senior Tourism in Post-COVID-19

COVID-19, which has created an immense shock in terms of seriously affecting cultural activities, recreation, and other consumer-facing sectors (Taloş et al., 2021) has provided the tourism industry, policymakers, and tourism researchers with vital lessons about the effects of global change. There are lessons to be learned, especially in accelerating the transformation to sustainable tourism (Gössling, Scott, & Hall, 2021). As an example, sustainability was a key theme in the United Kingdom's recovery plan (Jones, 2022). Based on the literature, in order to provide post-COVID-19 resilience in the tourism sector, G. D. Sharma, Thomas, and Paul (2021) suggested the following factors: "government response, technology innovation, local belongingness, and consumer and employee confidence." Additionally, diversification and specialization are considered significant in resilience and recovery (McCartney et al., 2021). Developing new business models together with the lessons learned from the pandemic is critical for the rapid recovery of the tourism sector. Tourism products and services need to be redesigned to accommodate the transition from mass to sustainable tourism. The pandemic should be considered as an opportunity to transition to more sustainable types of tourism. In addition, considering the contribution to be made to local stakeholders, it is meaningful to encourage chain strategy rather than destination strategy and to increase the contribution of each member of the value chain such as accommodation, transportation, food, and beverage to the visitor experience. This can also support the livelihood of local communities (Roxas, Rivera, & Gutierrez, 2022). Thus, adapting the products for senior tourists and getting the support of locals and other stakeholders can be beneficial. In this way, diversity can be ensured, and it can also help sustainability.

Since the impact of the pandemic was not only economical, governments had to consider other different dimensions. According to Orîndaru et al. (2021), in addition to supply side, support is also required for the demand, which is affected by psychological and economic factors. In this context, psychological factors, mainly including fear of contamination, affect willingness to travel and destination preferences while economic factors are associated with a decrease in household income, an increase in the propensity to save, or uncertain economic prospects. In the research of Yeh (2021), it was concluded that open communication, as well as government-sponsored loans, are critical for the survival of the industry in the COVID-19 pandemic. Within the scope of postpandemic recovery, the most mentioned feature in marketing messages was "safety" (Singh, Nicely, Day, & Cai, 2022). As an example of these efforts, in a study examining the destination development of Bali during the postpandemic period, it was understood that the destination competitiveness increased by organizing intensive workshops and training on international health procedures (Subadra, 2021).

Senior tourism needed new travel models in line with the "new normal." For example, travel experiences from home, smaller travel groups, less crowded destinations, or more sustainable tourism (Stončikaitė, 2021). Businesses that restructure their business models in line with economic, social, and technological changes can gain a competitive advantage (Khan et al., 2021). Therefore, emerging markets such as senior tourism should be followed closely.

It is thought that there is a need for a paradigm shift in destination management for possible future crises. DMOs should prioritize the digital transformation of tourism destinations, collaborate with companies, and maximize data usage. Therefore, tourism workforce skills need to be developed (Guerreiro, 2022). COVID-19 has affected the travel behavior of tourists (Hanafiah et al., 2021). Thus, after the pandemic, the functioning of the tourism sector and destination management models had to be reconsidered (Guerreiro, 2022). Innovativeness in tourism events influences tourists' revisit intentions (Rahimizhian & Irani, 2021). It is thought that the use of VR technologies can be beneficial in order to overcome the physical limitations applied during the pandemic period, help tourism destinations recover, and build tourism resilience (Kim, So, Mihalik, & Lopes, 2021). In this vein, Franco ve Mota (2021) studied augmented reality as a strategy to attract visitors to a tourist destination. Lu et al. (2022) studied virtual tourism for the tourism industry's recovery. Hence, virtual tourism was suggested as a solution to provide "virtual accessibility," especially for the elderly and disabled, and environmental sustainability.

In order to ensure the resilience in the post-COVID-19 period, tailor-made and age-friendly strategies for seniors should be organized by policymakers, taking into account the concepts of adaptation and innovation (Taloş et al., 2021). In the study by Wen, Zheng, Hou, Phau, and Wang (2022), tourism was seen as an alternative way to enhance the well-being of dementia patients in the context of positive psychology, and vulnerable groups were presented as a potential niche market to provide post-COVID-19 tourism recovery. In relation to this, applying tailored strategies and creating vulnerability-friendly destinations were recommended.

Conclusion

With the increasing number and variety of destinations, new tourist segments have emerged. Senior tourists are one of them. In this vein, the increase in the aging population makes it necessary to understand better the tourism and travel behaviors of the senior group (Filipe et al., 2021). It is also necessary that the senior tourists' segment is adequately understood by policymakers and managers, as this segment can help the recovery process and contribute to tourism revenues in the post-COVID-19 period (Handler, 2022). In addition, the active and healthy aging policy offers a significant market opportunity within the scope of EU silver economy policies. Improving recreation and leisure areas for the elderly can make the elderly population a more important market share (Taloş et al., 2021). In another aspect, travel has a positive effect on the elderly and contributes to maintaining a healthy lifestyle (Patterson et al., 2021). From this point of view, the support to be provided to senior tourism can be beneficial in terms of factors such as the development of tourism destinations, economic gains, and elderly health. Although it has not been studied enough in the literature, senior tourism is considered to be a potential part of COVID-19 recovery. It is decisive that the senior tourists' segment is adequately understood by policymakers and managers, as it can help the recovery process and contribute to tourism revenues in the post-COVID-19 period (Handler, 2022). In this aspect, this research aims to synthesize postpandemic strategies regarding tourism activities for seniors, one of the age groups most affected by the pandemic, in line with the relevant literature and policy documents. The preparation of regulations covering different tourist profiles is essential for the sustainability of tourism development. For this reason, understanding how the barriers created by the crisis are removed for senior tourists can be a guide for other destinations. In this context, it is assumed that the research can help understand the studies, policies, challenges, and strategies of destinations on providing resiliency, and assumed that the results of the study would contribute to policymakers, marketers, tourism businesses, and tourism researchers.

Today's senior tourists differ from previous generations as they participate more in overseas trips and travel for pleasure-related purposes (Patterson et al., 2021). For this reason, changing travel experiences of senior tourists should be considered when designing policy. An aging demographic cannot be ignored for destinations. Considering the travel experiences of this segment, it is critical to increase accessibility to tourism attractions and remove possible constraints (Wan et al., 2022). In studies handling senior tourism or new policies, it can be suggested to also consider caretakers who can be close relatives of elderly people sometimes. Destinations that are suitable for senior tourism can benefit especially domestic tourism activities as a new attraction. State sponsorship of domestic tourism trips among seniors can be promoted to aid tourism recovery.

Destination marketers should be aware that different age groups require different marketing strategies. For instance, social media for millenials, and self-presentation and social comparison for baby boomers (R. Sharma, Singh, & Pratt, 2022). Communication is essential for managing the fears and worries of tourists (Orîndaru et al., 2021). There are times when changing perceptions is more complicated than changing facts (Xu et al., 2021). People's perceptions of travel risk can change through intermediaries such as the media (Seyfi, Rastegar, Rasoolimanesh, & Hall, 2021). Thus, media regulations may be considered in policies, as they can change perception and trust toward the destination in the post-COVID era.

It has been understood that there is a need for a paradigm shift in destination management for possible future crises. In this period, it is necessary to act in accordance with the understanding of destination management, which encourages the coordinated management of all the elements that constitute the tourism destination and the efforts of the relevant stakeholders (Guerreiro, 2022). In the post-COVID phase, destination planners should coordinate health, sanitation, and public work services, provide hygiene and sanitation by applying safety measures of the Government, promote safety and relaxation through advertising, and take precautions against overtourism (Kala, 2021). The tourism industry and governments should be in coordination to support business establishments, especially the smallest ones, and the workers (OECD, 2020).

Rural tourism may be suitable for senior tourism in terms of providing social distance. For post-COVID-19 recovery, rural tourism can be suggested. However, it should be taken into account that there is a sensitive balance of competitive advantage attributes. Exceeding carrying capacity or cheapening of unique tourist attractions are possible outcomes in the occasion of unplanned development and over accessibility (Chin, 2021). In addition, seniors can move permanently to places they have visited before (Szromek et al., 2021). For this reason, the possible advantages and disadvantages of probable senior migration should be considered by policymakers.

There have been new contagious disease alerts already underway, and it is known that there is a risk of relapse of COVID-19. How ready international tourism is for new crises is a matter of debate. It is understood that there are not enough studies on senior tourists, which is a lucrative segment in terms of supporting tourism. For this reason, it may be beneficial to increase the number of studies in which technological developments are associated with senior tourism within the scope of innovation, and adaptation and new travel alternatives are produced.

References

Adams, K. M., Choe, J., Mostafanezhad, M., & Phi, G. T. (2021). (Post-) pandemic tourism resiliency: Southeast Asian lives and livelihoods in limbo. *Tourism Geographies, 23*(4), 915–936. doi:10.1080/14616688.2021.1916584

Aydın, İ., & Tütüncü, Ö. (2021). Pandemi sürecinde yaşlılık ve rekreasyon. *Anatolia: Turizm Araştırmaları Dergisi, 32*(1), 100–105. doi:10.17123/atad.948495

Bizzarri, C., Buonincontri, P., & Micera, R. (2022). Tourism for all: From customer to destination after COVID-19. In T. Abbate, F. Cesaroni, & A. D'Amico (Eds.), *Tourism and disability: An economic and managerial perspective* (pp. 129–153). Cham: Springer. doi:10.1007/978-3-030-93612-9_9

Campolo, M. G., De Pascale, A., Giannetto, C., & Lanfranchi, M. (2022). The determinants of length of stay of Italian senior tourists. In T. Abbate, F. Cesaroni, & A. D'Amico (Eds.), *Tourism and disability* (pp. 31–50). Cham: Springer International Publishing. doi:10.1007/978-3-030-93612-9_3

CDC. (2022). Older adults and healthy travel. CDC: Centers for Disease Control and Prevention. Retrieved from wwwnc.cdc.gov/travel/page/senior-citizens. Accessed on April 27, 2022.

Chin, C. H. (2021). Empirical research on the competitiveness of rural tourism destinations: A practical plan for rural tourism industry post-COVID-19. In *Consumer behavior in tourism and hospitality*. doi:10.1108/CBTH-07-2021-0169

Daoust, J.-F. (2020). Elderly people and responses to COVID-19 in 27 countries. *PLoS One, 15*(7), e0235590. doi:10.1371/journal.pone.0235590

Filipe, S., Barbosa, B., & Santos, C. A. (2021). Travel motivations and constraints of Portuguese retirees. *Anatolia, 32*(4), 591–603. doi:10.1080/13032917.2021.1999756

Franco, M., & Mota, L. (2021). Reopening for business post-COVID-19: Augmented reality as a strategy for attracting visitors to a tourist destination. *European Journal of Tourism, Hospitality and Recreation, 11*(1), 54–65. doi:10.2478/ejthr-2021-0006

Gössling, S., Scott, D., & Hall, C. M. (2021). Pandemics, tourism and global change: A rapid assessment of COVID-19. *Journal of Sustainable Tourism, 29*(1), 1–20. doi: 10.1080/09669582.2020.1758708

Guerreiro, S. (2022). Destination management in a post-covid environment. *Worldwide Hospitality and Tourism Themes, 14*(1), 48–55. doi:10.1108/WHATT-10-2021-0137

Hanafiah, M. H., Md Zain, N. A., Azinuddin, M., & Mior Shariffuddin, N. S. (2021). I'm afraid to travel! Investigating the effect of perceived health risk on Malaysian travellers' post-pandemic perception and future travel intention. *Journal of Tourism Futures, 1–16*. doi:10.1108/JTF-10-2021-0235

Handler, I. (2022). Can senior travelers save Japanese hot springs? A psychographic segmentation of visitors and their intention to visit Onsen establishments during COVID-19. *Sustainability, 14*, 2306. doi:10.3390/su14042306

Jones, P. (2022). A review of the UK's tourism recovery plans post COVID-19. *Athens Journal of Tourism, 9*(1), 9–18.

Kala, D. (2021). 'Thank you, God. You saved us'—Examining tourists' intention to visit religious destinations in the post COVID. *Current Issues in Tourism, 24*(22), 3127–3133. doi:10.1080/13683500.2021.1876643

Khalid, U., Okafor, L. E., & Burzynska, K. (2021). Does the size of the tourism sector influence the economic policy response to the COVID-19 pandemic? *Current Issues in Tourism, 24*(19), 2801–2820. doi:10.1080/13683500.2021.1874311

Khan, K. I., Nasir, A., & Saleem, S. (2021). Bibliometric analysis of post Covid-19 management strategies and policies in hospitality and tourism. *Frontiers in Psychology, 12*. doi:10.3389/fpsyg.2021.769760

Kim, H., So, K. K. F., Mihalik, B. J., & Lopes, A. P. (2021). Millennials' virtual reality experiences pre- and post-COVID-19. *Journal of Hospitality and Tourism Management, 48*, 200–209. doi:10.1016/j.jhtm.2021.06.008

Lu, J., Xiao, X., Xu, Z., Wang, C., Zhang, M., & Zhou, Y. (2022). The potential of virtual tourism in the recovery of tourism industry during the COVID-19 pandemic. *Current Issues in Tourism, 25*(3), 441–457. doi:10.1080/13683500.2021.1959526

McCartney, G., Pinto, J., & Liu, M. (2021). City resilience and recovery from COVID-19: The case of Macao. *Cities, 112*, 103130. doi:10.1016/j.cities.2021. 103130

McTeigue, C., Sanchez, C., Santos, E., Walter, C. E., & Au-Yong-Oliveira, M. (2021). A strategy for tourism growth, rebound, and revival: Promoting Portugal as a destination post-Covid-19. *Sustainability, 13*, 12588. doi:10.3390/su132212588

Mensah, E. A., & Boakye, K. A. (2021). Conceptualizing post-COVID 19 tourism recovery: A three-step framework. *Tourism Planning & Development, 1–25*. doi:10. 1080/21568316.2021.1945674

Mittal, R., & Sinha, P. (2021). Framework for a resilient religious tourism supply chain for mitigating post-pandemic risk. *International Hospitality Review*. doi:10. 1108/IHR-09-2020-0053

Mulder, N. (coord.). (2020). *The impact of the COVID-19 pandemic on the tourism sector in Latin America and the Caribbean, and options for a sustainable and resilient recovery* (No. 157-LC/TS.2020/147). Santiago: Economic Commission for Latin America and the Caribbean (ECLAC). Retrieved from Economic Commission for Latin America and the Caribbean (ECLAC): https://www.cepal.org/sites/default/ files/publication/files/46502/S2000751_en.pdf

OECD. (2020). Tourism policy responses to the Coronavirus (Covid-19). Retrieved from oecd.org/coronavirus

Orden-Mejía, M., Carvache-Franco, M., Huertas, A., Carvache-Franco, W., Landeta-Bejarano, N., & Carvache-Franco, O. (2022). Post-COVID-19 tourists' preferences, attitudes and travel expectations: A study in Guayaquil, Ecuador. *International Journal of Environmental Research and Public Health, 19*, 4822. doi: 10.3390/ijerph19084822

Orîndaru, A., Popescu, M.-F., Alexoaei, A. P., Căescu, Ș.-C., Florescu, M. S., & Orzan, A.-O. (2021). Tourism in a post-COVID-19 era: Sustainable strategies for industry's recovery. *Sustainability, 13*, 6781. doi:10.3390/su13126781

Otoo, F. E., Kim, S. (S.), Agrusa, J., & Lema, J. (2021). Classification of senior tourists according to personality traits. *Asia Pacific Journal of Tourism Research, 26*(5), 539–556. doi:10.1080/10941665.2021.1876118

Patterson, I., Balderas-Cejudo, A., & Pegg, S. (2021). Tourism preferences of seniors and their impact on healthy ageing. *Anatolia, 32*(4), 553–564. doi:10.1080/ 13032917.2021.1999753

Rahimizhian, S., & Irani, F. (2021). Contactless hospitality in a post-Covid-19 world. *International Hospitality Review, 35*(2), 293–304. doi:10.1108/IHR-08-2020-0041

Roxas, F. M. Y., Rivera, J. P. R., & Gutierrez, E. L. M. (2022). Bootstrapping tourism post-COVID-19: A systems thinking approach. *Tourism and Hospitality Research, 22*(1), 86–101. doi:10.1177/14673584211038859

Seyfi, S., Rastegar, R., Rasoolimanesh, S. M., & Hall, C. M. (2021). A framework for understanding media exposure and post-COVID-19 travel intentions. *Tourism Recreation Research, 1–6*. doi:10.1080/02508281.2021.1949545

Sharma, R., Singh, G., & Pratt, S. (2022). Exploring travel envy and social return in domestic travel: A cross-generational analysis. *Journal of Travel & Tourism Marketing, 39*(1), 58–72. doi:10.1080/10548408.2022.2045247

Sharma, G. D., Thomas, A., & Paul, J. (2021). Reviving tourism industry post-COVID-19: A resilience-based framework. *Tourism Management Perspectives, 37*, 100786. doi:10.1016/j.tmp.2020.100786

Shuja, K. H., Shahidullah, Aqeel, M., Khan, E. A., & Abbas, J. (2020). Letter to highlight the effects of isolation on elderly during COVID-19 outbreak [Letter to the editor]. *International Journal of Geriatric Psychiatry, 35*, 1477–1478. doi:10. 1002/gps.5423

Silva, D. S. (2020). Senior tourism and resilience and recovery of post-covid Sri Lanka tourism. Retrieved from https://www.researchgate.net/profile/Suranga-Silva/ publication/343050240_Senior_Tourism_as_a_Resilience_and_Recovery_ Strategy_for_Post-COVID_Sri_Lanka_Tourism/links/5f135daf92851c1eff1c4748/ Senior-Tourism-as-a-Resilience-and-Recovery-Strategy-for-Post-COVID-Sri-Lanka-Tourism.pdf. Accessed on May 6, 2022.

Singh, S., Nicely, A., Day, J., & Cai, L. A. (2022). Marketing messages for post-pandemic destination recovery- A Delphi study. *Journal of Destination Marketing & Management, 23*, 100676. doi:10.1016/j.jdmm.2021.100676

Spanaki, M. Z., Papatheodorou, A., & Pappas, N. (2021). Tourism in the post COVID-19 era: Evidence from hotels in the North East of England. *Worldwide Hospitality and Tourism Themes, 13*(3), 357–368. doi:10.1108/WHATT-01-2021-0013

Spencer, A. J., & Spencer, D. (2022). Cruising on choppy seas: The revitalization of Jamaica as a cruise destination post COVID-19. *Worldwide Hospitality and Tourism Themes, 14*(2), 99–114. doi:10.1108/WHATT-12-2021-0155

Stončikaitė, I. (2021). Baby-boomers hitting the road: The paradoxes of the senior leisure tourism. *Journal of Tourism and Cultural Change*. doi:10.1080/14766825. 2021.1943419

Subadra, I. N. (2021). Destination management solution post covid-19: Best practice from Bali – A world cultural tourism destination. In V. G. Gowreesunkar, S. W. Maingi, H. Roy, & R. Micera (Eds.), *Tourism destination management in a post-pandemic context (tourism security-safety and post conflict destinations)* (pp. 25–36). Bingley: Emerald Publishing Limited. doi:10.1108/978-1-80071-511-020211024

Szromek, A. R., Pytel, S., Markiewicz-Patkowska, J., & Oleśniewicz, P. (2021). Impact of tourist trips on seniors' migrations – Case study from Poland. *Journal of Tourism and Cultural Change, 1–15*. doi:10.1080/14766825.2021.1999460

Taloş, A.-M., Lequeux-Dincă, A.-I., Preda, M., Surugiu, C., Mareci, A., & Vijulie, I. (2021). Silver tourism and recreational activities as possible factors to support active ageing and the resilience of the tourism sector. *Journal of Settlements and Spatial Planning, SI*(8), 29–48. doi:10.24193/JSSPSI.2021.8.04

Wan, Y. K. P., Lo, W. S. S., & Eddy-U, M. E. (2022). Perceived constraints and negotiation strategies by elderly tourists when visiting heritage sites. *Leisure Studies, 1–19*. doi:10.1080/02614367.2022.2066710

Wen, J., Zheng, D., Hou, H., Phau, I., & Wang, W. (2022). Tourism as a dementia treatment based on positive psychology. *Tourism Management, 92*, 104556. doi:10. 1016/j.tourman.2022.104556

Xu, J. (B.), McKercher, B., & Ho, P. S. (2021). Post-COVID destination competitiveness. *Asia Pacific Journal of Tourism Research, 26*(11), 1244–1254. doi:10.1080/ 10941665.2021.1960872

Yeh, S.-S. (2021). Tourism recovery strategy against COVID-19 pandemic. *Tourism Recreation Research, 46*(2), 188–194. doi:10.1080/02508281.2020.1805933

Zambianchi, M. (2020). The collective traumatic event of COVID-19 pandemic and its psychological impact on beliefs and intentions of senior Italian tourists. *Almatourism – Journal of Tourism, Culture and Territorial Development, 11*(22), 45–60. doi:10.6092/ISSN.2036-5195/11653

Zielińska-Szczepkowska, J. (2021). What are the needs of senior tourists? Evidence from remote regions of Europe. *Economies, 9*, 148. doi:10.3390/economies9040148

Spirituality and Yoga for Well-being in a Post-disaster Scenario: Linking the Qualitative Facets of Traditional Indian Ways of Life

Manpreet Arora and Roshan Lal Sharma

Abstract

The pandemic has not only disturbed the economies but also eventually affected the way we think, act, or behave. The impacts had been so deep that the way the whole generation was living is completely changed. The impacts are not just physical, but the world is now more concerned about the mental and psychological impacts also. In this chapter the authors focus on spirituality, yoga, and meditation as strategies for well-being which have qualitative dimensions and are the basis of rich traditional lives. The qualitative analysis of the content on social media has been used as the base.

Keywords: Spirituality; yoga; well-being; pandemic; post-disaster; qualitative research

The coronavirus pandemic has not only disturbed the economies, it has also eventually affected the way we think, act, or behave. The impact has been so deep that it has changed the way the present generation has been living prior to the pandemic (Arora & Sharma, 2021). Besides taking a physical toll, the pandemic has also affected the mental and psychological well-being of people from across the world. The words "quarantine," and "social/physical distancing" have created psychological divides deep down in the lives of people. People of every age group have suffered immensely. The "new normal" being disturbingly abnormal is becoming worse with each passing day. While writing this chapter, the authors are surrounded by the fear of yet another omicron subvariant BA.2.75 known for its severity and transmissibility. Many countries are facing exponential increase in the coronavirus cases; the two groups, namely teenagers and elderly, are the worst effected as they have been confined indoors and forced to adopt a sedentary

Resilient and Sustainable Destinations After Disaster, 227–239
Copyright © 2023 Manpreet Arora and Roshan Lal Sharma
Published under exclusive licence by Emerald Publishing Limited
doi:10.1108/978-1-80382-021-720231016

lifestyle. Both the groups are facing problems of sleep disorders, depression, loneliness, low energy levels, and in some cases even obesity, eyesight issues, irritable bowel syndromes, erratic eating disorders, mood swings, lack of interest or enthusiasm, anxiety, depression, negative effects on vital organs in some cases, and the list keeps increasing. In such a scenario, taking medical advice is a good idea, but how long can one go on like this. The time-tested techniques of breathing exercise also known as *pranayam*, diet control, focusing of the mind by practicing meditation and yoga are basically the traditional Indian ways of life where the solution seems to lie. All other ways seem to have failed humanity repeatedly.

The tourism industry has a critical and vital role to play in making people from different countries of the world benefit from the time-tested techniques of spiritual, meditational, and yogic practices. There is ample evidence to show that these practices are known far and wide. In India, for the said purpose, a lot of tourist footprint has been there in the past, and the same has been adversely affected owing to the coronavirus pandemic. The outbreak of virus in 2019 and its subsequent proliferation through the variants like delta, omicron, etc., the world had no option but to fight back during the first and second waves, and it has to overcome even the impending third wave come what may. Once the devastation caused by COVID-19 is over, the world has to get back to normalcy.

As evident during the period after the second wave, there has been surge in tourist activity across the globe. Millennials left the claustrophobic spaces of their homes where they remained isolated and alienated for nearly 2 years. In fact, they experienced a sense of liberation as they moved to their choicest destinations across the world. India too experienced a surge in religious and spiritual tourism, and there has been a considerable increase in meditational and yogic practices not only in India but also across the world. The only reason that can be attributed to such exponential increase in spiritual, yogic, and meditational practices has been because the holistic and integral well-being of an individual can be attained only through these practices. It can be arguably claimed that such practices have not only resulted in physical, mental, and spiritual well-being but also served as powerful resilience strategies during the postpandemic/disaster scenario. It is really heartening to note that these practices entail the least capital investment but the gains are far more than we can imagine. India has a lot to offer to the world like several East Asian nations such as Thailand, Bhutan, etc. However, compared to these countries, India is a larger hub from the viewpoint of spiritual, yogic, and meditational practices, and these can offer everlasting benefits in the arena of holistic well-being.

Methodology and Research Questions

We will focus on spirituality, yoga, and meditation as strategies for well-being. The qualitative analysis of literature will serve as the base. The secondary data on various government portals will serve as the indicators. For content analysis on public domain, NVivo software will be used. The traditional Indian treatises and their excerpts will be used to support the arguments.

RQs

(1) What is well-being?
(2) How spirituality and yoga for well-being in the post-disaster scenario can serve as strategies?
(3) What are the Indian traditional ways of living for well-being?
(4) What role does the tourism industry play and how can it act as a bridge for achieving well-being in post-disaster times?

What Is Well-being?

The dictionary meaning of well-being is the "state of being comfortable, healthy and happy." The concept of well-being is very wide and holistic. It includes focus on good mental health, considering life-satisfying values, and a meaningful and purposeful life covering/benefiting everyone. The concept of well-being inherently includes focusing on happiness, coping with stress, and ensuring a peaceful and purposeful life (Slade, 2010). Another dimension of well-being is a positive state of mind. Well-being is not only physical well-being; it also includes mental well-being or wellness. Therefore, it is a holistic concept. The concept of wellness starts with psychological aspects that basically contribute a healthy and constructive state of mind. A healthy mind with positive and stress-free state leads to a healthy body free of illness and diseases (Munawar & Choudhry, 2021).

The state of well-being has positive outcomes, and is an indication that peoples' lives are full of happiness and good health, and that they live in conditions which are fundamental for healthy and peaceful living. It is not just related to physical living conditions but it is also related to inner satisfaction, positive state of mind, good feelings, and healthy, happy and depression-free lives (Shaw, 2020). Psychologists all over the world believe that the concept of well-being is holistic and encompasses mental as well as physical health (Lennon, 1994). It also helps in disease prevention and promotes good health.

Good health is related to a free and healthy mind, and it also signifies absence of any disease (Prime, Wade, & Browne, 2020). If one is healthy, we can realize our full potential, satisfy our desires, and cope with the environment and its challenges without much effort, which in turn helps us live a long, happy, and peaceful life (Ross, 1995). There are varied views about the concept of well-being, but as per the general agreement, well-being includes the following (Table 1):

The World Health Organization (WHO) describes "well-being" as a "resource for healthy living" and "positive state of health" that is "more than the absence of an illness" and enables us to function well – psychologically, physically, emotionally, and socially. In other words, "well-being" is described as "enabling people to develop their potential, work productively and creatively, form positive

Table 1. Elements of Well-being.

"Positive emotions
Good mood
Presence of feelings of contentment
Happiness
Absence of negativity
Absence of depression and anxiety
Satisfaction in life
Overall feelings of feeling good
Feeling of being energetic
Positive social relationships
Optimism
Extroversion
Self esteem"

Source: https://www.gov.uk/government/publications/mental-capital-and-wellbeing-making-the-most-of-ourselves-in-the-21st-century.

relationships with others and meaningfully contribute to the community" (www.cdc.gov/hrqol/wellbeing.html). The concept of well-being has various dimensions. For instance, social well-being can also be connected with mental, social, emotional, psychological, and spiritual dimensions of overall wellness. The sense of belonging to community and feeling a part of community, and doing good for community are all related to social well-being. On the other hand, when we experience good feelings, feel happy and contented, and positive emotions like love, joy, or compassion, it means that we are emotionally well and it is called emotional well-being. There are certain experiences of individuals which connect them with a higher power, higher purpose, and help them achieve a sense of emotional connectedness with divinity, lead them to the mystical world of eternal bliss and solitude, which is basically related to spiritual dimensions of wellness. The deeper implications of "well-being" help people cope with stress.

A content analysis was performed by the authors to see the public sentiments about the term "well-being." Twitter posts were extracted using NVivo software, using two different keywords such as "yoga" and "well-being." The search was performed on July 3, 2022. The Cloud Chart 1 and the Tree Chart 1 were created by using the posts of real-life tweets on the keyword "well-being." Data mining was done and the unnecessary words (like to, the, http, go, yes, etc.) were removed to get a real picture of the sentiments or words related to the well-being tweets. The prominent search word "well-being" came out to be the most frequently used word along with others such as wellness, care, cause, health, mental wellness, help, emotional, prosperity, people, support, and care. Indicating the relationship of well-being with people's prosperity, it becomes clearly evident that the term is related to mental wellness, supporting the world, caring about others, promoting health of people, focusing on mental health, and prevention from virus.

Word Cloud 1. Extracted by NVivo Software on Tweets on the Keyword Well-being (Dated: 3-07-2022).

#wellbeing	people	cause	#mentalh	covid	emotiona	world	human	healthy	country	commu	enorm	aware	family
					prosperity	self	research	years	month	focus	fantas	positiv	comp	future
			children	love	single	physica	educati	happy	reality	acco	brilli	learn	reso	infor	syste
	support	help		virus			society	india	stress	gove	living	comm	weal	pass	stabi
mental			#health		safety	amazin	environ	acces	benet	majo	work	conti	happ	sleep	activ
				sars	part	public	impact	suppo	progr	natu	body	busin	bless	plac	pray
	care	loss	#wellness	severe	social	young	togethe	doctor	econo	#self	excite	#min	#natu	surv	link
								welln	insur		whole	hope	statu	quality	art
											mom	little	avera	energ

Tree Chart 1. On Most Frequent Top 100 Words in the Tweets on "Well-being" Extracted Using NVivo Software on 3-07-2022.

Nature, sleep, positivity, family, emotions, amazing, future, mornings, young, social, and safety are some of the prominent and most frequently used words conveying the positive aspects/emotions by the tweets on "well-being" posted by the public on social media. As a matter of fact, people think of wellness, good health, prosperity, happiness, and positive thoughts when they talk about well-being. They seem to be concerned about well-being of their family and children due to virus as some tweets reflect their fear too. Many of the tweets are not just concerned about physical health vis-à-vis well-being but also about mental health, which endorses the fact that an important aspect of wellness is psychological wellness. While during lockdown we all experienced loneliness, isolation, and minimal human contact, it undoubtedly affected our minds much more than our bodies. Elderly people along with young adults lost connection/contact with the outside world due to ban on social activities, and as a result, they were confined to the four walls of their homes. They, in fact, became more vulnerable to mental and psychic pressures and as a consequence, sleep disorders and anxiety that are common even when everything is normal due to daily life stressors, which were worsened during pandemic as no physical activity made people overthoughtful, and thus eventually leading to increase in mental disorders.

How Spirituality and Yoga Can Serve as Strategies for Well-being During a Post-disaster Scenario?

Spirituality and yoga can be envisioned together despite being different technically. Whereas spirituality concerns our spirit, yoga alludes to physical postures known as *Asanas*, which besides benefitting our body also uplift our spirit/soul. Interestingly the pursuit of spirituality also has a lot to do with the material/physical dimension of our body. It is, in fact, this body of ours which contains the spirit/soul. In this sense, the former (body) is material and the latter (soul) is spiritual, which means that the first is concrete and the second abstract. If we assume that yogic exercises/*Asanas* have a tangible bearing on spirituality, it can be arguably proven. Likewise, if we claim that being spiritual is to a great extent being yogic in the sense of being inclusive, holistic, and integrating, it will not be untenable.

Spirituality and yoga thus are profoundly interrelated as well as interdependent. Undertaking spiritual quest or doing yoga can be employed as strategies to achieve diverse range of goals such as physical, material, medical/health-related, educational, financial, professional, or business-related (Arora, Sharma, & Kumar Walia, 2021). During the COVID-19 pandemic, there was ample evidence of the fact that in order to overcome the abysmally disastrous situation, a sizable chunk of world population turned either to spirituality or yoga or both for physical as well as mental well-being.

Now the question is as to how the notions of spirituality and yoga are connected to our mental health/well-being. Undoubtedly, yoga has a lot to do with our mind, mental health, and well-being. As stated above, the performative dimensions of yoga have a physical/outward character in the sense that in order to lend it actual meaning we have to involve our body and mind with equal intensity. In case we fail to combine our physical postures with mental focus, we cannot achieve the desired result. Even though it is hard to believe, yoga practitioners emphasize the fact that until body and mind are in total consonance while doing *yogic asanas*, neither our body nor mind can benefit.

Another way to understand the deeper connect between yoga and mental health can be to keenly observe our state of mind after doing yoga. Firstly, one experiences a deep sense of calm inside alongside experiencing the interconnectedness of everything within and around. It gives a great sense of meaningfulness and purposefulness in life. One also experiences that besides being individual to the core, one is also part of the larger cosmic/universal self. One also feels stronger psychologically and such a realization of mental strength helps one overcome the problems/ailments concerning the mind.

Thus, yoga is therapeutic in several ways, and moreover, it instills empathy and compassion in us and thereby enables us to transcend the narrow confines of our physical self, and thus realize our mental as well as spiritual being deep within ourselves. Spirituality too, like yoga, helps us overcome mental health problems such as schizophrenia, depression, obsessive compulsive disorders, attention deficit syndrome, paranoia, and other psychiatric ailments. The practice of spirituality may also vary, in diverse sociocultural climes. In addition to that, every religion has a distinct set of spiritual practices. Spirituality and religion technically vary; for instance, one does not need to be necessarily religious in order to be spiritual, and vice versa. However, religion and spirituality coexist harmoniously the world over. And therefore, at times one may be both, religious as well as spiritual.

Interestingly, the practice of spirituality directly affects and benefits our mental health. The precondition of being spiritual is: absence of selfishness, greed, and violence; absence of aggression, obsession, apathy, and indifference; and absence of contempt for others and self-centeredness. Until such negativities are overcome, one cannot enter the domain of spirituality. Spirituality besides demanding attention to know the self also pushes us to know the world around us better (Cohen, 2002). It also offers ways of dealing with stress, anxiety, and depression via training us to know who we actually are, and who we are supposed to be. Spirituality also inculcates spirit of pacifism, forgiveness, and simultaneous coexistence. It prepares us to deal with the devastating mental health issues caused by the postpandemic/disaster scenario.

It is worth emphasizing that India has been, since time immemorial, the locus of yogic and spiritual practices. By now, the world is familiar with the harbinger of yogic exercises, namely Pantanjali. He was the one who propagated yoga based on *Yogsutras* (formulas), and thereby showed the world as to how by overcoming our physical health, we can take care of our mental health and eventually, transcend this *mayavic* (illusory) world called *sansar*. The world, acknowledging the importance of yoga, celebrates International Yoga Day on 20 June every year. In fact, the UN realized how critical and crucial these Indian traditional yogic practices are. There are numerous *asanana* and *pranayams* (breathing exercises) that can rejuvenate and revitalize our sagging spirits and ailing body. There is a whole range of *asanas* and *pranayams* that have been distinctly unique to Indian traditional and cultural heritage.

A tree map was created by analyzing the content on the tweets on "Yoga" by using NVivo software on July 3, 2022. The NCapture extracted 8,900 tweets on "Yoga" and 14,075 on "well-being." Later, to see people's emotions/response on "well-being" and "Yoga," a sentiment analysis was also performed. The most frequent top 100 words after data mining of the words extracted by the software, a Tree Chart 2 was prepared, which shows words connected with yoga such as, calm, practice, happier, and athletic along with others, such as cure,

Tree Chart 2.   On Most Frequent Top 100 Words in the Tweets on "Yoga" Extracted Using NVivo Software on 3-07-2022.

determination, spirituality, poses, hope, positivity, workout, refreshing, wonderful, miraculous, respiration, Indian, incredible, *pranayama*, etc.

Table 2 shows the sentiment analysis of the tweets on yoga and well-being which give us a reflection of positive inclination of public toward both the words. Out of the tweets extracted on yoga out of the total posts more are on the positive side, 2,938 were moderately positive, and 1,931 are very positive. Similarly on the tweets extracted, 4,907 are on the moderately positive side and 2,204 are on the very positive side.

Indian traditional ways of living also known as Indian lifestyle majorly determines our physical as well as mental well-being. Tiwari and Pandey (2013), in their study on "the Indian concepts of lifestyle and mental health in old age," lucidly define lifestyle as the way people live, think, and behave. They characterize Indian lifestyles in terms of *karma* and *dharma*. *Karma* being action and *dharma* signifying righteous way of perform our duty. They also talk about how, life in India, was envisioned, in four stages, namely *brahamacharya, grihastha, vanprasth,* along with *sanyas.*

Whereas *bramhacharya* literally implies studentship, *grihasth* stands for householders, *vanprasth* implies dwelling in the forest, and *sanyas* stands for

Table 2. Sentiment Analysis on the Tweets on Yoga and Well-being.

File Path Downloaded by NCapture	A: Very Negative	B: Moderately Negative	C: Moderately Positive	D: Very Positive
1: Files\\(4) yoga – Twitter Search ~ Twitter	1,195	1,641	2,938	1,931
1: Files\\(4) well-being – Twitter Search ~ Twitter	2,027	2,910	4,907	2,204

Source: Extracted by using NVivo Software.

renunciation of this world of maya in the pursuit of the ultimate truth. According to traditional Indian lifestyle, the above four stages stands for an ideal life which is characterized by happiness, peace, and harmony; but if we ignore these stages and adopt a faulty lifestyle without exercising restraint, and are given to smoking and drinking, it affects our mental health adversely (Tiwari & Pandey, 2013).

The basic thrust of Indian traditional way of living remains on joint family setup. This has been an arrangement which is considered to be a thing of the past in contemporary times. The reason for such a view is preference for a nuclear family; however, a joint family system, arguably does better when all stakeholders/members operate with mutual understanding and cooperation. Traditionally, males have been, in the dominant role but with the passage of time the scenario has been changing rapidly as women too are given a place of privilege. The head of the family within such a setup has remained the key decision-maker, and the rest of the members tend to follow him. Nevertheless, it, in no way implies that individual opinions are ignored; on the contrary, the head of the family enjoys a privileged position to have the "final say" in most matters. It can be arguably proven that joint families are happier compared to nuclear ones, barring exceptions. The reason behind this is a sense of togetherness, feeling of mutuality, least space for isolation and alienation, scarce possibility of being left out, sense of healthy camaraderie, and overall sense of well-being despite tussles, tensions, bickering, and backbiting that comprise human frailty.

From the viewpoint of mental health too, being part of a joint family system/setup has its benefits in India as it is part of Indian ways of living steeped in culture. For instance, to deal with psychological problems in India such as stress, anxiety, despair, depression, paranoia, and other mental ailments, there are several methods of overcoming them such as meditation and self-help healing techniques, such *Vipasana*, and *pranayam*. *Ayurveda* also offers remedies for ill mental health with the help of various *rasayans* (chemicals) and medicines made of natural herbs and medicinal plants. Indian traditional way of living never allows excessive material thrust in life simply because it leads to psychological *vikaras* (problems). And therefore, to liberate from the clutches of *vikaras*, a healthy way of living characterized by a healthy body and stress-free mind are the prerequisites. Moreover, a *satvik* (vegetarian) way of life is much more preferred than non-*sativik* (nonvegetarian), way of life which lacks discipline, control, proper management, and freedom of mind, dietary restrictions, and intelligence of body and mind.

A rich community life, with an urge to participate in various cultural and social activities and thus contribute to the maximum possible extent, also plays a crucial role, in assuring of people's mental health and well-being. India is a richly diversely country and practices several faiths such as Hinduism, Buddhism, Sikhism, Islam, Christianity, etc., and every faith symbolically represents a unique way of life that is differentiated by its customs and ritual practices. The process of living, according to each faith, is a major determining factor of people's belief systems. The harmonious coexistence of different kinds of religious faiths/ways of living leads us to collective, sociocultural, and communitarian well-being, which profoundly impacts an individual's mental well-being. Be that cuisine, food, clothing, languages, or festivals, all of them strengthen diverse Indian ways of living making every region distinctly unique and different from others. People from different states partake of all these aspects of Indian living to enrich them, and in the process, end up being healthier, happier, more inclusive, and accommodating. These are the fundamental principles of mental happiness and well-being from the viewpoint of Indian ways of living.

Word Cloud 2.   Extracted by NVivo Software on Tweets on the Keyword Well-being (Dated: 3-07-2022).

The word cloud was prepared by doing content analysis of the tweets on the term "yoga," which supports the arguments proposed by the authors that yoga can be a successful means of promoting well-being as both are interconnected. The prominent words in addition to the keyword "yoga" came out to be, calm, mindfulness, determination, unperturbed, yoga for humanity, morning practice, composure, truth, healthy, spirituality, meditation, love, body, and seamless.

Well-being and Tourism

The concept of sustainability is closely connected with well-being. Highest attainable level of good health is a fundamental right, and every government should strive to take effective measures in order to ensure its citizens a healthy and sustainable life. Tourism industry has a great potential for not only promoting sustainability but also for promoting and encouraging good health and providing means of fostering healthy lives. There are so many things which, if connected to tourism, can encourage wellness and influence good health substantially. After the COVID-19 pandemic, the main thrust of tourists has been on health, safety and sanitization. It provides the tourism industry opportunities as well as challenges. In 2030, the agenda on the sustainable development, which was adopted by various governments in September 2015 at UN summit, two main and urgent challenges before the world were addressed, i.e., sustainability and development. Both of these are closely related with well-being of society and are interlinked with the tourism sector. A great deal of the aspects of sustainable development goals like End Poverty (Goal 1), Zero Hunger (Goal 2), Good health and Well-Being (Goal 3), Clean Water and Sanitation (Goal 6), Decent Work and Economic Growth (Goal 8), Sustainable Cities And Communities, Life below Water (Goal 14), Life on Land (Goal 15), etc. can be dealt with a focus on the tourism industry.

Promoting wellness is very important as it helps boost physical activity and promote good nutrition and mental well-being, so that our body remains in a fit/healthy condition. Tourism industry plays a pivotal role in promoting well-being as it boosts the revenue of the economy, helps and contributes to the infrastructural development of the country, fosters the promotion of cultural exchange between the foreigners and the citizens, and promotes happiness and camaraderie. Health and wellness tourism facilitates in lowering the risk of illness and is associated with the pursuit of maintaining and enhancing one's personal well-being. After the pandemic, a shift of tourists can be seen toward holistic health and prevention of diseases. And many of us are now adopting healthy lifestyles and wellness routines, even when we are away from our homes.

The wellness tourism sector is fast emerging. Its global size and economic impacts are far-reaching. According to the estimates of Global Wellness Institute, this industry was $639 billion in 2017, which has been increasing at a fast pace. Wellness tourism is associated with traveling for maintaining and enhancing personal well-being. Traveling gives us an opportunity to maintain and improve our holistic health and it is not just confined to medical tourism, it is also related with being in the midst of nature by which one can experience high level of internal bliss and solitude which is necessary for maintaining a happy and healthy body and mind. Wellness is basically a proactive approach wherein we maintain a healthy lifestyle, reduce our stress, take steps to prevent our diseases, and hence enhance our well-being. This aspect of wellness is motivated by tourism and travel, which help reduce stress and induce happiness in day-to-day routine. It is also motivated by the desire for living healthy without any disease and stress. There can be so many wellness experiences during travel wherein one can seek and achieve wellness. The motivation can be a destination hiking, mountaineering, yoga retreat, boot camps, sound walking, yoga safaris, etc.

Represented below with the help of Table 1 is a study conducted in November 2018 which highlights various unique parameters of destinations across the world which motivate and boost tourism activities. Some unique country-specific tourist activities reported in this study are compiled below (Table 3):

Table 3. Unique Parameters of Destinations Across the World.

Country	Unique Characteristics
Colorado	Hiking and mountain yoga retreats
California	Weight loss and detox retreat
Arizona	Destination spas
Mexico Temazcal	Resort beach spas
Caribbean	Wellness cruises
Costa Rica	Belize rainforest
Argentina	Spa retreats
Chile	Thermal resorts
New York	Urban healthy hotels and spas
United Kingdom	Weekend wellness retreats and boot camps
Austria	Alpine wellness hotels
France	Thalaso therapy
Morocco	Thermal hammams
Zambia	Walking yoga safaris
Norway	Nordic wellness
Egypt	Sand baths
South Africa	Health hydros, yoga, and wine retreats
Israel	Dead sea spa resorts
Turkey	Turkish baths
China	Hot spring resorts
Malaysia, Thailand	Executive checkups
India	Meditation, yoga, ayurveda retreats
New Zealand	Hot springs

Source: Global Wellness Institute Global Wellness Tourism Economy (2018).

The ambit of wellness tourism economy is very large. And it does not only include spas, wellness retreats, mineral springs, and boot camps, but one of the emerging aspects of wellness tourism is also maintaining a very healthy lifestyle which encompasses healthy eating exercises, fitness routines, and various kinds of mind and body practices. Experiencing nature, connecting with people, and learning from diverse cultures go a long way in benefiting us from the viewpoint of physical wellness and mental well-being. India offers a large variety of opportunities for wellness tourism which keeps ancient practices such as yoga and *Ayurveda* at the center for maintaining good overall health.

Conclusion

To conclude, we can say that spirituality and yoga have huge potential to benefit the suffering humanity in the postpandemic disastrous scenario via providing not just physical health but mental well-being as well. Indian ways of living, deeply intertwined with yoga, spirituality, and meditational practices, seem to be the best recourse in the post-disaster crisis caused by the COVID-19 pandemic. Yogic postures or *asanas*, meditation, spiritual practices, *pranayama*, and several other techniques of physical and mental well-being can offer sustainable solutions to the problems that have arisen due to the pandemic. Tourism industry too has an important role to play in this regard as wellness tourism has been working wonders ever since the concept was introduced, and India's role remains critically crucial in promoting it.

References

Arora, M., & Sharma, R. L. (2021). Repurposing the role of entrepreneurs in the Havoc of COVID-19. In *Entrepreneurship and big data* (pp. 229–250). Boca Raton, FL: CRC Press. doi:10.1201/9781003097945

Arora, M., Sharma, R. L., & Kumar Walia, S. (2021). Revisiting the inner self in times of debilitating distress: Gateways for wellness through spiritual tourism. *The International Journal of Religious Tourism and Pilgrimage, 9*(5), 26–36.

Cohen, A. B. (2002). The importance of spirituality in well-being for Jews and Christians. *Journal of Happiness Studies, 3*(3), 287–310.

Lennon, M. C. (1994). Women, work, and well-being: The importance of work conditions. *Journal of Health and Social Behavior*, 235–247.

Munawar, K., & Choudhry, F. R. (2021). Exploring stress coping strategies of frontline emergency health workers dealing Covid-19 in Pakistan: A qualitative inquiry. *American Journal of Infection Control, 49*(3), 286–292.

Prime, H., Wade, M., & Browne, D. T. (2020). Risk and resilience in family well-being during the COVID-19 pandemic. *American Psychologist, 75*(5), 631.

Ross, L. (1995). The spiritual dimension: Its importance to patients' health, well-being and quality of life and its implications for nursing practice. *International Journal of Nursing Studies, 32*(5), 457–468.

Shaw, S. C. (2020). Hopelessness, helplessness and resilience: The importance of safeguarding our trainees' mental wellbeing during the COVID-19 pandemic. *Nurse Education in Practice, 44*, 102780.

Slade, M. (2010). Mental illness and well-being: The central importance of positive psychology and recovery approaches. *BMC Health Services Research, 10*(1), 1–14.

Tiwari, S. C., & Pandey, N. M. (2013). The Indian concepts of lifestyle and mental health in old age. *Indian Journal of Psychiatry, 55*(Suppl 2), S288.

Smart Technologies and Tour Guides Beyond COVID-19

Gül Erkol Bayram, Jeetesh Kumar and Anukrati Sharma

Abstract

Tourist guides, one of the important service providers of tourism, have effected greatly by smart tourism technology during the COVID-19 period. It is thought that this trend will continue to increase in the future. Also, there are some challenges of smart tourism post pandemic on tour guides. In this context, the study aims to examine the levels of utilization of smart tourism applications by tourist guides, their activities in the COVID-19 period, and the transformation that tour guiding will undergo in the future. Within the scope of the study, existing smart tourism applications used in tours were examined with opportunities and challenges sides. In addition, the reflection of the guided cultural tours in the future was evaluated.

Keywords: COVID-19 pandemic; smart tourism; tour guides; smart tools; smart cultural tourism; tourism recovery

Introduction

Industry 4.0 which is a concept that has been frequently on the agenda in recent years and has led to concepts such as the internet of generations, artificial intelligence, sensors, cognitive technologies, nanotechnology, internet service, quantum computing, wearable technologies, augmented reality, smart cities, big data, 3D, and smart grid. After COVID-19, many areas such as education, trade, economy, and culture, especially in the health sector, have transformed with different aspects. Many services are now offered online. However, in the tourism sector, which acts together with technology, there have been some serious changes. Industry 4.0, a new era that brings significant changes in our lifestyle, economy, and society, has started with the introduction of new generation technologies such as the internet of things, artificial intelligence, virtual reality, and robots. With the rapid advancement of technology nowadays, most people

Resilient and Sustainable Destinations After Disaster, 241–250
Copyright © 2023 Gül Erkol Bayram, Jeetesh Kumar and Anukrati Sharma
Published under exclusive licence by Emerald Publishing Limited
doi:10.1108/978-1-80382-021-720231017

depend heavily on and rely on the internet to get information when traveling anywhere because of its use has penetrated deeply into people's lives. Another reason for using the internet is that it makes travel planning and traveling easier and more convenient. For example, travel planning can be done using smart-phones and applications, and at the same time instant travel needs can be met. Thus, next-generation technologies play a critical role in the travel and tourism industry. Huanga, Gooa, Namb, and Yoo (2017) emphasize that tourists are fully adapted to the use of online tools to facilitate their travel in terms of information search, travel planning, and booking procedures.

Huanga et al. (2017) state that tourists have fully adapted to the use of online tools to facilitate their travel in terms of information search, travel planning, and booking procedures. Currently, the vast majority of the travel preparation phase consists of internet searches for information, booking, and payment. The internet and some mobile applications provide tourists with rich, diverse, and useful information because they are easily accessible (Huanga et al., 2017). These developments show that the tourism industry is highly influenced by innovations in information and communication technologies (Avdimiotis et al., 2009; Bahar, Yüzbaşıoğlu, & Topsakal, 2019). Technology also supports tourism development in various ways (Garda & Temizel, 2016). Technology usage rates are increasing in most popular destinations. On the other hand, tourist guides are also known to play an important role in tourism (Chilembwe & Mweiwa, 2014). Although technological developments are increasing, human is accepted as the most important element in the tourism industry, where the service to people is essential and therefore a labor-intensive structure is exhibited (Solmaz & Erdoğan, 2014, p. 562). Also, Guide–tourist interaction emerges in tour programs (Eser, Çakıcı, Babat, & Kızılırmak, 2019). Tourist guides, one of the important service providers of tourism, have benefited greatly from technology during the COVID-19 period. It is thought that this trend will continue to increase in the future. In this context, the study aims to determine the level of utilization of smart tourism applications by tourist guides, their activities in the COVID-19 period and transformation that the profession will undergo in the future are to examine. Within the scope of the study, existing smart tourism applications used in tours were examined. In addition, the reflection of the guided cultural tours in the future was evaluated.

Literature Review

General View of Tour Guides

A tour guide explains his country and region to tourists, enables tourists to experience the historical, natural, and cultural accumulation of this region, helps them in many matters during their trips, takes care of them, gives accurate and complete information, and has the authority given by the Ministry of Culture and Tourism (Köroğlu, 2013). Tourist guides are a professional group that help guests during the tour, convey and make sense of the cultural and historical accumu-lation of its country, strengthen communication by building a bridge between local people and tourists, protect intangible and tangible heritage, and develop the awareness of conservation, develop a positive image and provide repeat visitation. In cultural tours, tourist guides not only who are interested with guests from the beginning to the end of the tour, or translate the language, but also help to ensure that tourists define and experience the culture visited and are informed about the natural, historical, and cultural history of that region (Erkol Bayram, 2016). According to the definition of the World Federation of Professional Tourist Guide Associations (WFTGA), "a tourist guide is a person who guides group or individual visitors from home or abroad to monuments, museums, the natural and cultural environment and historical places in a region or city in a language of their choice and conveys them to the visitors with an entertaining interpretation." Tourist guiding is an educational activity in which the ability to interpret has an important share (Rabotić, 2011).

According to Erkol Bayram (2017), a tour guide is a professional group that helps tourists with many issues during the tour, conveys the historical, natural, and cultural issues of its country and region most accurately and effectively, initiates and strengthens the communication process with local people and tourists, has a great role in the development of intangible and tangible heritage, is a leader to tourists for protecting the cultural and natural resources, and makes a great contribution to the development and strengthening of the positive image. In the tours carried out by the tourist guide in the travel agency, tour guides often take part in the tours on behalf of the travel agency with the tourists throughout the tour and deal with them on many issues, successfully undertaking many tasks such as translation, cultural brokerage, teaching, mediation, and leadership. Tourist guides, tour managers, and group leaders in charge of the realization of the tour program accompanying a group during the trip, such as field guides, and legal or routine procedures are confused with other sector workers who do or help them do it on their behalf (Türkmen, 2017, p. 914). A tourist guide is a professional group that includes many subjects and areas of expertise. They should be a psychologist when they see a worried tourist, an anthropologist when they see a tourist who is curious about cultures, and an archeologist when they see a tourist who has no ancient city left in his life and whose field of interest is the Sarcophagus. In addition to these, the tourist guide in general terms; must take responsibility for the tour during the tour, perhaps be a good educator as if they were telling someone who has never visited a museum in his life, be a friendly, hospitable, tolerant, unique host as if tourists had come to his own home, and he should know and be aware of where and when to use these skills (Ak, Kargiglioglu, & Bayram, 2019, p. 24; Ap & Wong, 2001).

Smart Tourism and Tour Guides: Issues, Challenges, and Opportunities

In general terms, smart tourism is a type of tourism supported by efforts in a city to collect data from physical infrastructure, social connections, state/organization resources, and the human mind. In addition, smart tourism includes tourism activities supported by ICT and smart technology. Smart tourism is a tourism system that uses smart technologies to create, manage, and deliver touristic experiences. It is defined as a tourism system that benefits from smart technologies. Smart tourism is different from smart destinations. Because smart tourism serves not only local people but also tourists, it also works for the benefit of tourists. Smart tourism is an important and triggering element for sustainable tourism. Because many tools that provide tourist satisfaction in a destination are available in smart tourism (Gretzel, Werthner, Koo, & Lamsfus, 2015). Smart tourism is defined as tourism which is based on the development of innovative mobile communication technologies and combines tourism resources with information communication technologies (ICTs) such as the internet of things, cloud computing, and artificial intelligence to provide accurate information and better service to tourists (Karamustafa & Yılmaz, 2019; Wang, Li, Zhen, & Zhang, 2016; Zhang, Li, & Liu, 2012). Smart tourism has created major changes in tourist behavior. In the tourist typology, a segment that is now accepted as the new tourist has been formed and the name is called "super-smart tourist." Among the most basic needs of these tourists are the weather, emergency numbers, Wi-Fi map, tourism information offices, hospitals, local governments, metro, buses, bicycles, tourist buses, railways, airports, road data, information about hotels, museums, tourist attractions, entertainment, and restaurants (Mussina & Oryngazhiyeva, 2018). The expectations of super-smart tourists are as follows (Wang et al., 2016 cited, Bahar et al., 2019);

- These tourists usually do their shopping online.
- They design travels online and schedule them on online platforms.
- They prefer the most practical, fast, and costly one to save time.
- They compare prices with different sites before buying travel products.
- It communicates with virtual travel communities and prefers to act together in a possible problem.

Although today's smart tourist prefers online platforms, the need for a tourist guide will exist now and in the future. Tourist guides are an indispensable part of cultural tours with leader, mediator, ambassador, and director roles (Zhang & Chow, 2004). They act as a bridge between the local population and the tourist group, especially in the destination visited by the tourists, by mediating the group of tourist guides (Howard, Smith, & Twaithes, 2001). However, the adaptation of tourist guides to the changing tourism services with technology is necessary for the sustainability of their professions. For example, thanks to technology, tourists can get information about the hotel they will stay in before going on a tour from the hotel's social media account and read the comments written by users about the hotel. Also, tourists quickly review good or bad reviews about the tour guide and travel agencies from complaint sites. Today, tourist guides should not be satisfied with classical methods, but also with devices such as smartphones, mobile technologies, tablets, mobile applications, GPS, and microphones to make their tour more interesting (Tekin, Bideci, & Avcıkurt, 2017). In this context, it is possible to express smart tourism applications, which can be the biggest assistant and the biggest competitor of the tourist guide in cultural tours, as follows (Çapar & Karamustafa, 2018):

Mobile Tourist Guides is a smart mobile application that allows the tourist to access information at any time, from any place, using an environment during the holiday, to get information according to their interests, and to make tours individually (Schwinger, Grun, Proll, Retschitzegger, & Schauerhuber, 2005). Mobile guide applications report location with the help of GPS and provide photos, maps, and descriptions of the region visited, and tourists use this application in museums and archeological sites. Mobile guides, which have functional features, especially in travels abroad, have several disadvantages. Mobile guides do not provide culturally, sociologically, or anthropologically information about the region, archeological site, or museum, and in fact, it offers information that almost anyone can find on the internet only in the application. For cultural tourists participating in experience tourism, a qualified tourist guide offers a superior service that cannot be compared with the infrastructure of mobile guides (Tekin et al., 2017).

Electronic Guides (Audio Guides): It is the system where tourists access information about archeological artifacts in the language they choose with radio, podcast, and telephone applications in museums and ruins (Weiler & Black, 2015). Audio guides are not preferred by tourists due to their limited knowledge. Tourists have questions about museums and ruins. But audio guides cannot respond to this or interact with the tourist (Eser et al., 2019).

Virtual Museums: Virtual museums are collections of digitally recorded images, audio files, text documents, and other historical, scientific, and cultural data that can be accessed through electronic media. Virtual museums do not have the permanence and unique feature of the institutional definition of the concept of a museum since they do not accommodate real objects. The majority of virtual museums exists under the sponsorship of corporate museums and depends on the existing collections of these museums. Yet the hyperlinking and multimedia capabilities of electronic information media, particularly the World Wide Web, the hypermedia system that operates on the internet, are digitized representations that are largely assembled by individual users for entertainment and work purposes (Rodriguez, 2017). The new formation connected to the technology, which is called a virtual museum created using multimedia devices and advanced computer-aided technologies, can be explained as the digitization of museum collections, which are tangible (Cited by Kahraman, 2021). Especially during the COVID-19 period, many museums have been exhibited virtually. Tourist guides have advertised online to do virtual guidance on various platforms.

Mobile technologies and Smart Applications: Thanks to smartphones, which are one of today's important tools, tourist guides use applications such as messaging, web browsing, weather data, phone book, alarm, calculator, chronometer, agenda, voice recorder, notepad, GPS, compass, camera, and flashlight on a single device. It is a great opportunity that many arguments that tourist guides should have with them during the tour are collected in one device. However, mobile technologies also offer great convenience for tourists (Düzgün, 2022).

Robotization: Robots used in different enterprises of tourism are not yet actively used in cultural tours. Also, it is assumed that if it is used, it can promote and direct museums and ruins in various languages in cultural tours. However, Boboc, Horatiu, and Talaba (2014) identified 27 ready-made robot tourist guides (Düzgün, 2022). If this number increases, tourist guides may face the danger of becoming unemployed.

Information Devices (info-kiosks): Kiosk is a system consisting of a microprocessor-controlled computer and touch screen that can be used comfortably in the outdoor environment. Kiosks, which are usually seen as information inquiry screens in museums, allow a visitor who has just entered the museum to have information about the whole museum (Harmankaya, 2010).

Augmented Reality: Augmented reality applications are related to the exhibition of the original state of the tangible and intangible cultural heritage elements of the past in museums and archeological sites with today's technology. In doing so, wireless connections are established with various devices such as digital cameras and GPS, and images are projected in three dimensions through computers, and the people who visit these places are tried to visualize them in their minds and to give the feeling of living in that period (Harmankaya, 2010). With such technological applications, it is aimed to establish a connection between visitors and cultural artifacts. Especially with augmented reality and virtual museum applications that provide distance from the routine in museums, the information that is pictorial or textual is almost three-dimensional with the help of virtual data. The cultural work is created as if it existed in the real environment (Styliani, Fotis, Kostas, & Petros, 2009 cited, Düzgün, 2022). According to United Nations reports, the average age of developed countries is increasing, birth rates are decreasing, and life expectancy is increasing. Generation Y is brave, a frequent traveler has a greater sense of wonder. This generation attaches more importance to the inner journey, to spiritualism. A guide who can be the answer to the inner quest is only possible with his knowledge and experience, and experience (Black & Weiler, 2005). Zátori (2013) holds the view that developments in the modern digital world will allow the physical disappearance of tourist guides. Most importantly, the fact that access to information has become so easy, thanks to technology, can be considered as a sign that the ability of guides to transfer information should now pass to the dimension of "experience marketing" and the probability of guides finding a job in the market in the future can be measured by the quality and experience in the field of "experience marketing" mentioned above rather than information. However, smart tourism is of such dimensions that it can take the place of tourist guides in terms of navigation, access, translation, and expression (Arslantürk & Gül, 2019; Weiler & Black, 2015). Tourists use smart tourism at almost every moment of their travel. Before the tour, they examine various travel blogs and social media platforms, do research, and shape their holiday plans after this research. In the survey of Bayram, Ak, and Erkol Bayram (2018), the top three social media tools that come to mind when it comes social media are Instagram, Facebook, and Twitter, and 89.8% of the participants are Instagram, 75.8% are Facebook, 58.5% are YouTube, 55% are Google+, and 50.3% are Twitter users. It was found that 57.6% of the participants spent 4–5 hours or more on social media. While 40.3% of the participants stated that they had previously made changes in their holiday plans by being influenced by social media, 60.3% stated that they could change their holiday plans by being influenced by social media. Tourists also have information about what to do at the destination they will visit, where to go, and what to eat through the same platforms. It is useful to emphasize the importance of the concepts of YouTuber and Instagrammable, which have increased recently, in travel preferences. Tourists rate and comment on the performance of tourist guides on web pages. So, tourist guides are better prepared for the tour, thanks to smart technologies. In addition, smartphones can communicate with travel businesses and other guides via WhatsApp and different platforms. Tourist guides facilitate their tour with a microphone, headset, navigation system, and tablets during the tour (Çapar & Karamustafa, 2018).

Conclusions and Discussions

Smart tourism often offers opportunities for the functions of guides to be fulfilled with information technologies. However, applications to information technologies should be considered as a supporting element for the presentation of tourist guides. Tourist guides need to be used as a tool to transform technological applications, tours, and narrations into more effective and enjoyable ones. It is considered a necessity for the guide to know the technological applications well and to support their narratives by using them actively for the contemporary tourists to be satisfied with their trips. In this way, guides will be able to find effective solutions to the problems they may encounter during the tour processes in a short time so that they can be effective on the tourists' holiday experiences. Although these practices seem interesting for tourists at first glance, tour guides' cultural background, knowledge, experience, and interpretation skills will ensure that the information is permanent (Çapar & Karamustafa, 2019). According to Bahar et al. (2019), smart tourism will see some changes for tour guides in the future. We can express them as follows;

- Smart tourist guides (applications) developed with new generation technologies will now be able to offer location-based guidance services to the visitor with more advanced software.
- Translation into alternative languages in a very short time through applications with very fast processors and guidance services in their language for tourists with different languages in the same group can be provided. For this reason, it

is very recently that the guidance service has become a service with a cultural content rather than a language-based service so that there is an adequate guidance certificate in any language. It will be possible for individuals to offer this service to everyone in the desired language.

* With the new generation of technologies, there will be a need for a visual guide instead of a physical guide. This emerging need will be able to be presented interactively in 3D through hologram guides.

References

Ak, S., Kargiglioğlu, Ş., & Erkol Bayram, G. (2019). Turist Rehberliği Mesleği. In B. Zengin, G. Erkol Bayram, & O. Batman (Eds.), *Turist Rehberliği Mesleği (Dünü-Bugünü-Yarını)*. Ankara: Detay Yayıncılık.

Ap, J., & Wong, K. K. F. (2001). Case study on tour guiding: Professionalism, issues and problems. *Tourism Management, 22*(5), 551–563.

Arslantürk, Y., & Gül, T. (2019). Turist Rehberliği Mesleği Dünü -Bugünü –Yarını. In B. Zengin, G. E. Bayram, & O. Batman (Eds.), *Turist Rehberliğinde Yeni Eğilimler ve Turist Rehberliğinin Geleceği* (s. 287–325). Ankara: Detay Yayıncılık.

Avdimiotis, S., Bonarou, C., Dermetzoupoulos, A., Karamanidis, I., Mavrodontis, T., Kelessidis, V., Kalonaki, E. (2009). *TOUREG: Global SWOT analysis. A report produced for Toureg project, deliverable D.2.1.*

Bahar, M., Yüzbaşıoğlu, N., & Topsakal, Y. (2019). The overview of future tourism guidance under the concepts of smart tourism and super smart tourist. *Journal of Travel & Tourism Research, 14*, 72–93.

Bayram, A. T., Ak, S., & Erkol Bayram, G. (2018). Üniversite Öğrencilerinin Tatil Tercihlerinde Sosyal Medya Kullanımı: Sinop Üniversitesi Örneği. *VII. Ulusal III. Uluslararası Doğu Akdeniz Turizm Sempozyumu* (pp. 1089–1099) (Tam Metin Bildiri/Sözlü Sunum) (Yayın No:4275738).

Black, R., & Weiler, B. (2005). Quality assurance and regulatory mechanisms in the tour guiding industry: A systematic review. *The Journal of Tourism Studies, 16*(1), 24–37.

Boboc, R. G., Horatiu, M., & Talaba, D. (2014). An educational humanoid laboratory tour guide robot. *Procedia, Social and Behavioral Sciences, 141*, 424–430.

Çapar, G., & Karamustafa, K. (2018). Turist Rehberliği ve Teknoloji. In S. Eser, S. Şahin ve A. C. Çakıcı (Eds.), *Turist Rehberliği içinde* (pp. 205–219). Ankara: Detay Yayıncılık.

Çapar, G., & Karamustafa, K. (2019). Turist Rehberliği ve Teknoloji. In S. Eser, S. Şahin, & Çakıcı (Eds.), *Turist Rehberliği* (pp. 205–220). Ankara: Detay Yayıncılık.

Chilembwe, J. M., & Mweiwa, V. (2014). Tour guides: Are they promoters and developers? Case study of Malawi. *International Journal of Research in Business Management, 2*(9), 29–46.

Düzgün, E. (2022). Turist Rehberlerinin Dijital Turizmdeki Gelişmelere Bakışı. *Turizm Akademik Dergisi, 9*(1), 193–208.

Erkol Bayram, G. (2016). Yabancı Dil Öğretim Yöntemlerinin Turizm Rehberliği Eğitimi Açısından İncelenmesi. *Eğitim ve Öğretim Araştırmaları Dergisi, 5*(4), 137. Issn: 2146-9199.

Erkol Bayram, G. (2017). Motivasyonun Demografik Ve Mesleki Özelliklere Göre Farklılaşması: Turist Rehberleri Üzerine Bir Araştırma. *Yaşar Üniversitesi E-Dergisi, 12*(48), 257–271. Retrieved from https://dergipark.org.tr/en/pub/jyasar/issue/31740/347869

Eser, S., Çakıcı, A. C., Babat, D., & Kızılırmak, İ. (2019). Turlarda Teknoloji Kullanımı: Turistler ve Turist Rehberleri Gözüyle Bir Değerlendirme. *Balıkesir Üniversitesi Sosyal Bilimler Enstitüsü Dergisi, 22*(41), 465–480. doi:10.31795/baunsobed.581982.

Garda, B., & Ve Temizel, M. (2016). Sürdürülebilir Turizm Çeşitleri. *Selçuk Üniversitesi Sosyal ve Teknik Araştırmalar Dergisi Sayı, 12*, 83–103.

Gretzel, U., Werthner, H., Koo, C., & Lamsfus, C. (2015). Conceptual foundations for understanding smart tourism ecosystems. *Comupters in Human Behavior, 50*, 558–563.

Harmankaya, M. B. (2010). *Müzelerde Elektronik Rehberlik Uygulamaları.* Unpublished Phd Thesis, T.C. Kültür ve Turizm Bakanlığı Kültür Varlıkları ve Müzeler Genel Müdürlüğü, İstanbul.

Howard, J., Smith, B., & Twaithes, J. (2001). Investigating the roles of the indigenous tour guide. *Journal of Tourism Studies, 12*(2), 32–39.

Huanga, C. D., Gooa, J., Namb, K. ve Yoo, C. W. (2017). Smart tourism technologies in travel planning: The role of exploration and exploitation. *Information & Management, 54*, 757–770.

Kahraman, Z. (2021). New approaches in virtual Museology. *Journal of Art Vision, 3*(2), 145–160.

Karamustafa, K., & Yılmaz, M. (2019). Konaklama İşletmeleri Yöneticilerinin Akıllı Turizm Teknolojilerinin Olası Faydalarına Yönelik Algılarının Değerlendirilmesi. *Journal of Tourism and Gastronomy Studies, 7*(3), 1669–1688. doi:10.21325/jotags.2019.442.

Köroğlu, Ö. (2013). Turist Rehberlerinin İş Yaşamındaki Rolleri Üzerine Kavramsal Bir Değerlendirme. *Pamukkale Üniversitesi Sosyal Bilimler Enstitüsü Dergisi, 16*, 91–112.

Mussina, K. P., & Oryngazhiyeva, M. R. (2018). Smart cities as a tourist destination for smart travelers. *Innovative Economy: Perspectives of Development and Improvement, 6*(32), 12–16.

Rabotić, B. (2011). Tour guiding as profession: Perceptions and self-perceptions of guides in Serbia. In *2nd International research forum on guided tours* (pp. 7–9). Plymouth: University of Plymouth.

Rodriguez, E. (2017). Virtual museum. Retrieved from https://www.britannica.com/topic/virtual museum

Schwinger, W., Grun, C., Proll, B., Retschitzegger, W., & Schauerhuber, A. (2005). Context-aware in mobiletourist guides-a comprehensive survey. *Technical report.* Johannes Kepler University.

Solmaz, S. A. ve Erdoğan, Ç. (2014, Aralık 5–8). Turizm Eğitimi Alan Ön Lisans ve Lisans Öğrencilerinin Turizm Endüstrisine Bağlılık Düzeylerini Belirlemeye Yönelik Bir Araştırma. *14. Ulusal Turizm Kongresi.* Erciyes Üniversitesi, Kayseri.

Styliani, S., Fotis, L., Kostas, K., & Petros, P. (2009). Virtual museums, a survey and some issues for consideration. *Journal of Cultural Heritage, 10*(4), 520–528.

250 Gül Erkol Bayram et al.

Tekin, Ö., Bideci, M., & Avcıkurt, C. (2017). Turist Rehberliği Üzerine Araştırmalar içinde. In Ö. Güzel, V. Altıntaş, & İ. Şahi (Eds.), *Turist Rehberliğinde Yeni Teknolojiler Kullanımı* (pp. 291–305). Ankara: Detay Publishing.

Türkmen, M. T. (2017). A research on determination of leadership orientations of tourist guides. *Gaziantep University Journal of Social Sciences, 16*(3), 913–927. doi: 10.21547/jss.314860.

Wang, X., Li, X. R., Zhen, F., & Zhang, J. (2016). How smart is your tourist attraction? Measuring tourist preferences of smart tourism attractions via a FCEM-AHP and IPA approach. *Tourism Management, 54,* 309–320.

Weiler, B., & Black, R. (2015). The changing face of the tour guide: One-way communicator to choreographer to co-creator of the tourist experience. *Tourism Recreation Research, 40*(3), 364–378.

Zátori, A. (2013). *Tourism experience creation from a business perspective.* Corvinus University of Budapest, Budapest.

Zhang, H., & Ivy Chow, Q. (2004). Application of importance-performance model in tour guides' performance: Evidence from Mainland Chinese outbound visitors in Hong Kong. *Tourism Management, 25*(1), 81–91.

Zhang, L., Li, N., & Liu, M. (2012). On the basic concept of smarter tourism and its theoretical system. *Tourism Tribune, 27*(5), 66–73.

Regenerative Tourism and Resilience in COVID-19 Pandemic: From Strategic Principles to Sustainability

Parag S. Shukla and Sofia Devi Shamurailatpam

Abstract

The connotation of sustainable tourism occupies prime importance in the light of prevalent pandemic situations across the globe. One such deliberation is the construct of regenerative travel, a type of "matured tourism" with restoration and rejuvenation of destinations as its pillars. With the COVID-19 pandemic, the tourism rate was dropped by nearly 65% across the world, leaving the countries' economies shattered and communities depending on tourism experiencing massive unemployment. However, regenerative tourism provides a way to secure a future of tourism and allows the communities to coexist with tourist attractions and sustain new models of tourism. This chapter examined the concept of regenerative tourism to build resilience particularly during the post-COVID-19 pandemic. The result shows various strategies for implementation of regenerative tourism, framework approach not recovery of tourism and renewing of tourism. Additionally, implications of regenerative tourism could be foreseen, and a roadmap is provided for the tourism stakeholders.

Keywords: Regenerative tourism; post-COVID-19 tourism; sustainable tourism; destination marketing; resilient tourism; destinations

Introduction

The term regenerative tourism encompasses a much wider concept than the sustainable tourism and includes notions like honoring the destinations, respect for local customs and traditions, conserving the habitats, protection of endangered species, and generating positive externalities in the destination with a judicious use of the natural resources for ecological balance of the travel destinations. Though the pandemic has caused a sudden halt in the tourism sector, the time is ripe to

Resilient and Sustainable Destinations After Disaster, 251–266
Copyright © 2023 Parag S. Shukla and Sofia Devi Shamurailatpam
Published under exclusive licence by Emerald Publishing Limited
doi:10.1108/978-1-80382-021-720231018

take a leap for taking advantage of this breakthrough by adopting a regenerative approach of tourism. Strategic actions for compensating carbon emissions; curbing environment impurities – air and water pollution; and restoring the carrying capacity of the region/area can reshape, regenerate, and rejuvenate the way toward recovery of balanced economy. Regenerative tourism is certainly catching attention, especially in COVID times although it's been around a while. Several countries are struggling to find a means how they can improve their economy after being affected by the COVID-19 pandemic. While the world is adapting to digitalization in various sectors, travel and tourism are among the sectors that can reap the advancement benefit technologically, economically, and socially so as to reduce the impact thereby resulting from the COVID-19 pandemic. Tourism can use the technology by integrating digital marketing, information and communication technology (ICT) and security issues while promoting tourism. Additionally, communities can be engaged in economic activities in tourist areas which could boost the Gross Domestic Product (GDP) and increase awareness as well as social responsibility in the preservation of social values, natural resources, and cultural heritage which are tourist attractions.

This chapter gives an outlook of regenerative tourism toward sustainability specifically in postpandemic periods that economies have to open for. In the next section a brief background of tourism and sustainability is reported. Section three gives about the review of literature on the relevant dimensions of tourism sustainability. Section four gives the conceptual framework established. The next section gives about discussion, priorities, and implications. The last section is the conclusion.

Background

Regenerative tourism goes beyond sustainable tourism to focus on "giving back" and contributing to the proactive regeneration of communities, cultures, heritage, places, landscapes, and so forth. Also, regenerative tourism approaches aim to push beyond traditional sustainable approaches: "The old ways are still focused on reducing the negative impact of human activity on the planet. Regenerative approaches that are systems based and align cultural and natural patterns are viewed as providing a way forward and are aimed at creating positive outcomes, not just "doing less damage" (Duxbury, Bakas, de Castro, & Silva, 2021). The tourism industry has drawn attention toward finding ways to make the tourism industry resilient. The tourism and hospitality industry has emerged as one of the key drivers of growth in the services sector. Also represents a sustainable way of traveling and discovering new places. Its prompt main goal for visitors is to have a positive impact on their holiday destination, leaving it in a better condition than how they found it. However, it is pivotal to understand the basic factors which resulted in the linkages between natural and social sciences and the notion of borrowing terms such as "sustainability" and "are regenerative" from natural sciences to social sciences, to avoid "green washing" and lack of consumer trust (Hussain & Haley, 2022). According to Pollock and Travel (2019), regeneration is a movement that sees people as part of nature's living systems, not dominant over them. It seems people's role as being that of stewards or guardians of the natural world across generations, honoring what we have inherited and taking responsibility for our legacy. Using the farming metaphor, it's about not just tending the soil, but about improving the soil so that it can provide better and more benefits than ever before. Regenerative tourism is an aspirational goal, a journey, a commitment, and a set of actions to secure all the conditions necessary to allow tourism, travel, and mobile living to coexist alongside, and in harmony with, the ability of nature and communities to sustain and continuously renew themselves (Major & Clarke, 2021).

Regenerative Tourism: The Natural Maturation of Sustainability

Regenerative tourism aims to restore the harm that our system has already done to the natural world, and by using nature's principles, to create the conditions for life to flourish. It views the whole and not parts and is a very different way of looking at the world. A regenerative approach to tourism starts at home within us, then our workplaces, and our communities, and depends on caring hosts willing to ensure their destination is healthy and full of life. Loretta Bellato, Frantzeskaki, and Nygaard (2022) expands their explanation by stating that is a holistic way of thinking in which all stakeholders build reciprocal, beneficial relationships, As Bellato explains, it is based on improving social and environmental systems and aligning everything toward sustaining the planet so that all beings can flourish.

Regenerative Tourism: By Following Nature's Principles

In regenerative tourism, each part (be it a plant, animal, ecosystem, person, business, or community) assumes its essential responsibility for ensuring it can thrive, health of the whole of which it is a part. When the prosperity of a community is synonymous with the health of all its parts and relationships, then the act of caring or stewarding ensuring that the conditions for life to thrive do exist is built into the system (Pollock, 2019).

Regenerative tourism focuses on the things in life that matter. By satisfying the primary needs of the community, regenerative tourism contributes to the quality of life of local people. Regenerative tourism offers an important set of solutions to rethink and rebuild the tourism industry (Galdini, 2007).

It also improves local economies and preserves local cultures and biodiversity while offering memorable, authentic life-changing experiences to the guests and allowing destinations to improve. For example, ecotourism is a burgeoning sector of the tourism industry offering a relatively guilt-free environment in which to satisfy the desire for travel and adventure. This ideology brings the design of ecotourism facilities which misses the opportunity to engage in a more productive and "regenerative" relationship with the place (Town & Owen, 2005). In some places, tourists produce up to twice as much waste as residents. This can put incredible strain on local waste management systems, causing landfills and sewage plants to overflow (Yusuff, 2022). The consequence of mass tourism is the large accumulation of waste that people don't differentiate. Inevitably, it creates a major environmental problem of disposal and pollution (Ferronato & Torretta, 2019). Overtourism destinations have caused an increase in water consumption, collection of huge litter masses, improper waste disposal, and air pollution due to vehicular and other sources owing to an upsurge in tourist activities (Gupta & Chomplay, 2021; Taiminen, 2018). Hence, most of the researchers discussed only about carbon dioxide and forget to speak about air quality and human exposure (Abbasov et al., 2019; Ciarlantini et al., 2022). The risk of solid waste generated also can increase due to the high level of the population (Mateu-Sbert, Ricci-Cabello, Villalonga-Olives, & Cabeza-Irigoyen, 2013). Sari and Nazli (2020) state that the risk of contagious disease, effects on the natural environment, and wastes have collaboration between the public health and the ecosystem.

However, there are so many different scenarios that happened during the pandemic (COVID-19) in the tourism industry and needed regenerative tourism to take a place, for example. The pandemic severely impacted travel and tourism globally, causing the industry a loss of almost US$ 4.5 trillion. Domestic visitor spending decreased by 45% while international visitor spending decreased by 69.4% compared to the spending in 2019 (Source: World Travel & Tourism Council, Economic Impact Reports 2020). Quarantine measures such as travel bans, border closures, and the patterns of previous crises can already foresee a massive loss in tourist revenues, especially at the international level. The World Travel and Tourism Council warned that the COVID-19 pandemic could cut a million jobs in the travel and tourism sector as traveling is expected to significantly drop worldwide in 2020 and could bring social and economic consequences to the communities. COVID-19 has also suspended many intangible cultural heritage practices with significant consequences for the social and cultural life of communities around the world. Although this situation makes tourism highly vulnerable, the sector is also in a unique position to contribute to broader and just recovery plans and actions. All over the world, tourism represents development opportunities and promotes solidarity and understanding beyond borders, while domestic tourism also helps to foster cohesion within nations.

Review of Literature

The tourism and hospitality industries are the worst affected industries globally and the continuous waves of the virus, and new variants, are forcing governments to impose strict lockdown (Asif, 2021). The pandemic has exposed massive vulnerabilities in the tourism operating system (Nanno, 2020). While the effects of which have fallen unevenly across different groups and subsectors of tourism (Developments and Challenges in the Hospitality and Tourism Sector, 2010), creative tourism initiatives can inspire new ideas and avenues of activity and contribute to the cultural vitality and potential regeneration dynamics through reinforcing distinctive elements of local identity, instigating flows and connections between the locale and the external, and serving as platforms for local collaboration, exchange, and development. In the time of COVID-19, enhancing connections with other organizations locally and regionally can contribute to wider initiatives and the development of community-based regeneration strategies, (Duxbury et al., 2021). Hence, human interventions are significant factors in the operations of tourism systems, where concepts are borrowed from natural sciences, to minimize the negative impacts of tourism; these concepts are often not fully understood (Hussain & Haley, 2022). While "human flourishing" offers merits as an alternative touchstone for evaluating the impacts of tourism on host communities, human flourishing has a long genesis and its contemporary manifestation, pushed by COVID-19 and applied to travel and tourism (Cheer, 2020). Brouder et al. (2020) state, that "ethics of probability" and "ethics of possibility," have been revealed through thought, behavior, and action. COVID-19 has fundamentally disrupted tourism. In dealing with the crisis, borders have been shut, lockdowns imposed, and international tourism curtailed (OECD, 2020). The pandemic foregrounded the renewal of social bonds and social capacities as governments acted to prevent economic and social devastation (Ibn-mohammed et al., 2020). Indeed, phenomena such as vaccine privilege and vaccine tourism are indicators that transformations must be enabled (Higgins-Desbiolles, Bigby, & Doering, 2021). Although misinformation and disinformation are making it harder for governments to implement strategies to contain the virus, it is significant to look up on the strategies to fight against the situation. The social distancing imposed by COVID-19 includes activities that reduce social contact and minimize tourism, which greatly affects people's assessment of leisure and travel activities (such as nature-based tourism activities) and personal leisure services (such as spas and catering), (Persson-Fischer & Liu, 2021). The impact of the COVID-19 pandemic on the international tourism market is manifested in the health risks and psychological risks perceived by tourists, which leads to negative emotions toward the tourism industry and other tourists (Rahman, Gazi, Bhuiyan, & Rahaman, 2021). Besides, the psychology movement is to ensure a deeper understanding of the tourism industry and its impacts on destinations and hosts, both in the short term and the long term (Asif, 2021).

Transformative tourism is offered to reset the global tourism system for good (Ateljevic, 2020). Innovation inherent in diverse economic practices (enterprise, exchange, labor, transactions, property, etc.) and illustrate their natural resilience as a result (Cave & Dredge, 2020). Furthermore, a partial-industrialized system using an adaptive cycle model as the key element of panarchy to explain a healthy social-ecological system. These new ways of being, knowing, and doing in the world are emerging as conscious citizens, consumers, producers, travelers, entrepreneurs, and community leaders who are calling and acting upon the necessary transformation toward the regenerative paradigm and regenerative economic systems. Results show that postpandemic tourism transformation must protect and promote local identities, and enhance and enrich visitor experiences with a focus on cultural and natural heritage (Fusté-Forné & Hussain, 2022). For example, three potential trends in food and drink tourism are identified, which are labeled as "Getting back to basics," "Valuing local and locals," and "Food for well-being" (Fountain, 2021).

The Perspective of Future Tourism

The world needs a positive psychology movement to ensure a deeper understanding of the tourism industry and its impacts on destinations and hosts, both in the short term and the long term (Asif, 2021). Existing trends, such as digitalization and globalization (enhancing the digital market), have been accelerated, and the industry faces new demands in areas such as health and safety protocols, complex web policy, regulation and infrastructure investment by the government. And also reform and recovery initiatives rolled out by the government in the region have immediate long term and far-reaching consequence for the industry (Asia & Pacific, 2022; GoK, 2020). Hence government can implement reform development of the tourism industry. The reform can be categorized in different perceptives such as the visa liberalization policy. The government can allow visitors or tourists to enter a certain country but not for a work permit or other benefit. Open Skies Agreement and Sky Policy will help the country to expand international passenger and cargo flights. Also enhancing job opportunities, economic growth, and expansion of the tourism sector are equally important. Simplification of rules and regulation; investment of Public–private partnership in infrastructure; and opportunities for PPP in tourism can offer both public service such as museums, historical artifacts, and national parks and private service such as hotels, themes parks, and entertainment, and also active promotion as a tourist destination (Gilauri, 2018; UNCTAD, 2021).

In addition, the future tourism must base on enacting pro-growth travel policies that will help to share benefits more equitably and can foster talent and a business environment, where it is necessary to enable travel and tourism to realize their potential for economic contribution, providing the rationale for the further protection of nature, habitats, and biodiversity (Jha, 2017). Also, global demographic trends including growing populations, increased life expectancy, aging populations, and urbanization present new opportunities and challenges for the tourism sector and its workers. In other words, with the changing dimensions in the distribution and composition of demographic transitions in the total population, there is a shift in the basket of goods and services, and tastes and preferences across travelers around the globe, and accordingly the structure of allocation of services available do imply significant changes and is also reflected on various macroeconomic variables and parameters in countries as a determining variable.

The Conceptual Framework of the Research Study

Despite all activities conducted with tourism particularly regenerative tourism is very important to make tourism active and reliable. In the tourism sector, there are stakeholders such as residents, activists, tourism developers, employees, local companies, government, competitors, tourists, business associations, and media. All these stakeholders make the tourism sector to be active and contiguous. Donors, government, and the private sector are the main stakeholders to initiate regenerative tourism, in general, to grow more, partnership in these three organs which can influence another aspect to be in better condition. The responsibility of the government in tourism is to find means to build good infrastructures either economically, socially, or politically to attract more tourists to visit a specific country. To generate policy and regulation, which will favor both parties (government, donors, and private sectors)? The private sector can be either under the government entity or stand on its own; most of the time in the tourism sector, the private sector is the one which conducts this business and pays some percentage to the government as revenue from what they got to the business. They play a major role in business, and it is their responsibility to use modernized ways of advertisement, to treat tourists well and also to ensure the tourism sector is attractable and manageable through conducting and taking care of regenerative tourism. Through the agreement between the government and private sector, this is where donors can work and penetrate to contribute to any sector because donors may help support the policy-making process at various levels and by building capacity in the regenerative tourism industry. So, by using a partnership of these three organs, they can support regenerative tourism in a different aspect. As mentioned in Fig. 1, technological, social, and economic aspects are factors/aspects we are looking for and every aspect has its variables (Fig. 2).

A good foundation for regenerative tourism must begin with the involvement of the community concerned because if the community is well integrated, it is easy

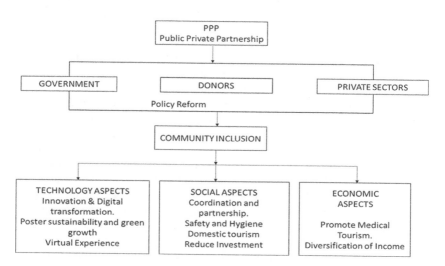

Fig. 1.   Conceptual Framework of Regenerative Tourism Post-COVID-19. *Source:* Prepared by Authors.

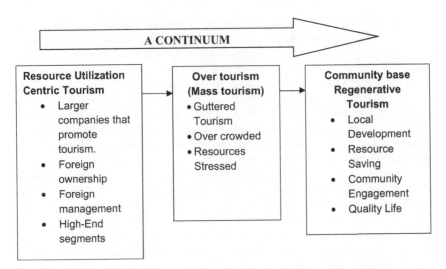

Fig. 2.   Continuum of Regenerative Tourism: A Journey From Resource Utilization to Resource Regeneration. *Source:* Prepared by Authors from various reports and literature cited.

to develop this sector in their areas. But also, community involvement makes it easier for the community to take care of the resources around them based on proper use. Communities agreeing to promote tourism leads to tourism growing in the area and leading to mass tourism, it is again the responsibility of the community concerned to maintain tourism through regenerative tourism because the more the tourist activities increase, the more damage occurs. It is easy for the respective communities to reap various benefits from tourism such as preserving local culture and heritage, strengthening community, provision of social service, commercialization of culture and art, revitalization of customs and arts forms, and tourists' income to set aside the projects which will bring employments to the society. So, all these benefits will prompt the community to conserve the resources around. Growth of tourism brings more positive impact to the sector accessibility of the investment can attempt large companies to be attracted to invest in tourism sector. The outcome of the investment will bring employment opportunities, opening of new market, diversification, and open social talents show case to the community. So, this is the new journey for the tourism sector to stand and grow because these invested companies will harmonize foreign ownership, foreign management, and high-end segmentation. Any development comes with a challenge; while we enjoy the fruitful growth of tourism sector, challenges also increase as well: controlling revenue and expenditure is the one of the challenges (local taxation), challenges of travel market will help to understand better what tourists want, infrastructure issue in order to increase efficiency of production and distribution of tourism service, security issue to maintain environmental threat and spread of infection disease, and cross-border regulation. Due to the framework above, this sector needs the third eye to grow and expand. The expansion of the sector based economically, socially, environmentally, technologically. All these will attempt tourism sector to attain local development, resources-saving, community engagement, and quality service.

Community involvement in the tourism sector is still very important, and in order for the community to participate fully, it requires the presence of utilization of local resources and relations between foreign and local supplier. The growth of this sector requires adequate monitoring and management. The community needs to be educated and gain training on the operation of this tourism sector, understanding the awareness of how they can benefit from local tourism and how they can participate in caring for the environment. Priority should be given to localities for them to own businesses and to conduct small activities inside the tourism center regarding the nature of participation and exposure to various tourist activities. Reduced environmental footprint and environmental protection are one of the most important areas as a community needs to know how to prevent or eliminate these challenges, all these will bring the improvement of carrying capacity of the tourism industry. Creating value chain of the tourism business will depend on government incentives which are taxes, breaks, reduction in bureaucracy, monitoring and evaluation that includes factors which will bring involvement of community in the sector, education and training which create awareness to community, preservation of environment (maintain natural resources), and the last but not least to reduce linkages and increasing the linkage from the local economy (Fig. 3).

Methodology

In this study, the data collection was based on the documentary survey methodology in completing the analysis using a secondary data literature review. Also, using the reviewed documents, the study was able to generate the concept of regenerative tourism and its aspects. The literature used was searched online, and two kinds of literature were kept into consideration: journal articles and official reports. The reports and journals available were checked for their relevance and credibility, the sample used in the study and the timing of the study. The reports from United Nations Conference on Trade and Development (UNCTAD) discuss reform development of the tourism industry, UNWTO state about the global trend in tourism, the consequence rising due to outbreak of the COVID-19 and economic fluctuation among the citizens, the OECD reports on tourism development and regenerative tourism post COVID-19 were the basis for the study. The relevant data from reports and articles helped to attain an understanding of the concept of regenerative tourism, how mass tourism affects the local economy and environmental ecology, and what acquire regenerative tourism during the pandemic crisis. Further, policy forums for making effecient and effective regenerative tourism during the post COVID-19 period to act economically, socially, technologically, and environmentally strong mechanisms. Moreover, the

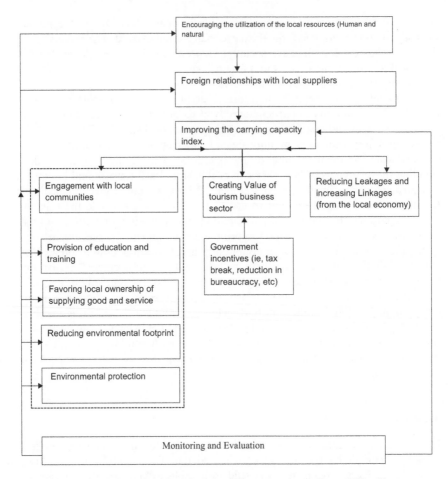

Fig. 3.   A Sustainable Model of Community – Based Tourism.
Source: Prepared by Authors based on various reports and review of literature cited.

model will justify the understanding of the connection of stakeholders, community inclusion, and other aspects of regenerative tourism. A list of primary documents are highlighted and explained in Table 1.

Discussions, Priorities, and Implications

Discussion: UNWTO (2019) reported that tourism was number three in global economic production while first is fuel and second is chemical. Whereby, approximately 7% of global trade was tourism, and 20% of GDP comes from

Table 1. Literature Review of Regenerative Tourism Based on Aspects.

Name	Title	Focus	Aspect
Jenny care and Dianne Dredge (2020)	Regenerative tourism needs diverse economic practices.	The diverse economic framework could enhance resilient communities and regenerative tourism.	Economic
Asif Hussain, Francesc, and Marie Haley (2021)	Is regenerative tourism the future of tourism?	How regenerative tourism can cover the current global crisis and the pathway to play future tourism.	Social
Asif Hussain (2021)	A future of tourism industry: conscious travel, destination recovery, and regenerative tourism	Conscious travel habits and positive psychology to reduce tourism adverse effect (Deeper understanding of tourism industry and its impacts on destination and hosts.	Social
Francesc Fuste-Forn and Asif Hussain (2022)	Regenerative tourism futures. A case study Aotearoa New Zealand.	The transformation of tourism must involve stakeholders in the creation of long-term socially, cultural, environmental and economically well-being. Future tourism needs management and market	Economic
OECD Tourism trend and policies (2020)	Rethinking tourism success for sustainable growth.	The needs of policymakers in tourism. Key policy consideration for tourism development and Implementation (Benefit and Costs)	Economic

Table 1. *(Continued)*

Name	Title	Focus	Aspect
Loretta Belloto, Niki, and Christian (2022)	Regenerative tourism: Conceptual framework leveraging theory and practice.	Knowledge system and practice in building regenerative tourism into regenerative development.	Technology
Loretta Bellato and Joseph M. Cheer (2021)	Inclusive and regenerative tourism and urban tourism: Capacity development perspectives.	Tactic knowledge and unique skills that can complement expert tourism knowledge and contribute to the development of more sustainable places and inclusive communities.	Technology

Source: Compiled by Authors from various relevant review of literature.

tourism globally. Also, the report indicated that in every 10 people, one person's source of income is from tourism, and on the island, 80% of citizens depend on tourism. Due to the outbreak of Covid 19 approximately 100 million to 120 million people, are at risk of losing their job. Hence, there is a rise of illegal hunting, vices and robbery activities, and the failure of tangible (handcraft) and intangible (festival) activities. Moreover, nearly 90% of museums were closed and 13% would probably not open again in the future. In the study, it has been found that regenerative tourism provided a new way of tourism which is more community-inclusive than in the past. A good example is a medical tourism as it is seen in the countries such as India and Turkey. For instance, India is using regenerative tourism to "promote medical tourism" through tax resumptions in medical treatment and pharmaceutical equipment. For Example; Johnson & Johnson Limited company, before COVID-19, imported medicine in India and paid a tax rate of 18% but after COVID-19 the tax rate this company paid was deducted 3% sometimes up to 0%. So, it brings a reduction in cost of transaction during the post-pandemic period for India as compared to other countries, especially for African countries – an initiative of regenerative tourism because they believe once a patient comes for treatment it's easier want to know more about India regardless of culture, taboos museums, and other factors not only for treatment. Further, the partnership among donors, governments, and the private sector has been reimagined and improved in regenerative tourism. Looking at the case of Africa, in Tanzania currently, there is an initiative of regenerative tourism by the government which connected three sectors (donor, government, and private sector). The three are taken as models which they can collaborate and work together for better tourism in the country. The product of such collaboration is the country's special program called "THE ROYAL TOUR," which is a tourism documentary led by the President of Tanzania, Hon. Samia Suluhu Hasan, who is the main character, supervised by TANAPA (Tanzania National Park) as a private institution tourism sector in Tanzania while different donors from outside and inside the country contribute their fund to ensure the program is succeeding.

Priorities (Road Map): For regenerative tourism to function well, the government has to come up with ways of mitigating the economic impact of the fall of tourism activities resulting from the COVID-19 pandemic, which mostly affected women involved in the tourist sector and comes with ways to empower them. Further, there should be a candid plan for boosting competitiveness and building resilience in tourism sector. For example, there could be diversification of income by creating new internal tourism (starting from domestic tourism and regional tourism itself) and also, by creating a conducive environment for small enterprises and to be allocated inside tourism centers as other big investors do. It is the easiest way to segment the tourists/customers according to their income. Rwanda is a good example of innovation in tourism; they went far away to advertise their country through football by using Arsenal football kits. With their slogan saying "VISIT RWANDA," they have accessed the majority of the people worldwide. In a digital transformation, regenerative tourism can use different ways, for example, airplanes, its international means of advertisement because it targets different people from different levels socially and economically. At the same time, it needed to foster sustainability and green growth. The stakeholders adopt green investment; instead of using generators for electricity, they should opt for solar panels and utilize the ecology for permanent consumption and help utilization of resources. Also, looking at carbon neutral, this can be done by reducing the emission of smoke in a tourism center, for instance, instead of using fuel car, which generates carbon air, we can use electricity car. With the change in regenerative tourism and the transformation of the sector, recovery must put people first and be easy to access. A few things that should be taken into consideration are safety and hygiene, taking the case of Tanzania mainland (Kilimanjaro) and Island (Zanzibar). During the outbreak of COVID-19, Zanzibar was among the earliest country to accept the vaccine while Kilimanjaro took time to decide on it. Due to this reason, most of the tourists in the report knew they were safe visiting Zanzibar than Kilimanjaro. Also, to reduce investment that was done directly into the sector, the revenue collected from tourism activities was directly deposited to the government, despite the amount of money they got. They must use effectively to reinvest to sustain recovery. Further, there should be the promotion of domestic tourism: According to the OECD, the percentage of the citizens who travel per year can be reported as follows: In Canada 20% of citizens were traveling and in German 50% of visitors travelled but dropped after COVID-19 while in the United Kingdom 73% of citizen dropped off after which can convert the domestic tourism for sustaining the chain of tourism sector and its significance towards building economic, social and environmental values.

Implications: Regenerative tourism brings a better position in the tourism sector, especially during pandemics (COVID-19). Improvement of local economies, sustainability and green growth, and safety and hygiene are the impacts of regenerative tourism. Regenerative tourism came up to renew the wealth creation, opportunity around the community, and prosperity. As COVID-19 hindered the tourism sector, regenerative tourism prompts the positive result to make tourism to be sustainable. The government and tour operators must reform their policy by looking at the value chain of the sector, Culture stewardship, environmental responsibility, and value addition. The industry needs a third eye to make alive by improving diversification of income, innovation and digital transformation, and green growth, and promoting domestic tourism.

Conclusion

The study discussed regenerative tourism and resilience in COVID-19 Pandemic from sustainability perspectives. However, due to the multidisciplinary nature of the subject, regenerative tourism can put better standards economically, socially, and technologically. Has been evidenced the positive impact of regenerative tourism on Covid 19. Medical tourism, public–private partnership, innovation and digital transformation, sustainability of green growth, domestic tourism, safety and hygiene, and investment reduction are the variables of regenerative tourism. Further, government, donors, and private sectors can collaborate in working together to create policies, rules, and regulations for the sector. The future of tourism, digitalization, and globalization enhance digital marketing which is an important area in the tourism industry, while visa liberalization policy, the Open Skies Agreement, and PPP are other factors for the future in this sector. The implications of the present study will be useful for policy imperatives of the government and for tour guides, including the community at large towards building tourism value chain, co-evaluation of the environmental factors and cultural stewardship of the country.

References

Abbasov, M., Brueggeman, R., Raupp, J., Akparov, Z., Aminov, N., Bedoshvili, D., ... Gill, B. S. (2019). Genetic diversity of *Aegilops L.* species from Azerbaijan and Georgia using SSR markers. *Genetic Resources and Crop Evolution, 66*(2), 453–463. doi:10.1007/s10722-018-0725-3

Asia, I. N., & Pacific, T. H. E. (2022). *Covid-19 and the future of tourism (Issue March).*

Asif, H. (2021). A future of tourism industry: Conscious travel, destination recovery and regenerative tourism. *Journal of Sustainability and Resilience, 1*(1), 1–25.

Ateljevic, I. (2020). Transforming the (tourism) world for good and (re)generating the potential 'new normal'. *Tourism Geographies, 22*(3), 467–475. doi:10.1080/1461668 8.2020.1759134

Bellato, L., & Cheer, J. M. (2021). Inclusive and regenerative urban tourism: Capacity development perspectives. *International Journal of Tourism Cities*, *7*(4), 943–961. doi:10.1108/IJTC-08-2020-0167

Bellato, L., Frantzeskaki, N., & Nygaard, C. A. (2022). Regenerative tourism: A conceptual framework leveraging theory and practice. *Tourism Geographies*. doi:10.1080/14616688.2022.2044376

Brouder, P., Teoh, S., Salazar, N. B., Mostafanezhad, M., Pung, J. M., Lapointe, D., ... Clausen, H. B. (2020). Reflections and discussions: Tourism matters in the new normal post COVID-19. *Tourism Geographies*, *22*(3), 735–746. doi:10.1080/14616688.2020.1770325

Cave, J., & Dredge, D. (2020). Regenerative tourism needs diverse economic practices. *Tourism Geographies*, *22*(3), 503–513. doi:10.1080/14616688.2020.1768434

Cheer, J. M. (2020). Human flourishing, tourism transformation and COVID-19: A conceptual touchstone. *Tourism Geographies*, *22*(3), 514–524. doi:10.1080/14616688.2020.1765016

Ciarlantini, S., Madaleno, M., Robaina, M., Monteiro, A., Eusébio, C., Carneiro, M. J., & Gama, C. (2022). Air pollution and tourism growth relationship: Exploring regional dynamics in five European countries through an EKC model. *Environmental Science and Pollution Research*. doi:10.1007/s11356-021-18087-w

Developments and Challenges in the hospitality and tourism sector. (2010, November 23–24). Issues paper for discussion at the Global Dialogue Forum for Hotels, Catreing and Tourism Sector, Geneva, 2010.

Duxbury, N., Bakas, F. E., de Castro, T. V., & Silva, S. (2021). Creative tourism development models towards sustainable and regenerative tourism. *Sustainability*, *13*(1), 1–17. doi:10.3390/su13010002

Ferronato, N., & Torretta, V. (2019). Waste mismanagement in developing countries: A review of global issues. *International Journal of Environmental Research and Public Health*, *16*(6). doi:10.3390/ijerph16061060

Fountain, J. (2021). The future of food tourism in a post-COVID-19 world: Insights from New Zealand. *Journal of Tourism Futures*, 1–14. doi:10.1108/JTF-04-2021-0100

Fusté-Forné, F., & Hussain, A. (2022). Regenerative tourism futures: A case study of Aotearoa New Zealand. *Journal of Tourism Futures*, 1–6. doi:10.1108/JTF-01-2022-0027

Galdini, R. (2007). Munich personal RePEc archive – Tourism and the city: Opportunity for regeneration tourism and the city: Opportunity for regeneration. *Tourismos: An International Multidisciplinary Journal of Tourism*, *2*(2), 95–111.

Gilauri, N. (2018). Future of tourism industry technological progress and tourism sector (1/2).

GoK. (2020). *Government of Kenya COVID-19 and travel and tourism Policy in Kenya brief* (p. 22). Retrieved from https://www.tourism.go.ke

Gupta, V., & Chomplay, P. (2021, December). Local residents' perceptions regarding the negative impacts of overtourism: A case of Shimla. *Overtourism as Destination Risk*, 69–80. doi:10.1108/978-1-83909-706-520211006

Higgins-Desbiolles, F., Bigby, B. C., & Doering, A. (2021). Socialising tourism after COVID-19: Reclaiming tourism as a social force? *Journal of Tourism Futures*, 1–12. doi:10.1108/JTF-03-2021-0058

Hussain, A., & Haley, M. (2022). Regenerative tourism model: Challenges of adapting concepts from natural science to tourism industry. *Journal of Sustainability and Resilience*, *2*(1), 1–14.

Ibn-mohammed, T., Mustapha, K. B., Godsell, J., Adamu, Z., Babatunde, K. A., & Akintade, D. D., ... Koh, S. C. L. (2020). A critical analysis of the impacts of COVID-19 on the global economy and ecosystems and opportunities for circular economy strategies. *Resources, Conservation and Recycling*. 2021 January. *164*, 105169. doi:10.1016/j.resconrec.2020.105169. Epub 2020 September 21.

Jha, S. K. (2017). Future perspective of tourism industry in India and impact of FDI. *International Journal of Creative Research Thoughts*, *5*(4), 422–426.

Major, J., & Clarke, D. (2021). Regenerative tourism in Aotearoa New Zealand – A new paradigm for the VUCA world. *Journal of Tourism Futures*, 1–6. doi:10.1108/JTF-09-2021-0233

Mateu-Sbert, J., Ricci-Cabello, I., Villalonga-Olives, E., & Cabeza-Irigoyen, E. (2013). The impact of tourism on municipal solid waste generation: The case of Menorca Island (Spain). *Waste Management*, *33*(12), 2589–2593. doi:10.1016/j.wasman.2013.08.007

Nanno, M. (2020). *The impact of the COVID-19 pandemic on the tourism sector in Latin America and the Caribbean, and options for a sustainable and resilient recovery* (Vol. 157, pp. 1–7). United Nations Publication. Retrieved from https://repositorio.cepal.org/handle/11362/46502

OECD. (2020). *Tourism policy Responses to the coronavirus (COVID-19)* (pp. 1–50). OECD. Retrieved from https://read.oecd-ilibrary.org/view/?ref=124_124984-7uf8n m95se&Title=Covid-19:TourismPolicyResponses

Persson-Fischer, U., & Liu, S. (2021). The impact of a global crisis on areas and topics of tourism research. *Sustainability*, *13*(2), 1–26. doi:10.3390/su13020906

Pollock, A. (2019). Flourishing beyond sustainability ETC Workshop in Krakow. February 6, 2019.

Pollock, A., & Travel, C. (2019). Flourishing beyond sustainability. 1–10.

Rahman, M. K., Gazi, A. I., Bhuiyan, M. A., & Rahaman, A. (2021). Effect of Covid-19 pandemic on tourist travel risk and management perceptions. *PLoS One*, *16*(9 September), 1–18. doi:10.1371/journal.pone.0256486

Sari, F. O., & Nazli, M. (2020). Exploring the effects of "excessive tourism growth" on public health and ecosystem. *Journal of Hospitality and Tourism Insights*, *4*(1), 1–17. doi:10.1108/JHTI-04-2020-0060

Taiminen, S. (2018). *The negative impacts of overtourism on tourism destination from environmental and socio-cultural perspectives* (p. 48).

Town, Y., & Owen, C. (2005). Regenerative Tourism: A case study of the resort. doi:10.1108/OHI-04-2007-B0005

UNCTAD. (2021, June). *Covid-19 and tourism an update* (pp. 1–23). Retrieved from https://unctad.org/system/files/official-document/ditcinf2021d3_en_0.pdf

World Tourism Organization. (2019). *International tourism highlights* (2019th ed.). Madrid: UNWTO. doi:10.18111/9789284421152

Yusuff, Y. (2022). Regenerative tourism: The future the tourism industry and our planet needs. In *Northeast Travel and Tourism Research Association (NETTRA) Annual Conference Research Colloquium, 2022* (pp. 1–6).

Revamping Hotel Industry in South East Asian Region: Outlook of Existing Situation After COVID-19

Syed Haider Ali Shah, Nosheen Rafique, Sharjeel Saleem, Rafia Amjad and Bilal Arshad

Abstract

The chapter is about the revamping of the hospitality and hotel industry in the South East Asian Region after the COVID-19 pandemic. The hotel industry contributes largely to the GDP of the economy. Therefore, the success of this industry is mandatory for the development of a country. The reconstruction of this sector depends upon the advanced techniques and practices to boost up this sector after crisis. Therefore, to implement such practices highly depends upon the highly educated and aware managers. This chapter focuses on how crisis management plan revamps this industry after the greatest destruction.

Keywords: Hospitality industry; hotel and tourism industry; crisis management practices; COVID-19; South East Asian; UNWTO

Introduction

Hospitality and tourism sector play a vital role in boosting the economy of developed countries as well as developing countries (Ali, Ciftci, Nanu, Cobanoglu, & Ryu, 2021; Assaf, Kock, & Tsionas, 2021). In the hospitality and tourism sector, the hotel industry is a very vibrant subsector with entrepreneurial approach to operations and activities (Ouyang, Liu, & Gui, 2021; Tunio et al., 2021a). Through an entrepreneurial approach, it contains many objectives like generation of wealth and maximization of profits, corporate social responsibility, and creation of employment opportunities (Li & Singal, 2021; Tunio et al., 2021b). Due to financial growth, several countries rely on the hotel industry to strengthen their economy (Tunio et al., 2021c). Developed countries like Italy,

Resilient and Sustainable Destinations After Disaster, 267–275

Copyright © 2023 Syed Haider Ali Shah, Nosheen Rafique, Sharjeel Saleem, Rafia Amjad and Bilal Arshad

Published under exclusive licence by Emerald Publishing Limited

doi:10.1108/978-1-80382-021-720231019

Germany, Switzerland, Norway, the United Kingdom, the United States, and Australia have major revenue generations from the hotel industry, and simultaneously, developing countries, mostly South Asian Countries like Afghanistan, India, Nepal, Bangladesh, Pakistan, Bhutan, Sri Lanka, and the Maldives critically depend upon hospitality and tourism, especially the hotel industry for major contribution to GDP (Marwah & Ramanayake, 2021). According to Pakistan Hotel Association (PHA), the hotel industry contributes 03% of its GDP (Pakistan Economic Survey, 2017–2018). However, there are also some countries that are taking initiatives to develop this industry.

The COVID-19 pandemic has brought major changes in the hospitality industry especially in the hotel industry (Rivera, 2020). The hospitality industry was adversely affected by the pandemic based on the interaction of guests and staff (Rivera, 2020). It suffered a loss of −90% on international accommodation in the first month of lockdown (Gössling, Scott, & Hall, 2020). To cope with such a scenario, the European Commission announced criteria and recommendations to ease restrictions on May 13, 2020. The impact from pandemic crises is not a national issue, but it needs international attention (Henderson & Ng, 2004). Therefore, there is a dire need to handle such conditions carefully, and well-aware and highly educated mangers are required in this industry to deal with such challenges (Benaben, Lauras, Trupil, & Salatage, 2016; Naser, Alhtarthi, & Khalifa, 2019). Crisis management is a distinctive part of management theory that deals with organizations and businesses in times of disasters (Pardeep & Clark, 2009). Crisis management is the preparation of survival before and after crisis (Israeli, Mohsin, & Kumar, 2011). It provides different tools and techniques to organizations and businesses to minimize the negative impacts of potential collapse (Benaben et al., 2016).

The COVID-19 pandemic emerged first in Wuhan, China, in December, 2019 and caused the death of 2 million people worldwide (Çoban & Özel, 2022). SARS-CoV-2 is a severe acute respiratory syndrome with symptoms of fever, cough, and shortness of breath. Tse, So, and Sin (2006) have listed down the classified crises in specific categories. According to them, external crises are caused by the social and natural environment. Natural crises start with a natural or man-made phenomenon such as floods, tsunamis, earthquakes, poisonings, and viruses.

By its nature the hotel industry is majorly affected by global crises (Vaishar & Šťastná, 2022). With the rapid spread of the pandemic, there has been a rapid increase in cancellation of trips, holidays, and flights due to prevention measures to stop the spread of the virus (Jin, Bao, & Tang, 2021). These measures include the introduction of national and international travel restrictions, the closing of border gates mutually in numerous countries, the introduction of curfews and quarantine practices, the cancellation of events, and the closing of many businesses connected to tourism, which have had a negative impact on national and international tourism (Fotiadis, Polyzos, & Huan, 2021; Fu, 2020; Gössling et al., 2020). Also many accommodation establishments have stopped providing services (Çoban & Özel, 2022). Some accommodation businesses on the other hand downsized their staff or completely closed due to the economic difficulties caused by the pandemic (Çoban & Özel, 2022).

This chapter aims to explore how functions and operations of the hotel industry are affected by COVID-19 and revamping strategies of the hotel industry to recover from losses and rebuild their reputation.

Background

For ages, humans have suffered from various pandemics, and these pandemics, such as SARS (2003), MERS (2015), Ebola (2014), and Zika (2014, 2016), have ingrained destructive impacts on every aspect of human life (Menegaki, 2020). Currently, this world is facing its deadliest pandemic in the form of SARS-CoV-2 that has killed millions of people all around the world and almost every state of the world announced lockdown which continued for several months which impacted all industries, especially the hotel industry. COVID-19 implanted far-reaching impacts on financial performance of the hotel industry, therefore; a significant number of employees from hotels lost their jobs. According to the United Nations Conference on Trade and Development (UNCTAD, 2020), the tourism industry including the hotel industry faced a loss of $1.2 trillion within 4 months due to COVID-19. Economists disclosed that the world's GDP declined by 3.8% in 2020 due to this pandemic (Marwah & Ramanayake, 2021). The estimated number of people who became unemployed from all around the world rose from 90 million to 110 million (Marwah & Ramanayake, 2021). In Nepal, there were 1,254 registered hotels (star and tourist categories) which were having a tough time sustaining their businesses during this period.

After COVID-19, the sustainability of the hotel industry is challenging for many counties, especially in the South Asian region. The world is still facing its fourth wave of pandemic, and it has learned to deal with such a situation. In the same way, stakeholders of the hotel industry are now looking at executive strategies for crisis management practices in response to the pandemic (Lai & Wong, 2020) so that this industry can ensure its sustainability during such a crisis in future as well. Currently, Pakistani prime minister Imran Khan is taking initiatives to boost tourism including the hotel industry. The purpose of this chapter is to reveal the current scenario of the hotel industry in the South Asian region and currently how these countries are taking measures to strengthen this industry and what will be the strategies to deal with such scenarios in future so that such a crisis cannot impact this industry.

Crisis management is a popular topic in the tourism and hospitality industry (Lai & Wong, 2020). Numerous studies proved the association between crisis and hospitality industry. De Sausmarez's (2007) study showed that the loss caused by the pandemic crisis threatens not only the national economy but also the livelihoods of many tourist destinations (Lai & Wong, 2020). Some crises are man-made such as economic crisis and terrorism (Lai & Wong, 2020). Some crises are natural disasters, such as epidemics (Lai & Wong, 2020). Safety is the top priority of tourists, where epidemic crises can decrease tourism activities (U & So,

2020) as well as demand for hotel bookings (Song, Lin, Witt, & Zhang, 2011) and occupancy percentage and hotel room rates (Kim, Chun, & Lee, 2005). Tsao and Ni (2016) also proved the severe impact of the epidemic crisis on the hospitality and tourism industry.

Numerous research studies have shown how to build a successful crisis management model (Lai & Wong, 2020). Kovaltchuk, Dedusenko, Blinova, and Miloradov (2016), for instance, analyzed these concepts and developed the crisis management model in the Russian hotel industry. Barbe and Pennington-Gray (2018) also provided insights into ways of using social media for hoteliers to develop crisis communication during a crisis.

Mikulić, Sprčić, Holiček, and Prebežac (2018) applied the principles of integrated risk management to make an exploratory assessment of salient risks for the Croatian tourism industry. Abo-Murad and Abdullah (2019) conducted a qualitative study to explore the influence of turnover culture on Malaysian hotels' crisis management. These studies are important for the hotel industry in the preparation of crises (Lai & Wong, 2020). Numerous studies on epidemic crisis management have pointed out the severe impact on the tourism industry and argued that more research should be conducted to understand the different aspects of an epidemic crisis (Lai & Wong, 2020). Zeng, Carter, and De Lacy (2005) viewed it as a short-term epidemic and examined the possibilities of new innovations after tourism recovery.

Financial damages led restaurants and hotels to reduce their staff that led to a tremendous social issue of unemployment (Lui-Lasters & Cahyanto, 2019; Shi & Li, 2017). Hong Kong restaurants had losses up to 03 billion in only a few months after the SARS crisis (Tse et al., 2006). Tse et al. (2006) discovered that Hong Kong's hospitality industry confronted the crisis caused by COVID-19 by following crisis management practices mostly associated with dynamic marketing and cost-cut practices. They also highlighted the importance of the creation of a crisis management team and a precrisis plan. Singapore successfully coped with the COVID-19 pandemic and turned the negative image into positive one by applying a series of crisis management practices that has helped Singapore to grow again gradually (Henderson & Ng, 2004). These practices were based on marketing and focused on domestic market, human resource management, hotel's infrastructure, and especially government's support (Henderson & Ng, 2004). These hotels started new advertising campaigns and new collaborations with travel agencies and airlines (Pavlatos, Kostakis, & Digkas, 2021). The hotel industry also promoted frequent travel controls and high standard of hygiene (Henderson & Ng, 2004). Numerous researchers and scholars suggested to implement crisis management practices and to analyze the importance of their usage (Israeli et al., 2011; Israeli & Reichel, 2003).

Main Focus of the Chapter

Research on tourism and the hospitality industry has become the center of attention of all the researchers and scholars (Zhao, Cheng, Yu, & Xu, 2020).

When epidemic crises occur, hotel industry stakeholders expect that crises will be over shortly and determine crises management practices based on such an assumption (Lai & Wong, 2020). 150 Hilton hotels in China were closed during the pandemic (HNN, 2020). Numerous studies declared it as tourism crises (Backer & Ritchie, 2017; Ritchie & Jiang, 2019). The major problem of pandemic crisis is unpreparedness of the hotel industry to deal with such scenarios. There are few studies that focused on the crises management of the hotel industry to cope with epidemic crises. In developing economies, hotel industries are not much stronger in financial perspectives; therefore, it cannot recover their loss within a short period of time. In such a scenario, governments of such economies have started to become more lenient in their policies and encourage this industry to bring innovative solutions to recover the loss in such situations.

This is a review article in which secondary source is used to collect the data from different databases like ResearchGate, Google Scholar, Emerald, etc. Along with scientific articles, reports and different periodicals are accessed to collect data about the target group of countries. As different waves of the COVID-19 pandemic were provoked with different intensities and still it was uncertain to say when the pandemic will end, the conditions to revert back to normal routine via vaccination and preventive measures are to be taken seriously. Thus, in order to check the current status of the hotel industry with respect to the pandemic, data are explored within the time bracket from December 2020 to December 2021, because before December 2020, the issue of the pandemic was at its peak where the whole world was under serious threat.

Solutions and Recommendations

COVID-19 impacted all the industries worldwide, but the most affected industry was the tourism and hotel industry. The hotel industry played a major role in strengthening the economy. But it suffered a huge loss due to the spread of COVID-19. To deal with such loss, there is a dire need to bring about highly advanced and highly affordable solutions. Developed economies developed new technologies with time such as to provide more focus on virus preventive measures. In the scenario of crisis management practices, Israeli and Reichel (2003) examined the association between the usage and importance of crisis management practices in the Israeli hospitality industry. They have conducted interviews for 13 managers and constructed four categories of practices. They referred to Mansfeld (1999) and developed the "marketing" category. They divided cost cuttings into "human resources" and "maintenance" and took "governmental assistance" as external support. Their framework consists of 21 items. Israeli and his coauthors extended the framework with minor revisions to the restaurant industry (Israeli, 2007), Indian luxury hotels (Israeli et al., 2011), and travel agency sectors (Perl & Israeli, 2011). Their research study suggested that stakeholders were reactive and managers strongly looked for support from the government. Quality, low cost, and the removal of harmful compounds are the factors that can be used to promote the revival of the hotel industry. The most significant use of these measures is the introduction of travel restrictions. In order to prevent the spread of the pandemic, 100% of tourism destinations across the world faced travel restrictions by closing their borders completely or partially and canceling international flights (UNWTO, World Tourism Barometer, 2020). This study helps in understanding how these countries are reshaping the industry after the pandemic situation. This study will be useful for the hospital and tourism sector, specifically the hotel industry, where government agencies are set policies and programs to support this vibrant sector in times of crises.

Future Research Directions

This chapter aims to focus on the quality solutions to revamp the hotel industry. Literature showed that to deal with epidemics there is a dire need to develop crisis management plans, but the major issue to cope with this scenario is the lack of focus on the new and innovative solutions to boost the industry. Another constraint is the lack of available resources to implement the latest technological solutions. This chapter helps to understand hotel industry revamp after COVID-19. This study is useful for scientists, researchers, academicians, students, and policymakers to adopt and apply novel approaches to deal with the pandemic crisis. Developing economies look for practices and policies to come out from this crisis situation to improve their financial performance of hotel industry. For future research studies, it is recommended to conduct applied researches to how hotel industry reconstructed its self to cope with such a situation. Researchers and scientists should consider the health protection element by reviewing a clear vision of the hotel industry. Organizations should adopt new practices and policies to enhance their service value and to improve health-related concerns.

References

2014–2016 Ebola Outbreak in West Africa | History | Ebola (Ebola Virus Disease) | CDC. (2019, March 8). Retrieved from https://www.cdc.gov/vhf/ebola/history/2014-2016-outbreak/index.html

2015 MERS outbreak in Republic of Korea. (2015, July 28). Retrieved from https://www.who.int/westernpacific/emergencies/2015-mers-outbreak

Abo-Murad, M., & Abdullah, A. K. (2019). Turnover culture and crisis management: Insights from Malaysian hotel industry. *Academy of Strategic Management Journal, 18*(2), 1–14.

Ali, F., Ciftci, O., Nanu, L., Cobanoglu, C., & Ryu, K. (2021). Response rates in hospitality research: An overview of current practice and suggestions for future research. *Cornell Hospitality Quarterly, 62*(1), 105–120.

Assaf, A. G., Kock, F., & Tsionas, M. (2021). Tourism during and after COVID-19: An expert-informed agenda for future research. *Journal of Travel Research.* doi:10.1177/00472875211017237

Backer, E., & Ritchie, B. W. (2017). VFR travel: A viable market for tourism crisis and disaster recovery? *International Journal of Tourism Research, 19*(4), 400–411.

Barbe, D., & Pennington-Gray, L. (2018, August 13). Using situational crisis communication theory to understand Orlando hotels' Twitter response to three crises in the summer of 2016. *Journal of Hospitality and Tourism Insights, 1*(3), 258–275.

Benaben, F., Lauras, M., Trupil, S., & Salatage, N. (2016, January). A metamodel for knowledge management in crisis management [Paper presentation]. *The 49th Hawaii International Conference on System Sciences (HICSS 2016)*, Koloa, HI.

CDC SARS Response Timeline | About | CDC. (2013, April 26). Retrieved from https://www.cdc.gov/about/history/sars/timeline.htm

Çoban, E., & Özel, Ç. H. (2022) Determining the crisis management strategies applied by hotel managers during the outbreak of Coronavirus (COVID-19). *Advances in Hospitality and Tourism Research, 10*(1), 27–48.

De Sausmarez, N. (2007). Crisis management, tourism and sustainability: The role of indicators. *Journal of Sustainable Tourism, 15*(6), 700–714.

The Economic Survey of Pakistan, 2017–2018, (Pakistan Economic Survey, 2017–2018).

Fotiadis, A., Polyzos, S., & Huan, T. C. T. (2021). The good, the bad and the ugly on COVID-19 tourism recovery. *Annals of Tourism Research, 87*, 103117.

Fu, Y.-K. (2020). The impact and recovering strategies of the COVID-19 pandemic: Lessons from Taiwan's hospitality industry. *Cogent Social Sciences, 6*(1), 1–12.

Gössling, S., Scott, D., & Hall, C. M. (2020). Pandemics, tourism and global change: A rapid assessment of COVID-19. *Journal of Sustainable Tourism, 29*(1), 1–20.

Henderson, J. C., & Ng, A. (2004). Responding to crisis: Severe acute respiratory syndrome (SARS) and hotels in Singapore. *International Journal of Tourism Research, 6*(6), 411–419.

HNN. (2020). Coronavirus effects color Hilton's 2020 outlook. *Hotel News Now*. Retrieved from www.hotelnewsnow.com/Articles/300258/Coronavirus-effects-color-Hiltons-2020-outlook. Accessed on 11 February 2020.

Israeli, A. A. (2007). Crisis-management practices in the restaurant industry. *International Journal of Hospitality Management, 26*(4), 807–823.

Israeli, A. A., Mohsin, A., & Kumar, B. (2011). Hospitality crisis management practices: The case of Indian luxury hotels. *International Journal of Hospitality Management, 30*(2), 367–374. doi:10.1016/j.ijhm.2010.06.009

Israeli, A. A., & Reichel, A. (2003). Hospitality crisis management practices: The Israeli case. *International Journal of Hospitality Management, 22*(4), 353–372. doi: 10.1016/S0278-4319(03)00070-7

Jin, X., Bao, J., & Tang, C. (2021). Profiling and evaluating Chinese consumers regarding post-COVID-19 travel. *Current Issues in Tourism*, 1–19.

Kim, S. S., Chun, H., & Lee, H. (2005). The effects of SARS on the Korean hotel industry and measures to overcome the crisis: A case study of six Korean five-star hotels. *Asia Pacific Journal of Tourism Research, 10*(4), 369–377.

Kovaltchuk, A. P., Dedusenko, E. A., Blinova, E. A., & Miloradov, K. A. (2016). Concept and procedures of crisis management in Russian hotel enterprises. *Journal of Environmental Management & Tourism, 7*(3 (15)), 473–480.

Lai, I. K. W., & Wong, J. W. C. (2020). Comparing crisis management practices in the hotel industry between initial and pandemic stages of COVID-19. *International Journal of Contemporary Hospitality Management, 32*(10), 3135–3156.

Li, Y., & Singal, M. (2021). Corporate governance in the hospitality and tourism industry: Theoretical foundations and future research. *Journal of Hospitality & Tourism Research.* doi:10.1177/10963480211011718

Liu-Lastres, B., & Cahyanto, I. P. (2019). Exploring residents' roles as risk insiders in tourism crisis management, *Travel and Tourism Research Association: Advancing Tourism Research Globally.*

Mansfeld, Y. (1999). Cycles of war, terror, and peace: Determinants and management of crisis and recovery of the Israeli tourism industry. *Journal of Travel Research, 38*(1), 30–36.

Marwah, R., & Ramanayake, S. S. (2021). Pandemic-led disruptions in Asia: Tracing the early economic impacts on Sri Lanka and Thailand. *South Asian Survey, 28*(1), 172–198.

Menegaki, A. N. (2020). Hedging feasibility perspectives against the COVID-19 for the international tourism sector.

Mikulić, J., Sprčić, D. M., Holiček, H., & Prebežac, D. (2018). Strategic crisis management in tourism: An application of integrated risk management principles to the Croatian tourism industry. *Journal of Destination Marketing & Management, 7,* 36–38.

Naser, M., Alhtarthi, A. N., & Khalifa, G. S. A. (2019). Business continuity management and crisis leadership: An approach to re-engineer crisis performance within Abu Dhabi Government Entities. *International Journal on Emerging Technologies, 10*(1a), 32–40.

Ouyang, X., Liu, Z., & Gui, C. (2021). Creativity in the hospitality and tourism industry: A meta-analysis. *International Journal of Contemporary Hospitality Management, 33*(10), 3685–3704.

Pardeep, R., & Clark, H. (2009). A framework for knowledge-based crisis management in hospitality and tourism industry. *Cornell Hospitality Quarterly, 50*(4), 561–577. doi:10.1177/1938965509341633

Pavlatos, O., Kostakis, H., & Digkas, D. (2021). Crisis management in the Greek hotel industry in response to COVID-19 pandemic. *Anatolia, 32*(1), 80–92.

Perl, Y., & Israeli, A. A. (2011). Crisis management in the travel agency sector: A case study. *Journal of Vacation Marketing, 17*(2), 115–125.

Ritchie, B. W., & Jiang, Y. (2019). A review of research on tourism risk, crisis and disaster management: Launching the annals of tourism research curated collection on tourism risk, crisis and disaster management. *Annals of Tourism Research, 79,* 102812.

Rivera, M. A. (2020). Hitting the reset button for hospitality research in times of crisis: Covid-19 and beyond. *International Journal of Hospitality Management, 87,* 102528.

Shi, W., & Li, K. X. (2017). Impact of unexpected events on inbound tourism demand modeling: Evidence of Middle East Respiratory Syndrome outbreak in South Korea. *Asia Pacific Journal of Tourism Research, 22*(3), 344–356. doi:10.1080/10941665.2016.1250795

Song, H., Lin, S., Witt, S. F., & Zhang, X. (2011). Impact of financial/economic crisis on demand for hotel rooms in Hong Kong. *Tourism Management, 32*(1), 172–186.

Tsao, C. Y., & Ni, C. C. (2016). Vulnerability, resilience, and the adaptive cycle in a crisis-prone tourism community. *Tourism Geographies, 18*(1), 80–105.

Tse, A. C. B., So, S., & Sin, L. (2006). Crisis management and recovery: How restaurants in Hong Kong responded to SARS. *International Journal of Hospitality Management, 25*(1), 3–11. doi:10.1016/j.ijhm.2004.12.001

Tunio, M. N., Shaikh, E., & Lighari, S. (2021a). Multifaceted perils of the Covid-19 and implications: A review. *Studies of Applied Economics, 39*(2).

Tunio, M. N., Yusrini, L., Shah, Z. A., Katper, N., & Jariko, M. A. (2021b). How hotel industry cope up with the COVID-19: An SME perspective. *Etikonomi, 20*(2), 213–224.

Tunio, M. N., Yusrini, L., & Shoukat, G. (2021c). Corporate social responsibility (CSR) in hotels in Austria, Pakistan, and Indonesia: Small and medium enterprise spillover of COVID-19. In *Handbook of research on entrepreneurship, innovation, sustainability, and ICTs in the post-COVID-19 era* (pp. 263–280). Hershey, PA: IGI Global.

UNCTAD. (2020). The coronavirus shock: A story of another global crisis foretold and what policymakers should be doing about it. Retrieved from https://unctad. org/en/PublicationsLibrary/gds_tdr2019_update_coronavirus.pdf

U, S. C., & So, Y. C. (2020). The impacts of financial and non-financial crises on tourism: Evidence from Macao and Hong Kong. *Tourism Management Perspectives, 33*, 100628.

Vaishar, A., & Šťastná, M. (2022). Impact of the COVID-19 pandemic on rural tourism in Czechia Preliminary considerations. *Current Issues in Tourism, 25*(2), 187–191.

World Tourism Organization (UNWTO). (2020). World Tourism Barometer. Retrieved from https://www.unwto.org/publications

Zeng, B., Carter, R. W., & De Lacy, T. (2005). Short-term perturbations and tourism effects: The case of SARS in China. *Current Issues in Tourism, 8*(4), 306–322.

Zhao, Y., Cheng, S., Yu, X., & Xu, H. (2020). Chinese public's attention to the COVID-19 epidemic on social media: Observational descriptive study. *Journal of Medical Internet Research, 22*(5), e18825.

Zika Virus. (2022, December 8). Retrieved from https://www.who.int/news-room/fact-sheets/detail/zika-virus?gclid=CjwKCAjwjYKjBhB5EiwAiFdSfieTuwGIEW3wdz wElgEWbMx1GdWCzMirnc8H40KQ2OhhP7AShK9k8BoCh-IQAvD_BwE

Harnessing the Potential of Ecotourism for Sustainability

Deeksha Dave

Abstract

The tourism has become more responsible in terms of tourists choosing environmentally friendly alternatives and resorting to green options in food, travel, and purchase. In view of this, "ecotourism" appears as a sustainable means of promoting tourism in the less explored areas which are endowed with esthetic beauty of nature. Ecotourism is based on the pillars of biodiversity, wildlife, natural wealth, rivers, and authentic cuisine. The proposed chapter is an attempt to explore the ecotourism potential of the Southern Rajasthan in India which has a rich heritage of natural wealth and cultural diversity.

Keywords: Ecotourism; sustainability; development; tribal; Rajasthan; culture

Introduction

Tourism is a multisectoral and multidimensional industry having potential for socioeconomic progress of any country (Kanga, Sharma, Pandey, Nathawat, & Sharma, 2013). It is one of the world's leading and rapidly growing industries which includes product improvement, marketing, rules and regulations, and human resource development, and opens a new horizon for much needed income and employment to the inhabitants of the place and foreign exchange fostering hotel, travel, food, and brewing industry (Ismail, Imran, Khan, & Qureshi, 2021; Sairam & Thilagaraj, 2017; Sharma & Arora, 2015).

Despite this, it is also true that the tourism-steered economic growth is addicted to the growth and often leads to ecological degradation, contributes to environmental pollution, and goes against the principles of sustainability (Azam, Alam, & Hafeez, 2018). Challenges like global climate change, threat of future pandemics, extremes of weather, loss of biodiversity, land degradation, and

Resilient and Sustainable Destinations After Disaster, 277–285
Copyright © 2023 Deeksha Dave
Published under exclusive licence by Emerald Publishing Limited
doi:10.1108/978-1-80382-021-720231020

environmental exigencies in the form of disasters are calling upon the environmentally and socially responsible tourism. This was realized long back when United Nations declared the year 2017 as the International Year of Sustainable Tourism (Khangarot & Sahu, 2019). According to World Tourism Organization (WTO), tourism and related activities play crucial role in achieving the Sustainable Development Goals (SDGs), particularly SDG 8: Decent Work and Economic Growth, SDG 12: Responsible Production and Consumption, and SDG 14: Life below Water (Suwanna, Pisitsenakul, & Passadee, 2019).

The pandemic hit the tourism industry hardest but the newer trends of staycation and workation by the tourists because of fear of contracting infection and search for solitude among the travelers has brought in fresh approaches to tourism and related activities. In this regard, ecotourism is an upcoming trend among tourists who are also nature lovers.

The term "Ecotourism" is made up of two words: Eco and Tourism. Eco means pertaining to environment and tourism refers to traveling and visiting distant places. (Jamal & Stronza, 2009). In view of this, ecotourism conveys tourism related to natural places like sanctuaries, bird parks, valleys, mountains, beaches, etc. without causing any harm to these destinations. However, ecotourism is not just visiting the natural environment but also aims to maintain the economic and social stability of the region. From these definitions, it can be interpreted that ecotourism is characterized by following three features (Ahmed, 2013).

- Conservation of environment in the form of protection of forests, wildlife, and other ecosystems.
- Community participation in the form of culture and social richness of the place.
- Sustainable in terms of maintaining continuity.

Earlier, Chesworth (1995) also included learning and experience and appreciation of local culture and traditions. To some researchers, ecotourism is responsible tourism (Singh, 2019) with incorporating social and environmental considerations (Chouhan, 2022). With the growing number of environmentally responsible tourists and increasing urgency to address environmental degradation, the ecotourism and related sector is expected to witness a boom in the future (Ketema, 2015).

The chapter explores the ecotourism potential of the Vagad region of the state of Rajasthan in India. The subsequent sections in the chapter describe the unexplored ecotourist spots in the region having environmental and social importance. Tourism here means an encounter with experiencing nature in the lap of rich cultural heritage. It underlies exploring the mixed deciduous forests, heritage forts, picturesque landscape, tribal communities, and discovering unmapped natural and sociocultural heritage highlighting the importance of sustainability.

The Study Area

The present study is confined to the southern region of Rajasthan known as Vagad region comprising of the districts of Banswara and Dungarpur. Banswara is known as the "City of Hundred Islands" because of the presence of small and big islands in the vicinity and is often referred to as the "Cherrapunji of Rajasthan" as it rains heavily during the rainy season. The name, Banswara, comes from "Bans wala" (bamboo forests), as bamboo was once found to be growing abundantly around this place. Dungarpur is known as City of Hills as it is surrounded by small hillocks on all the sides. The royal palaces in the city depict the glorious history of the region. The green marble of Dungarpur is exotic and is globally imported. The Swachh Survekshan 2021 (World's largest urban sanitation survey by the Government of India) ranked Dungarpur as the cleanest city in Rajasthan.

The Vagad region has a significant place in the world map, archives, and geography of India. The region abounds in the natural beauty like forests, valleys, rivers like Mahi and Som, rivulets, and much more. Land is wetter and more fertile here than other parts of the state. Summers are hot and winters are mild with rainfall occurring during the months of July to September. It is an unexplored region on the tourism map of the state and the country in spite of having immense potential. This may be due to more popularity of the nearby tourist destinations like Udaipur, Chittorgarh, and Mount Abu.

Out of the nine tourist circuits marked by the Department of Tourism, Government of Rajasthan, Vagad circuit comprising of Dungarpur and Banswara is also rich in tribal culture. Around 13% of the population in Rajasthan consists of tribal communities (Chouhan, 2022). In particular, the Vagad region is primarily tribal-dominated and is considered as a backward region. Bhil community is dominant in this region. (Doodwal, 2021). The tribes are simple, follow ancient rituals and traditions, and possess unique culture, taboos, beliefs, and activities forming cultural traits in the region. This is revealed by the art work and craft made from the natural products. Exotic fairs and festival celebration make the life of the people lively and colorful and attract tourists (Verma & Murdia, 2017). Bhil tribes of the region are skilled in archery, apt in guerilla warfare. A character called Eklavya in Mahabharata (Ancient Epic) who was an expert archer was also a bhil (Verma & Murdia, 2017). Damor tribes are found in Simalwara, Sagwara, and adjoining places of Banswara. Long back these tribes have suffered oppression, discrimination, and have been away from the main stream development models.

Ecotourism Potential of the Region

As compared to the past, where the tourists had a wide choice out of the canvas of palaces, forts, heritage buildings, deserts, and valor to choose from the state of Rajasthan, the current chapter throws light on the attractions which are undisturbed areas found in pristine environment. While the annual budget of the state government, 2020, mentions about the tourism development in the belt, the ecotourist destinations of the region deserve to be specifically developed. The ecotourism in the Vagad region comprises of both the natural landscape as well the cultural and social richness.

Forests and natural environment: The forests of Southern Rajasthan are found in hilly areas with luxuriant growth of teak forests, mango trees, etc. Beautiful valleys, meadows, flora, fauna, and pristine vegetation form a part of the protected region of the area. Some of these spots are visited by the people during monsoon to have an enthralling experience of nature's beauty. The Shyampura forest in the region is named as the oxygen hub, wherein it is proposed to develop walking track, cycling track, premarked nature trials to lure the tourists. It is a common belief that the rare species of large *Cocos nucifera* trees (commonly called Kalpa Virksha) located near Anand Sagar Lake (Bai Talab) fulfill the wishes of the people (Singh, 2005).

Owing to the presence of forests, vegetation, and water bodies, there are various ecologically rich zones present here. The geography and the terrain of the region are conducive to the growth of flora and fauna. The Tropic of Cancer passes through the Banswara district (23°30′N). Due to this, it is hot and humid supporting various life forms including the insects primarily found in winter and the water bodies in the region provide habitat to aquatic biodiversity. Another fresh water reservoir – The Mahi Bajaj Sagar Reservoir – is rich in fish diversity. In addition, the region is a heaven for the birding enthusiasts. The Mahi River, an important river of Central India, flows through the region and has several islands at various distances. The Vagad region is also known for the presence of big-sized water bodies like Surwania, Mahi Dam, Kadana Back water, and Anand Sagar Lake (Bai Talab). The region is a perfect weekend getaway especially during monsoons. The backwaters of Mahi River can serve as aqua or aero tourist hot spots (Rajasthan Tourism Policy, 2020). The activities which can be taken up include scuba diving, nature walking, traipsing forests, interaction with tribals, and enjoying the scenic beauty of nature. Water tourism like boating has already started at some places. However, it is important to demark only nonconsumptive water for entertainment and leisure activities.

Along with this, in this region, wildlife tourism, cultural tourism, weekend tourism, etc. may be explored. To keep the nature in its pristine state, one has to be careful to see that the basic civic facilities are provided inside the forests also. The movement of the big and small vehicles has to be restricted so as to not disturb the animals and damage the plants. It has been found that the tribal communities protect the plants growing in their vicinity through demarcating the region as sacred groves or using them in various rituals and festivals (Rana, Sharma, & Paliwal, 2016).

Religious and Cultural Heritage: The region is endowed with various sites of historical and mythological significance. It has immense scope to be developed as religious tourism hot spot of the country. Banswara is also known as "Lodhikashi" or little Kashi as it has eleven and a half Swayambhoo Shivalingas (Jat & Shrivastava, 2014). There is a famous Jain temple "Andeshwar Parshwanathji" located on a small hill which is very famous. Places of Hindu interest like Ram Kund, Radha Kund, and Bhim Kund present the mythological importance of the place. The temple of Goddess Tripura Sundari is one of the *"Shakti Peeths"* (Energy Centers) of the Hindus. The pilgrims of the nearby districts of the states of Madhya Pradesh and Gujarat visit the temples of the region and offer prayers especially during Navratri, Shivratri, etc. The region has a historical heritage value. Mangarh Dham which is the replica of the infamous Jallianwala Bagh Massacre is situated here. Here, in 1913, 1,500 tribals were killed by the British. It is strongly demanded by the tribals to set up a national memorial in this place to pay tributes to the martyrs. Further, Rajasthan Tourism Policy also recommended setting up Special Heritage Village or Special Crafts Village from the region. Cenotaphs and Chhatris made in the memory of those who died in the battle bring the feeling of valor, courage, and dignity among the tribals can be seen at various places in the districts. Other important places in the region are Arthuna and Galiyakot. While, the old architectural buildings are visited by the tourists to know about the valor and exemplary history of the region, the entry and movement of the vehicles inside the premises must be restricted. The old-walled cities of Dungarpur and Banswara are obscured by new structures, electric poles, and wires. There are many havelis, forts, and palaces in the region that can be developed into hotels, which would be of special attraction to tourists.

Tribal art and culture: The Vagad region is dominantly populated by the tribal communities. A look into their customs and way of living is an experience in itself. Main attractions include tribal fairs, culture, festivals, forts, and palaces; Baneshwar is an important destination known for the largest tribal fair organized in the region by the district administrations of Dungarpur and Banswara. The annual fair held in the month of January is called "Maha Kumbha" (Mega pilgrimage) of the *Vanvasis*. (Forest dwellers) is a great attraction for the tribes and is worth visiting. Baneshwar is called the "Prayagraj of Rajasthan" where the three rivers, Mahi, Som, and Jhakham meet. It is considered auspicious to take holy bath in the river and therefore is considered to be the Pushkar of Vagad. In the region, the celebration of festivals is not just a ritual but a reflection of various traditional elements. This can be seen while observing the manner in which the tribals celebrate festivals (Bagchi & Baranda, 2018). The place is ideal to learn about the various festivals and the celebrations which usually go on for 2–3 days and celebrated with zeal and enthusiasm. There is no commercialization of these local festivals and the outside world is not aware of this cultural diversity of the region. During the celebration, men can be seen wearing colorful *pagdi* (turban) and women are dressed in *gagra choli* (petticoat and blouse) with beautiful jewelry. The feast is made up of forest products and local cuisine is relished.

In the study it was revealed Banswara is also popular for the varieties of mangoes grown here which include the 18 Indigenous varieties. The food tourism can also be explored in this belt. By the use of locally grown crops such as minor millets, vegetables, sprouted grains, ragi (finger millet), and *til laddoos* (ball-shaped Indian sweet made from sesame seeds) and *sama kheer* (Pudding made of barnyard millet), the tribes maintain the nutrition level of their children (The Hindu, 27 August 2021). The minor millets are eaten in this region throughout the year. The local cuisine can be promoted through tickling the taste buds of the tourists coming in the region. Agritourism can be started here where the tourists can stay with the locals, taste the local foods, and can enhance their knowledge about farming along with relaxing and recreation. Depending upon the time of the visit, duration, etc., customized tourism can be promoted.

Socioeconomic Perspectives and Sustainability

From a socioeconomic and cultural point of view, ecotourism in the region offers a variety of opportunities. Various studies conducted in the past reveal that exploring sustainability in the tourism is a win–win situation for environment conservation and economic development (Eshun & Tichaawa, 2020). It can enhance livelihood opportunities, provide educational avenues, protect local culture, strengthen the identity of the communities, and promote sustainability (Mapp & Rice, 2019). The link between biodiversity conservation and community involvement believes that nature-based tourism managed by local people not only results in resource conservation but is also beneficial for their economic development (Chandel & Kanga, 2020; Coria & Calfucura, 2012).

Underestimating the potential of ecotourism in the region will result not just in economic loss but will keep the valuable assets unnoticed. Indigenous knowledge of the communities is also helpful in promoting the ecotourism in the area. Programs such as ARYA (Attracting and Retaining Youth in Agriculture) which are started for the first time in Banswara district in Rajasthan, utilizes the Indigenous knowledge system in goat farming (Choudhary, Gupta, Pramod, Bijarnia, & Kuri, 2022). Livelihoods of the people in the region are dependent on nature.

It has been observed that the tribals make optimum utilization of resources while preparing products and articles of day-to-day use. At Banswara and Dungarpur, Bhil communities still use mahua flowers (*Madhuca longifolia*) to brew the traditional liquor (Srivastava, 2016). The aspect of the circular economy can be noticed in the regenerative development model of the region. Ecotourism helps to conserve the resources utilized in the making of these products and provides enthralling experiences to the tourists (Day, Sydnor, Marshall, & Noakes, 2021). It also helps to boost local economy through creation of micro and medium enterprise through markets which are commonly known as "Haats."

Tourism products that are more sustainable are popular among tourists unlike the mass tourism through hoardings, advertisements, and promotional campaigns, etc. In view of this, tribal tourism can emerge as a special subset of ecotourism in the region. The artifacts, hand-made crafts, jewelry can attain market attention by developing a catalog of tribal products, guide books, etc. The promotion of tourism can also help in job creation in the region in the form of guides, tour operators, drivers, auto drivers, and so on.

The development of infrastructure, public–private partnership, and community participation can be instrumental in developing the region as ecotourist destination (Sharma et al., 2013). Geographical Information System (GIS) can be used to mark important tourist destinations on map. Materializing these suggestions requires interventions at various levels. Training, awareness camps, and introductory sessions need to be organized. An annual calendar of festivals can be prepared and displayed on websites. Ecotourism initiatives fail mostly when communities and local people are not involved. Special training should be organized for the tour operators, guides, hoteliers, and those who are directly or indirectly associated with the tourism in the area. Without proper training, there are chances of accidents and mishappenings. Multistakeholder perspective and multiinstitutional arrangement needs to be developed to leverage the ecotourism in the region (Ismail et al., 2021).

The study reflects that the promotion of tribal tourism will develop the locally generated goods, apart from the development of direct and indirect jobs, and will have essential multiplier effects as money is recycled into communities. Also, the development of ecotourism in the region will lead to substantial improvements in the tribal region development (Chouhan, 2022; Sangwan & Bhatia, 2020).

Challenges

Inspite of having immense potential of the development of ecotourism in the region, there are various hurdles and challenges. The increasing anthropogenic disturbances in the form of tree felling are destroying the beauty of the place. The bamboo (after which the "Banswara" is named) has been sacrificed in the run for developing the town (*Outlook* magazine, June 2022) Further, the summer months (March to June) are very harsh and less tourist activities are possible during this time. This may lead to a fragile and insecure source of income for the communities. It is for this reason that the tribals of Banswara and Dungarpur region mostly migrate to nearby places for livelihoods and the Indigenous life systems are diminishing fast. The places which have been identified for ecotourism are less traveled and less explored and so lack the connectivity problems. The ecotourism development in the region if not planned carefully may put strain on the local culture, violating their identities, and put economic and financial burden on the tribals. The present study reveals that in future these tourist destinations may be threatened due to urbanization and commercial activities. Facilities in the form of food, accommodation parking, etc. will put extra burden. The other downsides of tourism in the region may include economic abuse, cultural destruction, and environmental damage, etc.

Conclusion

The tribal region of Southern Rajasthan has hidden and undiscovered potential to be tapped to generate economy and also to conserve nature. The region is rich in natural wealth and has historical significance too. Exploring possibility of developing ecotourism in the region comes in the form of struggles and solutions. Sharing of information, use of technology, artificial intelligence, and community participation can prevent this heritage from eroding. Tribal communities of the study area are custodians of rich cultural ecological heritage, the knowledge of which needs to be preserved and appreciated. Technological innovations can help to bridge the gap between the various stakeholders to arrive at a common agenda for promoting ecotourism through knowledge sharing.

References

Ahmed, R. A. I. S. (2013). Desert ecotourism in Rajasthan: A case study of Jaipur. *South Asian Journal of Tourism Research, 6*(1), 159–168.

Azam, M., Alam, M. M., & Hafeez, M. H. (2018). Effect of tourism on environmental pollution: Further evidence from Malaysia, Singapore and Thailand. *Journal of Cleaner Production, 190*, 330–338.

Bagchi, T., & Baranda, Y. (2018). Celebration of Diwali festival in some Bhil villages of Udaipur, Rajasthan. *Journal of the Anthropological Survey of India, 67*(2), 239–251.

Chandel, R. S., & Kanga, S. (2020). Sustainable management of ecotourism in western Rajasthan, India: A geospatial approach. *Geo Journal of Tourism and Geosites, 29*(2), 521–533.

Chesworth, N. (1995). Ecotourism. In *Seminar paper delivered in the Institute of Environmental Studies and Management*, College, Laguna, UPLB.

Choudhary, K., Gupta, S., Pramod, D. C., Bijarnia, S. R., & Kuri, J. (2022). Suggestions of trainers to better run the programme of ARYA project in Banswara district. *The Pharma Innovation Journal, 11*(4S), 1868–1870.

Chouhan, V. (2022). Developing a sustainable tribal tourism model vis-a-vis the tribal region of Rajasthan. *Journal of Tourism, Heritage & Services Marketing (JTHSM), 8*(1), 58–63.

Coria, J., & Calfucura, E. (2012). Ecotourism and the development of indigenous communities: The good, the bad, and the ugly. *Ecological Economics, 73*, 47–55.

Day, J., Sydnor, S., Marshall, M., & Noakes, S. (2021). Ecotourism, regenerative tourism, and the circular economy: Emerging trends and ecotourism. In *Routledge handbook of ecotourism* (pp. 23–36).

Doodwal, S. (2021). Bhils of Southern Rajputana During British Raj. In *Tribe-British relations in India: Revisiting text, perspective and approach* (pp. 221–235).

Eshun, G., & Tichaawa, T. M. (2020). Community participation, risk management and ecotourism sustainability issues in Ghana. *Geo Journal of Tourism and Geosites, 28*(1), 313–331.

Ismail, F., Imran, A., Khan, N., & Qureshi, M. I. (2021). Past, present and future of ecotourism, a systematic literature review from last decade. *Studies of Applied Economics, 39*(4).

Jamal, T., & Stronza, A. (2009). Collaboration theory and tourism practice in protected areas: Stakeholders, structuring and sustainability. *Journal of Sustainable Tourism, 17*(2), 169–189.

Jat, D. N., & Shrivastava, L. (2014). Demographic structure in Banswara district. *International Research Journal of Management Sociology & Humanities, 5*(4), 37–47.

Kanga, S., Sharma, L. K., Pandey, P. C., Nathawat, M. S., & Sharma, S. K. (2013). Forest fire modeling to evaluate potential hazard to tourism sites using geospatial approach. *Journal of Geomatics, 7*(1), 93–99.

Ketema, T. D. (2015). Development of community based ecotourism in Wenchi Crater Lake, Ethiopia: Challenges and prospects. *Journal of Hospitality Management and Tourism*, *6*(4), 39–46.

Khangarot, G., & Sahu, P. (2019). Agro-tourism: A dimension of sustainable tourism development in Rajasthan. *The Journal of Indian Management & Strategy*, *24*(4), 21–26.

Mapp, S., & Rice, K. (2019). Conducting rights-based short-term study abroad experiences. *Social Work Education*, *38*(4), 427–438.

Rajasthan Tourism Policy. (2020). Ministry of Tourism, Government of Rajasthan. https://www.tourism.rajasthan.gov.in/content/dam/rajasthan-tourism/english/homepage/topslider/Rajasthan%20Tourism%20Policy%202020.pdf. Accessed on May 25, 2022.

Rana, S., Sharma, D. K., & Paliwal, P. P. (2016). Ritual plants used by indigenous and ethnic societies of district Banswara (South Rajasthan), India. *American Journal of Ethnomedicine*, *3*(1), 26–34.

Sairam, S., & Thilagaraj, A. (2017). Tourism - Strength to Indian economy. *Indian Journal of Applied Research*, *7*(1), 710–712.

Sangwan, S. R., & Bhatia, M. P. S. (2020). Sustainable development in industry 4.0. In *A roadmap to industry 4.0: Smart production, sharp business and sustainable development* (pp. 39–56). Cham: Springer.

Sharma, A., & Arora, S. (2015). Impact of events on Rajasthan tourism with reference to different fairs and festivals. *International Journal of Economics*, *5*, 9–22.

Sharma, S., Sharma, B. K., Kulshreshtha, S., & Johri, S. (2013). Ecotourism in Rajasthan: Prospects and perspectives. In *Faunal heritage of Rajasthan, India: Conservation and management of vertebrates* (pp. 353–398).

Singh, S. (2005). Secular pilgrimages and sacred tourism in the Indian Himalayas. *GeoJournal*, *64*(3), 215–223.

Singh, K. (2019). Scope of Eco Tourism through strategic approach: A review study of Rajasthan (India). *Journal of Emerging Technologies and Innovative Research*, *6*(3), 927–937.

Srivastava, S. (2016). Asian journal of multidisciplinary studies. *Asian Journal of Multidisciplinary Studies*, *4*(1), 58.

Suwanna, A., Pisitsenakul, S., & Passadee, L. (2019). Participatory Research in Preparing Sustainable Tourism Strategy Plan in Head Watershed of Chiang Mai, Thailand (pp. 0–16). (conference paper).

Verma, S., & Murdia, M. (2017). Highlighting tribal tourism potentials of Southern Rajasthan. *IRA-International Journal of Management & Social Sciences*, *6*(3), 384–390.

Rebuilding Tourism Industry Through Sustainability Practices and Opportunities in the Postpandemic Era

Shivani Trivedi and Santosh K. Patra

Abstract

COVID-19 was the most catastrophic pandemic in modern history. It has a massive impact on people's lives and a variety of sectors. One of the most impacted sectors is the travel and tourism industry. The tourism business was the first to be severely impacted by the epidemic, which had a wide range of effects on other parts of society. As a result, studying tourists' behavior as a core aspect of this industry and predicting their travel pattern variation after the COVID-19 outbreak has become a critical concern. To understand the damaging effects of this global calamity on tourism, this book chapter focuses on the concerns and perspectives of multiple stakeholders. It conducts a thematic analysis to investigate travelers' perceptions and travel issues after the COVID-19 pandemic.

Keywords: Domestic tourism; tourism industry; COVID-19; pandemic; sustainability; tourist behavior

Introduction

In the fiscal year 2019–2020, the Indian tourism sector contributed significantly to India's GDP by around 6.8%. It is an employment zone and provides about 39 million jobs, which equals 8% of all employment in India (Murali, Syiemlieh, & Govindan, 2021). The COVID-19 lockdown and imposed limits rendered the world vulnerable to job losses and salary deductions. According to the National Council of Applied Economic Research (NCAER), the lockdown caused a loss of 14.5 million employment in the first region, 5.2 million jobs in the second sector, and 1.8 million jobs in the third zone of the 2020–2021 fiscal year (Mathur, 2021). Additionally, it significantly impacts India's economy and employment situation in the travel and tourism sector. To improve the situation, governments have

Resilient and Sustainable Destinations After Disaster, 287–298

Copyright © 2023 Shivani Trivedi and Santosh K. Patra

Published under exclusive licence by Emerald Publishing Limited

doi:10.1108/978-1-80382-021-720231021

developed programs that cover the entire financial system and are highly targeted at tourism.

Furthermore, to support the tourism business, the government started to prepare for the return of inbound tourism and increase adaptive rules (IBEF, 2022). Travelers are anxious to experience new places and relax in peaceful settings where they may take in the scenery and feel at ease. It also makes it possible for the tourism sector to employ sustainable practices. In addition, many visitors want to travel with groups that engage in more environmentally friendly, socially responsible, and biological activities; sustainable tourism is essential (Murali et al., 2021). Despite the epidemic's negative impact on corporate operations, nature and the environment have evolved in the right ways. People are becoming more conscious of their environment, networks, and financial well-being.

Tourists favor regional sites due to affordability. It enables people to live and work in a sustainable environment after the coronavirus pandemonium, making them feel rejuvenated and revived and supporting the companies in recovering from pandemic-related losses (Antoniou, 2021). Most people think of local travel when they envision camping nearby, taking a family vacation nearby, or traveling within their nation. It has become a catchphrase because it promotes sustainable tourism by supplying low-priced and safe tour options in the home tourism bubble (Goncalves, 2020). However, domestic tourism is overgrowing as tourists assume to travel within the territory and stay in properly managed properties (Menon, 2021). The requirements for visitor enhancement are based on long-term sustainability norms, such as social, moral, and cultural considerations. According to (Van Vu, Tran, Nguyen, & Van Nguyen, 2020) the tourism industry needs to put forth a concerted effort toward long-term development and integration, considering ethical, cultural, and organizational factors. It is essential that the sector carefully analyze how its actions affect cultural assets and develop policies that align with those considerations. This chapter will discuss implementing postpandemic sustainable practices and how they could benefit India's travel and tourism sector. The two primary objectives of this study are:

(1) To recognize the impact of COVID-19 on the tour plan of tourists and what are the issues vacationers are considering even as finalizing the tour vacation spot.
(2) To discover the role of sustainable tourism practices in postpandemic destination finalization choices and vacationer notions after the pandemic.

The epidemic has forced everyone to confront the environmental issues that people have exacerbated. Vacationers would hold a crucial role in ecological concerns following the outbreak. The chapter will focus on the challenges and opportunities facing the travel industry following the COVID-19 situation.

Literature Review

Risk Perception

The concept of risk in tourism refers to analyzing a scenario about the potential for choosing a tour, buying, and ingesting travel-related goods or services

(Reisinger & Mavondo, 2005). According to Sonmez and Graefe (1998), perceived tourist risk is separated into four categories: financial, psychological, cultural threat, and time. Mäser and Weiermair (1998) also divided tour threats into four categories: natural disasters, hygiene and infections, crimes and injuries, and health concerns (Richter, 2003). However, a visitor's risk perception is influenced by various factors, including personal attributes and demographic considerations (Carr, 2001). Different elements include external and internal factors, including media, various statistics resources, and surrounding affect groups (Lepp & Gibson, 2003). In addition, "perceived threat" refers to one perception of susceptibility to an ailment and the severity of that sickness (Floyd et al., 2000). Susceptibility is described as one's influence on the risk of getting a disease, whereas perceived severity is defined as one's assessment of the ailment's severity (Deroche, Stephan, Brewer, & Scanff, 2007). The higher a person's impression of an ailment's susceptibility and severity, the more likely they are to participate in conduct that reduces the risk of contracting it (Hoon Kwak & Dixon, 2008). Additionally, travelers are more cautious when traveling to any region far from their home during the pandemic and the risk of catching the dangerous disease.

Travel Anxiety

According to McIntyre and Roggenbuck (1998) stress or anxiety is a subjective experience that results from exposure to actual or potential risk. It is frequently characterized as a feeling of unease, tension, stress, vulnerability, discomfort, disturbance, worry, or panic. Tourists believe they are less safe and choose not to travel (Gudykunst, Wiseman, & Hammer, 1977). Regarding anxiety, the expression of fear might be seen or concealed through physical or mental issues (Sin & Scully, 2008). Fear is a psychological problem (trouble or situation related to the future), and it includes uncertainty, worry, panic, hypervigilance, impatience, fatigue, insomnia, derealization, and depersonalization. As a result, after the unforeseen pandemic hit, travelers were anxious even when traveling for a unique experience.

Protection Motivation Theory

The protection motivation theory (PMT) examines how people respond to stressful or dangerous life situations and how they make decisions during those times. Making these choices is a means of self-defense against imagined threats. The idea tries to clarify and forecast what drives people to alter their behavior (Communication Theory, 2018). To understand (or mediate) behavior related to one's health, Rogers (1975) developed the PMT, an affective and cognitive model of behavior. As a framework for investigating how fear appeals affect the quality of human life. According to PMT, it's threat- and coping-appraisal components are essential for conceptualizing health-related action (Rather, 2021).

The risk evaluation evaluates risk using the concepts of perceived severity and vulnerability (Wilson & Little, 2008). While perceived vulnerability refers to the likelihood of a dangerous event, perceived severity refers to the extent of harm to a person because of an occurrence (Rogers, 1975). Afterward, individuals undergo a coping-appraisal process where they assess chance-coping techniques based on reaction efficacy and self-efficacy. This theory ideally relates to the pandemic situation as to how visitors cope and evaluate the risk factors while traveling.

Theory of Planned Behavior

The theory of planned behavior (TPB) explains how people behave when they have a goal in mind. TPB has been utilized in various industries to understand human or individual behavior, including advertising, fitness, and tourism. One of the ideas used in sociopsychology theories that anticipate human intention and action is the TPB. It was developed with the theory of reasoned action (TRA) (Fishbein & Ajzen, 1977); attitude and subjective norms that impact behavior goals – that is, an impact on actual conduct – are the main factors influencing reasoned action. Consequently, perspective, subjective norm, and comprehension within the TPB, behavioral control, and behavioral goal are the primary topics for explanation (Ajzen & Fishbein, 2000).

The COVID-19 pandemic may influence how visitors conduct their tours and may try to avoid traveling owing to the threat of the disease (Gupta, Cahyanto, Sajnani, & Shah, 2023), acquire a risk due to an outbreak (Lu, Wang, Lin, & Li, 2020), and alter their travel objectives or mindset. It can be concluded from this session that tourist behavior can change beliefs about perceived risk perception, types of holiday places, and types of tourism (Li, Zhang, Liu, Kozak, & Wen, 2020). In the postpandemic situation, travelers strived to visit a location with a lower risk of illness spread and steer clear of areas with a high risk (Gössling, Humpe, Fichert, & Creutzig, 2021). The COVID-19 pandemic has caused changes in human behavior and mental states, such as anxiety, fear, and suspicion (Zheng, Luo, & Ritchie, 2021).

Perceived Effectiveness

The term "perceived effectiveness" describes how customers perceive the impact of their environmental preservation efforts or activities on reducing damage to the environment (Han & Yoon, 2015). An environment-friendly person is more perceptive to environmental issues, feels collectively accountable for the issues, values environmental protection, and believes that sustainable actions and behaviors effectively resolve the issues (Judge, Jackson, Shaw, Scott, & Rich, 2007). Consumers' perceptions of the efficacy of their conservation efforts and activities unquestionably affect their proenvironmental consumption decisions and behaviors toward tourism products (Han & Yoon, 2015).

Methodology

To investigate the study's objectives, a thorough examination of postpandemic literature, news report, and interviews of stakeholders were collected to understand how India's tourism industry is changing. We conducted in-depth interviews with a few stakeholders, including travel agencies, the hotel industry, and tourists, to support the claims and explore the elements that impacted the tourism business. The theme analysis framework is used to analyze the gathered data. The purpose of the investigation was to identify the opinions and concerns of travelers. For the personal interview, a deductive approach was taken to comprehend the behavioral changes that visitors experienced postpandemic. Purposive sampling was used to conduct semistructured interviews with each of the eight respondents from India, those who traveled to local places after the pandemic and for whom the questions had been prepared following the theories.

Demographic Profile of Respondents

S. No	Occupation	Gender
1	Working professional	Male
2	Homemaker	Female
3	Student	Female
4	Working professional	Female
5	Working professional	Female
6	Hotel staff	Male
7	Travel agent/Travel business	Male
8	Travel agent/Travel business	Male

Analysis

The information gathered through in-depth interviews was archived with the respondents' consent. Audio recordings of the meetings were utilized to foster word-to-word transcripts. At last, the notes and records were assessed to meet the research objective.

Thematic content analysis was used to examine the data. This method helps the researcher to study vast amounts of textual data by systematically finding attributes such as the most frequently used keywords and identifying important communication content structures (Vaismoradi, Jones, Turunen, & Snelgrove, 2016). The following are the results of the study mentioned in Table 1.

Results

Following the assessment of the information, a structure (Table 1) was made considering the respondents' experiences and perspectives. Sustainable travel aims to improve the local population's social and economic standing while preserving the environment. The idea seeks to encourage long-term behaviors that assist in

Table 1. Data Coding and Thematic Classifications.

Quotes	Codes	Themes
"Before planning the vacation after the pandemic, we first collected all the details of the place on Google. We just want to assure that no COVID cases are increasing there and it's safe." "We maintain all the safety precautions while traveling to Gujarat like sanitizer, masks and COVID reports."	Secure places Information about COVID cases Lower risk Maintain social distance	Safety and hygiene factors
"After the pandemic, tourists are looking for risk-free atmosphere and for those places which are eco-friendly and nearby to visit. They became conscious of the environment; guests also started taking healthy measures." "Staying at home for a long time after COVID-19, people eagerly look for vacation and friendly places to travel." "To overcome the loss of pandemic, staff have been decreased, and to maintain the losses, precautions for reducing wastage have been taken care of." "I am looking for more eco-friendly options while planning a holiday, where I can also connect with local communities." "With my family, I prefer relaxed and not-so-crowded places."	Conserve environment Eco-friendly location Avoid using plastic Less water supplies Support local communities Relaxed surrounding	Sustainable practises
"The government has created strict rules and regulations for international travelers. Travelers select regional places for the holiday to get additional benefits and fancy holidays in their own country." "Because of the pandemic, I have been at home for so long. I was waiting to get over this and calm my mind and soul in a changed atmosphere." "I prefer local travel as it is a more convenient and low-cost trip."	Government restrictions Local benefits Affordable	Budget-friendly travel

Source: Author.

maintaining ecosystems and the local way of life. The essential thing is that they focus much on education for visitors and the local population. The themes discussed are as follows.

Safety and Hygiene Factors

According to Nazneen, Hong, and Ud Din (2020), safety and a sense of hygiene are essential factors to consider when traveling. As a result, to boost tourism demand, the government and businesses in the tourism sector should maintain the security and hygiene of touristic housing, food, and beverage. When discussing their postpandemic travel experiences, most participants shared the same concern.

Participant X mentioned, "I am afraid to travel although the restrictions have already been relaxed. My family and I waited for two days to avoid the crowds and travel safely while visiting a temple in Jaipur."

Participant Y also said they had "checked all the safety precautions before leaving, all the basic hygiene items we carried with us."

While pandemic constraints are announced, professionals in the travel business should evaluate the level of danger consumers feel when making trip plans and adjust their marketing strategy accordingly. Tourism professionals should investigate the factors affecting postpandemic travel intentions. As noted in the literature section, travelers' perceptions of travel risk and anxiety related to travel were on the higher side. According to PMT, vacationers talked about how tourists made decisions in the challenging COVID-19 environment. They evaluate the danger associated with traveling and how it might affect their judgment while making decisions.

Sustainable Practices and Government Initiatives

After the pandemic, everyone became more responsible and careful about the environment, and the United Nations' Sustainable Development Goals call for everyone to commit to achieving their aims by 2030 (Stombelli, 2020). Economic advancement, social progress, and environmental preservation are the three fundamental objectives of sustainability (Hakovirta & Denuwara, 2020). Travelers prefer domestic routes and believe in helping the local economy by buying goods from the residents.

Creating sustainable business environments that are beneficial to businesses is part of enhancing the lives of all living beings (Stombelli, 2020). When asked about sustainable practices after COVID-19, participants in the hotel industry also mentioned that they were searching for realistic solutions to minimize waste and conserve resources.

Participant Z said, "We avoid using plastic water bottles in the hotel and start providing eco-friendly disposable items to care for the hygiene issues and maintain sustainable practices."

Participant B mentioned, "I am receiving more demands for domestic tours after the pandemic, as it is feasible to travel locally with fewer restrictions and good government support for local places."

Moreover, the government has also created a few initiatives to encourage domestic travel using sustainable methods. Many tourism businesses understand the value of continuous conservation efforts to the visitor experience; more should be prompted to do so. Companies would be pushed to preserve habitats on their land and contribute financially or in kind to regional conservation efforts to support biodiversity. Tourists can also contribute financially to conservation efforts, becoming an increasingly significant source of cash. Visitors can also engage in beneficial activities, like taking conservation holidays. It should be simple and available for travelers to include sustainable in-destination activities and services in their trip plans (Ministry of Tourism | Government of India, 2022).

Additionally, TPB is used in the literature to describe how the epidemic changed people's behavior. The traveler feels guilty since they could contribute to the spreading a disease or harm the environmental resources. Following the pandemic, they adopted more responsible behaviors and altered their travel patterns to earn a living. They do this by gathering resources and providing support to the locals.

Budget-Friendly Travel and Local Community

Compared to international travel, there are fewer domestic or neighboring travel restrictions. Participants agreed that overseas travel is expensive and are entitled to more benefits and exceptionally luxurious services in their home countries. Providing the visitor with a different tour package also helps prevent over-crowding and creates extra comfort for the guest. After the unexpected circum-stances of an epidemic, international travel is risky and costly. Additionally, travelers can organize their journey for a long or short time when traveling locally. Although group travel is more affordable and enjoyable, it has become more popular since the pandemic.

As discussed by participant A, "Post pandemic condition, visitors are asking for a group travel package, so that their travel expenses will be less, and they can have more fun time with their friends and family."

However, hotels are also accommodating guests with affordable packages to cover their losses. The apparent effectiveness in the literature suggested that travelers were more environmentally conscious, believed in helping the local population survive after the epidemic, and did not want to destroy the natural resources in the wake of the COVID-19 pandemic attack. This opportunity will allow the locals to stay because many lost their way of life to COVID-19.

Managerial Implications

Planning should, in our opinion, be more comprehensive, inclusive, equitable, adaptive, and centered on what tourism and outdoor recreation sustain. Post pandemic, the industry experiences an increase due to the ongoing move toward ecotourism, a rapidly expanding sector focusing on environmental protection and local job development.

Another significant role technology plays in the tourism sector. Automation has been brought about by the use of technology to get rid of monotonous chores. Additionally facilitates online reviews, criticism, and suggestions. The tourist and hospitality sectors should apply the following initiatives in the wake of the pandemic.

- Creating eco-friendly travel and lodging options for guests.
- Developing travel regulations and community-building strategies.
- Enhancing local excursions to cultural places while conserving heritage sites.
- Offering attractive packages for extended stays during group visits.
- Using technology to give tourists assurance about their protection and security.

All stakeholders must involve and cooperate for the smooth functioning of the travel industry in the postpandemic scenario. While developing any travel policy, local communities should be encouraged to offer their views and support. Additionally, the government should maintain procedures for the travel industry while focusing on economic, social, and environmental issues to ensure the sustainability of the implementation.

Discussion

The sudden pandemic attack has entirely changed how people perceive it. Significant changes have been made in their attitudes and actions. People no longer desire challenging or risky travel over a period, and they now schedule their trips according to the level of risk. They constantly feared disease, uncertainty, and anxiety for a year. To be more mindful of these components and to address these challenges in the post-COVID-19 climate, it is crucial to rethink nature-based tourism and recreational activities. As a result, the travel business, hospitality sector, and destination management organizations (DMOs) could prepare all the criteria linked to security and healthy living.

The experience and mindset of anticipated holidaymakers following the pandemic were the top issues and initiatives of the present chapter. The themes that emerged from analyzing the in-depth insights of stakeholders include that the travel business will continue to expand since traveling is necessary for keeping people more relaxed and rejuvenated, not just because it is a demand. Still, after the outbreak, each person needs to practice mindfulness.

References

Ajzen, I., & Fishbein, M. (2000). Attitudes and the attitude-behavior relation: Reasoned and automatic processes. *European Review of Social Psychology, 11*(1), 1–33. doi:10.1080/14792779943000116

Antoniou, K. (2021). Post-pandemic travel: The trends we'll see when the world opens up again. *The Conversation.* Retrieved from https://theconversation.com/post-pandemic-travel-the-trends-well-see-when-the-world-opens-up-again-153401

Carr, N. (2001). An exploratory study of gendered differences in young tourists perception of danger within London. *Tourism Management, 22*(5), 565–570.

Communication Theory. (2018). Communication theory. Retrieved from https://www.communicationtheory.org/protection-motivation-theory/

Covid impact of tourism: 14.5 million jobs lost in 2020's Q1 alone. (2021). *The Economic Times.*

Deroche, T., Stephan, Y., Brewer, B. W., & Scanff, C. Le. (2007). Predictors of perceived susceptibility to sport-related injury. *Personality and Individual Differences, 43*(8), 2218–2228. doi:10.1016/j.paid.2007.06.031

Domestic tourism is reviving as visitors again throng popular destinations, even pilgrimage centres. (2021). *The Economic Times.* Retrieved from https://economictimes.indiatimes.com/industry/services/travel/domestic-tourism-is-reviving-as-visitors-again-thron

Fishbein, M., & Ajzen, I. (1977). Belief, attitude, intention, and behavior: An introduction to theory and research. *Philosophy and Rhetoric, 10*(2).

Floyd, D. L., Prentice-Dunn, S., & Rogers, R. W. (2000). A meta-analysis of research on protection motivation theory. *Journal of Applied Social Psychology, 30*(2), 407–429.

Goncalves, A. (2020). What is staycation: Discover the latest trend in sustainable tourism. *Youmatter.* Retrieved from https://youmatter.world/en/staycation-definition-stay-vacations-sustainable/

Gössling, S., Humpe, A., Fichert, F., & Creutzig, F. (2021). COVID-19 and pathways to low-carbon air transport until 2050. *Environmental Research Letters, 16*(3), 034–063.

Gudykunst, W. B., Wiseman, R. L., & Hammer, M. (1977). Determinants of the Sojourner's attitudinal satisfaction: A path model. *Annals of the International Communication Association, 1*(1), 415–425. doi:10.1080/23808985.1977.11923696

Gupta, V., Cahyanto, I., Sajnani, M., & Shah, C. (2023). Changing dynamics and travel evading: a case of Indian tourists amidst the COVID 19 pandemic. *Journal of Tourism Futures, 9*(1), 84–100.

Hakovirta, M., & Denuwara, N. (2020). How COVID-19 redefines the concept of sustainability. *Sustainability, 12*(9), 3727.

Han, H., & Yoon, H. J. (2015). Hotel customers' environmentally responsible behavioral intention: Impact of key constructs on decision in green consumerism. *International Journal of Hospitality Management, 45*, 22–33.

Hoon Kwak, Y., & Dixon, C. K. (2008). Risk management framework for pharmaceutical research and development projects. *International Journal of Managing Projects in Business, 1*(4), 552–565. doi:10.1108/17538370810906255

IBEF. (2022, September). *Indian tourism - India's tourism sector on the rise | IBEF.* India Brand Equity Foundation. Retrieved from https://www.ibef.org/blogs/indias-tourism-sector-on-the-rise

Judge, T. A., Jackson, C. L., Shaw, J. C., Scott, B. A., & Rich, B. L. (2007). Self-efficacy and work-related performance: The integral role of individual differences. *Journal of Applied Psychology, 92*(1), 107.

Lepp, A., & Gibson, H. (2003). Tourist roles, perceived risk and international tourism. *Annals of Tourism Research, 30*(3), 606–624. doi:10.1016/S0160-7383(03)00024-0

Li, Z., Zhang, S., Liu, X., Kozak, M., & Wen, J. (2020). Seeing the invisible hand: Underlying effects of COVID-19 on tourists' behavioral patterns. *Journal of Destination Marketing & Management, 18*(October), 100502. doi:10.1016/j.jdmm. 2020.100502

Lu, W., Wang, H., Lin, Y., & Li, L. (2020). Psychological status of medical workforce during the COVID-19 pandemic: A cross-sectional study. *Psychiatry Research, 288*, 112936.

Mäser, B., & Weiermair, K. (1998). Travel decision-making: From the vantage point of perceived risk and information preferences. *Journal of Travel & Tourism Marketing, 7*(4), 107–121. doi:10.1300/J073v07n04_06

Mathur, S. (2021). Covid impact of tourism: 14.5 million jobs lost in 2020's Q1 alone. *Times of India*. Retrieved from https://timesofindia.indiatimes.com/business/india-business/covid-impact-of-tourism-14-5-million-jobs-lost-in-2020s-q1-alone/articleshow/84573975.cms

McIntyre, N., & Roggenbuck, J. W. (1998). Nature/person transactions during an outdoor adventure experience: A multi-phasic analysis. *Journal of Leisure Research, 30*(4), 401–422. doi:10.1080/00222216.1998.11949841

Menon. (2021). Domestic tourism is reviving as visitors again throng popular destinations, even pilgrimage centres. *The Economic Times*. Retrieved from https://economictimes.indiatimes.com/industry/services/travel/domestic-tourism-is-reviving-as-visitors-agai

Ministry of Tourism | Government of India. (2022). Retrieved from https://tourism. gov.in/sites/default/files/2022-05/National%20Strategy%20for%20Sustainable% 20tourism.pdf

Murali, Syiemlieh, & Govindan. (2021). Tourism in the new normal post COVID-19: Is eco-tourism the solution? TERI. Retrieved from https://www.teriin.org/article/tourism-new-normal-post-covid-19-eco-tourism-solution

Nazneen, S., Hong, X., & Ud Din, N. (2020). COVID-19 crises and tourist travel risk perceptions. Available at SSRN 3592321.

Rather, R. A. (2021). Demystifying the effects of perceived risk and fear on customer engagement, co-creation and revisit intention during COVID-19: A protection motivation theory approach. *Journal of Destination Marketing & Management, 20*, 100564.

Reisinger, Y., & Mavondo, F. (2005). Travel anxiety and intentions to travel internationally: Implications of travel risk perception. *Journal of Travel Research, 43*(3), 212–225. doi:10.1177/0047287504272017

Richter, L. K. (2003). International tourism and its global public health consequences. *Journal of Travel Research, 41*(4), 340–347. doi:10.1177/0047287503041004002

Rogers, R. W. (1975). A protection motivation theory of fear appeals and attitude change1. *The Journal of Psychology, 91*(1), 93–114.

Sin, J., & Scully, E. (2008). An evaluation of education and implementation of psychosocial interventions within one UK mental healthcare trust: Practice development. *Journal of Psychiatric and Mental Health Nursing, 15*(2), 161–169. doi:10. 1111/j.1365-2850.2007.01202.x

Sonmez, S. F., & Graefe, A. R. (1998). Determining future travel behavior from past travel experience and perceptions of risk and safety. *Journal of Travel Research, 37*(2), 171–177. doi:10.1177/004728759803700209

Stombelli, V. M. (2020). Corporate social responsibility in hospitality: Are sustainability initiatives really sustainable? Case examples from CitizenM, Lefay and Six Senses. *Worldwide Hospitality and Tourism Themes, 12*(5), 525–545. doi:10.1108/WHATT-06-2020-0041

Tourism & Hospitality Industry in India. (2022). IBEF.

Vaismoradi, M., Jones, J., Turunen, H., & Snelgrove, S. (2016). Theme development in qualitative content analysis and thematic analysis. *Journal of Nursing Education and Practice, 6*(5). doi:10.5430/jnep.v6n5p100

Van Vu, D., Tran, G. N., Nguyen, H. T. T., & Van Nguyen, C. (2020). Factors affecting sustainable tourism development in Ba Ria-Vung Tau, Vietnam. *Journal of Asian Finance, Economics and Business, 7*(9), 561–572. doi:10.13106/JAFEB.2020.VOL7.NO9.561

Wilson, E., & Little, D. E. (2008). A "relative escape"? The impact of constraints on women who travel solo. *Tourism Review International, 9*(2), 155–175. doi:10.3727/154427205774791672

Zheng, D., Luo, Q., & Ritchie, B. W. (2021). Afraid to travel after COVID-19? Self protection, coping and resilience against pandemic "travel fear." *Tourism Management, 83*(October 2020), 104261. doi:10.1016/j.tourman.2020.104261

Zheng, B., Zhang, Q., Geng, G., Chen, C., Shi, Q., Cui, M., ... He, K. (2021). Changes in China's anthropogenic emissions and air quality during the COVID-19 pandemic in 2020. *Earth System Science Data, 13*(6), 2895–2907.

Index

Accommodation sector, 80–81, 90
Aceh Tsunami Museum, 101
ADB, forecast by, 113–114
Administrative environmentalism, 14
Agenda for Sustainability and
    Development and the Paris
    Climate Change Summit,
    2030, 44–45
Agritourism, 281–282
Air Zimbabwe, 81–82
Airports Council International (ACI),
    22
Alliance of Religion Conservation,
    139–140
Anchor investments, 42–43
Arouca Geopark, 48–49
Arouca Geopark Association, 58
Asia, 110–112
    change in GDP due to COVID-19,
        111–112
    Europe and Asian hospitality
        industry economical stats,
        112
    forecast by ADB, 113–114
    recommendations, 117–118
    strategies opted for rebuilding
        tourism after COVID-19
        pandemic in Asia, 114–117
Asian Pacific Context, post-disaster
    tourism in, 99–101
Attracting and Retaining Youth in
    Agriculture (ARYA), 282
Attraction, Accommodation,
    Accessibility, Amenities,
    and Activities (5 A), 189
Augmented reality, 35, 246–247
Average variance extracted (AVE),
    147–148
Awareness, 158, 171

Ayurveda, 235

Balanced business method, 43
Behavioral issue (BI), 145–146
Bhil community, 279
Black tourism, 97–98
Bramhacharya, 234–235
Brand development, 68
Branding, 71
Budget-friendly travel, 294
Bulawayo Cultural Festival, 65–66

Capitalist conservationism, 16
CARE mode and relevance to Oman
    tourism, 169
Central movement control orders
    (CMCO), 90
Chibuku Neshamwari Dance Festival,
    65–66
Chimanimani Arts Festival, 65–66
Climate change, 277–278
Cluster concept, 42
Cocos nucifera, 280
Communication, 69
    information flow works, 167–168
    significance of communication in
        community engagement,
        165–167
    strategy, 105
Community communication, 174
Community engagement, significance
    of communication in,
    165–167
Community participation, 102
Community-based recovery,
    105–106
Community-led approaches, 102
Comprehensive communication
    strategy, 167–168

Comprehensive systematic reviews, 182–183
Consolidation, 78
Convergence, 42
Corporate identification as well as genetic structure, 11–13
Costa Rica Tourism Institute, 206
Council of Ministers, 204
Country-of-origin effect, 129
Covergent validity, 148–149
COVID appropriate behavior (CAB), 128
COVID-19, 4, 19–20, 88, 109–111, 113–114, 116–117, 287–288
  change in GDP due to, 111–112
  effects of covid-19 pandemic on tourism, 20–21
  global guidelines to restart tourism, 23–25
  outbreak, 21, 114, 116, 157–158
  pandemic, 19–21, 121, 126, 157–158, 183, 195, 217, 241–242, 251–252, 268, 290
  pandemic crisis, 25–26
  priorities for tourism recovery, 21–23
  restarting strategies in destinations after, 21–25
  strategies opted for rebuilding tourism after COVID-19 pandemic in Asia, 114–117
Crises, 1
Crisis management, 104–105, 268–270
  practices, 269
Cross-cutting measures, 24
Cruise Lines International Association (CLIA), 22
Cultural heritage, 280–281
Culture, 281
Cumulative Resilience, 126–127

Dark tourism, 97–98, 102
Databases, 4, 182
Decarbonisation, 16
Demand–supply cycle, 123

Destination Consultancy Group, The, 82–83
Destination Management Organizations (DMOs), 104–105, 199, 295
Destination marketing, 130
  in Zimbabwe, 78–80
Destination Marketing Organizations (DMOs), 9–10, 69, 79–80
  role of, 82–83
Destinations, 26, 251–252
  image, 64
  management, 97–98, 199
  marketers, 64, 70
  strategy, 218
Development
  of ecotourism, 283
  of infrastructure, 282–283
Dharma, 234
Dhofar Municipality, 160
Differentiated methodological individualism, 13–14
Digital communication, 158
Digitalization process, 23
Disasters, 2–3, 6–7, 98
  knowledge, 105
  in tourism, 195
Divergent validity, 148–149
Document analysis technique, 5
Domestic tourism, 288
Doom tourism, 97–98

e-Medical Attendant Visa, 124–125
EBSCO, 4
Ecological Threat Register (2020) (ETR), 99
Economic autonomy, 43
Economic capital, 99
Economic sustainability, 45
Ecotourism, 253–254, 278
  challenges, 283
  industry, 13–14
  potential of region, 279–282
  socioeconomic perspectives and sustainability, 282–283
  study area, 278–279

Electronic guides, 245
e–Medical Visa, 124–125
Emerald, 271
Employability, 42
Entrepreneurial approach, 267–268
Environmental management, 14
Epidemics, 2
Essential uncertainty, 12–13
Europe and Asian Hospitality Industry
    Economical Stats, 112
  travel and tourism share regionwise,
    112
European Geoparks Network (EGN),
    48–49
European space, 47
European Union, 47
Event brand communication, tourism
    festival and, 69
Event brand development, tourism
    festival and, 68
Event brand implementation, tourism
    festival and, 69
Event brand tracking, tourism festival
    and, 70
Event destination brand awareness,
    tourism festival and, 70–71
Event destination brand equity,
    Zimbabwe tourism festival
    and, 70–72
Event destination brand image,
    tourism festival and, 71
Event destination brand loyalty,
    tourism festival and, 71–72
Event destination brand positioning,
    tourism festival and, 68
Event destination brand quality,
    perceived tourism festival
    and, 71
Event destination branding process,
    67–70
Event destination market analysis,
    tourism festival and,
    67–68
Event destination personality, tourism
    festival and, 68–69

Faith tourism, 140–141

Fear, 289
Five-point Likert scale, 143–144
Forests, 280
Fornell–Larcker Criterion, 148–149
Future tourism, perspective of, 256

Geographical Information System
    (GIS), 282–283
Geoparks, 48, 58
Global Guidelines to Restart Tourism,
    32–33
Global guidelines to restart tourism,
    23–25
Global health emergency, 19–20
Global innovation ecosystem, 23
Global Tourism Crisis Committee, 20
  of WTO, 21
Google Scholar, 4, 182, 271
Government, 124–125
Government Communication Centre,
    158–159
Government of India, 124–125
Great Depression, 76–77
Great East Japan earthquake and
    tsunami (2011), 101
Green tourism, 81
Grihasth, 234–235
Gross Domestic Product (GDP),
    251–252
  GDP due to COVID-19, change in,
    111–112

Haats, 282
Harare International Festival of Arts
    (HIFA), 65–66
Harare International Food Festival,
    65–66
Healthcare sector, 125
Healthcare system, 125
Healthcare tourism, 133–134
Healthcare workers (HCWs), 123
Heritage Reserve Platform, 48
Heterogeneous constructionist method,
    10–11
Heterotrait–Monotrait Ratio
    (HTMT), 148–149
Hindu pilgrim centers, 143–144

Hinduism, 140–141
Hong Kong's hospitality industry, 270
Hospitality, 24, 267–268
  industry, 270–271
  sector, 112
Hotel industry, 267–268
  background, 269–270
  future research directions, 272
  solutions and recommendations,
     271–272
Hotline for Tourism Micro-Business
     Liquidity, 205
HTMT ratio, 148–149
Human capital, 99

Image-building process, 174
India's tourism industry, 290–291
Indian Ocean earthquake, The, 101
Indian tourism sector, 287–288
Indigenous medicine, 122–123
Industry, 9–10
Industry 4.0, 241–242
Information and communication
     technologies (ICTs), 26,
     243–244, 251–252
Information devices, 246
Information-oriented (IO), 145–146
Infrastructural issue (INI), 145–146
Innovative tourism, 166, 173
Institutional capital, 99
Integrated risk management, principles
     of, 270
Interdisciplinary research approaches,
     130
Internal marketing process flow, 125
International Air Transport
     Association (IATA), 22
International Civil Aviation
     Organization (ICAO), 22
International Labor Organization
     (ILO), 22
International Maritime Organization
     (IMO), 22
International Monetary Fund (IMF),
     19–20
International tourism, 20

sector, 20
International tourists, 21
International Year of Sustainable
     Tourism, 44
Intwasa Arts Festival koBulawayo,
     65–66

Jikinya Dance Festival, 65–66
Jiuzhaigou National Scenic Spot, 101

Kalpa Virksha (*see Cocos nucifera*)
Karma, 234
Kiosk, 246

Local community, 166, 294
Local resiliency knowledge, 105
Local tourism, 99
Long-term economic viability, 44
Low–density territories, 42

Mahi Bajaj Sagar Reservoir, 280
Mahua flowers (*Madhuca longifolia*),
     282
Management ecology, 14–16
Market analysis, 67–68
Market-led approach, 141–142
Marketing strategies, 3
Media, 69
Medical tourism ecosystem, 123–124
Medical Value Travel (MVT), 122–123
Medical Visa, 124–125
Meditation, 228–229
Medium-term recovery plans, 200
Micro clusters, 42–43
Midlands Arts and Culture Festival,
     65–66
Millennium Development Goals
     (MDGs), 10–11
Millennium Improvement Goals
     (MIGs), 10
Ministry Of Environment, 10–11
Ministry of Heritage and
     Tourism, The, 158,
     169, 170
Ministry of Tourism, The (MoT),
     124–125, 153

Mission Unit for the Enhancement of the Interior (UMVI), 48
Mobile technologies, 245–246
Mobile tourist guides, 245
Monetary issue (MI), 145–146
Monkeypox, 109–110, 113
Movement control orders (MCO), 90

National Arts Council of Zimbabwe (NACZ), 65–66
National Council of Applied Economic Research (NCAER), 287–288
National differentiated approach, 88–89
National innovation ecosystem, 23
National Program for Territorial Cohesion (PNCT), 42
National Recovery and Resilience Plan, 203–204
National UNESCO Commission, 49
Natural environment, 280
Neoliberal approaches, 15–16
Neoliberalism scientific management, 15
New offerings, comparative analysis of old and, 89–90
New public management (*see* Neoliberalism scientific management)
Niche tourism, 181
Nontherapeutic medical tourism, 122–123
Nvivo software, 5

Oil Crisis, 76–77
Oman
    CARE mode and relevance to Oman tourism, 169
    communication information flow works, 167–168
    findings and results, 173–174
    implications and future direction, 174–175
    limitations and directions for future studies, 175
    methodology, 169–170
    overall sultanate tourists' data from 2010 to 2018, 160–164
    significance of communication in community engagement, 165–167
    as spectacular tourist destination, 158–160
    tourism, 157–159
Oman government, The, 165, 167
Omran (Oman tourism development company), 160
Online traveling agencies, 117–118
Open Skies Agreement, 256
Overtourism destinations, 253–254

Pacific tourism, 201–202
Pakistan Hotel Association (PHA), 267–268
Pandemics, 2–3, 6–7, 110–111, 227–228
    comparative analysis of old and new offerings, 89–90
    of COVID-19, 113
    recommendations and future avenues, 92
Passenger locator forms (PLFs), 90
People's Republic of China (PRC), 113
Perceived effectiveness, 290
Perceived severity and vulnerability, 289–290
Personal Protective Equipment (PPEs), 125
Pilgrimage tourism, 140–141
Political sustainability, 45
Post-COVID destinations, 214
Post-COVID-19 tourism
    lessons to destinations for senior tourism in, 218–219
    recovery, 214
Post-disaster, 229
    methodology and research questions, 228
    RQs, 229
    spirituality and yoga, 232–236
    tourism, 236–238

well-being, 229, 232, 236, 238
Post-disaster tourism, 98
  in Asian Pacific Context, 99–101
  definition and concepts of, 98–99
  development, 104–105
  framework development on resilient
    and sustainable
    communities, 102–106
  parameters of, 99
Postpandemic era, 130
Postpandemic tourism transformation,
  255–256
Pranayam, 235
Principal Component Analysis (PCA),
  47–48
Product planning, 182–183
ProQuest, 4
Protection motivation theory (PMT),
  289–290
Publicity crisis
  accommodation sector, 80–81
  destination marketing in Zimbabwe,
    78–80
  exploring tourism globally, 76–78
  role of DMO, 82–83
  travel sector, 81–82
Public–private partnerships (PPPs), 4,
  169, 189

Qualitative method, 5
Quantitative method, 5

RACE Model, 174
Rajasthan, 279
Rajasthan Tourism Policy, 280–281
Rebuilding tourism after COVID-19
    pandemic in Asia, strategies
    opted for, 114–117
Recovery
  case study, 183–186
  methodology, 182–183
  purpose of study, 182
  responsible sustainable tourism
    product planning and
    design, 188–190
Recovery plans, 196

and strategies of countries, 199–206
Regenerative tourism, 251–252
  background, 252–254
  conceptual framework of research
    study, 256–260
  methodology, 259–260
  natural maturation of sustainability,
    253
  nature's principles, 253–254
  priorities, and implications, 260–264
  review of literature, 254, 256,
    261–262
Regional competitiveness, 42
Regional movement control orders
    (RMCO), 90
Regional policy objectives, 42
Religious heritage, 280–281
Religious tourism, 140–141
ResearchGate, 271
Resilience, 126–127, 196–197
  in tourism, 198–199
Resilient and sustainable destinations,
  3
Resilient communities, framework
    development on, 102–106
Resilient ecosystem for medical
    tourism, 127
Resilient medical tourism
  appropriateness of service triangle
    model, 125
  aspects of medical tourism, 122–123
  concept of medical tourism,
    122–123
  implications, 130–134
  pull and push factors relevant with
    medical tourism, 123
  rationale and relevance of WRQoL,
    126
  recommendations, 126–134
  role and relevance of various
    stakeholders, 124–125
  synthesis, 127–130
  theoretical background, 123–126
Resilient medical tourism ecosystem,
  123–124
Resilient tourism communities, 97–98

Resource management, 14
Responsible sustainable tourism
    product planning and
        design, 188–190
Responsible tourism, 180
    concept of, 180
    product development, 189
Restart tourism, global guidelines to,
        23–25
Restarting strategies in destinations
        after COVID-19 pandemic,
        21–25
Robotization, 246

Sacred tourism, 140–141
Sanatana Dharma, 140–141
Sanyas, 234–235
SARS-CoV-2, 268
Scale techniques, 143–144
Scopus, 182
Security and safety (SS), 145–146
Semantic scale, 143–144
Senior tourism, 214–215
    lessons to destinations for senior
        tourism in post-COVID-19,
        218–219
    policy implications for tourism
        sector, 215–216
    seniors and, 216–218
Service businesses, 183
Service marketing concepts, 125
Service triangle model, appropriateness
        of, 125
Shoko Festival, 65–66
Short-term actions, 199–200
Sky Policy, 256
Small and medium-sized enterprises
        (SMEs), 29, 31, 100–101,
        199
Small-scale economies, 42–43
Smart applications, 245–246
Smart city concept, 26
Smart City Wheel model, 28
Smart destinations (SDs), 20, 25–26, 29
    benefits of SDs considering
        restarting strategies, 21–23

effects of Covid-19 pandemic on
        tourism, 20–21
    literature review, 20–21
    restarting strategies in destinations
        after COVID-19 pandemic,
        21–25
Smart economy, 27, 29, 31
Smart environment, 27–28, 32–33
Smart governance, 27, 31–32
Smart living, 28, 33
Smart mobility, 27, 32
Smart people, 27, 32
Smart tourism, 242
    issues, challenges, and
        opportunities, 243–247
    literature review, 242–243
Social capital, 99
Social capitalism, 102–103
Social isolation, 116–117
Social Mention (semantic search
        engines), 143
Social well-being, 229–230
Sociedad Mercantil Estatal para la
        Gestión de la Innovación y
        las Tecnologías Turísticas
        (SEGITTUR), 26–27
Solutions, Information, Value, and
        Access (SIVA model), 128
Spatial sustainability, 45
Spiritual tourism, 140–141
Spirituality, 228–229, 232, 236
Stagnation, 78
Stakeholders, 47, 123–124, 181,
        189–190
    role and relevance of various,
        124–125
Standard operating procedures (SOPs),
        90–92
Strategic approach, 4
Strategic Initiatives & Government
        Advisory (SIGA), 140–141
Structural equation modeling (SEM),
        141–142
Sultanate tourists data from 2010 to
        2018, 160–164
Super Typhoon Rolly, 100–101

Susceptibility, 288–289
Sustainability, 45, 277–278
Sustainable communities, framework
     development on, 102–106
Sustainable design concepts, 182
Sustainable development
  applied to territories, 44–45
  in tourism, 45, 181–182
Sustainable Development Goals
     (SDGs), 44–45, 181–182,
     277–278
Sustainable Improvement Goals
     (SIGs), 10
Sustainable local tourism communities,
     4
Sustainable pilgrimages, 142
Sustainable resource management,
     32–33
Sustainable Smart Cities Initiative
     groups, The, 27–28
Sustainable tourism, 2, 15–16, 181,
     251–252, 288
  communities, 97–98
  corporate identification as well as
     genetic structure, 11–13
  differentiated methodological
     individualism, 13–14
  indicators, 46
  as management ecology, tourism
     and SIGs, 14–16
  product, 181
Systematic scoping review, 182–183

Technology, 242
Territorial cooperation, 42
Territories, sustainable development
     applied to, 44–45
Thailand Special Tourist Visa, 205
Thematic content analysis, 291
Theory of planned behavior (TPB), 290
Therapeutic medical tourism,
     122–123
Tour operators, 24
Tourism, 1–2, 14, 16, 26, 44, 88, 98–99,
     109–110, 140–141, 169, 180,
     236, 238, 251–252, 277–278

  comparative analysis of old and new
     offerings, 89–90
  development, 103–104
  effects of Covid-19 pandemic on,
     20–21
  enterprises, 196
  establishments, 197
  industry, 228
  micro cluster, 43
  planning, 180
  policymakers, 9–10
  recommendations and future
     avenues, 92
  risk in, 288–289
  scholars, 9–10
  sector, 2, 21, 33, 35, 117–118,
     267–268, 288
  tourism-steered economic growth,
     277–278
  types, 290
Tourism agencies, 190
Tourism Area Life Cycle (TALC),
     75–76
Tourism business, 89, 142–143, 196,
     288
  management, 189
Tourism destinations, 76–77, 214
  management, 50
  marketing, 80
Tourism festival
  concept, 63–64
  and event brand communication, 69
  and event brand development, 68
  and event brand implementation, 69
  and event destination brand
     awareness, 70–71
  and event destination brand image,
     71
  and event destination brand image
     in Zimbabwe, 64
  and event destination brand loyalty,
     71–72
  and event destination brand
     positioning, 68
  and event destination market
     analysis, 67–68

and event destination personality, 68–69
process, 67–70
tourism festival and event brand tracking, 70
Tourism industry, 1–2, 10, 99, 112, 121–122, 269, 278
analysis, 291
budget-friendly travel and local community, 294
demographic profile of respondents, 291
literature review, 288–289
managerial implications, 294–295
methodology, 290–291
perceived effectiveness, 290
PMT, 289–290
results, 291–294
risk perception, 288–289
safety and hygiene factors, 293
sustainable practices and government initiatives, 293–294
TPB, 290
travel anxiety, 289
Tourism Life Cycle (TLC), 75–76
Tourism products, 181, 282
development, 189
Tourism recovery, 103–104
priorities for, 21–23
Tourism share regionwise (2019), 112
Tourism stakeholders, 167–168
Tourism Strategic Plan (2027), 46
Tourism Strategy (2027), 49–50
Tourism sustainability, 44
indicators, 45–55
Tourism sustainable planning
sustainable development applied to territories, 44–45
tourism sustainability indicators, 45–55
Tourist guides, 242
general view, 242–243
issues, challenges, and opportunities, 243–247

literature review, 242–243
Tourists, 89, 242, 288–289, 294
behavior, 181–182, 290
destinations, 25–26
industry, 12
stakeholders, 180
Tourists' harassment during pilgrimage
data analysis, 149–152
methodology, 142–149
objectives of study, 142
outcomes of study, 152
review of literatures, 140–142
suggestions, recommendations, and future scope of study, 153–154
Transformative tourism, 255–256
Transition, 98
Travel agencies, 24
Travel anxiety, 289
Travel planning, 241–242
Travel sector, 81–82
Travel sector, 117–118
Travel share regionwise (2019), 112
Traveler locator's forms (TLF), 90
Travelers, 288
Tribal art, 281
Tribal communities, 279
TripAdvisor, 142–143, 152
reviews, 143–144
website, 4–5
Triple bottom line, 133–134
Tropic of Cancer, 280
Tropical Cyclone Pam, 100
Tsunami Educational Park, 101
Tsunami hit Aceh, 101
Tsunami Inundation Monuments, 101

UN 2040 Agenda for Sustainable Development, 10
UN body, 9–10
UN's official International Year of Sustainable Tourism for Advancement, 9–10
UNESCO Geoparks, 44–45
UNESCO National Community, 50

United Arab Emirates (UAE), 109–110
United Nations (UN), 44, 181–182
  Organization, 44–45
  Sustainable Development Goals,
    293
United Nations Conference on Trade
    and Development
    (UNCTAD), 114, 116,
    259–260
United Nations World Tourism
    Organization (UNWTO), 3,
    10–11, 14–16, 44, 180,
    271–272
  World Tourism Barometer, 157–158
United States Agency for International
    Development (USAID),
    76–77

Vagad region, 279–280
Value chain creation process, 124
Vanprasth, 234–235
Vanuatu Tourism Office (VTO), 100
Victoria Falls, 77
Vipasana, 235
Virtual accessibility, 219
Virtual museums, 245
Virtual reality, 35
Virtual tourism, 219
Volatile, uncertain, complex, and
    ambiguous (VUCA), 5
Vulnerability in tourism, 195–197

Web of Science, 182
Well-being, 229–232
  elements, 230
Wellness medical tourism, 122–123
Wordle. com (semantic search
    engines), 143
Work-Related Quality of Life
    (WRQoL), 125
  rationale and relevance of, 126
World Bank (WB), 22
World Commission and Environment
    and Development, The, 44
World Economic Forum, 44

World Federation of Professional
    Tourist Guide Associations
    (WFTGA), 242–243
World Health Organization (WHO),
    19–20, 110–111, 229–230
World Tourism Organization (WTO),
    157–158, 277–278
World Travel and Tourism Council
    (WTTC), 10

Yoga, 228–229, 232, 236

Zimbabwe, 76–77
  destination marketing in, 78–80
  tourism destination marketing,
    79–80
  tourism festival and event
    destination brand image in,
    64
  tourism industry, 79–80
Zimbabwe International Film Festival,
    65–66
Zimbabwe Tourism Authority (ZTA),
    76–78
Zimbabwe Tourism Development
    Corporation (ZTDC),
    79–80
Zimbabwe tourism festival and event
    destination brand equity,
    70–72
  perceived tourism festival and event
    destination brand quality,
    71
  tourism festival and event
    destination brand
    awareness, 70–71
  tourism festival and event
    destination brand image,
    71
  tourism festival and event
    destination brand loyalty,
    71–72
Zimbabwe's tourism image and
    publicity crisis
  accommodation sector, 80–81

destination marketing in Zimbabwe,
78–80
exploring tourism globally,
76–78
role of DMO, 82–83
travel sector, 81–82

Zimbabwean accommodation sector,
80–81
Zimbabwean tourism, 3
marketing, 76–77
Zimbabwean Tourism Authority, The,
82–83